A Peace Reader

❖

A Peace Reader

Edited By

E. Morris Sider
Professor Emeritus of History and English Literature
Messiah College

Luke Keefer Jr.
Professor of Church History
Ashland Theological Seminary

Evangel
Publishing House
Nappanee, Indiana 46550

Toll-free Order Line: (800) 253-9315
Internet Website: www.evangelpublishing.com

Unless otherwise noted, Scripture quotations taken from the HOLY BIBLE, NEW INTERNATIONAL VERSION. Copyright © 1973, 1978, 1984 International Bible Society. Used by permission of Zondervan Publishing House.

Cover Design by Ted Ferguson
Copyediting by Meg Cox

Publisher s Note: We have preserved the style of items reprinted from other sources to assure the integrity of previously copyrighted material. For this reason, the reader will find a variety of capitalization, punctuation, and spelling styles in this volume.

Publisher's Cataloging-in-Publication Data
(Provided by Quality Books, Inc.)

A peace reader / edited by E. Morris Sider, Luke Keefer, Jr. — 1st ed.
    p. cm.
    Includes bibliographical references.
    LCCN 2001099478
    ISBN 1-928915-30-2

    1. Peace—Religious aspects—Christianity. 2. Peace—Bibliography. I. Sider, E. Morris. II. Keefer, Luke L.

BT736.4P43 2002   261.8'73
                                   QBI33-582

Printed in the United States of America
5 4 3 2 1

Table of Contents

Part III:
Applications of Christian Peacemaking

Acknowledgments

"The Politics of Jesus," by J.R. Burkholder, is excerpted from *Children of Peace*. Foundation Series Curriculum © 1982 by Evangel Press, Nappanee, Ind. 46550 and by Mennonite Publishing House, Scottdale, Pa. 15683. Used by permission.

"Does the New Testament Sanction War?" by G.H.C. MacGregor, is abridged from chapter 2 of *The New Testament Basis of Pacifism*, by G.H.C. MacGregor © 1954 by Fellowship Publications. Reprinted with permission of the Fellowship of Reconciliation, Nyack, N.Y. 10960 (www.forusa.org).

"The Gospel of Peace," by Marlin E. Miller, is reprinted from *Mission and the Peace Witness*, edited by Robert L. Ramseyer © 1979 by Herald Press, Scottdale, Pa. 15683. Used by permission.

"Judging the Just War," by Howard J. Loewen, is reprinted from chapter 12 of *the Power of the Lamb*, by John E. Toews and Gordon Nickel, eds. © 1986 by Kindred Press. Used by permission. All rights reserved.

"Biblical Faith and the Unborn," by Ronald J. Sider, reprinted by permission from chapter 2 of *Completely Pro-Life*, by Ronald J. Sider, copyright © 1987 by Ronald J. Sider.

"Peacemaking and Economics," by Ronald J. Sider, reprinted from *Christ and Violence*, by Ronald J. Sider, copyright © 1979 by Herald Press, Scottdale, Pa. 15683. Used by permission.

"Racial Reconciliation: From Anger and Guilt to Passion and Conviction," by Spencer Perkins and Chris Rice, reprinted from chapter 10 of *More Than Equals*, by Spencer Perkins and Chris Rice, copyright © 2000 by Nancy Perkins and Chris Rice, revised edition. Used by permission of InterVarsity Press, P.O. Box 1400, Downers Grove, Ill. 60515. Website: www.ivpress.com

"The War Prayer," by Mark Twain is from *The Plough Reader*, Winter 2001. Used by permission.

"Guidance: An Adventure in Failure," by E. Stanley Jones, is reprinted from *A Song of Ascents*, by E. Stanley Jones, copyright © 1968 by Abingdon Press. Used by permission.

"From Pearl Harbor to Calvary," by Mitsuo Fuchida, is reprinted by permission of BLI, formerly Bible Literature International, Columbus, Ohio. Readers may request a free copy of the brochure, "Finding Forgiveness at Pearl Harbor," by logging onto www.bli.org or by calling 1-800-326-9673. In addition, printable versions of the testimonies of Jacob DeShazer and Mitsuo Fuchida are available at www.bli.org.

Introduction

JOHN ADDINGTON SYMONDS, a nineteenth-century British poet and historian, told of going into a small store in Italy to examine old artifacts. The owner brought from the back room a wooden crucifix some twenty inches in length, which he had bought from a convent when it closed. Carved on the crucifix was the body of Christ; Mary, Jesus' mother, smiled from a medallion. Surely, thought Symonds, the church had used the crucifix many times and in varying ways—priests had brought it to the bedside of the dying, criminals had kissed it on their way to the scaffold, devout people had bowed before it in prayer.

The owner invited Symonds to press a button on the back of the crucifix. The cross sprang apart. From one of the sections the author drew a small dagger. "What had been a crucifix," Symonds wrote, "became a deadly dagger in my hand, and the rust upon it, in the fading light, looked like blood."[1]

This joining of dagger and cross is a startling image. But on second thought it seems symbolic of the relationship that has often existed over many centuries between the church, the state, and war. Clearly there has been a need to more closely examine that relationship, and the need is as great today as ever.

This *Peace Reader* is designed to address that need, as well as other issues involving conflict and violence. The continuing prevalence of local and international conflicts (and of racial, domestic, even congregational tensions) means that Christians must always be asking how they should respond to such situations. The need is all the more acute because societal pressures to accept violent solutions, to avoid the way of reconciliation, are difficult for many Christians to resist, even those in peace churches. This collection of readings joins the call to Christians to be peacemakers rather than to succumb to what is normal in the surrounding culture.

The readings discuss peace on a variety of levels. Relations between nations and within nations; tensions within families and congregations; and the treatment of criminals, the poor, and the unborn are within the book's range of issues. The breadth of the *Reader* is also indicated by its various parts: The authors discuss biblical and theological themes, church history and issues of peace; they suggest applications for peacemaking;

---

[1]Quoted in Culbert G. Rutenber, *The Dagger and the Cross: An Examination of Christian Pacifism* (Nyack, N.Y.: Fellowship Publications, 1958), 90.

they offer stories as illustrations; and they reflect on the events of September 11, 2001.

Each of the readings contains an introduction that provides context, identifies the author, and offers questions for discussion. A bibliography at the end of the volume lists books and, to a lesser degree, articles for further reading. The list is not exhaustive; our intent is to indicate some of the most helpful and available sources rather than to provide a complete bibliography of everything published on the various subjects.

We have included some readings by writers who are not from the historic peace churches and would not classify themselves as standing in the peace tradition. However, all of the authors are committed to pursuing peace from a Christian perspective. As editors, we do not fully agree with the view or approach taken by every author; however, we consider each author to have something important to say that is worthy of discussion.

This *Reader* is intended for use by various groups, among them students of Christian colleges and universities. It is also directed toward adult Sunday school classes and adult study groups. The didactic and issue-oriented articles in the *Reader*, together with the stories, make the volume an appropriate teaching and learning tool for these and other groups.

Books are never produced without valuable assistance from other people. We owe thanks to several colleagues for their help in preparing this volume. Luke Keefer Jr. expresses appreciation to the following people at Ashland Theological Seminary: librarians Christine O'Dell, Sylvia Locker, and Russell Morton for locating articles; Amy Ailes and Dawn West, faculty secretaries, for entering items into the computer in preparation for publication; and Onalee Burkhard, his teaching assistant for the 2001–2002 school year, for help in preparing the bibliography. At Messiah College, Dori Steckbeck, Director of the Brethren in Christ Historical Library and Archives, assisted E. Morris Sider in a variety of ways—always with her usual good cheer.

As editors, we are appreciative that Evangel Publishing House readily accepted the basic concept and plan for the book. Joseph Allison, the publishing manager at Evangel, worked with us in a spirit of cooperation, courtesy, patience, and—fittingly—peace. We are also grateful for the many readers of the draft proposal, who made excellent comments and helped to shape what the book became.

E. Morris Sider

Luke Keefer Jr.

Part I

❖

The Biblical
and Theological Themes
of Peace

❖

Peace
in the Old and New Testaments

John R. Yeatts

For many people, the validity of the peace position can be maintained, at best, only by prooftexting—that is, by selecting passages here and there from the Bible for support—a method which, in the end, provides only scattered proof. They claim that in the Old Testament one must strain very hard to find any text to uphold the concept of peace. Their teaching from the New Testament, where admittedly more scriptures seem to support a peace view, is so high as to be too idealistic; it is fitting only for some future time when conditions will allow the lamb to lie down with the lion.

John Yeatts, Professor of the Psychology of Religion at Messiah College, takes a different view. He argues from many references in both the Old and the New Testament that instead of being an abstraction that is peripheral in the Christian's life, practiced only where suitable and easily possible, peace is central to the gospel, and thus to each of our lives.

What does this mean in practical terms? Are there any areas of our personal and public lives that cannot be ruled by the gospel of peace? Aside from attitudes toward war, what does a gospel of peace mean, for example, for the conduct of business, for interaction with a difficult neighbor, for responding to bullies—on the playground and later in adult world—indeed for all of life?

A Mennonite acquaintance of my father-in-law was a conscientious objector. During World War II, he worked at the Hamilton Watch Company in Lancaster, Pennsylvania. At times, his job required him to make timing devices to be used in detonating weapons. When asked how as a conscientious objector he could participate in the war effort through weapon production, his response was: "If I do not pull the trigger, I am not violating my non-resistant position."

This man had a very limited understanding of the concept of peace, defining it narrowly as being a pacifist and refusing to go to war. Of course, the peace message of the Bible does preclude participation in war, prompting the Christian to make extremely complex decisions related to military involvement. In times of war, nearly everyone is a participant. Even Mennonite farmers who produce food for troops are participating in the war effort.

Similarly, the Bible has a very broad definition of peace. It goes beyond the refusal to participate in the military to include all aspects of life. In the Hebrew Bible, the word *shalom* refers to safety, security, welfare, health, and contentment in all aspects of life. No distinction is made between military peace and physical or spiritual health. In the New Testament, the word *eiréné* is the opposite of armed conflict and denotes peace in contrast to war. Yet, this word carries the symbolic meaning of harmony and order.

Indeed, peace is a concept that incorporates all of life. It refers to a contentment that comes not from accumulating possessions, but from trusting in God. Peace resides in the rejection of materialism. Peace also brings harmony to all relationships—family, church, and even government. The biblical concept of peace cannot be limited to the absence of military conflict, although it certainly has application there; in the Bible, peace is integral to all of life.

Peace in the Old Testament

Much has been written about war and peace in the Old Testament. Susan Niditch has provided an informed and helpful summary of the various positions.[1] Terry Brensinger concludes that "a theology of peace" can be grounded in the Old Testament. While admitting "the Old Testament is clearly not a pacifistic document," he argues that it "seeks...to transform and even abolish" war "much as it does...slavery, polygamy, and the subjugated roles of women."[2] Although Brensinger is correct that the Hebrew scriptures move in the direction of the prophetic renunciation of war, he defines pacifism too narrowly in this statement, and thus concedes too much in saying that the Old Testament is not a pacifistic document. The theme of peace permeates its pages.

Indeed, the word *shalom* in its variety of forms in the Old Testament means "peace" or "well-being." When used of an individual, it carries the meaning of "bodily health" or "satisfaction." When used of a group or nation, which is more common in the Old Testament, it refers to "prosperity" or "stability."[3] In ancient Israel, nomadic people greeted friends and strangers in the desert with: "Peace, peace to you" (1 Chron. 12:18; also Judg. 6:23; Isa. 57:19). When they met, they would inquire about the peace of persons and their families and associates (Gen. 43:27; 2 Sam. 18:29; cf. 20:9). When they parted, they would be said to go in peace (Gen. 26:29; Ex. 18:23; Judg. 18:6; 1 Sam. 20:42; also Isa. 55:12). Far more than a greeting, this usage of the word *peace* indicates that Israelites were to live a quiet and peaceable life (2 Sam. 20:19), to "seek peace and pursue it" (Ps. 34:14), and to have peaceful conversation with their neighbors (Ps. 28:3). Indeed, peace is included in the solemn blessing placed by Eli upon Hannah after she was promised a son (1 Sam. 1:17), by the priests upon all the people of Israel (Num. 6:24–26), and by the group of leaders from the province of Trans-Euphrates upon King Darius (Ezra 5:7).

Shalom certainly carries a military, political meaning when it refers to the absence of war (Lev. 26:6; Judg. 11:13; 21:13; 1 Sam. 7:14; 16:4–5; 29:7; 1 Kings 2:5; 4:24; 22:17; 2 Kings 9:17–31; 18:31; 20:19; Ps. 120:7; Eccl. 3:8; Isa. 32:18; 33:7; 39:8; Ezek. 7:25; Mic. 3:5). Although military peace is ultimately from God (Job 25:2), political security may come immediately through military vic-

[1] Susan Niditch, *War in the Hebrew Bible: A Study in the Ethics of Violence* (New York: Oxford University Press, 1993). See also my review of this book in *Review of Religious Research* 35, no. 3 (1994): 279–80.

[2] Terry L. Brensinger, "War in the Old Testament: A Journey towards Nonparticipation," *Brethren in Christ History and Life* (December 2001): 415–16, 428.

[3] Gerhard von Rad, "שלום in the OT," *Theological Dictionary of the Old Testament*, vol. 2 (Grand Rapids: Eerdmans, 1964), 402–403.

tory (Josh. 10:21; Judg. 8:9; 11:31; Jer. 43:12), surrender (2 Sam. 10:19; 1 Kings 20:18; 1 Chron. 19:19), or a peace agreement (Deut. 2:26; 20:10–12; Josh. 9:15; 10:1, 4; 11:19; Judg. 4:17; 1 Kings. 22:44; 1 Chron. 19:19). Nevertheless, peace more often comes from a relationship with God (2 Sam. 20:19; 1 Kings 8:61; 15:3, 14; 2 Kings 20:3; 1 Chron. 28:9; 29:19; 2 Chron. 15:17–19; 16:8–9; 19:9; 25:2; Job 22:21; Prov. 16:7; Isa. 38:2–3; Ezek. 37:26), which is rooted in God's love and compassion (Isa. 54:10) and brings even nature and society into covenant (Lev. 26:6; Job 5:23; Psa. 72:3; Ezek. 34:25).

In spite of this overwhelming message of peace, the frequency of warfare in the Old Testament cannot be disputed. For example, in response to the capture of Lot and the plundering of Sodom and Gomorrah, Abram's troops routed the enemy and rescued his nephew (Gen. 14:1–16). Nevertheless, the self-control of Israel's leaders is remarkable. After Philistines stopped up the well that Abraham had dug and seized two wells dug by Isaac's servants, Isaac did not retaliate violently; he simply moved on and dug another well (Gen. 26:18–22). After being repeatedly tricked by his father-in-law, Laban, Jacob rejected violence in favor of a covenant with him (Gen. 31:43–54); to avoid retribution over the birthright controversy, Jacob sent gifts to his brother Esau (Gen. 32:13–21). His sons contemplated bloody revenge after Shechem raped their sister Dinah, but Jacob held his peace (Gen. 34:5).

Although Israel's monarchy had a reputation for violence, King Solomon was a "man of peace," and for that reason he was permitted to build the temple and establish a royal throne in Israel that was to last forever (1 Chron. 22:9). An example of Solomon's character is evident in his peaceful agreement with the Phoenician King Hiram of Tyre; Hiram provided Israel with cedar and cypress timber for building the temple, and Solomon provided Lebanon with wheat and oil (1 Kings 5:7–18). Even in the context of military campaigns, peace is valued. Moses attempted to make peace with King Sihon of Heshbon to allow the Israelites to pass through his territory in peace (Deut. 2:26–30). In the war between Israel and Judah, Jehoshaphat of Judah made peace with King Ahab of Israel (1 Kings 22:44). When hosts were encamped against Judah, Isaiah said: "You will keep in perfect peace him whose mind is steadfast, because he trusts in you" (Isa. 26:3).

Symbolically, *shalom* sometimes has the sense of material prosperity (Isa. 54:12–13; 66:12; Hag. 2:9). Although the psalmist at times sees prosperity as something to be desired, he also attributes it to the wicked (Ps. 37:10–11; 73:3). Ezra counsels the returning exiles to reject treaties with corrupt peoples, because that sort of peace will inhibit their possession of the land (Ezra 9:12; see also Job 15:21).

More often, *shalom* carries the meaning of welfare, sometimes in the context of battle: the conflicts between Gideon and the Midianites (Judg. 6:23), Micah and the Danites (Judg. 18:6, 15), and David and Nabal (1 Sam. 25:6, 35); the military campaign when David stole Bathsheba from Uriah the Hittite (2 Sam. 11:7); the conflict in which David's son Absalom was killed (2 Sam. 18:28–29); and Jehu's defeat of Ahab and Jezebel (2 Kings 9:11, 17–19, 22; 10:13). Even in military conflict, the Old Testament gives glimpses of divine peace. Indeed, the psalmist says that such peace should be the goal (Ps. 72:7; 122:6–8).

It is perhaps surprising to note that *shalom* occurs even more often in the context of family relationships. Examples are Jacob's relationships with his father-in-law Laban, his wife Rachel (Gen. 29:6), and his eleven brothers (Gen. 37:4, 14; 43:23, 27–28; 44:17); Moses' relationship with his father-in-law and his kinfolk in Egypt (Ex. 4:18; 18:7); David's provision for his seven brothers in battle (1 Sam. 17:18); Adonijah's attitude when his half-brother Solomon was chosen king over him (1 Kings 2:13); and Gehazi's concern for the welfare of the family of the Shunammite woman in the story of Elisha (2 Kings 4:26). The peace between Israel and Edom is couched in the idea that they are family (Deut. 23:7).

Moreover, peace is also used in the context of human relations beyond the family (Gen. 26:29; 1 Sam. 29:7; 2 Sam. 15:27; Ps. 28:3; 35:20; 41:9; 55:20; Jer. 20:10; 38:22; Obad. 7; Zech. 6:13). For example, *shalom* occurs in the context of the friendship between David and Jonathan (1 Sam. 20:7, 21).

Peace in the symbolic sense of welfare involves safe sleep (Ps. 4:8), posterity (Ps. 37:37–38), length of life (Prov. 3:2), and a peaceful death and burial (Gen. 15:15; 2 Kings 22:20; 2 Chron. 34:28; Isa. 57:2; Jer. 34:5; cf. Judg. 6:23; 1 Kings 2:6). It is used in the sense of being safe, sound, or uninjured (Gen. 28:21; 33:18; Job 5:24; 8:6; 9:4; Isa. 38:17; cf. Psa. 38:3; Jer. 16:18). More generally peace denotes a quiet contentment (Ex. 18:23; Job 21:9; Isa. 32:17–18; Jer. 12:5; cf. Jer. 25:37; Zech. 8:10), which can even be found in difficult times like the exile of Judah (Jer. 29:7; cf. 38:4). Such peace comes from observing God's teachings and keeping the commandments (Deut. 7:9–10; Prov. 3:1–2).

This inner, spiritual peace comes from God (Num. 6:26; Ps. 4:8; Isa. 45:7) and is rooted in a relationship with God (Num. 25:12; Judg. 6:24; Ps. 29:11; 35:27; 85:8, 10; 125:5; 128:6; 147:14; Isa. 27:5; 53:5; 54:10; 55:12; 60:17; 66:12; Jer. 16:5; 29:11; 33:9; Hag. 2:9). Peace is promised to those who trust in the Lord (Isa. 26:3). The prophets call this a covenant of peace (Ezek. 34:25; 37:26; Mal. 2:5–6). It includes pardon from sin (2 Kings 5:18–19;

Ps. 34:14; cf. Isa. 57:19–21; 59:8), the healing of wounds (Isa. 57:18–19; Jer. 33:6; cf. Jer. 6:14; 8:11; 12:12; 14:19; 30:5; Ezek. 13:10, 16), strength (Ps. 29:11; cf. Ezek. 7:25), joy (Prov. 12:20; Isa.55:12), and the assurance of answered prayer (Gen. 41:16). A concrete example of the latter is Eli telling Hannah to "Go in peace" after God had granted her petition for a son (1 Sam. 1:17). Furthermore, peace is closely tied to our righteousness (Ps. 72:7; 85:10; Isa. 32:17) and obedience to God's commandments (Est. 9:30–31; Ps. 119:165; Isa. 48:18). To be at peace is to be upright (Isa. 57:2; Mal. 2:6), faithful (2 Sam. 20:19; Ps. 85:8), an upholder of the truth (Zech. 8:19), and a person of justice (Isa. 59:8) and truth (Zech. 8:16). Moreover, peace is the antithesis of wickedness (Ps. 34:14; Isa. 48:22; 57:21).

Certainly, the concept of peace is central to the thought of the Old Testament and the people of Israel. Indeed, the name of the city Jerusalem includes the word *shalom;* Jerusalem is the city of peace. The psalmist calls for prayer for the peace, security, and prosperity of Jerusalem (Ps. 122:6–9; 128:5–6). Moreover, God promises peace for David, his descendants, and their throne for ever (1 Kings 2:33). Indeed, peace is tied to Israel's salvation (Ps. 85:8–9; Isa. 52:7; Nah. 1:15). The prophets anticipated a future time of peace (Isa. 26:12; Jer. 14:13; 28:9; Mic. 5:4; Zech. 8:19). Ezekiel even notes that the prophets predict peace when there is no peace (Ezek. 13:16).

Peace is central to the messianic hope of the Kingdom of God. The Messiah is the Prince of Peace (Isa. 9:5–7; see also Mic. 5:4–5), who will bring warfare to an end: "I will take away the chariots from Ephraim and the war-horses from Jerusalem, and the battle bow will be broken. He will proclaim peace to the nations" (Zech. 9:10). In the messianic age, nations and peoples "will beat their swords into plowshares and their spears into pruning hooks. Nation will not take up sword against nation, nor will they train for war anymore" (Isa. 2:4). Even the Messiah's human suffering is the "punishment that brought us peace" (Isa. 53:5). While war is not eradicated in the Old Testament, it is clear that peace, both personal and political, is central to its message.

Peace in the New Testament

Peace is even more integral to the message of the New Testament. Willard Swartley has produced a fine corpus of books on the topic of peace in the New Testament.[4] The word *eiréné* carries the sense of a "time of peace" or a "state of peace," an interlude in the perpetual state of war that seems to dominate ancient and modern societies. Indeed, it is regularly used as the opposite of *war*. This immensely rich term also refers to a "treaty of peace" or a "peaceful attitude."[5]

As in the Hebrew scriptures, in the New Testament the word *peace* is used as a greeting. When Jesus appeared to His disciples after His resurrection, He greeted them with: "Peace be with you" (Luke 24:36; John 20:19, 21, 26). More than a greeting, the phrase involves the bestowal of peace (Matt. 10:13; Luke 10:5–6). Jesus promised that when He went to His Father's house, He would leave His peace with them: "Peace I leave with you; my peace I give you" (John 14:27). It is paired with grace in the entreaty that the grace and peace of God be on other believers (Rom. 1:7; 1 Cor. 1:3; 2 Cor. 1:2; Gal. 1:3; 6:16; Eph. 1:2; 6:23–24; Phil. 1:2; Col, 1:2; 1 Thess. 1:1; 2 Thess. 1:2; 3:16, 18; 1 Tim. 1:2; 2 Tim.

1:2; Tit. 1:4; Philem. 3; 1 Pet. 1:2; 5:12, 14; 2 Pet. 1:2; 2 John 3; Rev. 1:4).

The greeting can take the form of an exhortation. Jesus exhorted Jairus's daughter after her healing, the sinful woman after she was forgiven, and the woman in the crowd after her healing to "go in peace" (Mark 5:34; Luke 7:50; 8:48). The Philippian jailer told Paul to "go in peace" after Paul was delivered from jail (Acts 16:36). Yet, James cautions against telling persons to "Go in peace" without meeting their bodily needs (James 2:16). After the members of the Jerusalem Council delivered its results to the believers in Antioch, they were sent on their way in peace (Acts 15:33). Simeon gave a self-exhortation when he declared that he could die in peace because he had seen God's salvation (Luke 2:29).

Like the Hebrew scriptures, the New Testament clearly recognizes the reality of fighting (Rev. 13:4), warfare (Luke 14:31; Heb. 11:34), and battle (1 Cor. 14:8; Rev. 9:7; 16:14; 20:8). A show of force is even seen as a positive thing (Luke 11:21). Jesus says that we can expect that the future will bring "wars and rumors of wars" (Matt. 24:6; Mark 13:7; see also 1 Thess. 5:3; Rev. 11:7; 12:17; 13:7; 17:14). But when Christ goes to battle, His only weapon is the sword that comes out of His mouth (Rev. 19:11–16).

The New Testament word for peace, *eiréné*, is the opposite of war and armed conflict (Matt. 10:34; Luke 12:51). In warfare persons ask for terms of peace (Luke 14:32; Acts 12:20) while others take peace away (Rev. 6:4). The word also refers to

---

[4]Willard Swartley, *The Love of Enemy and Nonretaliation in the New Testament* (Louisville: Westminster/John Knox, 1992); *Slavery, Sabbath, War, and Women: Case Issues in Biblical Interpretation* (Scottdale, Pa.: Herald, 1983); *War and Peace in the New Testament*. Aufsteig und Niedergang der Romischen Welt (Rise and Decline of the Roman World), ed. Wolfgang Haase and Hildegard Temporini. 2.26.3:2298–408 (New York: de Gruyter, 1996).

[5]Warner Foerster, "The Greek Concept of εἰήνη," *Theological Dictionary of the Old Testament*, vol. 2 (Grand Rapids: Eerdmans, 1964), 400–401.

keeping the peace among those who are quarreling (Acts 7:26). We should pray for kings and political authorities so we can lead a peaceable life (1 Tim. 2:2). Both Jesus and Paul exhort their followers to live at peace with one another and, indeed, with everyone (Mark 9:50; Rom. 12:18; 2 Cor. 13:11; Eph. 4:3; 1 Thess. 5:13).

Like *shalom, eiréné* also carries the connotation of welfare or health. The centrality of the concept of peace in the New Testament is perhaps best expressed in the concept of the "gospel of peace" (Rom. 10:15, KJV). Although in the world Christians are persecuted, in Jesus they have peace (John 16:33). Therefore, they are to preach the gospel of peace (Act 10:36; Eph. 6:15) that Jesus Christ proclaimed to them (Eph. 2:17). Indeed, peace is said to encompass our entire relationship with God; peace is central to the entire message of the gospel. We were alienated from and hostile enemies of God (Rom. 5:10; Eph. 4:18; Col. 1:21). Those who were under the power of sin had not known the "way of peace" (Rom. 3:17). Jesus mourned Jerusalem because she did not recognize the things that make for peace (Luke 19:42). Nevertheless, justification by faith brought peace with God through the blood of Jesus Christ (Rom. 5:1; Col. 1:20). As a result of this peace with God, new believers "turn from evil and do good" and "seek peace and pursue it" (1 Peter 3:11). Indeed, the tender mercy of God "guide[s] our feet into the path of peace" (Luke 1:79). As a result, Christ is called our peace (Eph. 2:14–15), and true children of God are called peacemakers (Matt. 5:9; see also James 3:18). As such, they are to be among those who "come between two contending parties and try to make peace."[6]

Warner Foerster argues that, far from being peripheral or an addendum to the process of coming to faith in Christ, the New Testament concept of peace is "salvation in a deeper sense."[7] Peace with God is said to be the sum total of the blessings experienced in Christ (Rom. 5:1). Paul speaks of the peace of God (Phil. 4:7), as well as the peace of Christ (Col. 3:15). God is the God of peace (Rom. 15:33; 16:20; 2 Cor. 13:11; Phil. 4:9; 1 Thess. 5:23; Heb. 13:20; see also Heb. 7:2) and the Lord of peace (2 Thess. 3:16). God's wisdom is peaceable (James 3:17). God promises peace on earth (Luke 2:14) and in heaven (Luke 19:38). Christ is that peace (Eph. 2:14). Peace is the gift of Jesus for the troubled hearts of His followers (John 14:27). Moreover, Jesus leaves peace with His disciples before His crucifixion (John 14:27).

Therefore, Christians are exhorted to strive to be at peace (2 Peter 3:14). This sort of peace is at the heart of the message of the New Testament. Paul says that the cross of Christ has brought peace between Jews and Gentiles:

> For he is our peace; in his flesh he has made both groups into one and has broken down the dividing wall, that is, the hostility between us. He has abolished the law with its commandments and ordinances, that he might create in himself one new humanity in place of the two, thus making peace, and might reconcile both groups to God in one body through the cross, thus putting to death that hostility through it. So he came and proclaimed peace to you who were far off and peace to those who were near. (Eph. 2:14–17, NRSV).

Peace is among the fruits of the Holy Spirit along with "love, joy,...patience, kindness, goodness, faithfulness, gentle-

---

[6]Ibid., 419.

[7]Ibid., 411.

ness and self-control" (Gal. 5:22; see also Rom. 14:17; 15:13; 2 Cor. 13:11; 2 Tim. 2:22). Peace is also closely tied to righteousness (Rom. 14:17; James 3:18), glory and honor (Rom. 2:10), life (Rom. 8:6), safety (1 Thess. 5:3), and holiness (1 Thess. 5:23; Heb. 12:14). Disciplined holiness yields the peaceful fruit of righteousness (Heb. 12:11): "Pursue peace with everyone, and the holiness without which no one will see the Lord" (Heb. 12:14, NRSV). This peace among believers leads to their mutual upbuilding (Rom. 14:19). Therefore, peace should dominate Christian worship (1 Cor. 14:33), family life (1 Cor. 7:15), and church relations (Rom. 14:19). Indeed, the church is an institution of peace when it lives "in the fear of the Lord and in the comfort of the Holy Spirit" (Acts 9:31, NRSV).

Foerster concludes that in the New Testament God has called us to peace, the normal, healthy state of things that corresponds to the will of God in the present life of the Christian. Nevertheless, peace is also connected to our ultimate salvation, which comes from God and brings peace with God. When Jesus came into the world, He brought peace on earth (Luke 2:14). When Jesus rode triumphantly into Jerusalem, the crowd proclaimed, "Peace in heaven" (Luke 19:38). Although hidden now, God's peace will ultimately be revealed (Luke 19:42). Ironically, the God of peace will crush Satan (Rom. 16:20), thus allowing peace to rule in the hearts of believers (Col. 3:15). Indeed, this peace is the protection of those who are in Christ Jesus (Phil. 4:7). Peace is the salvation of the whole person—body and soul (Heb. 13:20–21). Without doubt, peace is integral to the entire message of the New Testament and, as we have seen, the entire Bible.[8]

Conclusion

The concept of peace is central, rather than peripheral, to the message of the Bible. The concept of peace infuses the entire Old Testament. Although warfare is common, God's people show remarkable restraint, and King Solomon is admired as a person of peace, thus qualifying him to build the temple of God. In the New Testament, peace is at the heart of every aspect of the message of the gospel. In order to bear witness to the gospel, Christians are called to exhibit peace in their relationships.

Moreover, the biblical message of peace is comprehensive, relating to all of life rather than limited to the context of military violence. Peace describes the well-being of the person and the nation—both political well-being and a secure relationship with God. Indeed, the word *peace* denotes a harmony in all relationships. The Old Testament highlights peaceful relations among family members and close friends. The New Testament adds that peace brings hope at the end of life. Indeed, Christians who live in peace can anticipate living eternally in the peaceable kingdom of God. The Bible portrays peace as integral to all of this life as well as the life that lies beyond.

---

[8]Ibid., 412–17.

Chapter Two

War in the Old Testament: A Journey toward Nonparticipation

Terry L. Brensinger

Is the Old Testament a collection of books promoting war? Many Christians find support for the just war theory within its pages. But not Terry Brensinger, formerly chair of the Biblical and Religious Studies Department at Messiah College, now senior pastor of the Grantham Brethren in Christ Church. He does not see the Old Testament as a pacifist document, but he sees within it messages that call for transforming, eventually even abolishing, war. He offers proof for his views in three aspects of Old Testament history: first, God's insistence on reducing the size of Israel's troops (it is God, not humanity, who wins battles); second, the constraints put on Israel's natural inclination toward militarism; and third, the call for a future when peace, not war, will be normative for all of life.

The author calls on us to imagine such a future and to think of ways in which to give effect to our imagination. What would a free play of our imagination on the subject yield? Is the author correct in saying that the place to start is within the church? Translating the author's view of Old Testament developments to our own time and place, how could the church encourage reduction in the size of our military programs (or do we think a strong, defensive military program is necessary?), and, relatedly, how could we help to convince those in the seats of power that their reputation does not necessarily depend on how strong they make the nation militarily?

In March of 1994, on the second day of Purim, a thirty-eight-year-old physician named Baruch Goldstein strolled into the Mosque of Abraham in the West Bank town of Hebron and proceeded to massacre twenty-nine Palestinian worshipers. In the aftermath of this apparent atrocity, Israeli Prime Minister Rabin personally contacted his avowed enemy, PLO chairman Yasar Arafat, and confessed: "As an Israeli, I am ashamed of this deed."[1] Yet the atrocious character of Goldstein's act was not so apparent to the militant Jewish settlers with whom he resided in Kiryat Arba, a small town situated just outside of

---

[1]Russell Watson, "Massacre in a Mosque," *Newsweek* (March 7, 1994), 35.

Terry L. Brensinger, "War in the Old Testament: A Journey Towards Nonparticipation," *Brethren in Christ History and Life* 24, no. 3 (2001): 414–29.

Hebron. To them, Goldstein was nothing less than a hero of biblical proportions, for his annihilation of the Palestinians constituted a reenactment of Samson's warring exploits against the Philistines.

Before judging Goldstein and his fellow Jewish settlers too harshly, however, we at least need to be reminded that the Hebrew Scriptures have inspired the Christian Church throughout its history to engage in similar military adventures. In describing the capture of Jerusalem by the crusaders, for example, Raymond of Agiles wrote:

> Some of our men (and this was more merciful) cut off the heads of their enemies; others shot them with arrows, so that they fell from the towers; others tortured them longer by casting them into the flames. Piles of heads, hands, and feet were to be seen in the streets of the city.... Indeed, it was a just and splendid judgment of God, that this place should be filled with the blood of the unbelievers, when it had suffered so long from their blasphemies.[2]

He goes on to describe the mood of the crusaders upon arriving at the Church of the Holy Sepulchre: "Now that the city was taken it was worth all our previous labors and hardships to see the devotion of the pilgrims at the Holy Sepulchre. How they rejoiced and exulted and sang the ninth chant to the Lord."[3] Throughout such crusading episodes, a favorite text of the participants was Jeremiah 48:10: "Cursed be he that keepeth back his sword from blood"(KJV).

More recently, the Puritans at times saw their conflict with the "aboriginal natives" here on American soil in similar terms. In 1704, for example, Herbert Gibbs preached a sermon following Puritan advances; in it he joyfully acknowledged "the mercies of God in extirpating the enemies of Israel in Canaan."[4] Still later, World War II General Montgomery prayed "that the Lord mighty in battle will go forth with our armies, and that his special providence will aid us in the struggle."[5] Just a few years ago, a student in one of my seminars casually but seriously remarked: "If killing was good enough for Joshua, then it's good enough for me!"

For most of us, such blatant applications of Old Testament passages concerning war immediately strike a raw nerve. Yet the issue remains: What is a Christian, distanced from the Old Testament by both culture and further revelation, to do with these texts? People who accept the justification of war, at least under certain circumstances, often use them to add validity to their claims. Those from peace traditions tend, with exceptions, to assign them to a pre-New Testament period, a period since surpassed by the teachings of Jesus. Is there, however, another alternative?

In seeking such an alternative, it must be stated up front that the Old Testament is clearly not a pacifistic document. On the contrary, wars abound in the traditions of ancient Israel, often in graphic and seemingly barbarous forms. At issue, however, is whether the Old Testament consistently accepts war as an inevitable and at times appropriate human activity, or whether it seeks instead to transform and even abolish it (much as it does, in the minds of many readers at least, with

---

[2]Roland Bainton, *Christian Attitudes toward War and Peace* (Nashville: Abingdon, 1960), 112–13.

[3]Ibid., 113.

[4]Ibid., 168.

[5]Quoted in Peter C. Craigie, *The Problem of War in the Old Testament* (Grand Rapids: Eerdmans, 1978), 33.

such matters as slavery, polygamy, and the subjugated roles of women). Can we find emerging from the pages of the Old Testament what Susan Niditch refers to as an "Ideology of Nonparticipation?"[6] In order to address this question, three general issues will be discussed: reducing the troops; constraining the king; and imagining the unimaginable.

Reducing the Troops

Wars, once again, are extremely common in the Old Testament, as they are in texts throughout the ancient Near East. War, in other words, was a standard part of the landscape. What requires our attention, then, is the manner in which Israel and her neighbors portrayed their wars.

To begin, the writers of Scripture seek to present the various wars in which Israel engaged as divinely ordained campaigns. According to this prevalent trajectory, Israel's wars were in fact a primary means through which God judged the sinful nations of the world (Lev. 18:25–28; 20:22; Deut. 18:9–14; 2 Kings 21:9). Accordingly, such war narratives have more in common with the biblical account depicting the divine destruction of Sodom and Gomorrah than they do with contemporary conflicts between warring nations. Rather than simply portraying adversarial nations defending or expanding their borders, the war stories of the Old Testament reveal God distributing his justice through human instruments. In short, God instructs Israel when and where to fight (Deut. 7:2; 20:17; Josh. 10:40; Judg. 1:1–2). Wars initiated by and for Israel herself are doomed to fail.

Beyond this, Israel's military victories were divinely propelled. In other words, the narratives consistently attribute Israel's victories to divine intervention. God sends the plagues upon the Egyptians (Exod. 7–12). God destroys the walls of Jericho (Josh. 6:20). God causes the sun to stand still during Israel's fight against the Amorites (Josh. 10:12–13). God sends rain in order to stymie the Canaanite coalition (Judg. 5). God confuses the bewildered Midianites (Judg. 7). God blinds the Arameans (2 Kings 6:18). God strikes the blood-thirsty Assyrians (2 Kings 19:35–37). God ambushes the invaders from the east (2 Chron. 20). Again and again, God manipulates the forces of history and nature and victoriously intervenes on Israel's behalf.

Importantly, then, the writers of the Old Testament invite us to see Israel's wars as divinely inspired and divinely propelled confrontations in which God accomplishes his purposes. Interestingly enough, such a conception is essentially how Israel's neighbors viewed war as well. Continually, the records from Egypt, Mesopotamia, Anatolia, and Syro-Palestine reveal the widespread conviction that the gods of these people also fight in battle. They too ordain military conflict, and they too intervene in order to assure victory. Consider just a few examples in which the gods miraculously intervene on behalf of their subjects:

A. Hittite Texts

1. Report from the reign of Muršiliš II:

> But as I marched, as I reached there to the mountain of Lagaša, there the proud Weather-god, my lord, showed his divine power, and he attached a thunderbolt there. And my army saw the thunderbolt, the land of Arzawa also saw it, and the thunderbolt went forth there, and struck the land of

---

[6]Susan Niditch, *War in the Hebrew Bible: A Study in the Ethics of Violence* (New York: Oxford University Press, 1993), 134.

Arzawa, it also struck the Lhhaluis city of Apasa. (*KBo* III 4 II 5–19)[7]

2. *Report from Muršiliš II, who was in pursuit of Sunupassaer:*

The proud Weather-god, my lord, stood beside me. It rained all night so that the enemy could not see the campfire of the troops. But as soon as the weather became clear in the early evening, the proud Weather-god suddenly raised the storm and brought it and it went before my troops, making them invisible to the enemy. So I arrived at the land of Malazzia and burnt and destroyed it utterly. (*KUB* XIV 20 11–22)[8]

B. Egyptian Texts

From Rameses II during a Syrian campaign in bad weather:

His majesty considered, and took counsel with his heart: How will it be with those whom I have sent out, who have gone on a mission to Syria, in these days of rain and snow which fall in winter. Then he made a great offering to his father Seth, and with it pronounced the following prayer:

Heaven rests upon your hands; the earth is under your feet. What you command, takes place. [May you cause] the rain, the cold wind and the snow [to cease] until the marvel you design for me shall have reached me. Then his father Seth heard all that he had said. The sky became peaceful and summer-like days began (*Aub Simbel* 1:36:39).[9]

Clearly, the war narratives of the Old Testament and those of Israel's neighbors have a great deal in common.[10] What appears to be lacking in the ancient Near Eastern accounts, however, is the strong emphasis that the Old Testament places upon the theme of God warring on behalf of a weak and perpetually overmatched group of people. We find, for example, Deborah and Barak encountering the chariot-possessing Canaanites, Gideon the camel-riding Midianites, and David the awe-inspiring Goliath. Likewise, the Chronicler repeatedly calls attention to the weaknesses of those whom Yahweh assists (2 Chron. 14:9–15; 16:8; 20:12). "O our God," Jehoshaphat cries, "will you not execute judgment upon them [invaders from the east]? For we are powerless against this great multitude that is coming against us. We do not know what to do, but our eyes are on you" (20:12, NRSV). In each instance, the Israelites are woefully underequipped—torches, trumpets, pottery, slings, or nothing at all. Although David was granted permission to use Saul's armor, he found it too cumbersome for battle (1 Sam. 17:38–39).

Significantly, this theme of God warring on behalf of the weak is so prevalent in the Old Testament that in a few instances when Israel's own resources might lead them to believe that they could win the battle on their own, an act of reduction occurs. As a result, Gideon confronts the innumerable Midianites with but a fraction of his original forces (Judg. 7), and Amaziah is left to face the Edomites without the aid of the Ephraimites (2 Chron. 25:5–7). To make matters even worse, the troops left for Gideon to em-

---

[7]Albrecht Goetze, *Die Annalen des Muršiliš* (Leipzig: Hinrichs, 1933), 46–47.

[8]Ibid., 194–95.

[9]H. Te Velde, *Seth, God of Confusion* (Leiden: Brill, 1977), 133.

[10]For a more complete collection of ancient Near Eastern texts relating to war, see Sa-Moon Kang, *Divine War in the Old Testament and in the Ancient Near East* (Berlin: Walter de Gruyter, 1989).

ploy are the least competent of those originally summoned.[11] Unmistakably, only Yahweh deserves the credit for Israel's military victories.

The war narratives of the Old Testament, then, resemble those of Israel's neighbors in several crucial respects. God directs the fighting, and it is he who intervenes in battle. However, unlike the accounts from the surrounding nations, Israel's texts place particular attention on the weaknesses of the people and their occasional need for reduction. That such a theme of weakness and reduction occurs at all is noteworthy. That it occurs with respect to a group of people who find themselves in what is perhaps the most war-torn region of the world is potentially profound. Rather than celebrating their own military accomplishments, the Israelites are instructed to wait and view Yahweh alone as their protector and deliverer. While these contrary tendencies undoubtedly tell us something about God, they likewise reveal something about the way his people are to function within the world.

Constraining the King

With a significant number of the war narratives canonically situated prior to Israel's request for a king in 1 Samuel 8, it is apparent that such a request places Israel's position as Yahweh's uniquely chosen people in jeopardy. Kings, after all, typically become self-serving, consolidating within their grasp all power and authority. This tendency, observable throughout the ancient Near East, lies behind the list of warnings that follows Israel's request. In reality, a king will institute a military draft, force the Israelites to work against their will, confiscate property, and impose burdensome taxes (1 Sam. 8:11–17). While such royal practices may be common and even appropriate elsewhere, they are clearly not what the Israelites anticipate.

In order to prevent the actualization of these self-serving tendencies, kingship in Israel is uniquely situated within a set of theological parameters. According to Deuteronomy 17, Israel's kings were to avoid three practices so characteristic of monarchy elsewhere. First, they should not amass many horses, the attaining of which would signify military security. Second, they should not acquire many wives, a reference most likely to the marrying of foreign women in order to formalize international alliances. Such an act would symbolize political security. Third, they should not accumulate large amounts of silver and gold, the gaining of which would constitute financial security. Israel's kings, as such, were to redirect their energies in entirely new directions.

And what were they to do? Sit on the throne and study Torah day after day! In the words of Walter Brueggemann: "The biblical tradition and Israel in her reflection on monarchy are peculiar in affirming that the fundamental religio-political reality is not king but Torah, not human distribution of power, but divine vision for society."[12] This is, needless to say, a scandalous redefinition of power and monarchy. As Herbert Huffmon casually comments, the gods of the ancient Near East "bud into the affairs of earthly kings in order to oversee their activities, but to so limit kingly responsibilities is unusual indeed."[13]

---

[11]Following the reading of the LXX for Judges 7:7, those who alertly knelt down and drank with "their hands to their mouths" were sent home. The MT preserves a less coherent reading, placing the phrase "with their hands to their mouths" in connection with the lappers in v. 6.

[12]Walter Brueggemann, *Living toward a Vision* (Philadelphia: United Church Press, 1976), 92.

[13]Telephone conversation with Herbert Huffmon, Drew University, Madison, N.J. (September 1995).

Given these theological parameters, it is significant to note that two of the three relate directly to warfare. The prohibition against amassing horses is self-evident—Israel is not to base either her identity or security on military might. However, the prohibition against marrying many wives and thereby ratifying alliances also relates to warfare because it deliberately limits Israel's military maneuverability during moments of crisis. In the same way that the ruling nations of the ancient Near East stipulate that their vassals not enter into agreements with competing forces, so too are the Israelites bound by treaty to Yahweh alone. They were not to rely on anything or anyone else. In *The Mighty from Their Thrones,* J.P.M. Walsh captures this same idea:

> The tradition insists on this: Yahweh wars on behalf of Israel. But what is Israel to do? The tradition is clear on this, too: "Be still" (Exod. 14:13–14). If Israel relied on military might they would be arrogating *mišpat* ("having the say") to themselves and rejecting the *sedeq* ("sense of rightness") of Yahweh. They would be living by the same sense of *sedeq* that caused the kings to amass armies and multiply horses and chariots: of *sedeq* rising, and validating obsession with security and freedom from risk. For Israel to rely on power and strategy would mean rebellion against Yahweh.[14]

Importantly, however, these theological parameters rarely prevented the type of self-serving tendencies so prevalent among kings elsewhere. As a result, the Old Testament repeatedly levels criticism against a vast array of violators. Within the so-called Deuteronomistic History, David himself, the paradigmatic king, is harshly rebuked for counting his fighting men (2 Sam. 24). Apparently, the taking of such a census is analogous to an aging person fretfully anticipating retirement, only to discover that a larger-than-expected return on an investment makes anxiety, and faith, unnecessary. David's troops, not God, ensure the quality of his advancing years. Similarly, the historian attributes the decline of Solomon's seemingly glorious reign to his blatant disregard of all three of these parameters (1 Kings 10:26–29; 11:1–13). While it is true, as M.H. Segal points out, that Solomon receives direct criticism only for his innumerable marriages to foreign women, the clear connections with Deuteronomy 17 make explicit editorial comment unnecessary.[15] Solomon self-destructed by absolutizing himself.

In the prophetic literature, related pronouncements appear with some regularity. Consider these:

Their land is filled with silver and gold,
    and there is no end to their treasures;
their land is filled with horses,
    and there is no end to their chariots.
Their land is filled with idols;
    they bow down to the work of their hands,
    to what their own fingers have made.
        (Isa. 2:7–8, NRSV)

For thus said the Lord GOD, the Holy One of Israel:
In returning and rest you shall be saved;
    in quietness and in trust shall be your strength.
But you refused and said,
"No! We will flee upon horses"—
    therefore you shall flee!
and, "We will ride upon swift steeds"—
    therefore your pursuers shall be swift!
        (Isa. 30:15–16, NRSV)

Because you have trusted in your power
    and in the multitude of your warriors,

---

[14]James P.M. Walsh, *The Mighty from Their Thrones* (Philadelphia: Fortress, 1987), 68.
[15]M.H. Segal, *The Pentateuch and Other Biblical Studies* (Jerusalem: Magnes, 1967), 79.

therefore the tumult of war shall rise against your people,
 and all your fortresses shall be destroyed.
    (Hosea 10:13–14, NRSV)

In that day, says the LORD,
 I will cut off your horses from among you
 and will destroy your chariots.
    (Mic. 5:10–13, NRSV)

In each of these and other passages, Israel and Judah defy the principles embodied in Deuteronomy 17 and trust instead in horses and chariots. Significantly, such behavior is included in lists that also mention sorcery and idolatry in its various forms (Mic. 5:12–15).

Similar texts could be cited in which the establishing of treaties with foreign nations receives prophetic condemnation (Isa. 31:1; Jer. 2:36; 37:7–8; Hos. 5:13; 7:11; 8:9; 12:1). Isaiah 30:1–3 serves as an example:

Oh, rebellious children, says the LORD,
who carry out a plan, but not mine;
who make an alliance, but against my will,
 adding sin to sin;
who set out to go down to Egypt
 without asking for my counsel,
to take refuge in the protection of Pharaoh,
 and to seek shelter in the shadow of Egypt;
Therefore the protection of Pharaoh shall become your shame,
 and the shelter in the shadow of Egypt your humiliation. (NRSV)

In such instances, military alliances constitute a violation of Israel's covenantal identity, a deplorable compromise of their calling to "be still."

While it is true, as some have argued, that such passages criticize the misplacing of one's confidence in military might and alliances rather than war itself, the point remains that Israel testifies to a rather peculiar notion of monarchy and its employment of power. Once again, while this notion unmistakably tells us something about God, it surely implies something about the intended character of Israel in the world. As Willard Swartley suggests,

> The pervasive prophetic criticism of kingship with its military power indicates that the Old Testament points to another way, the establishment of justice through the Torah and the way of the suffering servant, which refuses and judges the military war.[16]

Imagining the Unimaginable

In spite of the attempts to reduce the troops and constrain the king, the Old Testament bears witness to Israel's increasing propensity to fend for herself. In the process, the king, whose task was to promote peace and justice, became instead the author of chaos. Such chaos brought with it a continuing prophetic critique as well as a deepening conviction that the same God who freed Israel from Egypt would at some point free her from the monarchical abyss into which she had fallen. Yahweh would raise up someone who would succeed where previous kings had failed.

What gradually emerges, then, is a prophetic vision of a righteous kingdom ruled by a righteous king. For Isaiah, such a kingdom is characterized by endless peace, justice, and righteousness (9:6–7). Micah envisions hope for the weak and marginalized (4:6–13). Jeremiah speaks in terms of safety, of people actually living with genuine security and confidence (23:5–8). In each instance, this quality of life will be guaranteed by an anticipated ruler sitting upon the throne of David.

---

[16]Willard Swartley, *Slavery, Sabbath, War, and Women: Case Issues in Biblical Interpretation* (Scottdale, Pa.: Herald, 1983), 116.

Perhaps the most remarkable description of this longed-for kingdom appears in Isaiah 11:6–9. Seemingly grasping for appropriate metaphors, the prophet stretches language to the limits in portraying things to come:

The wolf shall live with the lamb,
  the leopard shall lie down with the kid,
the calf and the lion and the fatling together,
  and a little child shall lead them.
The cow and the bear shall graze,
  their young shall lie down together;
  and the lion shall eat straw like the ox.
The nursing child shall play over the hole of the asp,
  and the weaned child shall put its hand on the
  adder s den.
They will not hurt or destroy on my holy mountain;
for the earth will be full of the knowledge of the
LORD
  as the waters cover the sea.
    (NRSV)

Everything has been turned upside down, and the unthinkable become commonplace.

Eventually, however, the disappointment of exile and the apparent fragmentation after the return no doubt caused considerable pause. Yet the imaginative glimpse lived on in apocalyptic depictions of things still to come. In Zechariah 9:9–10, for example, the anticipated king triumphantly enters Zion. Unlike earlier passages, which consciously associated the coming king with David, this ruler is decidedly unlike David in certain respects. The king of Zechariah 9 lacks military might, and the horses and chariots of Solomon have given way to a colt. This king, so it appears, has intentionally disarmed. Upon his arrival, his kingdom will similarly disarm:

He will cut off the chariot from Ephraim
  and the war horse from Jerusalem;
and the battle bow shall be cut off,
  and he shall command peace to the nations;
his dominion shall be from sea to sea,

and from the River to the ends of the earth.
  (Zech. 9:10, NRSV)

In place of monarchical chaos, peace will carry the day.

Importantly, while many of these passages envisioning a peaceful kingdom focus specifically on Israel, various texts clearly present a glimpse of future peace in which the surrounding nations are also direct participants and benefactors. In Isaiah 19:18–24, for example, Israel and her longtime foes, Egypt and Assyria, share equally in divine blessing. Likewise in both Isaiah 2:1–4 and its parallel in Micah 4:1–3, the nations of the world mutually participate in the actualization of God's righteous kingdom. At that time, God will judge fairly between all people, and all will walk together in the ways of the Lord. Among other things,

they shall beat their swords into plowshares,
  and their spears into pruning hooks;
nation shall not lift up sword against nation,
  neither shall they learn war any more.
    (Isa. 2:4, NRSV)

Suggestively, the journey from reducing the troops and constraining the king leads eventually to disarming the nations. In Isaiah's mind at least, such a journey would progress far more smoothly and quickly if Israel would herself begin to enact the vision, for he continues his oracle with a striking exhortation:

O house of Jacob,
  come, let us walk
  in the light of the LORD!
    (Isa. 2:5, NRSV)

Rather than constituting a mere eschatological hope, beating swords into plowshares serves here as a daring appeal for God's people to enact that longed-for age of peace within the present world.

30 ✤ *A Peace Reader*

Issues for Reflection

The Old Testament, without argument, does not portray a pacifistic community. War predominates throughout the ancient Near East, and Israel clearly participates. Yet, the nature of the materials indicates that "something is in the works." By suggesting both an outrageous understanding of power and might as well as depicting an imaginative alternative of peace, the Old Testament does indeed bear witness to an emerging ideology of non-participation. From this, several implications can be drawn:

First, the life and ministry of Jesus, which for many serves as a paradigm of non-violence, need not be viewed as an absolute break from the seemingly militant orientation of the Old Testament. At the same time, neither must the Old Testament be considered an embarrassment for those who seek to embrace a theology of peace. While the Old Testament does not present a crystalized view of pacifism as such, it does present what Niditch refers to as an "extended and self-consciously critical treatment of warring behavior."[17] This treatment, in combination with a prophetic and apocalyptic vision of peace, provides the soil for a more developed theology of pacifism based upon the New Testament.

Second, that the Old Testament does in fact give witness to a non-violent alternative should come as no surprise to us in so far as Jesus himself expressed dismay over the failure of his fellow Jews to receive him. This rejection, so most commentators suggest, resulted from a Jewish expectation for a politically oriented Messiah who would forcibly free his people from Roman oppression. Furthermore, such an expectation must have arisen from an Old Testament context which predicted the violent overthrow of Israel's enemies.

The alternative question, however, focuses on the fact that Jesus apparently expressed surprise at being rejected. Why would he be so surprised if the Jews had no theological framework with which to recognize him? Indeed, the fact that recognition was deemed possible suggests an emerging view within the Old Testament of a king who would turn power and violence on its head.

Third and finally, one striking issue remains: What does all of this mean for the contemporary Christian church? To begin with, it is essential to affirm that the church, not the United States or any other nation, inherits the mantle of modeling the kingdom of God within the world. It is the church, therefore, that must reduce its power-oriented equipment, constrain its aspiring kings, and present to a warring world an imaginative alternative to violence, manipulation, and coercion. Doing so will involve at least these three things:

a. serving as a prophetic-consciousness within the world, a consciousness that criticizes warring behaviors and challenges the violent policies that our respective nations so often embrace;

b. promoting peace, both by articulating insightful alternatives to war as well as by actively supporting and engaging in non-violent ministries, even in the most war-torn areas of the world; and

c. modeling genuine peace within all levels of the church itself, even when working through difficulties and disagreements. A church continually at war with itself, as at times seems to be the case, has little to say to a warring world.

---

[17]Niditch, *War in the Old Testament*, 138.

In reflecting upon Isaiah 11:6–8, Walter Brueggemann suggests that the images there are unheard of and abnormal; wolves do not live with lambs, cows do not graze with bears, and children do not play with poisonous snakes. "But then I look again," Brueggemann continues, "and notice something else. The poet means to say that in the new age, these are normal things. And the effect of the poem is to expose the real abnormalities of life, which we have taken for granted. We have lived with things abnormal so long that we have gotten used to them and we think they are normal."[18]

Violence is a part of life, so everyone around us says. War is inevitable. Killing is everywhere. The abnormalities of violence and war, so drastically opposed to life as God intended it, have become so normal that the world cannot imagine anything else. The world cries out for alternatives. The world needs an imagination. Therein lies a portion of our task.

Yet this is precisely where the Church has often failed to leave its mark. Rather than decrying the evils of war, we seek to justify it. Rather than imaginatively and creatively exploring the possibilities of promoting peace, we settle for common realism and cope with what we presently have. Rather than providing a drastically different alternative that at least gives onlookers the opportunity to say, "There is a better way," we model more of what the world already sees in itself. A theology of peace, the groundwork for which has been laid in the Old Testament, might at first glance appear to be unrealistic and frighteningly abnormal. Admittedly, embracing it requires a renewed imagination.

---

[18]Brueggemann, *Living toward a Vision,* 44–45.

Chapter Three

The Politics of Jesus

J.R. Burkholder

J.R. Burkholder is a respected Mennonite educator and author. He has been a provocative theologian within the peace tradition, challenging it and attacking popular assertions. His underlying concern has been for a peace position that stands the scrutiny of exacting biblical scholarship.

This chapter is taken from the book *Children of Peace*, written by Burkholder and John Bender. It is part of the Foundation Series Curriculum, designed by and for various "peace church" denominations.

The author asks us to consider what kind of kingdom Jesus established through His life, death, and resurrection. This is crucial for Christian thought and action. It determines both the meaning of salvation and the way we live as those who are members of and who work for God's kingdom.

Several questions may help us get at the heart of the issues Burkholder is addressing. In what way was Jesus being political?[1] In terms of Jewish expectations, what other kinds of kingdoms might Jesus have established? Are there times when Christians have tried to achieve versions of the kingdom that are closer to those desired by the Jewish parties of Jesus' day than to the kingdom He actually is establishing?

Our chapter title will surely cause some readers to suspect a fad or a bandwagon when they see once again the connection of Jesus and politics. For they know that the last decade has produced a number of books and articles (including John H. Yoder's *The Politics of Jesus*) using the language of politics to speak about Jesus.

Is this indeed a legitimate or necessary angle of approach to the central figure of our faith? To answer these questions, we must first be clear about our use of *politics*. We are not talking about caucuses in smoke-filled rooms, nor even about the conventional electoral processes. Rather, we use the word in its classic sense, as having to do with the life of the *polis,* the

---

[1] See John Howard Yoder, *The Politics of Jesus* (Grand Rapids: Eerdmans, 1999).

This chapter originally appeared as J.R. Burkholder, "The Politics of Jesus," in J.R. Burkholder and John Bender, *Children of Peace* (Nappanee, Ind.: Evangel Press, 1982), 36–46.

city—that is, the ordered social life of humans. When we use *politics* in this chapter, we are talking about relationships, about questions of power and authority, of order and structure, of justice and responsibility.

We have established that *shalom*, the peaceable kingdom, has to do with societal questions of law and justice, as well as with inner attitudes of harmony and tranquility. There can be no real peace without structures of order. The central problem of the Old Testament revolved around the competing patterns of order represented on one hand by the covenant-and-law model from Mt. Sinai, and on the other by the kingship model from David onward. This is obviously a political question.

We have seen that the gospel of the kingdom is basic to the New Testament; it was the heart of the message that Jesus came preaching. Now *kingdom*, of course, implies a king, a ruler—and that, too, is political language.

Our religious usages have tended to obscure the fact that *Christ* is a political term; it's simply the Greek form of *Messiah*—the anointed one, the coming king expected by hopeful Jews for generations. When Jesus was born in Bethlehem, wise men from the East came inquiring, "Where is he who has been born king of the Jews?" (Matt. 2:2, RSV). Crafty King Herod knew what to make of that kind of political query and promptly dispatched his extermination crew to eliminate the threat to his own power.

Messianic Expectations under Roman Rule

First-century Palestine was filled with longing for the coming of a deliverer who would restore the power and glory that they recalled from the ancient monarchy. Old Testament prophecies and particularly the inter-Testamental literature had supported these hopes by portraying various ways in which the messianic rule would be established. Some texts were interpreted to encourage the hopes of violent revolutionaries.

For centuries Palestine had been ruled by Egyptian and Syrian foreigners. They imposed heavy taxation and at times threatened the religious and cultural independence of the Jewish people with their promotion of Greek culture. The extreme policies of the Syrian ruler, Antiochus Epiphanes, triggered the Maccabean revolt in 167 B.C.; its surprising success enabled nearly a century of partial independence, until the coming of the Romans in 63 B.C.

Thus, Jesus' homeland was occupied territory. Oppressive governors and hated collaborators created an unsteady situation where questions of political freedom were very much alive. The memory of the Maccabean freedom fighters was a vital force. Stubborn nationalists, the Zealots, trained as guerrilla fighters, were poised to strike a blow for freedom against impossible odds, believing that Yahweh would send his legions of angels to assure victory. But their frequent uprisings only resulted in massive retaliation from the Romans, in the form of crosses—capital punishment for revolutionaries—on hillsides.

Into this troubled world Jesus was born.
They all were looking for a king
*   to slay their foes and lift them high.*
Thou camest, a little baby thing
*   That made a woman cry.*

These moving lines from the Scottish writer George MacDonald point up the surprise element in the manner of the Messiah's coming. But the powerless babe nevertheless evoked forceful lyrics from those closest to the event: "He has put down the mighty from their thrones, and exalted those of low degree" (Luke 1:52, RSV).

The words of Mary, along with those others recorded in the first chapters of Luke—from the angel, from Zechariah, from Simeon at the temple—all speak of expected social and political change. They refer to a new system of order and justice and right relationships. Add to this the proclamation of the forerunner, John the Baptist, and the stage is set for the politics of Jesus, a program that will indeed be much different from conventional expectations—yet it *is* a politics, a pattern for social order.

Political Dimensions in the Ministry of Jesus

How does one build a messianic politics, a kingdom of shalom? Or for an even sharper focus, let us ask: How did Jesus go about being king?

One initial clue came at His baptism, when the voice from heaven was heard: "Thou art my beloved Son; with thee I am well pleased" (Luke 3:22). For those who knew the Hebrew Scripture, the allusions here were startling. The two phrases bring together the themes of kingly enthronement (Ps. 2:7–8) and the suffering servant of Isaiah (Isa. 42:1). With the likely emphasis on the call to mission that sonship implies in this setting, we have the direction set for a new kind of kingship.

Next, we find that the encounter between Jesus and the devil in the wilderness may well represent a series of temptations centered on the critical question—How be king? What are the choices one faces in claiming influence and authority? To make bread out of stones is hardly an appropriate way to end a forty-day fast, but it does suggest the use of economic resources as a way to power. Feeding the masses could make one a welfare king, and indeed Jesus later rejected precisely that temptation (John 6:15).

The second temptation is most obviously political in character (Luke 4: 5–8). From the mountain vantage point, rulership with all its majesty and glory beckons. But the way is satanic—surrender to a false allegiance, to the old way of force and coercion. Jesus declares categorically that only one Lord is worthy of worship and service.

Then there came the religious test (Luke 4:9–12), perhaps rooted in Malachi 3:1, which speaks of the messenger of God making a sudden appearance at the temple. Such a messianic revelation, a miraculous feat of daring, would undoubtedly have brought the priests and scribes to attention, and guaranteed that the masses would fall in line. But Jesus chose instead to work among the peasants of Galilee, Judea, and even Samaria, teaching, preaching, and healing. He deliberately avoided direct messianic claims, speaking often in riddles and parables. Persons were thus forced to make a decision based on faith, not on fanciful acrobatic display.

Next in Luke's narrative comes Jesus' sermon in the synagogue at Nazareth (Luke 4:16–30). His use of the text from Isaiah 61 sets forth the platform for a public ministry in explicit social and political terms as well as in personal and spiritual expressions. To liberate the poor, the captives, and the oppressed is what the expected deliverer-king is all about. How will these claims be fulfilled?

Jesus' quotation from Isaiah comes to a climax with the phrase "the acceptable year of the Lord" (RSV), best understood as a reference to the year of jubilee (Lev. 25). Jubilee called for a regular schedule of crossing off debts and redistributing land in an effort to bring about social justice and equality. If, as some significant recent biblical scholarship suggests, Jesus points to the jubilee as a blueprint for his activity and teaching, then it is easy to understand why he provoked so much hostility. For the requirements of jubilee had been generally neglected in Israel;

even the religiously scrupulous had chosen to emphasize ritual and petty detail rather than the basic questions of justice (Luke 11:42). Surely one of the motives that stirred those who plotted Jesus' crucifixion was his call for a radical reordering of society and its economics. If his claim that the kingdom of God is now breaking in meant that the accumulated social inequities of the centuries must now be swept aside, a powerful backlash was inevitable.

Jesus now moves out into public ministry, signaled by his words: "I must preach the good news of the kingdom of God" (Luke 4:43, RSV). Crowds follow, people are astonished at his teaching authority, his power to heal and his claim to forgive sins. Some are disturbed and angry (Luke 5:21, 30; 6:11); others leave all and begin to follow him; they are called disciples. After a night of prayer, Jesus chooses twelve whom he names apostles (Luke 6:12–16).

Here is a deliberate political act. Jesus came out of the wilderness alone, he went to the synagogue alone, but now he is the leader of a movement. A radically new teacher standing alone is hardly a threat, but an organization represents a political reality; it is the nucleus of a new social order!

The Four Groups

What will be the strategy of this new movement? The politics of the Messiah can be better understood by contrast with the existing socio-politico-religious groups on the scene in Jesus' time. There are four: the "establishment" (Sadducees), the "proper religionists" (Pharisees), the "isolationists" (Essenes), and the "violent revolutionaries" (Zealots).

Sadducees were the aristocratic elite, the group to which most temple priests belonged. Though relatively small in size, the group represented influence and power. They had achieved a satisfactory mode of accommodation with the occupying Roman forces; moderation and compromise were their values. They were "responsible" collaborators who didn't want any trouble. Religiously, they held to the written Torah only, rejecting the oral tradition of the rabbis.

Pharisees, whose name means "separated," were dedicated to thorough observance of the Mosaic law. They were largely responsible for the development of the elaborate oral tradition surrounding the law, through their scholarly leaders, the scribes. Further, they sought to make the rules of ritual purity binding on all Jews, not just the priests. This fixation on law could be exemplary and devout; it could also become self-serving and even hypocritical. Though they stood in the political tradition of Jewish nationalism, their rigorous concern for purity produced a segregated way of life that resulted in indifference and acquiescence to Roman rule. As long as they could preserve their religious priorities, they chose to be neither cooperators nor revolutionaries.

While the Essenes do not appear as such in the biblical texts, we know about them from both ancient sources (Josephus and Philo) and the discoveries in this century of the Dead Sea Scrolls at Qumran. This highly organized community gave itself to prayer and self-discipline, seeing themselves as the only faithful remnant of God's people. Politically, they were isolated, but awaited the call to the climactic messianic war that would establish the final kingdom.

The Zealots, labeled for their zeal for God's law, reflected the Maccabean heritage, but traced more directly to the uprising against Rome in A.D. 6, led by Judas the Galilean. They were firmly convinced, to the point of suicidal violence, that Roman rule was blasphemous and had to be resisted. Zealots inspired frequent guerrilla attacks and assassinations of Romans and their collaborators, thus creating a climate of fear and unrest. Their final revolutionary outburst in A.D. 66 resulted in the conquest of Jerusalem.

This brief survey of the options before Jesus leads to two important observations. First, these four views all have their modern counterparts; anyone concerned with matters of shalom and justice must choose among available social strategies. Establishment politics is an ever-present fact and usually enjoys the blessing of religious spokespersons, regardless of the nature of the government that receives the support of their words and actions. The separatism of proper religion seeks to draw clear lines between the "spiritual business" of the church and the realm of "social action"; for such persons, only private morality is a Christian concern. Withdrawal continues to be available in various forms: Amish separatism, isolated rural villages, even artificial segregation into homogeneous suburban communities. And of course there is no shortage of religious advocates for revolutions, even violent ones, of either the right or the left, with the usual justification—our cause is righteous, "they" understand only force!

Our second point is to stress that Jesus rejected all four of the existing ways. The establishment never tempted him; indeed, the chief priests appear as the most prominent group opposed to him. While Jesus surely shared the Pharisees' concern for rigorous faithfulness, he rebuked their petty legalism and could not agree with their "inward migration" regarding the larger socio-political issues of the time. Again, there is no evidence that Jesus was ever attracted to a planned isolation; rather, he carried his ministry to the very center of society—Jerusalem.

Zealotry, however, may have represented a temptation for Jesus. In his debate with the devil in the wilderness effort to crown him king, and finally as he faced the cross in Gethsemane, the way of violence could have appeared as an attractive shortcut. We must look more thoroughly at the question of Jesus and violence, because it belongs to the heart of our discussion.

Jesus and Violence

There are, of course, many elements in the Gospels upon which to base the claim for a peaceful, nonviolent Jesus. The language of peace and good will at his birth (Luke 2:14), his teaching on love of enemies and turning the other cheek (Matt. 5:38–48), his blessing of peacemakers (Matt. 5:9), his rebuke of Peter's use of the sword in the garden (John 18:11), and his nonresistant acceptance of his own death (John 18:36) all stand as sufficient testimony for undergirding the Christian pacifist conviction.

There are, however, aspects of his ministry that have posed problems. What shall we make of apparently violent language such as "I have not come to bring peace, but a sword" (Matt. 10:34, RSV) or harsh exchanges with his opponents (Matt. 23; Luke 12:1), or actual involvement in conflict, such as the clearing of the temple (Luke 19:45)?

Throughout the history of the church since it lost its early nonresistance, many writers have argued from these few instances that Jesus approved of, or at least accepted, violence. We cannot go into detail here on these passages; the standard books on biblical pacifism offer extended helpful commentary. The important summary finding is that there is no evidence that Jesus ever advocated or used physical violence against persons.

Of course, if one's picture of Jesus is of a person who is only "gentle, meek, and mild," then these instances of confrontation and divisive action are indeed troublesome. But such a Jesus is a distortion! Jesus in the Gospels is forthright and assertive, but, we repeat, there is no record of his approving physical violence. Always his actions are in the context of love and concern.

Yet when we view his ministry from the perspective of the messianic role, the politics of the kingdom, we recognize how often the option of Zealot violence recurs in the gospel narrative. We noted above several such instances; others could be cited. Most interesting are the indications that Zealot thinking prevailed among those closest to Jesus—the chosen apostles. Peter is the first to recognize that Jesus is the Messiah (Matt. 16:13–20), yet he cannot accept the way of the cross that Jesus then foretells. "The promised king dare not suffer execution!" he declares. "We faithful disciples will not stand for that!" Surely Peter here reveals his Zealot orientation. But Jesus soundly scolds him as a mouthpiece of the devil.

The disciples were slow to learn. When some Samaritans were inhospitable, James and John called for vengeance. But Jesus rebuked them (Luke 9:51–56). And finally in the garden arrest, Peter is still swinging his sword in Maccabean style. Once again, Jesus reversed the act in both deed and word (Luke 22:49–51; John 18:10–11). "Love your enemies, do good to those who hate you" (Luke 6:27, RSV).

The suspicion of Zealotry, however, was so thick around Jesus that the Romans could go along with the charge that he plotted rebellion. It is clear that he was executed in the manner prescribed for political rebels, with the inscription of the charge against him "The King of the Jews" (Mark 15:26, RSV).

The Messianic Community

Is this the answer to our question of "How be king?" Death on a cross? In one very basic sense, yes. As John Howard Yoder writes: "The cross is not a detour or a hurdle on the way to the kingdom, nor is it even the way to the kingdom; it is the kingdom."[2] We will be exploring the manifold implications of the cross and its

meaning for kingdom faith and life in other chapters of this book. But to conclude this chapter, let us pick up another question left unanswered: What is the social strategy of the new movement that Jesus started? For this is fundamental to the politics of the Messiah.

On the way to the cross, Jesus began to gather a distinct people, an intentional community, and to teach them a new way to live. This new society offered:

instead of vengeance—forgiveness (Matt. 6:14–15; Luke 17:3–4; 23:34);

instead of violence—readiness to suffer (Matt. 5:38–39);

instead of greed—sharing (Luke 12:33–34; 18:22);

instead of domination—service (Luke 22:24–27);

instead of hatred—love (Matt. 5:43–45; Luke 6:27–31).

These are the signs of the kingdom. But the learners who gathered around Jesus were slow to grasp his startling message. At their last fellowship meal, they were still arguing over pride of place (Luke 22:24). Jesus had to admonish them, both by word (Luke 22:25–27) and by example (John 13:1–20) that the model for the coming kingdom was the suffering servant. And yet he entrusted them with his mission to the world: "I confer on you a kingdom, just as my Father conferred one on me" (Luke 22:29).

The seeds for the politics of the Messiah had been planted. Later, the waiting disciples would receive the Spirit of Peace (John 20:19–23). In the power of that Spirit, they would recall his words and build on his model as they proclaimed the rule of justice and peace.

[2]John Howard Yoder, *The Politics of Jesus* (Grand Rapids: Eerdmans, 1972), 61.

The Sermon on the Mount and the Doctrine of Nonresistance

Glenn A. Robitaille

Glenn Robitaille came to the Brethren in Christ Church from a nonpacifist church tradition. He has pastored for twenty years in both Ontario, Canada, and Ohio. Nearly two-thirds of his pastoral experience has been in church planting, where a Christian peace stance was not readily understood. His counseling experience throughout his pastoral service led to the foundation in 1999 of the Barnabas Christian Counseling Network, which provides therapy online through certified Christian counselors. The chapter reflects his academic and pastoral insights on Matthew 5, as well as his personal faith journey.

The article asks us to decide whom Jesus had in mind when He told us not to resist evil in violent ways: personal enemies, public criminals, or national aggressors. Are there different types or degrees of Christian pacifism? Are all interpretations of Matthew 5 equally valid?[1]

For the last five years, I have been privileged to serve the Brethren in Christ Church as a member of the Commission on Ministry and Doctrine. Among the duties assigned to members is that of evaluating the responses of ministry candidates to questions of doctrine and practice. My observation has been that the one area of doctrine in which the answers are consistently weak is peace and nonresistance.

I did not grow up in a peace church. My father was a captain in the Ohio National Guard most of my early life, and the idea of violence being anything but necessary under certain circumstances never occurred to me. My challenge came in my early twenties as a neophyte Brethren in Christ pastor seeking credentials within the church. Because of my weakness in this understanding, it was suggested by my senior pastor, Dale Shaw, and my bishop, Harvey Sider, that I spend time discussing the issue with E.J. Swalm—a patriarch of the peace position in his day.

The conversion I experienced to the position of peace was as radical and life-changing as my conversion out of the Roman Catholic Church. I have since come to believe that the doctrine transcends the issue of violence and addresses

---

[1]See the fine collection of articles in *The Love of Enemy and Nonretaliation in the New Testament*, edited by Willard M. Swartley. (Louisville: Westminster/John Knox, 1992).

This chapter originally appeared as Glenn A. Robitaille, "The Sermon on the Mount and the Doctrine of Nonresistance," *Brethren in Christ History and Life* 20, no. 3 (1997), 272–90.

deeper issues of ultimate meaning. Indeed, it is an essential understanding in shaping the believer in the pattern portrayed in the Gospels, and in the image of Christ himself.

In these complicated days of global competition and ideological confusion, a position of peace is not very popular. Even those who embrace the view find it hard to be consistent, as it is challenged by often brutal and painful realities. Differences exist even among those who hold the doctrine about how to apply their conviction of peace. This reality above all others is the motivation behind this paper.

I have often described myself as the world's most reluctant pacifist. Very little of what flows in my veins resonates with the notion of peace; but I cannot deny that peace forms one of the central pillars in the teaching and example of Christ. No other command of Jesus more requires me to "deny self" or to "take up my cross and follow" him than does this one, and no other doctrine requires deeper trust. Perhaps that is why it is so easily dismissed by so many.

In the first section of this paper I shall examine the relevant passages from the Sermon on the Mount which provide the foundation for this doctrine. In the second, I shall examine the various views prevalent in the Brethren in Christ Church and provide an overview of their meanings.

I offer this paper in the hope that it will be helpful in underscoring the importance of the doctrine of peace, and that it will provide a framework for discussion among those who hold to the varying views. I do so believing that peace in its different forms is more than an intellectual acknowledgment; it is an attitude of the heart that holds within its core one of the greatest mysteries and challenges of the

Christian faith. In practice, it is about peace; but in essence, it is about love.

The Biblical Basis
for the Doctrine of Nonresistance

The biblical validation for what has been historically called the doctrine of nonresistance is found primarily in Matthew 5:38–48 and its companion passage, Luke 6:27–36. While the sequence is different, the material itself, regarded by most scholars to have its origin in the hypothetical source Q, is essentially the same in both Gospels.[2] For the purposes of this article I shall be focusing on that material which appears in Matthew's Gospel as part of the Sermon on the Mount.

The basis for the doctrine flows from two complementary pericopes—portions of Scripture—which appear in succession: Matthew 5:38–42 and 5:43–48.

> You have heard that it was said, "Eye for eye and tooth for tooth." But I tell you, *Do not resist an evil person.* If someone strikes you on the right cheek, turn to him the other also. And if someone wants to sue you and take your tunic, let him have your cloak as well. If someone forces you to go one mile, go with him two miles. Give to the one who asks you, and do not turn away from the one who wants to borrow from you (Matt. 5:38–42).

It is commonly accepted among most scholars that Jesus is setting this teaching over against the *lex talionis*—the principle of retribution—as it is described in Exodus 21:24, Leviticus 24:19–20, and Deuteronomy 19:21. These texts were not condoning the notion of vengeance, which the law explicitly forbade (Lev. 19:18). The intention appears to be to provide the judicial system with a ready formula of punishment with the intention of terminating vendettas.[3] The *principle of*

---

[2]Frank E. Gabelein, gen. ed., *The Expositor's Bible Commentary,* vol. 8 (Grand Rapids: Zondervan, 1984), 155.

[3]Ibid.

retribution, therefore, was a step forward in matters of justice for the people of God. It would also appear from Christ's words in this section that a further step was needed.

In determining Christ's intent in making this comment, one must establish what is meant by "an evil person," for it is such a person the Christian is called upon not to resist. Some have suggested that it is not a person at all who is to be the object of our nonresistance, but something else—an evil *presence* of some kind. This thought is not well supported by the text. Scripture expressly commands us to "resist the devil" in James 4:7, and Paul commands us to "not be overcome by evil, but overcome evil with good" (Rom. 12:21). Even so, John Chrysostom maintained that *to ponero*—the evil—did refer to Satan personally, and both Luther and Calvin interpreted it as a neuter force of "injustice."[4] This, however, cannot be reconciled with the use of the verb *rhapizei*—to strike—in the following verse, which indicates that the one "striking on the cheek" is a very real person doing so with the palm of the hand,[5] and not a spiritual or composite force.

When *poneros* is used of persons in the ethical sense, it means wicked, evil, bad, base, worthless, vicious, degenerate.[6] This kind of person seems to be the intended object of nonresistance identified in this passage. According to Clifton Allen, *"Do not resist* through violent means of self-

defense, *one who is evil"* (RSV) is the correct translation, not "evil in the abstract."[7] Even the worst of human beings is not to be resisted, in contrast to what is said in the Mosaic law, the Code of Hammurabi, and the Roman law, all of which required the wrongdoer to be visited with as much as he gave.[8]

The other question that must be asked is, what is meant by "do not resist"? Jesus offers four examples as illustrations of his intent. The first example is, "If someone strikes you on the right cheek, turn to him the other also"(v. 39). A blow on the cheek was an insult delivered with the back of the hand, so that the palm of the hand could return with a blow to the left cheek.[9] The implication inherent in this is that "Jesus' disciples will gladly endure the insult again," rather than seeking recompense at law under the *lex talionis*.[10]

The second example is, "And if someone wants to sue you and take your tunic, let him have your cloak as well"(v. 40). Here the connection to the legal system is more specifically mentioned. Under Mosaic law the outer cloak was an inalienable possession (Ex. 22:26, Deut. 24:13), and could not be obtained through litigation.[11] That point notwithstanding, Jesus enjoined his disciples to willingly part with that which they were legally entitled to keep.

The third example likely refers to the Roman privilege of commandeering civilians to carry the luggage of their

[4]Heinrich A.W. Meyer, *Meyer s Commentary on the New Testament: Gospel of St. Matthew* (New York: Funk and Wagnalls, 1884), 137.

[5]William D. Mounce, *The Analytical Lexicon to the Greek New Testament* (Grand Rapids: Zondervan, 1993), 406.

[6]Ibid., 690.

[7]George A. Buttrick, ed., *The Interpreter s Bible,* vol. 7 (New York: Abingdon-Cokesbury, 1951), 301.

[8]Ibid.

[9]Ibid.

[10]Gabelein, *Expositor s Bible Commentary,* 156.

[11]Ibid.

military personnel one Roman mile. "If someone forces you to go one mile," Jesus says, "go with him two miles" (v.41). This is not a hardship of the same degree as the first two, but clearly an indignity to Christ's audience, who experienced this as humiliation. Nevertheless, Jesus invokes his disciples to go the required mile and more.

The fourth example is, "Give to the one who asks you, and do not turn away from the one who wants to borrow from you" (v. 42). The intent of this instruction is that the Christian is to have a generous spirit. No attempt is made to discern whether or not "indiscriminate almsgiving is wise, or whether one has responsibilities to family that supersede other such obligations; the point is simply that Christ's followers will have generous impulses, and will act on them."[12]

What we see in this section, therefore, is a call to nonresistance and generosity whether in reference to a mortal enemy or a friend, without much attempt at clarifying such instructions for specific circumstances. They are broad, sweeping, general principles. As Dorothy Jean Weaver observes,

> At this point the saying ends. There are no motive clauses and no further words of explanation. After his listing of illustrative imperatives (5:39b–42) Jesus simply moves on to the sixth and final "antithesis" (5:43–48). But here in this final "antithesis" Jesus puts into words that which until now has remained unspoken. The motive clause that is missing from the command "not to resist the one who is evil" finds clear expression in the saying that follows:

You have heard that it was said, "Love your neighbor and hate your enemy." But I tell you: *Love your enemies* and pray for those who persecute you, that you may be the sons of your Father in heaven. He causes his sun to rise on the evil and the good, and sends rain on the righteous and the unrighteous. If you love those who love you, what reward will you get? Are not even the tax collectors doing that? And if you greet only your brothers, what are you doing more than others? Do not even pagans do that? Be perfect, therefore, even as your Heavenly Father is perfect (Matt. 5:43–48).[13]

The command to "love your neighbor" would not have been foreign to Christ's audience, as it was part of the Mosaic law (Lev. 19:18), but the notion of loving one's enemies was new. It can be said that the law required a certain fairness with respect to how *aliens* were treated, but it was not a prescription anywhere in the law that enemies should be loved. Rabbinic literature was no more generous.[14] It is not surprising then that the Sadducees and the Pharisees were not the least bit sympathetic to such an inclusive doctrine of love. The Qumran community commanded love for "those whom God had elected," meaning the community itself, but hatred for the outsider,[15] and the attitude of the Zealots was clearly antagonistic to enemies in every way. Thus when Jesus made this declaration, he was propounding a new concept.

This imperative is not presented in this text for its shock value; rather, it is offered as a condition for being "the sons of your Father in heaven" (Matt. 5:45). The phrase *hopos genesthe huioi tou patros humon tou en*

---

[12]Buttrick, *Interpreter s Bible,* 302.

[13]In Willard M. Swartley, ed., *The Love of Enemy and Nonretaliation,* 57.

[14]Gabelein, *Expositor s Bible Commentary,* 157.

[15]Ibid.

ouranois is a conditional clause—"so that you [all] may become sons [children] of your Father in heaven." The force of the thought is revealed in the comparative interrogatives that follow, which can be paraphrased: "What great virtue and accomplishment are yours if you merely 'love' and 'greet' those who love and greet you? Are not even the 'tax collectors' and 'pagans' capable of that?" Theodore Robinson comments on this point:

> If men merely *love those who love* them, and *salute* their *friends,* they are still on the level of novices. They have, in fact, not yet entered into the competition. Instead of attaining to a higher class in *goodness* than the scribes and the Pharisees who gave their whole lives to the subject, they have not risen above the *tax collector* and the *pagan* who know little about *goodness,* and perhaps care less. It is not thus that (people) enter the *realm of heaven.*[16]

The force of this section seems to find its resolution in verse 48: "Be perfect, therefore, as your heavenly Father is perfect." The form of this verse is exactly like Leviticus 19:2, with "holy" being displaced by "perfect."[17] The force of the future *esesthe,* literally "you will be," is imperatival[18] which would indicate an expectation on Christ's part that the hearer would take this instruction seriously and *become* what the passage is calling for in the measure possible. What we are to become is perfect—*teleioi*—which can be rendered "mature" or "full grown" in some instances, but makes no sense according to that definition when used in reference to our heavenly Father who is offered as our example of this quality. More likely,

> Jesus is saying that the true direction in which the law has always pointed is not toward mere judicial restraints, concessions arising out of the hardness of men's hearts, still less casuistical perversions, nor even the "law of love." No, it pointed rather to *all the perfection of God,* exemplified by the authoritative interpretation of the law bound up in the preceding antitheses. This perfection Jesus' disciples must emulate if they are truly followers of him who fulfills the Law and the Prophets."[19]

The call, therefore, is for the serious disciple of Christ to transcend legalistic approaches to the law, and to emulate his or her heavenly Father who "causes his sun to rise on the evil and the good, and sends rain on the righteous and the unrighteous" (v. 45), without regard for the recipient's attitude toward him.

> The perfection demanded by Jesus (v. 48) is not the legalism of the Pharisees or the Qumranites but a deeper and radical understanding of the Law's intention. Matthew finds sinless perfection only in Jesus, but he does not flinch in representing Jesus as making radical, ultimate, and absolute demands upon his followers.[20]

Practical Responses to Violence and Evil

It is probably true that the teaching of Jesus found in Matthew 5:38–48 is the

---

[16]Theodore H. Robinson, *The Moffat New Testament Commentary: The Gospel of Matthew* (London: Hodder & Stoughton, 1928), 45.

[17]Gabelein, *Expositor s Bible Commentary,* 160.

[18]Clifton J. Allen, gen. ed., *The Broadman Bible Commentary,* vol. 8 (Nashville: Broadman, 1969), 112.

[19]Gabelein, *Expositor s Bible Commentary,* 161.

[20]Allen, *Broadman Bible Commentary,* 112.

most difficult in all of Scripture. Accordingly, it is among the most defining. Serious questions have been raised about the validity of the section by many, calling it everything from "hyperbole"[21] to "inadequate."[22] Others see it as the key consideration in identifying the true follower of Christ.[23]

In my reflection on this doctrine, I have found it most helpful to consider the various views through the lens of resistance, and the degrees and kinds of resistance deemed acceptable. I have organized these views as follows:

1. Nonresistance.

Among those who hold to a strict nonresistance, any form of violence or resistance is deemed unacceptable regardless of the cause or motive. The center of this doctrine is the *self* and how one's personal relationship with God and others would be affected by an act. By "center" I mean that part of the belief that is held most sacred, or that forms the motivation underlying the view. Many of our Brethren in Christ ancestors were nonresistants, declaring that they could not be moved to violence even in defense of their wives or children. Some were imprisoned for their beliefs during World War I and threatened with execution.[24]

Nonresistants make no demands of the violator and expect no accountability; rather they leave issues of justice to God.

2. Passive Resistance.

This view, often described as nonviolent resistance, is one centered on *justice*. Resistance is acceptable under this view as long as it does not involve acts of violence. Henry David Thoreau popularized this concept in his classic work, *Civil Disobedience*. According to Thoreau, "A minority is powerless while it conforms to the majority; it is not even a minority then; but it is irresistible when it clogs by its whole weight."[25] In the twentieth century, Ghandi and Martin Luther King Jr. led successful reform movements based on the principles set forth in Thoreau's work and a nonviolent, passive resistance approach to Christ's teaching on the subject. King eloquently makes the point by saying,

> We cannot in all good conscience obey your unjust laws, because non-cooperation with evil is as much a moral obligation as is cooperation with the good...but be assured that we will wear you down by our capacity to suffer....We shall so appeal to your heart and conscience that we shall win *you* in the process, and our victory will be a double victory.[26]

---

[21]Gabelein, *Expositor s Bible Commentary,* 157.

[22]Robert G. Clouse, ed., *War: Four Christian Views* (Downers Grove, Ill.: InterVarsity Press, 1991), 123.

[23]Stanley Hauerwas, *The Peaceable Kingdom: A Primer in Christian Ethics* (Notre Dame, Ind.: University of Notre Dame Press, 1983), xvi.

[24]For examples, see E.J. Swalm, *Nonresistance under Test: A Compilation of Experiences of Conscientious Objectors as Encountered in Two World Wars* (Nappanee, Ind.: E.V. Publishing House, 1949), 27–57; Carlton 0. Wittlinger, *Quest for Piety and Obedience* (Nappanee, Ind.: Evangel Press, 1978), especially chapter 16; E. Morris Sider, *The Brethren in Christ in Canada: Two Hundred Years of Tradition and Change* (Fort Erie, Ont.: The Canadian Conference, Brethren in Christ Church, 1988), chapter 10.

[25]Henry David Thoreau, *Civil Disobedience* (New York: Penguin Classics, 1983), 399.

[26]Martin Luther King Jr., *Strength to Love* (New York: Harper & Row, 1963), 40.

Of course, the victory King had in mind was a political one relating to equal rights, not salvation. This is not the case with the third form of resistance.

3. Reverse Resistance.

Reverse resistance is a *conversion-centered* approach focused on the transformation of the aggressor. With this view, the teachings of Christ are usually combined with Paul's instruction in Romans 12:9–21, with special emphasis on verses 20–21:

If your enemy is hungry, feed him;

if he is thirsty, give him something to drink.

In doing this, you will heap burning coals on his head.

Do not be overcome by evil, but overcome evil with good.

Heinrich Meyer espoused this view, suggesting,

> This idea, which is that of love, yielding and putting to shame in the spirit of self-denial, and overcoming evil with good, is concretely represented in those examples (Matt. 5:38–42; John 18:22ff.), but has, in the relations of external life and its individual cases, the *measure* and the limitation of its moral practice.[27]

John H. Yoder agrees:

> If I am the child of a Father who loves both good and evil children, if I am a witness for a God who loves his enemies, then when I love my enemy I am *proclaiming that love.* I am not just obeying it; I am communicating it. And I cannot communicate it any other way.[28]

I see evidence of this view in the philosophy and practice of Mennonite Central Committee and its subsidiary, Mennonite Disaster Service. Those who risked their lives during the recent Gulf War to be witnesses for peace by becoming a buffer between the two factions are also of this persuasion. Their resistance was proactive and offensive rather than reactive and defensive, with the ultimate hope of effecting a change of heart in the warring parties, or of being a living example of the love of Christ.

4. Limited Resistance.

Limited resistance is a *person-centered* approach focusing on issues of human well-being. With this view, resistance—even violence—is acceptable if human well-being is being threatened. According to Paul Ramsay,

> While Jesus taught that a disciple in his own case should turn the other cheek, he did not enjoin that his disciples should lift up the face of another oppressed man for *him* to be struck on *his* other cheek. It is no part of the work of charity to allow this to continue to happen. When choice *must* be made between the perpetrator of injustice and the many victims of it, the latter may and should be preferred—even if to do so would require the use of armed force against some evil power.[29]

Under this scenario, resistance, violence, even war is permissable providing human well-being is being threatened. Proponents may find justification in the war against Nazi Germany and the Napoleonic wars, and question the American Revolution and the Crusades. Erasmus of Rotterdam—a pacifist by nature—would have been a proponent of this view.[30]

---

[27]Meyer, *Meyer s Commentary,* 137.

[28]John H. Yoder, *He Came Preaching Peace* (Scottdale, Pa.: Herald, 1985), 52.

[29]Paul Ramsay, *The Just War* (Savage, Md.: Littlefield Adams, 1983), 143.

[30]Roland H. Bainton, *Christian Attitudes toward War and Peace* (New York: Abingdon, 1960), 131.

5. Active Resistance.

Those who espouse this view are *rights-centered* in their approach to resistance. Proponents might argue that Jesus was talking to a defeated people in the Sermon on the Mount who lacked the means to resist. Some might compare the biblical presentation on the subject to its discussion of slavery, which is seemingly accepting of the norms of the day but clearly in violation of the spirit of what Christ taught.[31]

While some who hold to what has been described as the just war theory are more *limited* in their approach than *active,* it is the active definition that more frequently describes the ideology of those who have most often laid claim to the title. A just war is any war where an ideal of any kind is being protected, more often than not in the name of God. During the Protestant Reformation, Luther, Zwingli, Calvin, and Pope Leo IV all found justification in the theory for their own violence against the Anabaptists and other detractors, and even against one another. In our own day, a shortage of oil is justification enough.

Within the family of peace churches, adherents of the first three views can most often be found in both pure and blended forms. The Brethren in Christ Church—once strongly nonresistant—is now more adequately defined as a church of the second category: passive resistance. This is evident in such General Conference actions as the approval of the Board for Brotherhood Concerns' "Statement on Lotteries and Gambling," which suggests in its third recommendation that "we use our influence to help in the formation of *public policy* that eliminates gambling and lotteries as sources of public revenue."[32]

Similar recommendations were adopted during the 1986 General Conference with respect to pornography and abortion,[33] all of which move away from a position of not resisting evil to one of proactively confronting it in a peaceful, nonviolent way.

Also conspicuous by their growing numbers are those holding to a position of *limited resistance,* as is evidenced by the growing number of ministry candidates who express this view on doctrinal questionnaires, and the discussion that often occurs around the subject of nonresistance on the floor of General Conference.

The question that is begged by these developments is whether or not limited resistance should be regarded as a legitimate view in light of the two pericopes we have examined. The heart of the issue rests in whether or not Christ's comments are to be interpreted as ideals, or as strict definitions of literal behavior. Qualifying Christ's teaching on this subject as idealism allows for a certain subjectivity, opening the door to "dilutions by endless equivocations."[34] Is this something peace churches really want to do?

Whether or not one agrees with how others interpret this material, Romans 14 suggests that a person's first responsibility in a "disputable matter" is to respect his or her own conscience without violating the conscience of another (vv. 13-19). At all times and in every way, the committed Christian must do what he or she believes God desires to be done, and allow others the same privilege. Thoreau is very nearly correct in saying, "The only obligation which I have the right to assume, is to do at any time what I think

---

[31]Ramsay, *Just War,* 151.

[32]*General Conference Minutes,* 1988, 98–99.

[33]*General Conference Minutes,* 1986, 97–98.

[34]Gabelein, *Expositor s Bible Commentary,* 157.

[35]Thoreau, *Civil Disobedience,* 387.

right"[35]—a notion that goes over very well in the individualistic West. There is a wide chasm, however, between doing what "I think right," and what Scripture indicates God desires to be done. Nevertheless, the issue of peace and nonresistance is primarily an issue of conscience, and something good is compromised when the freedom to follow one's conscience is displaced by any kind of legalism, regardless of how noble its intent.

The freedom to follow Scripture according to one's conscience is a hallmark of Anabaptist thought, and must therefore be included in the list of considerations in determining one's response to the existence of violence and evil. This subject is disputable by the breadth of diversity in the question, and by how dependent responses seem to be on issues of culture, context, and social location.

To my thinking, the relative merit of a particular view is best established by examining the center that is engaged by it. The center of *nonresistance*—a concern about remaining faithful to the will and purpose of God in relationships—is certainly biblical and worthwhile. John Yoder asserts,

> No one created in God's image and for whom Christ died can be for me an enemy, whose life I am willing to threaten or to take, unless I am more devoted to something else—to a political theory, to a nation, to the defense of certain privileges, or to my own personal welfare—than I am to God's cause: his loving invasion of this world in his prophets, his Son, and his church."[35]

This is the position with which all more permissive views must reckon.

The center of *passive resistance* is justice. This too is an ideal well supported in the New and Old Testaments. If Jesus intended that even evil in the church not be

resisted, a passage like James 2 where rich oppressors are confronted, or Galatians 2 where Paul confronts Peter's duplicity with the Gentiles, would be against the principle Christ taught in the Sermon on the Mount. Also, Paul would have been wrong for appealing to Caesar, if justice was never an issue in selecting a response. Therefore, biblically, justice is a concern that must be considered in determing how we must honor God in conflict.

It is also worth noting that political vehicles for confronting social injustice did not exist at the time the New Testament was being written. In our present day, with global awareness of justice issues growing, does the church not have a responsibility to use all of the peaceful means available to it to speak for the disadvantaged, both at home and abroad, including political pressure? Proponents of passive resistance would argue that we do, quoting such authorities as God himself through the prophet Isaiah:

Is not this the kind of fasting I have chosen:
to loose the chains of injustice
     and untie the cords of the yoke, to set the
     oppressed free
     and break every yoke? (Isa. 58:6)

It seems that *passive resistance* is a biblical view that deserves consideration, despite the fact that evil is resisted in a passive, yet forthright way.

The center of *reverse* resistance—conversion—is also well supported in Scripture. The aforementioned passage, Romans 12:17–21, would indicate that to aggressively attack hatred with love with the intention of bringing others to Christ is consistent with the heart and mind of God. Proponents may well overlook an issue of injustice in order to demonstrate the love of God to an oppressor. They would argue that to make justice the cen-

---

[36]Yoder, *He Came Preaching Peace,* 20.

ter of the process is to make justice more important than the salvation of the unjust.

Support for this view can be found in the instruction Paul gives to slaves in Titus 2:9–10:

> Teach slaves to be subject to their masters in everything, to try to please them, not to talk back to them, and not to steal from them, but to show that they can be fully trusted, so that in every way *they will make the teaching about God our Savior attractive.*

Conversion is also a matter to be considered in evaluating conflict.

The center of *limited resistance* is human well-being. This is also an ideal well established in Scripture as being close to the heart of God. When Christ verbally attacked the Pharisees and scribes in Matthew 23, much of his diatribe focused on their abuse of people—their neglect of the "more important matters of the law—justice, mercy and faithfulness" (v. 23). The question, therefore, becomes: is there any indication in Scripture that Jesus practiced or advocated violence against another as part of protecting human well-being? Some appeal to Christ's comment in Luke 22:36 as evidence of this: "But now, if you have a purse, take it, and also a bag; and if you don't have a sword, sell your cloak and buy one."

But without further explanation, one must resort to extrapolation in determining Christ's intent. If the subject is considered in light of gospel teaching and the example of Christ found therein, no compelling argument can be found for violence being justified under any circumstances. *Limited resistance* is not a gospel doctrine.

The more profound consideration in this discussion is Romans 13:1–7 where Paul urges submission to the governing authorities, declaring, "he does not bear the sword for nothing. He is God's servant, an agent of wrath to bring pun-

ishment on the wrongdoer" (Rom. 13:4). If nothing else, this suggests that the "sword" and its violence can be used in the service of God when it metes out punishment on the wrongdoer. It is also worth noting that this very observation directly follows the injunction: "Do not be overcome by evil, but overcome evil with good" (12:21), and is followed by a call for love: "The commandments…are summed up in this one rule: 'Love your neighbor as yourself.' Love does no harm to its neighbor, therefore love is the fulfillment of the law" (Rom. 13:9–10).

If, therefore, a concession is being made for violence in the name of justice, it is not being done at the expense of the higher call for "love," and for "overcoming evil with good." Nor can it be argued that support for war of any kind is rooted in this pericope. What can be argued is that civil authorities including the police have a divine mandate to protect truth and justice, and that violence under such circumstances is permissible. Therefore it is possible to include those who hold to a view of limited resistance that extends as far as civil law within the family of peace.

Whether or not a Christian should be a civil servant is not answered in this text; it remains a matter of conscience. What is clear is that a civil servant is "an agent of God" by virtue of his or her office, and that being such an agent does not parallel being a Christian. The implication is that God is the one who holds an ultimate concern in the area of justice, and those who act in the interests of justice are accountable to him.

Accordingly, whether or not one agrees with the acceptability of violence under any circumstances, those who hold to a high view of Scripture must agree that biblically allowance is made for some to oppose violence and evil with the sword without compromising their standing as "servants" of God. It must also be agreed that this same respect for Scripture compels us to note the absence of any New Testament support for the possibility of a Christian participating in war. Active resistance is not a New Testament view.

The balance seems to be found in the recognition that God calls us to "peace" (Heb. 12:14, 1 Cor. 7:15), and to be "peacemakers" (Matt. 5:9), and also to be "just" (Phil. 4:8, NRSV; Titus 1:8, NASB). In our seeking of these ideals, he further calls us to respect one another in our differences, and to recognize that he is the one before whom every servant must "stand" (Rom. 14:4). It is significant to me that this chapter arrives on the heels of Paul's discussion of these very controversial issues.

There are no easy alliances between peace and justice, and the questions raised are not easily answered. God, however, calls us to peace most of all with one another. I resonate with Dale Brown when he says,

> It should be recognized that there are different kinds of pacifist responses. Some advocate a style of non-resistance. Some would attempt to deal with the attacker in a calm spirit of reason and prayer. Others would defend their families physically to the point of eliminating their attacker if necessary. Some of these would do everything short of actually killing the adversary. Some pacifists would participate in police action but not in war. Others could not participate in police action themselves but would grant its legitimacy for the state in an evil world. Thus we have seen that a pacifist stance....is held by a wide variety of people whose beliefs about their personal responses to force vary.[37]

Conclusion

Whatever one's philosophy is in this area, it is probably uncertain how one will react in times of conflict until the conflict has arrived. My personal conviction around the pericopes examined is a more literal one, but I am not so arrogant as to think that I know how even I would respond under certain circumstances. What I do know is that I desire to be a person of peace who is willing to die if necessary to preserve the sacred ideals of the Lord Jesus Christ who died for me.

---

[37]Dale W. Brown, *Brethren and Pacifism* (Elgin, Ill.: Brethren Press, 1970), 116.

Chapter Five

Does the New Testament Sanction War?

G.H.C. MacGregor

G.H.C. MacGregor was a professor of divinity and biblical criticism at the University of Glasgow and thus was a voice in the pacifist movement in the United Kingdom at the time of World War II. Nonpacifists point to a list of New Testament texts that they assert condone Christian uses of violence in the cause of justice or in occasions of international conflict. MacGregor examines several of these alleged texts and refutes the contention that they justify Christian participation in warfare.

Many pragmatic arguments can be advanced for and against participation in war, and they have their place in ethical deliberation. However, as MacGregor says in the preface of his book, war for the Christian is a moral problem that can be resolved only upon theological grounds.[1] Thus, the case for pacifism stands or falls on the biblical witness.

What does Jesus teach regarding conflict and its resolution? Do the so-called violence passages of the New Testament advocate war?[2] If not, then what do they mean?

Both sides to the present controversy must plead guilty to the unfortunate practice of quoting isolated texts, often wrested from their context; and in view of the constant and light-hearted misapplication of certain well-known passages, it will be well to deal with them, before entering upon a more positive and constructive study of the New Testament evidence. The passages will first be quoted from the Revised Version; the use made of them by certain apologists for militarism will then be indicated, and, where necessary, a corrective will be provided. We shall confine ourselves to the New Testament. Admittedly much use is made in certain quarters of passages drawn from

---

[1]G.H.C. MacGregor, *The New Testament Basis of Pacifism and The Relevance of an Impossible Ideal* (Nyack, N.Y.: Fellowship Publications, 1954), 5.

[2]See also the excellent discussion by Jean Lasserre on the "violence passages" of the New Testament in *War and the Gospel* (Scottdale, Pa.: Herald, 1962).

This chapter is an abridgment of chapter 2 in G.H.C. MacGregor, *The New Testament Basis of Pacifism*, which is bound together with another treatise by MacGregor, *The Relevance of an Impossible Ideal* (Nyack, N.Y.: Fellowship Publications, 1954), in which he critiques the position of Reinhold Niebuhr.

the more war-like sections of the Old Testament; the question whether the will and the hand of God are to be traced in the aggressive wars of Israel is one that must be frankly faced. But our present task is not the philosophy of history but the interpretation of Scripture, and if the New Testament is always to be understood in the light of the Old, rather than the Old Testament re-interpreted in the light of the New, then we may well despair of any progress towards the truth.

> For the man who relates the question of Christianity and War to the whole Bible, while regarding the Bible as a unity, the whole of which lies on one level, the problem is insoluble. But he for whom the Scriptures are not a static unity, but an organic (for an organism passes through phases of growth), a progressive and ever fuller revelation of God's being and will, *he* will be able to see an ascending line, which finds its goal and zenith in Jesus Christ.[3]

Moreover it often seems to be forgotten that Jesus prefaces the most crucial of all our passages with the words, "Ye have heard that it was said by them of old time...But I say unto you" (Matt. 5:21–22, 27–28, 33–34, 38–39, 43–44, KJV). Could Jesus have possibly indicated more clearly that He claimed, and was indeed exercising, the right to correct the misconceptions even of the Old Testament Scriptures themselves? As Windisch again well says: "The brutal dictates of War and State in the Old Testament simply do not arise for the man who has grasped the antitheses of the Sermon on the Mount."[4]

The Cleansing of the Temple (Mark 11:15–18; Matt. 21:12–13; Luke 19:45–46; John 2:13–17): especially John 2:15:

"And he made a scourge of cords, and cast all out of the temple, both the sheep and the oxen."

Jesus, it is argued, was no pusillanimous Pacifist, but a man capable of righteous anger, which expressed itself in an act of aggressive personal violence against the desecrators of the Temple. What better justification does a Christian need even for aggressive warfare in a just cause?

This scene admittedly indicates a reaction against evil on the part of Jesus much more strenuous than the meek acquiescence which is commonly misrepresented as Pacifism. But we are not concerned to deny that there is room in Jesus' ethic for a discriminating use of force. Note, however, the following points:

(1) It is the Fourth Gospel alone which mentions the "scourge." Jewish tradition held that the Messiah at his coming would bear a lash for the chastisement of evil-doers (cf. the winnowing "fan" in Matt. 3:12). Scholars are agreed that the whole significance of the scene in this Gospel is Messianic, and the Evangelist's well-known love of symbolism suggests that the "scourge" is to be regarded as an emblem of authority rather than as a weapon of offence. But even if the word is to be taken literally, a correct rendering of the Greek makes it clear that the whip was used only on the ani-

---

[3]Gerrit Jan Heering, *The Fall of Christianity: A Study of Christianity, the State, and War*, trans. J.W. Thompson (London: Allen & Unwin, 1930), 19.

[4]Hans Windisch, *Der Sinn der Bergpredigt: Ein Beitrag zum Problem der richtigen Exegese* (Leipzig: J.C. Hinrichs'sche Buchhandlung, 1929), 154.

mals.[5] Finally, the word[6] which in its English dress "cast out" gives the impression of extreme violence, is frequently used in the New Testament without any such suggestion, e.g., "Pray ye therefore the Lord of the harvest, that he *send forth* labourers into his harvest" (Matt. 9:38). The parallel verse in Mark might quite legitimately be translated without any hint of exceptional violence: "He entered into the temple, and began to *send out* them that sold and them that bought in the temple" (Mark 11:5).

(2) Had Jesus used violence, He must inevitably have provoked retaliation and been overpowered by superior numbers. Much more probably it was the compelling "authority" of His words which overawed His opponents; their conscience condemned them, and they withdrew in disorder. Moral authority, unarmed, triumphed where violence would have been futile. There would seem to be an argument here for Pacifism at least equal to that against it.

(3) In any case, the passage has no relevance whatever to war. "My house," says Jesus, "shall be called a house of prayer *for all the nations,* but ye have made it a den of robbers" (Mark 11:17).

Probably the scene of the desecration was the outer Court, which was open to Gentiles. The foreigner was being robbed of his right of approach to Israel's God. An incident which is so often adduced as an apology for war can in fact be read as a protest by Jesus on behalf of international goodwill.

The Centurion at Capernaum (Matt. 8:5–10; Luke 7:1–10): "Jesus marvelled and said to them that followed, Verily I say unto you, I have not found so great faith, no, not In Israel."

It is pointed out that Jesus commends the centurion, and never hints that there is anything wrong in the occupation of a soldier, or that the centurion should give up the profession of arms. Jesus, then, would give no countenance to Pacifism. A similar use is made of Luke 3:14, where John the Baptist answers the soldiers' questions without condemning their calling. Thus Augustine, quoted by Calvin with approval: "If Christian discipline condemned all wars, when the soldiers asked counsel as to the way of salvation, they would have been told to cast away their arms....Those whom he orders to be contented with their pay, he certainly does not forbid to serve."[7] In reply we may note:

---

[5]The Greek here is πάντας ἐξέβαλεν ἐκ τοῦ ἱεροῦ, τα τε πρόβατα καὶ τοὺς βόας. Note (a) a common and correct use of the particles τε...καὶ is to subdivide a subject or object, previously mentioned, into its component parts. Here πάντας "all of them" (i.e., all the animals), is further defined as consisting of "sheep" (πρόβατα) and "oxen" (βόας) Cf. Mathew.22:10: πάντας σὗς εὖρον, πονηρούς τε καὶ ἀγαθούς. Another good example is Rom. 2:9–10, where the construction occurs twice. Cf. also Luke 22:66. (b) It is sometimes objected that, if πάντας referred only to the animals, it should naturally be in the neuter gender agreeing with πρόβατα (the nearest word), rather than the masculine agreeing with βόας; being masculine it must refer to the men. But the grammatical rule is that, when one adjective qualifies two nouns of different genders, it will agree with the masculine or feminine noun rather than with the neuter noun, irrespective of position. A good example is Heb. 3:6: εἀν τὴν παρρησίαν καὶ τὸ καύχημα τῆς ἐλπίδος μέχρι τέλους βεβαίαν κατάσχωμεν.

[6]ἐκβάλλειν.

[7]There is a certain unconscious humour in the fact that in the *Westminster Confession,* Chapter XXIII, the first New Testament authority cited in support of the proposition that "Christians...may lawfully, now under the New Testament, wage war upon just and necessary occasions" is Luke 3:14: "And soldiers also asked him saying, And we, what must we do? And he said unto them, *Do violence to no man.*"

(1) It was the centurion's faith, not his calling, which Jesus commended. Moreover this is one of the very few occasions on which Jesus is said to have "marvelled." The chief impression left by the story is that Jesus was greatly surprised to find faith in so unlikely a quarter, though doubtless this was chiefly because the man was a heathen.

(2) An "argument from silence" is always precarious, and never more so than when applied to the Gospels....As Dr. Martin Dibelius says, "The first Christians had no interest in reporting the life and passion of Jesus objectively to mankind....They wanted nothing else than to win as many as possible to salvation in the last hour just before the end of the world, which they believed to be at hand. This salvation had been revealed in Jesus, and any morsel of information about Jesus was full of meaning for them *only when it pertained to salvation.*" "The aim of the Gospels is to furnish proof of the message of salvation which has been preached."[8] Moreover, the story of the centurion belongs to a group of what have been called "Pronouncement Stories," whose "chief characteristic...is that they culminate in a saying of Jesus which expresses some ethical or religious precept."[9] In other words, the interest of such stories is focused upon one particular motif, in this case upon the centurion's faith and Jesus' response to it. We have no right, therefore, to expect to find in it an estimate by Jesus, either favourable or otherwise, of the supplicant's military calling, nor to deduce anything from His silence. In the same chapter in Luke (7:36ff) Jesus commends "a woman in the city, which was a sinner," but He is not

supposed to condone her prostitution because He is silent about it. He commends Zacchaeus the tax-collector (Luke 19:9) without referring to his profession: must He be held therefore to condone "graft"? The New Testament contains no word of protest against slavery: are we to conclude, therefore, that slavery is in accordance with the Christian ethic, and that those who led the protest against it were perverting the Gospel?

(3) The question of war hardly arises here. The Roman soldiery in Palestine corresponded rather to a police-force; and Jesus could not have publicly condemned such service, even had He desired to do so, without coming into premature conflict with Rome, and ultimately identifying Himself with violent revolt, to the stultification of His own pacifist ethic....

(4) It should surely be obvious that one may gladly recognize splendid qualities in individual soldiers, as in all other professions, without thereby committing oneself to approval of their calling....

"Think not that I came to send peace on earth: I came not to send peace, but a sword" (Matt. 10:34; cf. Luke 12:51).

It is often argued from this saying that Jesus foresaw the inevitability of war under the Christian dispensation, and indeed conceived that the purpose of His mission would find its fulfilment in war rather than in peace. It is part of the presumption of Pacifism to assume that the Kingdom must be one of universal peace. But:

(1) Does this verse really express *purpose*? More probably it is a good example of a common Semitic idiom whereby what is really a consequence, especially a

[8]Martin Dibelius, *Gospel Criticism and Christology* (London: I. Nicholson & Watson, 1935), 16, 31. Italics mine.

[9]See Vincent Taylor, *The Formation of the Gospel Tradition: Eight Lectures* (London: Macmillan, 1935), 63ff.

[10]A good example from the Old Testament is Hosea 8:4: "Of their silver and their gold have they made them idols, that they may be cut off," i.e., "with the result that they have been cut off."

tragic one, is ironically expressed as a purpose.[10] Jesus means, "I came on a mission of mercy, and the only result, alas, is a sword."

(2) As a matter of fact there is no reference whatever in the verse to war. Are we seriously to picture the daughter using the "sword" upon her mother? Instead of "sword" Luke here much more literally has "division" (διαμερισμός), the same word as in Hebrews 4:12: "The word of God is living, and active, and sharper than any two-edged sword, and piercing even to the *dividing* of soul and spirit." Just as the word of God is said to sift the component parts of a man's being, so will Jesus' mission sift the true from the false in human society. The context shows that the "division" in question has nothing to do with war, but refers to the misunderstanding and even persecution to be endured by the loyal Christian at the hands of those who should be his best friends. The words might find a true illustration, not in a war supposedly sanctioned by Jesus, but far more fittingly in the conscientious objector to war, ostracized by society, disowned even by his own family, on account of loyalty to Jesus' teaching as he understands it.

"When ye shall hear of wars and rumours of wars, be not troubled: these things must needs come to pass" (Mark 13:7 and parallels).

With this saying may be compared the various prophecies of war in the Apocalypse (Rev. 6:4–8; 11:7 ff; 12:7 ff; 13:7; 16:16; 17:14; 19:11–21). What right, it is asked, has the Christian to renounce war, when Jesus Himself foretells that "it must needs come to pass"? "I would very much

like to know," runs a typical "letter to the Editor," "what justification writers have for their extreme pacifist views. Whether we wish it or not, we still have the Battle of Armageddon to face. Will these friends then, when the great battle of Christ's forces against anti-Christ takes place, be pacifists?"[11] We may remark in reply:

(1) It is hardly necessary at this time of day to caution the intelligent reader against fantastically literal interpretations of the Book of Revelation....

(2) The warning of a dire succession of wars has proved only too tragically true....It is not necessary to conclude that, contrary to the whole trend of His teaching, Jesus has laid upon His disciples the obligation to take part in such wars, which are due in part, as He Himself suggests, to the emergence of "false Christs and false prophets" who will "lead astray, if possible, even the elect" (Mark 13:22).

(3) As for the warlike passages in the Book of Revelation, since the "Messiah of the apocalypse fights with angels at his side, and not with men, this action in no way affects the example which the Christ of the Gospels has left behind. 'Heavenly beings and superhuman heavenly powers alone wage war on God's behalf. When men fight, they are doomed to destruction; only the devil lets men fight for him.' The author of Apocalypse is convinced of that."[12]

"But now, he that hath a purse, let him take it, and likewise a wallet; and he that hath no sword, let him sell his cloke and buy one. For I say unto you, that this which is written must be fulfilled in me. And he was reckoned with transgressors: for that which concerneth me hath fulfilment. And they said, Lord, behold, here are two swords. And he said, It is enough" (Luke 22:36–38).

---

[11]*British Weekly,* August 30, 1934.

[12]Heering, *Fall of Christianity,* 30, quoting Adolf von Harnack, *Militia Christi: Die chistliche Religion und der Soldatenstand in den ersten drei Jahrhunderten* (Tübingen: Mohr, 1905), 6, and Hans Windisch, *Der messianische Krieg und das Urchristentum* (Tübingen: Mohr, 1909), 76.

A typical comment from the anti-pacifist viewpoint is that of the German theologian Spitta during the war: "See! Jesus has summoned His followers to armed defence! He was no tender pacifist."[13] Is there any reply?

(1) It must be frankly confessed that the passage is one of the most puzzling with which we have to deal, and it has always perplexed scholars, even when they have no axe to grind in connection with the present controversy. Thus Weiss writes in his famous *Commentary*: "The martial note in this word is in direct contradiction to many others which definitely forbid resistance. It is in direct opposition to the whole spirit of primitive Christianity." If Spitta's comment is justified, then it is very hard to explain Jesus' complete change of front when His disciples take Him at His word and put up an armed defence in Gethsemane: "Put up again thy sword in its place: for all they that take the sword shall perish with the sword" (Matt. 26:52).

(2) Short of a definitely pacifist explanation, much the best interpretation is one suggested to me by my colleague Principal W.A. Curtis:

> It is evident that Jesus had not forbidden the disciples in their journey from Galilee to Jerusalem to carry weapons and that these weapons were nothing but the customary means of protection which travellers have always used *when beyond the reach of law* and armed protection. In Jerusalem they were *under the shadow of the law,* Jewish and Roman, and their arms were in abeyance. In the passage quoted the traveller's sword is like the purse, and the wallet, and the sandals, and the cloak, a symbol of homeless wandering on an urgent and dangerous mission, far more formidable than

their shorter and safer errands hitherto at His bidding. It may be inferred that Jesus had taken no exception to them bearing the ordinary means of self-defence when travelling in bandit-infested country *beyond the protection of armed authority*. (Italics throughout are mine.)...

This exegesis is admittedly attractive: but there are serious difficulties:

(a) The command to "buy a sword" appears to be given with the prospect of Jesus' coming arrest and death definitely in view, and with the purpose of meeting some eventuality connected with this coming crisis: verse 37, *"For...that which concerneth me hath fulfilment,"* makes this quite plain.

(b) Yet, if anything is certain, it is that the command cannot have been given with a view to resistance at the arrest; Jesus' rebuke, "Put up thy sword again into its place," rules this out.

(c) It is difficult, again, to see how the approach of Jesus' death, or even the Crucifixion itself, should be thought of as so altering the disciples' circumstances that, whereas formerly they travelled under the protection of common law, where no "sword" was needed, they would henceforth be travelling (as this interpretation assumes) "beyond the protection of armed authority," where possession of arms might be permitted....

(3) Many modern scholars have accordingly suspected the passage, and even the connection of verse 36 with verse 38 is questioned....

(4) If this be considered too drastic a cutting of the knot, we are left with three alternatives. The command to "buy a sword" must be taken either:

(a) Quite literally and seriously, as the opponents of Pacifism assert. But, as J.M. Creed in our foremost commentary in

---

[13]Spitta, *Theol. Rundschau*, 1915, 235; quoted by Heering, *Fall of Christianity*, 24.

English on St. Luke's Gospel puts it, "It is unlikely that Jesus seriously entertained the thought of armed resistance, which indeed would be in conflict with the whole tenor of His life and teaching."[14] Similarly F.C. Burkitt: "It is impossible to believe that the command to buy a sword was meant literally or seriously."[15] It should perhaps be remarked that neither of these scholars is a Pacifist.

(b) Seriously, but metaphorically. "It seems better," writes Dr. Creed, "to assume that Jesus intended the words of verse 36 to be accepted in a general sense as a warning that disaster is coming [cf. Matt. 10:34; Luke 12:51] and that the disciples misunderstood Him."[16] Then Jesus, in despair at the denseness of His hearers who have taken him up literally and produced two swords, breaks off the conversation with the common Semitic formula, "It is enough!" (See Deut. 3:26 and the similar phrase in Mark 14:41)— as we might say, "That will do!"

(c) Literally, but ironically—the words being spoken by Jesus in what Dr. Burkitt calls a mood of "ironical foreboding." The words "it is enough" might then be taken as a semi-playful reminder to the literally-minded disciples. The absurdly inadequate "two swords" are "enough" with which to resist the might of Rome! So far from being a summons to armed defence, Jesus' words are rather a wistful reminder of the utter futility of armed resistance.

Our conclusion then is that these words have been made to carry much greater weight than is legitimate. But it must be allowed that, so far as this context goes (if it is read apart from the sequel in Gethsemane), we cannot cite Jesus as definitely discountenancing the

recognized habit of carrying arms in self-defence. But, even so, is it necessary to suppose that, where a Livingstone was content to go armed only with the Gospel of love, the Master Himself and His company, in contradiction to the whole spirit and trend of His teaching, would rely upon "swords"?

"All they that take the sword shall perish with the sword" (Matt. 26:52).

This is quite commonly interpreted as meaning that the aggressor, no doubt, is to perish; but how, if not by the "sword" of the defender? It is argued that Jesus thus sanctions defensive warfare as an instrument necessary for the accomplishment of God's just and holy purpose.

But the saying can be thus misused only when it is wrested from its context by the omission of the first clause, "Put up again thy sword in its place!" For it is precisely the *defensive* "sword" which is here coming under condemnation. The sword, even when used in defence, will recoil upon him who uses it. There are not two "swords" in view, the unrighteous sword of the aggressor and the righteous sword of the defender. The "perishing by the sword" is inherent in the very use of the sword, not a penalty exacted by a third party. It is true that there is an echo of this saying in the warlike Book of Revelation, where it appears to be misunderstood in much the same way as it is by our militarists: "If any man shall kill with the sword, with the sword must he be killed," but the words as spoken by Jesus are regularly interpreted by early Christian writers as an absolute prohibition of military service. Here, for example, is Tertullian: "Shall it be held

---

[14]John Martin Creed, *The Gospel according to St. Luke: The Greek Text with Introduction, Notes, and Indices* (London: Macmillan, 1953), 270.

[15]F.C. Burkitt, *The Gospel History and Its Transmission* (Edinburgh: T. & T. Clark, 1911)

[16]Creed, *Gospel according to St. Luke*, 270.

lawful to make an occupation of the sword, when the Lord proclaims that he who uses the sword shall perish by the sword?"[17]

"When the strong man armed guardeth his own court, his goods are in peace" (Luke 11:21).

From this it is argued that according to Jesus Himself the only true security is to be armed to the teeth. To refute such exegesis it is only necessary to read on: "But when a stronger than he shall come upon him, and overcome him, he taketh from him his whole armour wherein he trusted, and divideth his spoils" (v. 22). If security lies in arms, then it is only when each man is stronger than all his neighbours! The whole stress is upon the futility of "the armour wherein he trusted." In any case there is no reason to suppose that Jesus blesses war merely because He uses a simile drawn from arms. Is He to be thought to bless burglary when He compares the coming of the Son of Man with the breaking in of a thief? (Matt. 24:42ff).

"If my kingdom were of this world, then would my servants fight" (John 18:36).

Jesus is explaining that a Kingdom such as His is not one which is defended by force of arms, for "it is not of this world." Yet the inference has actually been wrung from the verse that conversely, when the issue *is* one of loyalty to a worldly kingdom, Jesus *would* have His servants fight. Even Luther argues from this passage that Jesus had no quarrel with war itself, provided it were waged by the Sovereign for just ends. Were Jesus a worldly Sovereign, He would do the same.

But the saying begins, "My kingdom is NOT of this world." One might as well argue that, if Jesus' view of His mission and purpose were the opposite of what in point of fact it is, then His ethical teaching would be likely to suffer a similar metamorphosis— which is obvious, but not very helpful! The very essence of the New Testament challenge is surely that the Christian is to practise here in the world an ethic which is not of the world.

"But the king was wroth; and he sent his armies, and destroyed those murderers, and burned their city" (Matt. 22:7).

Together with this verse we may consider other similar parabolic illustrations (Matt. 18:34ff; 22:13; 24:50ff; 25:30; Mark 12:9; Luke 19:27, etc.).

It is sometimes argued that various allusions in Jesus' parables, for example descriptions of kings and masters inflicting severe penalties on offending subjects, must be held to imply that Jesus would approve a similar application of armed violence and other forcible social sanctions to wrongdoers in real life. A correct appreciation of the whole trend and method of Jesus' teaching will decisively negative any such suggestion. In his parabolic illustrations Jesus can be held neither to approve nor condemn the actual practices from which they are drawn. He always uses these illustrations to underline some one fundamental moral or spiritual truth. For example, Luke 17:7–10 has as its central thought the truth that the Christian is always on duty. It does not teach that the Christian himself may own and overwork slaves!

"Put on the whole armour of God" (Eph. 6:10–17) and numerous other Pauline military metaphors (cf. Rom. 13:12; 2 Cor. 6:7;

---

[17]Tertullian, *de Corona*, xi.

1 Thess. 5:8; 1 Tim. 1:18; 6:12; 2 Tim. 2:3ff).

Surely, it is argued, Paul must approve of warfare, or else he would not so constantly use military metaphors to describe the Christian way of life.

Once again a study of the context is sufficient refutation. The emphasis is regularly upon the *contrast* between ordinary warfare and the Christian way of life: "Our wrestling is NOT against flesh and blood" (Eph. 6:12). The Christian will fight only with the weapons of the Spirit. It would be truer to argue that Paul deliberately uses the figure of military warfare in order to stress the point that the warfare of the Christian is something wholly different. The Christian must discover "the moral equivalent of war." It is "the good fight of faith" which is in question (1 Tim. 6:12). No early Christian would have dreamed of appealing to such metaphors in justification of war; the very reverse is the truth. "I am a soldier of Christ," cried a soldier-convert martyred for refusing military service, "and may not fight; the weapons of blood are discarded, that the weapons of peace may be girded on."[18]

"Greater love hath no man than this, that a man lay down his life for his friends" (John 15:13).

War may sometimes be justified, so it is said, if only because it calls forth the supreme expression of this Christ-like love....

We may remind ourselves:

(1) Jesus did *not* say, "that a man kills his enemies for the sake of his friends." Reverently though one acknowledges that multitudes have so laid down their lives in battle for the sake of their friends, so to do is not the aim and object of the soldier's training and profession. The soldier is trained to protect himself and to kill others, and the better soldier he is, the more successful will he be in doing both. The self-sacrifice is but an inevitable by-product of the soldier's main task, and we must not allow sentiment to blind us to that fact.

(2) An even higher expression of this Christ-like love is envisaged in the great words of Paul: "God commendeth His own love towards us, in that, while we were yet *sinners,* Christ died for us." Jesus died not only for His "friends." "When we were *enemies,* we were reconciled to God by the death of His Son" (Rom. 5:8, 10).

(3) The essence of this Christ-like sacrifice is that it should be wholly voluntary: "Therefore doth the Father love me, because I lay down my life.... No man taketh it away from me, but I lay it down of myself" (John 10:17ff). Though one humbly, yet proudly, agrees that thousands have died on the battlefield in such a spirit, what can there possibly be in common between such an ideal and a war-system which conscripts free human personalities to be the instrument of mass-slaughter and in the end to become themselves "cannon-fodder"? We gain nothing by mincing words.

(4) It is easy to come perilously near to blasphemy when we thus appeal to the Cross in the name of Mars. "The Cross," says Erasmus, "is the banner and standard of Him who has overcome and triumphed, not by fighting and slaying, but by His own bitter death. With the Cross do ye deprive of life your brother, whose life was rescued by the Cross?"

---

[18]Quoted by Heering, *The Fall of Christianity,* 53.

Chapter Six

The
Gospel of Peace

Marlin E. Miller

Marlin E. Miller served as a Mennonite missionary in Paris, France, working among African university students. He then returned to the United States in 1975 to become a professor of theology and also the president of Goshen Biblical Seminary (now known as Associated Mennonite Biblical Seminary, located in Elkhart, Indiana).

The article probes the relationship between peace and missions, primarily from the perspective of the gospel of reconciliation. While it does not trace out all the implications of reconciliation as a leading biblical metaphor for salvation, it does establish that peace is rooted in God's redemptive action. It is for us to ask the application questions. Should peace be part of the initial evangelistic message or introduced later as an issue of discipleship? Dare missionaries teach peace when they are discipling people who are trying to escape from the chains of colonialism or a repressive regime? How does warfare affect missions around the world? Does Jesus call His disciples to be His warriors or His witnesses?

Many contemporary evangelical Christians refer to "the gospel" as if the word had a narrowly circumscribed content. "Preaching the gospel" presumably means proclaiming the message of forgiveness from past sin and guilt through the atoning work of Christ on the cross, inviting sinners to repent and accept God's plan of salvation, and extending the promise of eternal life to those who accept Christ as personal Savior. Within the broader Protestant context of evangelical Christianity, "the gospel" also carries the connotation of pure grace, devoid of any ethical demands

which might be construed as prerequisites for salvation or as conditions for remaining in a state of peace. Discipleship as the shape of Christian obedience is seen at best as secondary, as a fruit of faith's response to the gospel. It is, however, not understood as integral to the gospel message as such. Major dogmatic definitions have thus attached to the biblical term "gospel," a particular content which provides a capsule statement of the message to be preached. This content is intended also to be a critical safeguard against liberal deviations, for example, against tendencies to seek man's salvation by edu-

---

This chapter appeared as "The Gospel of Peace" in *Mission and the Peace Witness: The Gospel and Christian Discipleship*, ed. Robert L. Ramseyer (Scottdale, Pa.: Herald, 1979), 9–23.

cation, material welfare, or social change rather than by preaching "the gospel."

The New Testament however employs a variety of terms to describe the comprehensiveness of the good news. Jesus Himself proclaimed the gospel of the kingdom. The Apostle Paul speaks about the gospel of God, the gospel of Jesus Christ, the gospel of the glory of Christ, the gospel of salvation, and simply the gospel. Both Peter (Acts 10) and Paul (Eph. 2:6) refer to the gospel of peace. This variety of New Testament terms certainly may not be construed to mean that there are several "gospels" which differ markedly in form and substance. The gospel of God is none other than the gospel of Jesus Christ. The gospel of salvation is the same as the gospel of peace. Even on the most superficial level, this multiplicity of descriptions should caution against too readily limiting our understanding of the gospel to one facet of the New Testament message or against reducing all other dimensions of the good news to one particular aspect. Such reductionist interpretations almost inevitably end up with a truncated gospel, an amputated Christ, and a crippled church. We should rather seek to understand the particular point of reference of each description and its roots and place within the global vision of the good news.

Within the limits of this essay, I will focus on the description of the good news as "the gospel of peace." This focus is prompted not by an attempt to reduce the good news to a gospel of peace, but by specific shortcomings in broad streams of Protestant and evangelical thought and practice. Sometimes the gospel of peace has simply been omitted from the message as preached. Perhaps more often, "peace" has been reduced to the inner calm of an assuaged conscience, interpreted as "peace with God." Perhaps even more often "peace" has been separated from the gospel and assigned to

Christian social ethics. As such it may arise when the topic is discipleship or Christian action in the society at large, but peace is not seen as the immediate focus of the gospel. This theological axiom has also been reinforced in the minds of many Mennonite missionaries as well as congregational members by the institutionalized division of labor between denominational mission boards and the Peace Section of the Mennonite Central Committee. In all of these ways, sometimes more explicitly, other times more implicitly, reconciliation of former enemies and the establishment of peace where prejudice, conflict, and injustice characterize human relations and social structures are not understood as integral to Christ's saving work on the cross.

In comparison to these omissions and interpretative schemes, we may summarize our thesis as follows: Peace as a present social and structural reality as well as an inner tranquility and future promise inherently and explicitly belongs to a biblically adequate understanding of salvation through Jesus the Messiah. It therefore also inherently and explicitly belongs to a mission theology and practice which accepts the New Testament description and proclamation of the good news as normative for Christian mission in our time.

In its major forms, the word for "peace" appears over 100 times in the New Testament. The contexts of its usage also demonstrate its significance to the biblical message. God is repeatedly called the God of peace; Jesus is named the Lord of peace; the Holy Spirit is recognized to be the Spirit of peace. After Jerusalem's rejection of the messianic peace offered by Jesus, He gave it instead to His disciples. "Peace" was the characteristic greeting of the early Christians. In using this greeting, they most likely meant to follow Jesus' own practice and to witness to the fulfillment of the messianic peace. When he addressed Cornelius, a Gentile with whom faithful Jews were to have no close association, the Apostle Peter summarized God's message to His people as "the good news of peace through Jesus Christ" (Acts 10:36). The Apostle Paul encouraged the Christians in Ephesus to "stand firm" with their "feet fitted with the readiness that comes from the gospel of peace" (Eph. 6:14–15). In the same epistle, he summarized the purpose of Jesus' coming and of His death on the cross as the making of peace between Jew and Gentile.

We do well to remember that Jesus and His disciples stood in the tradition of the Old Testament law and prophets (Matt. 5:12). When they spoke about peace and identified the good news of salvation with the gospel of *peace,* they used the term in the Hebraic sense of *shalom.* John Driver has aptly summarized this understanding of peace in *Community and Commitment,* from which we quote extensively:

> *Shalom* is a broad concept, essential to the Hebrew understanding of relationship between people and God. It covers human welfare, health, and well-being in both spiritual and material aspects. It describes a condition of well-being resulting from sound relationships among people and between people and God. According to the prophets, true peace reigned in Israel when justice (or righteousness) prevailed, when the common welfare was assured, when people were treated with equality and respect, when salvation flourished according to the social order determined by God in the covenant which He had established with His people. In fact, the prophet understood that God's covenant with Israel was a "covenant of life and peace" (Mal. 2:5).

On the other hand, when there was greed for unjust gain, when judges could be bought for a price, when there was not equal opportunity for all, when suffering was caused by social and economic oppression, then there was no peace, even though false prophets insisted to the contrary (Jer. 6: 13–14).

For the Hebrews, peace was not merely the absence of armed conflict. Rather shalom was assured by the prevalence of conditions which contribute to human well-being in all its dimensions. Not mere tranquility of spirit or serenity of mind, peace had to do with harmonious relationships between God and His people. It had to do with social relationships characterized by His people. It had to do with social relationships characterized by justice. Peace resulted when people lived together according to God's intention. Peace, justice, and salvation are synonymous terms for general well-being created by right social relationships.[1]

To be sure, the concept of peace in the New Testament differs in significant ways from this composite image of shalom in the Old Testament. In this respect, the New Testament fulfills and transforms the expectations of the Old. But this fulfillment and transformation does not amount to replacing the Hebraic vision of peace with Greek or Roman views of peace, even though these may be more familiar to those of us shaped by Western culture and accustomed to thinking with its categories. In contrast to a predominantly Greek view, the New Testament does not focus on peace as inner calm and tranquility at the expense of peace as reconciliation in social relations and structures. Nor does the New Testament consider peace to be the balance of

---

[1]John Driver, *Community and Commitment* (Scottdale, Pa.: Herald, 1976), 71.

self-interest between power groups regulated by an extensive legal system and maintained by military might. Such a view is part of the Roman legacy to Western culture. All too often Christianity has adopted this notion of peace when it has identified itself with a particular group or nation. The differences between the Old and New Testaments have to do rather with the way in which Jesus fulfilled the messianic expectations of the Old and the way in which shalom took shape in the church as the messianic community. These differences transform but do not eliminate the structural and social dimensions of peace understood in the Hebraic sense of *shalom.*

The messianic peace inaugurated by Jesus and characterizing the Christian community springs from Christ's sacrifice on the cross. As a mature missionary-theologian, the Apostle Paul summarizes in Ephesians 2 and 3 the "mystery" about the present age made known to him by revelation. According to the revelation of this mystery—something which had previously remained hidden from the sight and knowledge of humanity—God's intent at the present time is that His "manifold wisdom" be made known "to the rulers and authorities in the heavenly realms" through the church (Eph. 3:10). As made clear in the apostle's summary, he does not mean simply that the church should transmit a particular message which in some curious way will be communicated to angelic powers. God would hardly have needed such a devious route of communication with angelic hosts. The crucial issue is rather that the church now exists as the messianic community made up of both Jew and Gentile. Those who had previously been divided by an insurmountable hostility of religious, social, cultural, and political dimensions now were reconciled and participated on an equal basis in the messianic *shalom.* The community made up of former enemies is itself the message—visible as well as verbal—of God's intent in creation, as in the cross of Christ. In the Ephesians summary, reconciliation and peace between former enemies even provide the context in which both may live in "peace with God." The peace between Jew and Gentile is the realm in which the reality of peace with God may be experienced—rather than a possible secondary and derivative consequence of a purely transcendent peace with God. The messianic peace encompasses both the reconciliation of enemies on the social level as well as the common access to the presence of God.

Contrary to several strands in the Old Testament expectations as well as among the Jewish people of the first century, Jesus as the Messiah made peace by suffering and death, rather than by righteous vengeance and the domination of the enemies of God's people. "But now in Christ Jesus you who once were far away have been brought near through the blood of Christ. For he himself is our peace, who has made the two one and has destroyed the barrier....His purpose was to create in himself one new man out of the two, thus making peace, and in this one body to reconcile both of them to God through the cross, by which he put to death their hostility" (Eph. 2:13–16). The peace established by Jesus as the Messiah thus retains and even goes beyond the Hebraic understanding of shalom as including the social relations among God's people and between the people and God. It includes the realization of reconciliation and community unattainable by human efforts and therefore relegated to a utopian future age. What had been considered utopian had now through the cross become present reality.

Traditional doctrines of the atonement have usually focused on the language of sacrifice and have understood the work of Christ for the salvation of humankind above all in relation to His death on the cross. Whether of Anselmic or Abelardian leanings, whether explaining Christ's death on the cross as a ransom paid to the devil or as a demonstration of His power over the evil one, and whatever else their strengths or weaknesses, the classic understandings of the atonement have overlooked or neglected any direct relation between the crucifixion and the social reality of the messianic peace. They have focused rather on the enmity between the sinful or guilty soul and God, thus abstracting from both the social reality of sin as well as of reconciliation.

The language of Paul's summary however emphasizes that the work of Christ inherently means the making of peace between human enemies as well as providing their common access to God. Peacemaking between enemies thus belongs fundamentally to the death and resurrection of Jesus Christ—not only to Christian social ethics—once the enmity with God has been overcome. This making of peace includes both a destructive and a constructive action.

By His death on the cross, Jesus "has destroyed the barrier, the dividing wall of hostility, by abolishing in his flesh the law with its commandments and regulations" (Eph. 2:14–15). Peacemaking in the sense of the biblical shalom means first of all negation of whatever division and hostility. It begins at the point of offense in the situation of conflict and confronts that offense rather than simply calling for greater toleration or balancing of one offense against another. The offense between Jew and Gentile was founded on "the law with its commandments and regulations." What had originally been given to the Jewish people as a part of God's covenant with His people had become a means of perpetuating and justifying division from and enmity with the Gentiles. The uniqueness of Jewish existence and of its relation to God was defined in such a way that it meant division from and enmity with the Gentiles. This division and hostility continued to shape the mood and actions of many early Christians—even though contrary to the leading of the Holy Spirit as recounted in Acts. But as Paul rightly insists, the fulfillment of the messianic peace in the Christian community means the destruction of the occasion for enmity and prejudice. The crucifixion of Jesus as the representative of God's chosen people means that He has taken the initiative to destroy the barrier between His people and their enemies rather than compelling the outsiders to submit to the spiritual and social domination of His people, or rather than simply leaving them outside the scope of His peace. In solidarity with Jesus, Jewish Christians were thus freed to die to the presumed necessity of finding their identity in a religious, social, and cultural reality which ratified enmity with all those outside their own ethnic group.

Nothing less than the cross of the Messiah could overcome a hostility as profound and pervasive as that between Jew and Gentile. In situations of radical enmity, the conflict may be overcome only by the elimination or defeat of the enemy. The elimination of the enemy, whether in personal or social conflict as experienced on the human level, however, rules out any reconciliation between the opposing parties. The defeat of the enemy in such conflict situations only reinforces the resentment on the part of the defeated and relegates him to the status of subjugated or second-class citizen in relation to the victor. The defeat of the enemy only reinforces, on the part of the victor, his own personal or social identity, now further strengthened by the experience of having conquered the one who threatened that identity. These examples may serve as partial analogies to the way in which only the death of Jesus on the cross could overcome the hostility between Jew and Gentile. "Through the cross" this conflict was destroyed without relegating the Gentiles to second-class citizenship in the messianic community. "Through the cross" the hostility was defeated without reinforcing the kind of Jewish existence which necessarily implied enmity with the Gentiles or spiritual or political subjugation to the Jews.

The making of peace and the reconciliation of former enemies has a constructive side. In destroying the barrier of hostility, Jesus' purpose "was to create in himself one new man out of the two, thus making peace." This constructive side confirms the Hebraic understanding of shalom which goes beyond mere absence of conflict to a reordering and restructuring of social relations between former enemies and between them and God. In this aspect of making peace the Messiah is the representative of a new humanity. He is the new "image of God" who incarnates a human identity in which reconciliation and peace rather than strife and division become a visible and social reality. Paul's language here is rooted in the creation account, but now oriented around the new creation in the Person and corporate existence of the Messiah. Both Jew and Gentile are given a new basis for existence. Rather than perpetuating their uniqueness as experienced and defined over against each other, they are granted a new common existence in Christ. The new humanity created by the Messiah is His own corporate existence, the messianic community in which hostilities are overcome and former enemies live in peace. The messianic peace thus includes a change of attitude, but an equally fundamental restructuring of social realities in the messianic community. National, racial, and cultural division and enmity are replaced by a peace which overcomes such divisions and reflects the unity of humankind in Jesus Christ.

The creation of a new corporate existence in which hostility and conflict give way to a new social and religious identity does not however amount to a kind of cosmopolitan universalism in which the "Gentiles" gain the upper hand. The new community in which the messianic peace takes on social reality is not the realization of a humanistic universalism, but the participation of former enemies in the particular corporate existence of the Messiah. The Apostle Paul can therefore speak of Gentiles, Jews, and "the church of God" (1 Cor. 10:32). Nor does the fulfillment of the messianic shalom provide a rationale for the elaboration and imposition of a "Christian culture" upon all. The peace of the messianic community is a dynamic rather than a static reality which begins ever anew at the points of offense and hostility between conflicting peoples with the message of reconciliation between themselves and God. As such, the messianic community by its corporate and social existence points toward the final peace and reconciliation of all creatures, which God will establish in His name (Col. 1).

In addition to the continuity with the Hebraic vision of peace and the Pauline summary of Christ's work on the cross as reconciliation between former enemies, the broader testimony of the New Testament speaks for the structural and social dimensions of the messianic peace. In the messianic community, peace and reconciliation include the creation of new relations between men and women, relations which had been marked by alienation and structures of domination since the fall as described in Genesis. Shalom means a new social and structural relation of mutual service between men and women rather than hostility or domination based on sexual difference. The work of Christ similarly transformed the structure of relations between slaves and masters in the messianic community. Even though the legal and economic structures which perpetuated the "institution" of slavery continued in the broader society, the social reality of these relations began to take on the shape of shalom in the messianic community (Philem., 1 Cor., Eph.).

The social dimensions of the messianic peace also extend to the economic area, where wealth becomes another form of power which engenders hostility, oppression, and conflict. The Apostle Paul, who proclaimed the gospel of peace between Jew and Gentile, also helped organize the redistribution of material resources between Jewish and Gentile Christians. Not only was this redistribution to respond to the particular material needs under which Jewish Christians suffered, but it was to be carried out according to the "rule of equality" (2 Cor. 8). Far from being limited to a subjective attitude about the charitable sharing of excess wealth, the collection organized by Paul was a means of making the final equality between former enemies part of the messianic peace. Even though the economic inequalities and divisions of the broader society continued to engender hostility and conflict, the church began to live out this dimension of reconciliation and peace. In making material sharing according to the "rule of equality" part of the gospel of peace, the Apostle Paul continued the tradition of the early Jerusalem Christians who had "all things in common."

The gospel of peace thus integrally belongs to the good news about Jesus Christ. The message of peace means that through no merit of our own, we are in Christ reconciled to our enemies and called to participate in the social realities of a new community where old structures of personal, social, and economic hostility are replaced by those of reconciliation. In this sense the gospel of peace is a social gospel. It differs from other social gospels, however, which would attempt to establish peace and overcome conflict by domination and power rather than by inviting men and women to participation in the messianic community. The gospel of peace is also the proclamation of a present reality which has begun to take shape in a world characterized by strife, injustice, and power struggles—not simply a utopian vision of a desirable future. Finally the gospel of peace is both a message and a corporate existence. The credibility of the message will therefore depend in large measure upon the community which proclaims it.

Understood as part of the gospel of peace, several New Testament passages, usually cited as support for an almost exclusively individual and subjective understanding of reconciliation and peace with God, in fact express a more comprehensive perspective. For example, most translations of 2 Corinthians 5 encourage an understanding of God's reconciling work in Christ as limited to an inner and personal transformation. Instead of the familiar "if anyone is in Christ, he is a new creature" (or an equivalent rendering), a more accurate translation of verse 17 would read "therefore, if anyone is in Christ, (there is a) new creation—the old has gone, behold the new has come." Through reconciliation in Christ there is thus a whole new perspective, a whole new way of looking at the world. Rather than others being judged from the worldly perspective of status, nationality, culture, class, gender, or race, they are now seen as befits their common participation "in Christ." Reconciliation thus means peace with God as well as with those previously considered enemies. Another example is the familiar opening verse of Romans 5.

"Therefore, since we have been justified through faith, we have peace with God through our Lord Jesus Christ." Even though the immediate context of Romans 5:1 does not explicitly refer to the social dimensions of shalom, it does not exclude them either, particularly in view of the Hebraic understanding of shalom which includes both spiritual and social reconciliation. Moreover the broader setting of Romans 5 has to do with the theological foundations of the gospel addressed to both Jew and Gentile. Just as the shalom of the messianic community may not be reduced to a purely social reality, so this social dimension may not be excluded from the peace with God incarnate in Jesus Christ.

A renewed vision of the gospel of peace as an integral part of the good news of Jesus Christ would have far-reaching consequences for missionary thought and practice. It would mean a theological reorientation with respect to central, traditional, doctrinal formulations which have not been foundationally shaped by the social dimensions of the good news. It would mean an understanding of the Apostle Paul as a peacemaker, continuing the teaching of Jesus on peace as well as His reconciling of the cross in the cities of the Roman Empire. It would mean an extension of the missionary proclamation in our time to include the messianic peace addressed to situations of enmity and injustice. It would mean giving priority to theological and missionary efforts which focus points of conflict and reconciliation rather than reinforcing or totally undergirding given social and economic conflicts and enmity. It would mean the renewal of the church as a messianic community whose basis for existence derives not from national, ethnic, or cultural givens, but from an ever new corporate identity in Christ. To all of this and more we are called and freed by the "good news of peace through Jesus Christ."

Part II

Church History
and Issues of Peace

The Christian Church and Peace through the Centuries

Robert G. Clouse

Beginning with the Old Testament, Robert G. Clouse, Professor of History at Indiana State University and minister of the First Brethren Church in Clay, Indiana, surveys attitudes of followers of the Bible toward the wars of their time. One of the significant values of this article is the author's account of the changing nature of warfare and how such change affected the Christian response to war. He graphically describes modern warfare, the nature of which, he points out, has led to significant loss of support for the historic just war theory. Many denominations in North America are now officially making provision for those of their members who are conscientious objectors to war.

What factors appear to have led the church to abandon its pacifist stance in the early centuries after Christ? Do you agree with the author that the just war theory no longer can justify Christians' participation in war? What relationship has existed between those in power (political, social, and economic) and war? Does such a relationship exist today? Have Christians too easily accommodated to rationales for warfare, especially during times of war? Where does your denomination stand on recognition and support of conscientious objectors?

The Christian response to war is a difficult study because of the difference between the Old and New Testament approaches to the subject. The Old Testament contains many statements that have been used to support participation in armed conflict. The words of Moses in such passages as Deuteronomy 7:16 constitute a warrant for Israel to engage in aggressive "holy" wars to seize the Promised Land. In Deuteronomy 20:10–18 rules of conquest are given that command the Israelites to exterminate all those who live within the Holy Land. Deuteronomy chapters seven and twenty, along with the war narratives of Joshua, Judges, and Samuel, make it clear, as Peter Craigie shows, that aggressive wars were carried out "at the command of God, in the name of God and with the help of God. And even if it is argued that the Biblical 'historical' narratives have a legendary character to them, and that the wars of conquest described therein did not actually take place, still the problem remains. For although the historical reality of the wars of conquest may perhaps be removed in this manner, the theological ideal remains."[1]

---

[1]Peter C. Craigie, *The Problem of War in the Old Testament* (Grand Rapids: Eerdmans, 1978), 50.

The Old Testament teaching of aggressive war has encouraged many Christians to engage in armed conflict. These individuals, however, fail to realize that Israel was a theocratic state that went to war at the command of God. In modern times there is no state whose king is God. The Israelites not only fought to take the land according to divine promise, but they also struggled to execute judgment on the people who lived there. The reasons for this are cloaked in mystery because it cannot be established historically that the Canaanites were more morally corrupt than other ancient peoples. It is simply stated that they were especially deserving of punishment. God used the Israelites to conquer them as He was later to use foreign nations to bring judgment on His own people.

Such passages as the war texts of the Old Testament remind the reader that some laws given to ancient Israel cannot be used today. The war regulations were specifically applicable to the Hebrew kingdom of God. In the teachings of Jesus the kingdom takes on a different emphasis. It is no longer confined within the boundaries of a single state but exists wherever Christ is accepted and acknowledged as Lord. The change in the form of the kingdom means that care must be taken in applying Old Testament laws to the new situation.

Another point that should be noticed is that much of the Old Testament teaching emphasizes peace as well as war. In Isaiah 2:4 and 9:5–6, Micah 4:1-3, and Zechariah 9:9–10 the prophets refer to the Redeemer of Israel, the future Messiah, as one who would begin a new government of Israel and would end the militaristic ways of the world by establishing a pacifist society. These texts indicate that military industries would be converted for the production of agricultural implements and that existing weapons and armaments would be destroyed. Also military preparations, training, and enlistment would cease in the new kingdom. This golden age of peace on earth would lead to economic and cultural advances such as the world has never experienced.

The New Testament broadens the believer's understanding of the kingdom of God. When Jesus replied to Pilate, who asked if He was a king, He stated: "My kingdom is not of this world" (John 18:36). The Roman governor of Judea could not understand the idea of a person being a ruler over some intangible realm. He was confused, but then he decided that Jesus was no threat to Roman rule, so he wanted to free Him. Jesus reinforced His teaching that violence is no solution to human problems when He was arrested by the Roman soldiers. Peter, wishing to defend Him, drew his sword and struck the servant of the high priest, cutting off his ear. "Put your sword back in its place," Jesus told him, "for all who draw the sword will die by the sword. Do you think I cannot call on my Father, and he will at once put at my disposal more than twelve legions of angels?" (Matt. 26:51-53). In the Sermon on the Mount, His longest sermon, Jesus makes His clearest statement concerning the Christian and nonviolence as He states:

> You have heard that it was said, "Eye for eye, and tooth for tooth." But I tell you, Do not resist an evil person. If someone strikes you on the right cheek, turn to him the other also.... If someone forces you to go one mile, go with him two miles. Give to the one who asks you, and do not turn away from the one who wants to borrow from you. You have heard that it was said, "Love your neighbor and hate your enemy." But I tell you: Love your enemies and pray for those who persecute you, that you may be sons of your Father in heaven." (Matt.5:38–45)

The historical context of this passage is that of a people living in a land occupied by the Roman army. Although these soldiers kept the peace in Palestine, it was a mixed blessing. Most Jews hated the foreign conquerors of their land and at times Jews violently retaliated against them. Then the Romans would crush the Jewish resistance even more forcefully. Jesus commanded His followers to live in peaceful coexistence with the Roman occupiers of their land. He taught that the way of peace is the only method to achieve harmony and toleration.

Armed conflict in the cause of God is thus terminated and the spiritual kingdom of the New Covenant prophesied by Isaiah, Micah, and Zechariah is established by the Messiah, Jesus of Nazareth. The concept of pacifism and nonresistance under the Prince of Peace thus replaces the military struggles of Israel in the Old Testament. It is especially wrong for the believer to engage in a conflict against a sister or brother in Christ, and those who belong to Christ's kingdom come from every tribe, nation, and language. Jesus Christ instituted peace and harmony among those who believe in Him. They are to be examples of peace and loving-kindness among all people regardless of race, nationality, or doctrinal differences. Christians are to follow in His steps, as Peter stated: "He committed no sin, and no deceit was found in his mouth. When they hurled their insults at him, he did not retaliate; when he suffered, he made no threats. Instead, he entrusted himself to him who judges justly" (1 Pet. 2:22–23).

For the Christian, the New Testament explains that the war that one ought to wage is a spiritual conflict. Military terms and metaphors are used to describe this struggle: as Paul wrote, "Finally, be strong in the Lord and in his mighty power. Put on the full armor of God so that you can take your stand against the devil's schemes. For our struggle is not against flesh and blood, but against the rulers, against the authorities, against the powers of this dark world and against the spiritual forces of evil in the heavenly realms" (Eph. 6:10–12). The real enemy is the evil found both inside and outside the Christian believer. The fight against lust, sin, and the impulse to lash out against others constitute the Christian struggle, as James realized: "What causes fights and quarrels among you? Don't they come from your desires that battle within you? You want something but don't get it. You kill and covet, but you cannot have what you want. You quarrel and fight. You do not have because you do not ask God" (James 4:1–2). This spiritual war can be won only with the gospel of peace, which is spread by acts of loving-kindness and personal witness to the good news about the saving ministry of Christ.

The quality of love found in the life and ministry of Christ was not lost on the early church. These believers saw an incompatibility between love and killing. Consequently, the early Christians would not serve in the Roman army. There is no evidence of a single Christian soldier after New Testament times until about A.D. 170. Because the Romans did not have universal conscription and because there was no pressure on Christians to serve, there was little need even to discuss military service. Toward the close of the second century the situation began to change, and there are records of Christians in the army despite the condemnation of the theologians. Many soldiers were converted to Christianity because of its increasing popularity, and they wondered if they should continue their military service.

Thoughtful Christians were not pleased with the blurring of distinctions between the church and the world. These people condemned participation in warfare and urged believers to wage a spiritual conflict rather than a carnal one. Origen dealt with the problem by citing the words of Christ to Peter: "For all who draw the sword will die by the sword" (Matt. 26:52). He explained that one must be wary because warfare and the vindication of our rights might lead believers to "take out the sword, [and] no such occasion is allowed by this evangelical teaching."[2] The Canons of Hippolytus, written by a Roman Christian as a guide for church disciples in the third century, indicate that a follower of Christ who is a soldier "must be taught not to kill men and to refuse to do so if he is commanded."[3] The apparent contradiction between being a soldier and not killing is resolved when one understands that it was possible for a person to be in the Roman legion for a lifetime and never kill anyone. The army performed many of the public services provided by the police force and the fire department in our present age.

Some have also suggested that Christians did not join the army because it involved taking an idolatrous oath of allegiance to the emperor, but most believers would not participate in violence in the second and third centuries because it contradicted the teachings and example of Christ. Justin Martyr, Irenaeus, Clement of Alexandria, Tertullian, Cyprian, and Lactantius all caution their fellow Christians to remember their spiritual calling and that they owe their allegiance to a spiritual kingdom. The same scruples that kept Christians out of the army led them to decline to serve in other governmental positions. They refused to take part in the civil state because of the participation in sacrifices, oath taking, and torture that Rome demanded of civil servants. Just as there is no evidence for the

presence of Christians in the Roman army before the end of the second century, so there is no record of believers in positions of authority under the Roman government until about A.D. 250. The early followers of Christ also thought of themselves as a new community that cut across political boundaries and included all who followed the true God. In a sense they had a rival organization that replaced the old imperial ties.

The church father Origen defended Christians against charges of disloyalty to the Empire that often led to persecution. His apology is found in the book *Contra Celsum,* which is a response to an elaborate attack on Christianity written about 178 by Celsus, a pagan philosopher. Celsus argued that if everyone behaved as a Christian and refused to enter the imperial forces, Rome would fall into the hands of savage barbarians and the church would be destroyed along with the rest of the classical world. Origen responded by stating that if all the Romans were converted and the barbarians invaded the Empire, it would be saved in a supernatural way. Christ promised that two or three agreeing in prayer would receive what they prayed for. Imagine what the entire Empire united in prayer could accomplish! Just as the Israelites were saved at the Red Sea while the armies of Pharaoh were destroyed, so the Romans would be saved by divine power.

Origen, however, did not evade the dilemma of the actual situation, in which the Christian minority profited from the Roman state while seemingly not contributing to its defense. In response to this challenge he claimed that Christians gave the empire alternative service by improving the moral fiber of society and by

---

[2]Quoted in Stan Windass, *Christianity versus Violence: A Social and Historical Study of War and Christianity* (London: Sheed & Ward, 1964), 12.

[3]Quoted in Roland H. Bainton, *Christian Attitudes toward War and Peace* (New York: Abingdon, 1960), 78.

praying for the government. Prayer involved believers in spiritual combat against the forces of evil that caused wars and incited people to violence.

Despite the arguments of the church fathers such as Origen, there was increasing pressure on Christians to serve in the government and the army. When Emperor Constantine made Christianity the official religion during the early fourth century, the church fell away from its teaching with regard to warfare. About half a century later, Augustine wrote as a product of the merger between church and state. At the time he wrote, Christians had been serving in the army for almost two hundred years, and their participation had been accepted as normal. Also, the Empire was threatened with annihilation by destructive groups such as the Vandals. Augustine was asked by a Roman officer who commanded the armies in North Africa whether he should lead his troops in battle or retire to a monastery. Influenced by the new developments, Augustine answered by teaching that a person could serve in the army and also follow the Lord.

Augustine's "just war" theory consisted of rules of warfare worked out by classical thinkers such as Plato and Cicero, but with a Christian emphasis. War, he claimed, should be fought to restore peace and to obtain justice. It must always be under the direction of the legitimate ruler and be motivated by Christian love. Such love, he believed, is not incompatible with killing because nonresistance is identified with an inward feeling. Augustine explained his position as follows: "If it is supposed that God could not enjoin warfare because in after times it was said by the Lord Jesus Christ, 'I say unto you, Resist not evil,'...the answer is that what is here required is not a

bodily action but an inward disposition. ...Love does not preclude a benevolent severity, nor that correction which compassion itself dictates."[4] Augustine also taught that a just war was to be conducted in an honorable manner. Faith was to be kept with the enemy, and there were to be no unnecessary violence, massacres, burning, and looting.

Despite his rationale for the just war, Augustine felt the tension between the pacifism of the early church and the need for Christians to serve in the army. There is a gloomy mood about much of his teaching on the state. This is seen in his discussion of the Christian judge who must employ torture in the examination of accused criminals. The suspect in the case Augustine cites turns out to be innocent and has been unjustly tortured. Yet Augustine defends the participation of Christians in the practice by stating: "If then such darkness shrouds social life will the wise judge take his set on the bench? That he will. For human society, which he cannot rightly abandon, constrains him to do his duty. He will take his seat and cry 'From my necessities deliver thou me.'"[5]

Despite the just war theory advanced by Augustine, which seemed to harmonize participation in conflict with Christian values, the pacifism of the early church remained a living force within the community of faith. Those who killed in war were forced to do long terms of penance, and there was no glorification of the holy Christian knight until the eleventh century. The situation in Europe changed due to the breakup of the empire and the influx of Germanic peoples. A new militant attitude was formed in the church. The Germans placed a great emphasis on warfare, as is common among primitive groups. Their greatest virtues,

[4]Ibid., 97.
[5]Ibid., 98.

such as devotion to gods of battle and the desire to die in conflict, were those of the warrior. A fusion of the Germanic religion of war and the religion of peace took place among the Christians of Western Europe.

The most famous results of the new warlike outlook were the Crusades. In 1095 at the Council of Clermont, in response to appeals for help from the Eastern emperor at Constantinople, Pope Urban II preached a sermon urging his listeners to undertake an expedition under papal leadership to free the Middle East from pagan control. He stirred his audience by describing how the Turks had disemboweled Christian men, raped women, and desecrated churches. Urban appealed for unity in the face of the enemy and promised forgiveness of sins for anyone who would fight to free the Holy Land. The crowd responded enthusiastically to his sermon, shouting: "God wills it! God wills it!"

Historians have pointed out several reasons for the Crusades. One of these was the desire of the papacy to reduce the scale of violence in Western Europe. If the knights could not be persuaded to stop struggling with each other, perhaps they could be encouraged to fight against some other enemy.

There were really two groups involved in the expeditions that were later called the First Crusade. The first expedition was made up of lower-class people under the leadership of popular preachers such as Peter the Hermit. They wandered through Europe killing Jews, begging, and stealing. Many deserted the cause or died on the way, but a surprisingly large number reached Asia, where the Turks massacred them.

The second group of Crusaders was composed of nobles who understood the situation better than the poor people did. Led by some of the most important men in Europe, they spent a year making preparations for their journey and arrived in Constantinople in 1097. These knights fared better than the peasants and won a series of victories that culminated in the capture of Jerusalem in 1099.

The First Crusade led to the establishment of four European states on the shores of the eastern Mediterranean. Tradition has numbered the later Crusades, but actually there was a continual coming and going of European knights to the Holy Land. The purpose of the later Crusades also changed; in one of them Crusaders conquered Constantinople in 1204, and others were directed against papal foes in Europe. Even the loss of Western holdings in the eastern Mediterranean with the fall of Acre in 1291 did not stop the movement, which continued into the fifteenth century.

It is clear from the Crusades that what finally overpowered the early Christian teaching against violence was not merely a just war theory but rather a merger of violence and holiness at all levels of Christian life. Many other examples could be given of the new favorable attitude toward violence in the church. The liturgy was expanded to include the blessing of weapons and standards. Knights were consecrated by ceremonies that often were a continuation of old pagan customs. There were even new religious orders, such as that of the Templars, who promised to fight the enemies of God in addition to taking the normal vows of poverty, chastity, and obedience.

Throughout the Middle Ages there was a tendency on the part of Christian writers to accept war as part of the necessary condition of society. There was little serious dispute about the necessity of fighting the Turks or the enemies of the faith in Western Europe. The just war teaching of Augustine was put into a legal form by Gratian in the twelfth century and repeated in a scholastic fashion by Thomas Aquinas during the thirteenth century. Surprisingly little time was spent in discussing the problem. Aquinas has only one question on war in his massive theological work, compared with twenty-four questions about angels.[6] At the same time the theologians were ignoring the problem of war, the growth of the chivalric ideal was exerting a powerful influence on the emerging hero image of Europeans. In *The Canterbury Tales,* Chaucer described the knight as the natural leader of the pilgrims and made him the embodiment of all that was graceful and noble in an individual.

During the fifteenth and sixteenth centuries, several factors created a new situation in which war again received the attention of thinking Christians. Among these developments was the growth of a new technology that led to the decline of medieval methods of warfare. The most important aspect of this change was the use of gunpowder in weapons that could destroy the walls of castles and cities, thus taking away the security of the feudal lords. Later these cannons were adopted for field use, and the knight in armor was made obsolete. These changes in weaponry were grimly prophetic of further advances that would lead to the three-dimensional nuclear warfare of the twenty-first century. Another change that affected Christian attitudes toward war during the Renaissance period was the division of Europe into dynastic monarchies, from which the contemporary pattern of national states has emerged.

The new style of warfare met with vigorous opposition from such leading Christian humanists as Thomas More, Erasmus, and John Colet. These individuals rediscovered the relevance of the New Testament to many matters, and this led them to condemn war. The greatest of them, Erasmus of Rotterdam (1469–

1536), used his impressive talents to condemn violence. He believed renewal and reform could come to the church if individuals would study the Bible and live a simple life in imitation of Christ. To him nothing was more basic to the philosophy of Christ than hostility to war. His satire *In Praise of Folly* ridiculed the theologians who drew a justification for violence from Jesus' advice to his disciples to sell their clothes and buy swords.

The church, Erasmus believed, had accepted the idea of the just war along with the whole body of Roman civil law, which was not in harmony with the law of Christ. Also, he added, once wars are accepted as just, they tend to become glorious. In short, he and the other humanists accused the church of accepting the just war teaching, missing the true meaning of Scripture, and becoming the servant of the bloodthirsty ambitions of the princes.

The era of the Renaissance was also the age of the Reformation. Despite their brilliant rediscovery of the gospel, the early Protestants did not bring peace to Earth. The confessional rivalry, when added to the new weapons technology, resulted in bloody warfare that was not to be equaled until the twentieth century. The Protestant leaders Luther, Zwingli, and Calvin accepted the use of violence and warfare. The European religious wars that lasted from about 1550 to 1648 seriously discredited the Reformation in many quarters.

One group of the Reformers, however, did not accept the use of violence. The Anabaptists differed widely among themselves, but they were more radical than the other Protestants and rejected the state church. Beginning about 1560 they espoused pacifism because they believed Christ had initiated a new order of love

---

[6]Thomas Aquinas, *Summa Theologica II,* ii. Q. 40. For a helpful recent edition of Aquinas's work, see *An Aquinas Reader,* ed. M.T. Clark (Garden City, N.Y.: Doubleday, 1972).

and meekness in which there should be no constraint. The Christian must imitate Christ and not resist when mistreated. After all, Jesus referred to his followers as sheep: "A sheep is a suffering, defenseless, patient beast, which has no other defense save to run so long as it can and may. A sheep is no more comparable to the governance of the sword than to a wolf or lion."[7] The behavior of Christians is to be wholly different from that of worldly people. Said one Anabaptist leader, "Our fortress is Christ, our defense is patience, our sword is the Word of God, and our victory is the sincere, firm, unfeigned faith in Jesus Christ. Spears and swords of iron we leave to those who, alas, consider human blood and swine's blood well nigh of equal value."[8]

In the years that followed the Peace of Westphalia (1648), which settled the last of the religious wars, dynastic states such as France under Louis XIV became the centers of power in Europe. These states suppressed local war bands and organized national standing armies. The new forces permanently replaced the nobles as the fighting element in society. At the same time the rising middle class was challenging the privileges of the old chivalric class in other fields. Faced with changing conditions, many nobles who were accustomed to warfare and had a tradition of authority took command of the growing military power of the nations. Throughout Europe in the early modern period the nobility came to monopolize the positions of command in the armed forces, and they developed a strong vested interest in increasing the military establishment.

Despite the popularity of military values, during the eighteenth century the impact of the Enlightenment and the inefficiency of the monarchies of Europe tended to check the growth of warfare. During the seventeenth and eighteenth centuries the Christian pacifist tradition was kept alive by at least three groups, the Mennonites, the Religious Society of Friends (Quakers), and the Church of the Brethren. The Mennonites were the descendants of the Anabaptists, while the Church of the Brethren originated with the ministry Alexander Mack, who in 1708 combined Anabaptism and Pietism. The Quakers grew from the preaching of George Fox of Cromwellian England, who wished to follow the Sermon on the Mount in a literal way. These peace churches in their various divisions have kept up a continuing witness against war as well as a refusal to participate in it.

The coming of the French Revolution and the struggles that followed broke the comparative calm of the age of reason and led to the birth of modern war. The revolution was diverted from its original goals by Napoleon (1769–1821) and transformed into an effort to conquer Europe. An artillery officer who graduated from a military academy in Paris, Napoleon skillfully manipulated the masses to form an alliance, joining their democratic idealism and nationalism with the ambition and militarism of the aristocracy. He put the entire nation of France into the service of war.

The Napoleonic wars of conquest humiliated the Prussians and inspired them to copy the French methods. It was a teacher at the Prussian military academies, Karl von Clausewitz (1780–1831), whose theories of warfare were accepted as the standard in modern times. He articulated the concept of "total war," the necessity to push conflict to the "utmost bounds" of violence in order to win. As Clausewitz explained: "He who uses force unsparingly, without reference to the

[7]Bainton, *Christian Attitudes*, 153.
[8]Ibid.

bloodshed involved, must obtain a superiority if his adversary uses less vigor in its application. The former then dictates the law to the latter, and both proceed to extremities, to which the only limitations are those imposed by the amount of counteracting force on each side.... To introduce into a philosophy of war a principle of moderation would be an absurdity. War is an act of violence pushed to its utmost bounds."[9] These teachings became influential throughout Europe. It seems that the Prussian writer conspired with history because the Industrial Revolution of the nineteenth century greatly increased the power of armaments and made it possible to totally defeat an enemy.

Despite these ominous developments, after the settlement of the Napoleonic Wars the history of warfare marked time throughout most of the nineteenth century. In fact, before World War I broke out, there were many indications that international cooperation and humanitarianism might reduce the need for conflict. A strong Christian influence led to international gatherings such as the Hague Conferences of 1899 and 1907. From these meetings came decisions that limited the nature of war, protected the rights of prisoners of war, affirmed the need to care for the sick and the wounded, promised protection of private property, and guaranteed the rights of neutrals.

These principles were violated by both sides during World War I. Despite the fact that the war was not fought over basic ideological issues, it became necessary to use ideologies to justify the slaughter and monotony of the seemingly endless war effort. Because of technological advances, Clausewitz's total or absolute war could now be fought. Modern artillery, machine guns, poison gas, submarine warfare,

aerial bombardment, and extensive use of land mines broke the rules of war so confidently set forth at the Hague Conference of 1907. Economic warfare and blockades that led to widespread food shortages affected millions of people who were not soldiers in the traditional sense. War became three-dimensional, and its ability to strike at civilian populations was vastly increased. The conflict had started with a great deal of lighthearted, irresponsible patriotic fervor on the part of the Allies, and Christians joined in the spirit, but later the mood toughened into a bitter nationalism.

The governments managed to drag their people through the war, but the armistice laid the basis for another conflict. While totalitarian regimes grew in Germany, Japan, and Russia, the mood turned to discouragement in much of the Western world. Under the League of Nations, which was formed to prevent a repetition of World War I, collective security and peaceful settlement of disputes were to control international relations. But a world government without the full support of its members could not operate successfully. So a Second World War came and brought even more severe horrors.

That war differed from World War I because it was a battle to the end between different, antagonistic social and political systems. The demand for unconditional surrender and the rejection of a negotiated peace demonstrates the triumph of the logic of violence. To achieve the total suppression of the enemy, the techniques of violence were perfected. New rockets and nuclear weapons that seemed to represent the ultimate in destructive capabilities were produced.

Despite these trends, there were important pacifist reactions to the violence.

---

[9]Karl von Clausewitz, *On War,* quoted in Alfred Vagts, *A History of Militarism* (Cleveland, Ohio: Meridian, 1959), 182.

The Fellowship of Reconciliation (F.O.R.), an international, interdenominational body, was founded on the eve of World War I in England by Henry Hodgkin, a Quaker, and spread to the United States in 1915. Convinced that war violated Christian principles, F.O.R. opposed American intervention in World War I. It aided conscientious objectors who were often mistreated by the government and finally concluded that war is not an aberration, but a logical outcome of a capitalist society. Despite pressure to become solely a humanitarian movement, it has kept its Christian witness and was active in the anti-Vietnam War movement of the 1960s and 1970s.

With the end of World War II, the threat to world peace continued in the rivalry between the United States and the U.S.S.R. The arms race became a part of everyday life, and the satisfaction of defense needs was woven into the very texture of industrial technological society. When the Soviet empire collapsed and it seemed that a new era of peace might result, many pacifists were encouraged, but the new American campaign against terrorism has revived the war emphasis.

Since World War II many Christian groups have joined the historic peace churches in a pacifist stance because of the danger to all of human civilization caused by nuclear weapons. This threat started with large-scale bombing of civilian populations during the 1930s, when the Spanish town of Guernica was destroyed and the Japanese used similar tactics on Chinese cities. The world responded to these tactics with moral outrage. Both President Franklin Roosevelt and Prime Minister Winston Churchill condemned such actions as atrocities.[10] Yet later, in response to Luftwaffe attacks on British cities, the Royal Air Force began to raid German industrial cities. In 1942 the British started a policy of "obliteration bombing" intended to terrorize the German people and reduce their "will to resist." By 1943 the U.S. Air Force had joined the British in obliteration bombing.

On August 3, 1943, after Hamburg had been pounded by ten days of concentrated air raids, sixty thousand acres of the city caught fire. In the resulting "fire storm," the entire city began to function as a huge furnace. Those who had taken refuge in shelters were gradually roasted alive as the temperature mounted, and others, who tried to escape the inferno, were carried back into its center by high winds. The effect at Hamburg was unintended, but the obliteration bombing of Dresden in 1945 was deliberately planned. The city was crowded with refugees, and despite later claims that it was the center of poison-gas production, in reality it was of slight military importance. Waves of British bombers laid a fire storm over eleven square miles of the city. Temperatures soared to one thousand degrees centigrade and hurricane-strength winds swept people and objects into the core of the city. The number of bodies was so enormous that it took weeks to dispose of them, and estimates of dead vary between one hundred thousand and a quarter of a million.

During the summer of 1945 the U.S. Air Force unleashed an aerial attack on Japan that exceeded even the bombing of Germany. The culmination of this offensive came on August 6, 1945, when the first effective atomic bomb was dropped on the city of Hiroshima. This blast destroyed over half of the city of 320,000, killing over seventy thousand and maiming many more. All utilities and transportation services were put out of

---

[10]See Robert C. Batchelder, *The Irreversible Decision: 1939–1950* (Boston: Houghton Mifflin, 1962).

commission, and only three of the city's fifty-five health-care units were able to function. The heat was so intense that stone walls, steel doors, and asphalt pavements glowed like molten iron. More than a mile from the center of the blast the intense heat fused kimono patterns onto women's bodies and children's stockings were burned onto their legs. The now familiar mushroom-shaped cloud hovered over the city as a symbol of the spectacular and disastrous attack. Three days later another atomic bomb was dropped on Nagasaki with similar horrible results.

Another development of the post–World War II era that has radically changed the world condition in which the just war theory operates is in the field of rocketry. In 1957 the Russians orbited Sputnik, and by 1961 they were able to put a manned rocket into orbit. In the same year President John F. Kennedy announced a program to put a man on the moon by 1970. These efforts, although launched for a variety of reasons, were basically a continuation of the arms race between the Eastern and Western military blocs. Space satellites were launched that could be used to rain death on the enemy at a moment's impulse.

Not only has the delivery system for weapons improved, but the arms have also been perfected. The bombs that destroyed Hiroshima and Nagasaki produced mere pinpricks compared to the potential effects of present-day thermonuclear weapons. The original atomic bombs could level a city and leave a radioactive fallout in the immediate area for about a week. A twenty-megaton hydrogen bomb of the type now available can destroy a city the size of Washington, D.C., and cause serious damage over an area extending from Harrisburg, Pennsylvania, to Norfolk, Virginia. Such an explosion could send radioactive fallout over an even larger area, depending on the winds. The contamination would seriously affect human beings and the earth for many generations. Stripped of emotional patriotic arguments, the potential use of thermonuclear bombs makes a mockery of the just war theory because they would automatically cause the slaughter of noncombatants. These weapons invalidate war as a rational instrument of national policy.

Challenged by the growing possibility of a nuclear holocaust and the futility of violence to solve human conflicts, many denominations that have historically accepted the just war theory and the crusading ideal as the only position on war have also issued pacifist statements. Two notable examples of this are the Pastoral Constitution on the Church in the Modern World issued by Vatican and the declaration of the United Presbyterian Church (USA) titled, "Peacemaking: The Believer's Calling." A book recently issued by the National Board for Conscientious Objectors identifies dozens of groups that allow for conscientious objection to violent conflict.[11] It is important to notice that many of those groups encourage some kind of alternative nonviolent service to our fellow human beings.

---

[11]Beth Ellen Boyle, ed., *Words of Conscience: Religious Statements on Conscientious Objection*, 10th ed. (Washington, D.C.: NISBCO, 1983).

Judging
the Just War

Howard J. Loewen

The just war theory, never a formal doctrine of the church, was proposed by Augustine (354–430) and used in early medieval thought both as a substitute for early Christian opposition to war and as a means of limiting the evil effects of war that Europe was experiencing at the time.

The theory historically demanded that several conditions be fulfilled before war is justified. Among them are the following: (1) the war must be defensive—a response to unjust aggression; (2) success must justify all wartime sacrifices; (3) there must be some proportion between the moral and physical costs of the hostilities and the peace and better social order sought after; (4) only military targets, not unarmed civilians, can be the targets of military strikes; and (5) force may never be used as a means in itself to brutalize the social order and the military personnel.[1]

In recent years, the just war theory has come under attack. Even non-Christians can agree that in a nuclear age some of the historic requirements for a just war cannot be met. Others have attacked the theory on the basis that even so-called Christian nations can easily find justification for participation in war.

Howard Loewen, Dean of the School of Theology and Professor of Theology and Ethics at Fuller Seminary, explains objections to various elements of the just war theory and ends by insisting that the only just war is the War of the Lamb.

Is the author correct when he says, in effect, that self-interest prevents us from being able to determine when a war is just? What might be elements of such self-interest (e.g., desire to protect what we have gained in material goods and property)? If you oppose the just war theory, how would you answer the person who insists that World War II was just because an evil Hitler had to be defeated? How do you respond to the thinking of early Anabaptists that in war a Christian might kill another Christian on the enemy side, and that a non-Christian enemy who is killed has been deprived of an opportunity for redemption?

---

[1]*Concise Dictionary of Theology* (New York: Paulist, n.d.).

During World War II, the U.S. Navy desperately needed chaplains. Hence someone suggested that they recruit men directly from theological seminaries and put them into the chaplaincy without any previous pastoral experience. It was a mistake they never repeated. But I was one of the forty they recruited.

Within a week after graduation I was in the Navy. And in a few months I was in the South Pacific, assigned to the First Marine Division. Being in a war posed no theological problems for me. Reformed theology had long since eased my conscience with its "just war theory." I felt that my participation with the Marines—trained for assault operations— was pleasing to God. I carried no weapon, so would not personally do the enemy any harm. Besides, I was an evangelical, and those Marines needed the gospel of Jesus Christ. My burden was the possibility of their dying without the knowledge of his salvation.

Our first operation was against a Japanese stronghold (Cape Gloucester, New Britain). On Christmas Eve (1943) I gathered with quite a few Marines on the deck of our L.S.T. The assault was scheduled before dawn the next day. We sang some carols. I read the Christmas story, spoke of God s condescension, and we prayed. All were inwardly "ruminating the morrow s danger." So far as the Marines were concerned it was to be "Merry Christmas to the Nips!"

A day or so later I was advancing along with some others over the area that had been hotly contested. It was raining. I recall the mud, the debris on the battlefield, and the stench of human flesh rotting in the tropical heat. Then to my right I saw what had been an enemy strongpoint. The treadmarks of one of our tanks went right over it. It had been crushed and some bodies were scattered about.

My attention was particularly drawn to what had been a Japanese soldier, lying in the mud. His head was missing The sight was altogether revolting. I turned aside, but then found myself almost unconsciously drawn back to him. For what caught my attention, and what piqued my curiosity was a little book half buried in the mud alongside where his head should have been. I had to see what that book was. I can still recall the revulsion and the smell as I forced myself to reach down and grasp the book.

You guessed! It was a Japanese New Testament. Had this horrible refuse been my brother? I was greatly troubled. A verse of Scripture came to mind: Galatians 6:10, "While we have opportunity, let us do good to all men, and especially to those who are of the household of faith" (NASB). What was I, a Christian, doing there at Cape Gloucester? Somehow, the "just war theory" on that day and in that place seemed like so much unwarranted nonsense. And you can be sure that I ve not been the same since![2]

The just war theory (J.W.T.) does have moral value. Its intention is to limit violence, even though there is little evidence of its effectiveness. In the history of the church the J.W.T. has usually functioned to justify war rather than to judge it.

Yet it is better to have some kind of restraint on the conditions and means of war than none at all. In a world that will always be riveted with violence and war it is still possible to hope that the J.W.T. could be used to steer the church and society toward more peace. That is one of the challenges today for Christians who hold this view.

Perhaps the present dangers of nuclear and revolutionary wars can help the

---

[2]Arthur Glasser, Professor of Missions, Fuller School of World Mission, June 25, 1985.

This chapter originally appeared as Howard J. Loewen, "Judging the Just War," in *The Power of the Lamb*, ed. John E. Toews and Gordon Nickel (Hillsboro, Kans.: Kindred Press, 1986), 107–116.

J.W.T. become an ethical instrument to reject rather than justify war. Could it direct people toward a biblical perspective that judges all wars in a nuclear age to be wrong? A consistent application of the J.W.T. criteria today renders both nuclear and revolutionary wars unjustifiable—more clearly so than with regard to other kinds of war in history.

Above all, the church and society must be strongly encouraged actually to *use* the J.W.T. Perhaps this would lead the church back once again to the prophetic position of the early church regarding war and peace—namely, a biblical pacifism.

Yet on the whole the J.W.T. has not and does not sufficiently represent a thorough-going Christian ethic. The following criticisms demonstrate its serious inadequacy as the ground for Christian actions and attitudes toward war and peace in our day.

Inadequate for the Realities of War

Mass Destruction

The horror of modern warfare makes J.W.T. ineffective. Although J.W.T. condemns any use of weapons of mass destruction, it breaks down completely when weapons are designed to destroy nameless civilians indiscriminately. Therefore, the technology of modern warfare alone puts the J.W.T. out of date.

Similarly, the technology and tactics of modern guerrilla warfare make the criteria of J.W.T. virtually impossible to apply. The widespread and massive destruction of such warfare, and the even more serious destruction of the established authorities seeking to squelch revolutions, violates every rule of the J.W.T.

International Christians

Christians should not and cannot be involved in killing other Christians. Christians are one in the body of Christ. The long his-

tory of warfare in the "christianized" West has repeatedly violated this fundamental truth. Christians have repeatedly killed each other.

Now, in the nuclear age, this killing can be increased in geometric proportions. If then we apply the J.W.T. rules we would have to condemn all wars in which Christians participated—past, present, and future. In the same way, revolutionary warfare increases many times over the reality of Christians killing Christians.

Official Condemnation

Never has a body of bishops or a major denominational body officially condemned a war. Since its beginning in the fourth century the J.W.T. has remained a theory. It has never really worked. The implementation of the J.W.T. criteria represents a history of failure.

However, there are some signs today that official religious bodies and leaders are willing to take positions against the nuclear threat based on the J.W.T. Unfortunately, this emerging pacifism is frequently cancelled out by a corresponding willingness on the part of northern hemisphere Christians to support and justify counter-revolutionary violence in the southern hemisphere in the name of justice.

Moral Function

The J.W.T. has seldom been used as a tool for moral guidance. Until recent times, proponents of the J.W.T. usually have been able to justify the wars of their own nations. The theory was originally formulated to show that some wars might be an exception to the gospel, yet it has become a tool to justify every war that comes along.

In addition, nations serve as judges in their own cases during the threat of war. Therefore, who is to say that all alternatives have been exhausted? The J.W.T. implies that there will be truthful presentation of all the facts by a nation to its people before and during war, allowing Christians to make informed judgments. However, this has never happened.

Finally, the J.W.T. simply has too many loopholes. Proponents can find ways to justify any war. For the appeal of the J.W.T. to be credible, its criteria must be stated more clearly and firmly, and its effectiveness demonstrated in actually limiting war.

Self-Righteous Justification

The J.W.T. assumes that one side will be just and the other unjust. Yet in times of war, without exception, both sides claim their cause to be just. Perhaps we should conclude from this that no nation can be just. There is much that is unjust on both sides.

The injustice on both sides is only heightened when today there are two super-powers each sufficiently armed to annihilate human civilization. Each has self-righteously driven the other to the point of mutually assured destruction.

Fusing Church and Society

The J.W.T. was born in a church established and supported by the Roman Empire under the emperor Constantine. It therefore has a conservative bias regarding the relation of the church to the state. Its vision of church-state relations is one which links together the church and society in such a way that the church is supportive of the state.

In this environment the church can justify the use of force to bring about its desired ends for society. It comes to see war as a police function which maintains peace and order and resists violence and tyranny.

The J.W.T. continues to function with this understanding of the Constantinian vision. This is true whether it is the church in the northern hemisphere joined to a capitalist society which can justify nuclear war, or whether it is the church in the southern hemisphere joined to a Marxist movement which can justify revolutionary wars in the name of Christ.

Both the classical just war and the contemporary just revolution waged in the name of Christ exemplify the Constantinian orientation of the J.W.T. which fuses church and society as ethical agents of change in a questionable way.

Natural Law Tradition

The J.W.T. is too extensively grounded in the natural law tradition of the Greeks and Romans. Reliance on natural law means that you appeal to that point of view in society which makes the most political sense. That is true whether one lives in a Constantinian, capitalist, or communist society.

To be politically realistic, people appeal to that which makes the most sense in the context of a given society. Therefore Christians—whether in ancient or modern society—have justified war in terms of defending the world and culture in which they lived because that made the most sense to them and they had the most to gain from it.

The origins of the J.W.T. in this natural law tradition have provided the basis for the Christian church invariably and uncritically to support wars fought by nation states or national movements.

This kind of strong reliance on national politics has overshadowed the primary source of authority to which Christians and the church claim to appeal in judging questions of war and peace— namely, biblical revelation.

Must not the origin of the Christian position on war come from the Bible? Does not the teaching of Scripture, and that of Jesus Christ in particular, clearly challenge the very basis on which the J.W.T. is built? Is not the biblical vision of peace and the early church's witness to peace a sign of the true biblical and theological position for our age?

These questions focus the most fundamental criticism against the J.W.T.—that it is not sufficiently biblical and theological in its orientation.

Falls Short of the Bible

The assumptions of the J.W.T. are not rooted deeply enough in the biblical vision of the gospel of peace and salvation. Therefore the moral power of the J.W.T. has eroded during the present time. The Christian politics of medieval Europe and modern America, which have nurtured this tradition, have essentially collapsed. As a result the J.W.T. increasingly has become an inadequate moral instrument to deal with the most profound ethical issue of our nuclear age.

The Sinfulness of Human Nature

One of the major weaknesses of the J.W.T. is its understanding of human nature. On the one hand, it tends to use the argument of the fallenness of human nature to justify the use of force to contain violence. On the other hand, it appeals to enlightened human reason in applying the criteria of the J.W.T. so that fighting a just war is possible.

What is not sufficiently clear in the J.W.T. is that warfare has its roots in the fallenness of human nature, and that war itself is the climax of rebellion against God and humanity. In the Bible sin as disobedience, violence as an outcome of deep insecurity, and warfare as an expression of human hatred are very closely related. The rapid escalation of violence from Adam to Cain to Lamech to Noah to Nimrod in Genesis supplies convincing evidence of this sinfulness.

Today the murder of Abel by Cain has the possibility of being magnified to include the entire human race. The J.W.T. does not sufficiently contribute to the recognition that modern societies have produced a nuclear Cain. Nuclear weapons provide a devastatingly clear picture of human cursing and murdering. The human heart, not God, is the root of all destruction. The inner attitude of collective hatred has led to the self-righteous building of murderous weapons that can annihilate an entire population of Abels.

The Sovereignty of God, the Warrior

The J.W.T. does not sufficiently affirm that God has entered the arena of human conflict as a warrior to eliminate violence rather than justify it. God has chosen to participate in the sinful history of humanity in order to defeat the evil forces contributing to violence, injustice and chaos. The holy wars of God recorded in the Bible are fought toward this end. Thus God fights both for and against Israel. Here the sovereignty and lordship of God the warrior are demonstrated. The focus is on *his* involvement and control in war rather than on human involvement and control.

God's wars in biblical history are ultimately fought by the Word of God, by miracle, and by faith, not with sword and armies under human control. When Israel begins to replace her dependence on God as warrior with an idolatrous dependence on the nation and the king as warrior, she comes under the judgment of God, and the Lord fights—that is, brings judgment—against her.

The J.W.T. does not sufficiently recognize the idolatry of national sovereignty. The nation state has become one of the main gods of our civilization. There exists a tendency, deeply rooted in our culture, to preserve that god at any cost. The J.W.T. frequently has contributed to this idol worship.

The idolization of the nation state and the bomb increasingly propel us toward self-destruction. The J.W.T. does not have a sufficiently realistic grasp of the fact that the nation state is an agent of the principalities and powers of this world. Modern rebellious and idolatrous states are now willing to sacrifice any number of human beings on the altar of the god of national sovereignty.

If the false god is not clearly identified in the assumptions of the J.W.T., neither is the nature and way of the true God. Accordingly, in the J.W.T. the reality of God's judgment regarding the warring ways of the nations is severely minimized. What the J.W.T. does not recognize is that God's judgment is a far more awesome threat than the menace of a nuclear enemy or a revolutionary movement.

The illusions by which nation states live are foolishness in God's eyes. The J.W.T. does not bring this perspective to bear on today's nuclear situation. Instead it has contributed to the development of the bomb which reflects the colossal self-righteousness of nuclear nations.

From the perspective of the biblical vision, the judgment of God lies in allowing these nations to head toward self-destruction. As in the days of Noah, God may choose to let this rebellion be limitless, even to the point of self-annihilation and ultimate separation from God himself. The J.W.T. is not an adequate moral instrument to see us through the nuclear age.

The Kingdom of Christ, the Lord

The J.W.T. operates from assumptions that do not adequately take into account the vision of God's kingdom as manifested in Jesus Christ and the apostolic church. God entered the fray of human history to reverse the increase of violence and to establish a vision of peace. The substance of this vision involved establishing one community of God's people where peaceful living would provide an alternative to the injustice, violence, and warring of sinful humanity.

Thus in Jesus Christ, God entered into the brickyards of human society to reverse the curse of Cain and to release his people from bondage. In Jesus, God continues to be the warrior contending against the principalities and powers of evil. This Jesus resisted evil by loving the enemy and preaching the gospel of peace. He came to inaugurate a new kingdom, a new spiritual and social community of people.

Jesus Christ conquered the temptation to be an international leader, yet his new kingdom community ultimately posed a threat to the Roman Empire itself as it proclaimed, taught and imitated the way of the cross, the way of humility and service. This was the nonviolent way of Jesus who has absorbed and who will absorb the violence of the nuclear and revolutionary Cain. He was and is the supreme defense of us all. We look to his defenselessness on the cross as a model and to his resurrection as a source of power.

Jesus Christ as victor and victim stands with all the victims of humanity in the nuclear age and holds back doom while offering hope. Out of that victory Christians must call together a faithful remnant of God's people who will say a resounding "NO" to nuclear destruction. Such a people will bear witness to the fact that the very attitude which drives the nations toward nuclear war speaks a big "NO" to the gospel of Jesus Christ in our time and provides an occasion for God's judgment.

But the members of the kingdom of Christ must also resist frantic activity which simply draws people into a survivalist movement in the face of the nuclear threat. Likewise, they must resist a fatalistic pessimism that is resigned to accepting the inevitable. For the kingdom of God speaks a message of resurrection hope. Its members must call people everywhere to repentance for attitudes and actions that betray our rebellious nature. That is the mission of the church of Christ. It must speak and live a gospel that states that Jesus Christ is victor over the rebellious powers.

Christians must reckon with the day of the Bomb and the bullet, but they must not be overcome by it. We must pray that the evidence of Christ's triumph might be present even after such an unthinkable event. That will be the most difficult of all times to live the way of the cross. Yet the church will be called upon to suffer with the Lamb.

The War of the Lamb is the only justifiable war. All other wars only lead the human family deeper into the cycle of revenge and murder. The J.W.T. has not been able to break that cycle. It has only led us more deeply into it. For it has not adequately understood the fundamental conflict between the kingdom of Christ and the kingdom of the anti-Christ, and the victory of the former over the latter. The only defense for Christians today is to continue to pray "thy kingdom come here on earth."

Chapter Nine

First Pure,
Then Peaceable

Daniel R. Chamberlain

Daniel R. Chamberlain has had a distinguished career in Christian higher education, serving as Dean of Upland College and later Messiah College, then as the President of Houghton College. He has been known for both his innovative leadership and his incisive thought.

In this article he reflects on the pacifist conviction of the early Wesleyan Methodist Church in America. Then he records how the Civil War eroded the peace stance of the denomination. He notes that the chance to rid the United States of the plague of slavery was deemed to be an overriding issue of justice, one that called for modifying the pacifist stance. He implies at the end that this represented a loss of the original denominational vision.

This historical sketch of one denomination's brief experiment with pacifism is of considerable interest. Should we view this loss of vision as a compromise of the gospel? Or should it be seen as a just failure of idealistic pacifism that cannot solve issues of justice in society? Such questions lie at the heart of the Christian debate concerning peace and justice. How do we resolve the conflict?

The Wesleyan Methodist Church was born out of a serious conflict, a conflict of conscience over the issues of slavery and the role of the Methodist Episcopal Church in terminating human bondage. Generally the Methodist Episcopal Church counseled containment, appeasement, and a reluctant tolerance of slavery, which it regarded primarily as a political and economic issue. Those who founded the Wesleyan Methodist Connection of America (later the Wesleyan Methodist Church of America) believed the issue involved such profound biblical and moral principles that individuals as well as the corporate church should cry out against the evil and press for abolition through acts of legislation, if possible, and civil disobedience, if necessary.

The resultant conflict of conscience produced its first major withdrawal of congregations from the Methodist Episcopal Church in Michigan. On May 13,

---

This article was previously published as "First Pure, Then Peaceable: The Position of the Wesleyan Methodist Church on War and Peace from its Founding to the Civil War," in *Within the Perfection of Christ: Essays on Peace and the Nature of the Church in Honor of Martin H. Schrag*, ed. Terry L. Brensinger and E. Morris Sider (Nappanee, Ind.: Evangel Press, 1990), 217–29.

1841 these congregations joined together to form an annual conference using the name "The Wesleyan Methodist Church." A year and a half later, in December 1842, a similar withdrawal of abolitionists from the Methodist Episcopal Church occurred in New England and New York, when these groups held a Wesleyan Anti-Slavery Convention in Andover, Massachusetts. Six months later (May 31–June 8, 1843) they held a Wesleyan General Convention in Utica, New York, to form a new denomination opposed to slavery and episcopacy. The newly created denomination held its first general conference on October 2–12, 1844; within two years the church had grown to 245 stationed ministers and 14,600 members.[1]

The 1842 Wesleyan Anti-Slavery Convention not only organized a new denomination, it also authorized the publication of a weekly church periodical titled *The True Wesleyan*. The first edition was printed on January 7, 1843, and carried the motto: "First Pure, Then Peaceful." A week later, on January 14, 1843, the motto was modified to read: "First Pure, Then Peaceable" (an obvious reference to James 3:17), and those words appeared on every subsequent weekly edition until well into the twentieth century.[2]

Evidence suggests that this motto was a very careful and deliberate choice which was intended to express the position and the spirit of the new church. In fact, a front page editorial appearing in the very first edition of *The True Wesleyan* entitled "Withdrawal from the Methodist Episcopal Church" stated: "Hence we have come to the deliberate conclusion that we must submit to things as they are or *peaceably retire* [emphasis added]. We have unhesitatingly chosen the latter."[3]

The primary task of the first General Conference was the preparation and approval of its *Discipline of Doctrine and Governance*. This new discipline was similar in its content to that of the Methodist Episcopal Church; in fact, most of the articles of religion were essentially the same. However, the Wesleyan *Discipline* differed dramatically from its parent body on the issue of war and peace. The singular reference to war, peace, or the military in the Methodist Episcopal *Discipline* of 1840 and 1844 was to include military chaplains in the list of those ministers exempt from the maximum two-year ministerial appointments. By contrast the organizers of the Wesleyan Methodist Church appointed a Committee on Peace to present a report which was entitled "The Duty of Christians on the Subject of Peace." The Committee presented its report on October 9, 1844, and ten days later *The True Wesleyan* records:

> Christian duty can only be determined by an appeal to the law and to the testimony. Other standards are assumed, however, by many. The right to decide our duty by the circumstances of the case, or the supposed results of action, has been argued by learned and wise men. The consequence is the justification of actions which debase and destroy mankind and dishonor God. Among these acts is the practice of war.

---

[1] Ira F. McLeister and Roy S. Nicholson, *Conscience and Commitment* (Marion, Ind.: Wesley Press, 1976), 49.

[2] *The True Wesleyan* was founded by Orange Scott in 1842; its first issue was published on January 7, 1843. In 1844 the General Conference of the Wesleyan Methodist Church approved the editorial policy of *The True Wesleyan*, purchased the paper, and made it the official organ of the denomination.

[3] J. Horton and O. Scott, eds., "Withdrawal from the Methodist Episcopal Church," *The True Wesleyan*, January 7, 1843, 1.

Duty on this question is clearly set forth in the laws of Christianity, as the following extracts will show. "Love your enemies. Bless them that curse you. Do good to them that hate you, and pray for them that despitefully use and persecute you. See that none render evil for evil to any man. Recompense to no man evil for evil, but overcome evil with good. Lay aside all malice. Be gentle, showing all meekness to all men. But if you forgive not men their trespass, neither will your Father forgive you. Forgive, if ye have ought against any. God has called us to peace. Live in peace."[4]

The article proceeded to note that the observance of these "provisions of Christian law"

> would prevent, not only the practice of offensive and defensive war, but it would prevent those dispositions of the mind and those customs which tend to foster and perpetuate the war spirit. (Such is our opinion of Christian character, that we believe the practice of war in any of its forms, or those customs which tend to foster and perpetuate the war spirit, should disqualify any person for membership in the Christian Church.)[5]

The True Wesleyan goes on to report that, "After a spirited discussion of a few minutes, which promised to be quite protracted, the debate was closed by an agreement to drop off the sentence in brackets."[6] This decision of the General Conference was then referred to the Com-mittee on Revisals to develop specific language for including this decision in the *Discipline* of 1844. The result was Article XXXII, entitled "On Peace": "We believe the gospel of Christ to be every way opposed to the practice of war, in all its forms; and those customs which tend to foster and perpetuate the war spirit to be inconsistent with the benevolent designs of the Christian religion."[7]

This denominational position remained unchanged until the General Conference of 1867. While the position was not as strong as the Committee on Peace had desired or recommended, it did align the Wesleyan Methodist Church with the peace movement and helps to account for the many articles, letters, and editorials on the subject which appeared in *The True Wesleyan* from 1843 to 1862. These articles most frequently appealed to scriptural authority for their opposition to war, although references to the early church fathers (of the first two centuries of the Christian church) were also common. These biblical and historical foundations led the Wesleyan Church to express strong anti-war sentiments and positions during the Mexican War (1846–1848). The following samples are typical of articles appearing in *The True Wesleyan* during this period.

> At this moment drums are beating and fifes playing, and men dressed in military costume are marching with mechanical exactness through our streets, beating up for volunteers to go to the frontiers of Mexico, while hundreds of half-grown men and boys, captivated by

---

[4]This reference clearly implies that Wesleyans subscribed to the Reformation doctrine of *sola scriptura*. While Scripture was an important source of authority for them, scholars generally agree that Wesleyans accepted a quadrilateral basis of authority: Scripture, tradition, experience, and the guidance of the Holy Spirit.

[5]*The True Wesleyan*, October 19, 1844, 167; taken from a report of the first General Conference of the Wesleyan Methodist Church.

[6]Ibid.

[7]*The Wesleyan Discipline*, 1844, 87.

the trappings of men who wear long sharp knives at their sides, with which to cut each others' throats, march before or follow after, full of hilarity and glee.

How fearful the thought, that in the nineteenth century, in "the most enlightened and Christian nation on earth," where there are thousands of men employed from year to year to instruct the people in the religion of Christ, the Prince of Peace, that men should still be found, who are willing for the paltry sum of three shillings per day, to hire themselves as wholesale butchers of their race—to murder, burn, maim, and destroy all that comes within their reach. When, oh when will men beat their swords into plowshares, and their spears into pruning hooks?

I believe ALL war, for any and every purpose wrong: wrong in its beginning; wrong in its progress; wrong in its results. If I look to Jesus, He is all peace and tenderness; if I look to His true disciples, I see the reflection of His image....Instead of that, we have slaughtered husbands, murdered sons, heartbroken wives, polluted daughters, burning cities, ruined commerce, devastated fields, and damned spirits, to say nothing of the baneful influence on morals at home—far from the seat of war....

As the Connection [the commonly used name for the Wesleyan Methodist Church at that time], we profess to believe all war anti-Christian, and have published our sentiments to the world. Shall we, in this emergency be true to our principles? I pray God it may be so. May no Wesleyan be found either spilling the lifeblood of his brother or giving encouragement to others to do

so. Our testimony is demanded by the God Whom we serve, by the religion we profess, by the souls we seek to save. I know it will be a time to try men's souls, but if we suffer as Christians, happy are we....Let the language of every Christian be, when drafted or otherwise, that of the time-honored Maximillian, "I am a Christian and cannot fight."

Are we not under special obligations at a time like this to exert ourselves in the spread of peace principles, through the press, by the pulpit, and every other means within our reach? Let us remember the only way by which we are allowed to kill our enemies is, by heaping coals of fire, acts of kindness, upon their heads.[8]

The same issue of *The True Wesleyan* carried a moving article by an author (identified only as "Mary") which presents a Wesleyan woman's reaction to the Mexican War.

For the last few weeks my mind has been deeply afflicted by illuminations, cannonadings, and the enlisting of volunteers for the army. Many young men of good families have gone and left the sweets of home, under a false idea of patriotism, and "my country right or wrong." They are now lying on the cold damp ground, sick and weary, with no kind mother, sister or wife to administer to their wants, or to wipe the cold sweat from their brow. They die almost like the beasts that perish, or, if fortunate enough to escape the diseases of the country, they are led on blindfolded as it were, for a sacrifice to the god of war. Oh! When will our nation learn to do justice, love mercy, and convert the instruments of death into implements of husbandry. When love to God and

[8]R.S. Ensign of Zanesville, Ohio, "War," *The True Wesleyan*, July 10, 1847, 109.

all mankind shall be the ruling passion of our hearts; then, and not til then war and bloodshed shall cease from off the face of the earth; and Christ will reign over nations, as He now does over saints.

The author went on to protest the perversion of public sentiment that allowed people to rejoice at the honors of the war:

Many thousands have been slain on the field of battle; hundreds are still in the agonies of death, and we rejoice! Many are lingering in hospitals, maimed and wounded, and we rejoice! How many widows and orphans are deprived of husband and father, and thrown on the cold charities of the world, and we rejoice! Cities are ravaged and desolated, men, women and children are slain and we rejoice!…How unlike the peaceable gospel of our Saviour, which was heralded by the angels, peace on earth, goodwill to men! The love of conquests has chilled the heart of the nation, to every better feeling of our nature; they seem to forget there is a God in Heaven, Who will bring every secret, thought, and act into judgment. What a fearful retribution awaits that so-called Christian nation, who wages an unjust war, on a feeble, half-distracted sister republic. Surely the demons themselves cannot be actuated by worse principles and feelings, than the leader and the abettors of this unholy and cruel war.[9]

During the first eight months of 1847, no fewer than seven articles appeared in *The True Wesleyan* opposing war and urging Wesleyans to promote their peace position in their churches and with government officials. Beginning in August, the periodical began reprinting, a chapter at a time, a book entitled *War and Peace* by Scrutator. The chapter titles included such topics as "The Cost of War," "The Horrors of War," "The Vices and Crimes of War," and "The Causes of War."

The Second General Conference, held in October 1848, saw renewed efforts to strengthen the *Discipline* article "On Peace." The General Conference *Book of Minutes* reports a memorial "from the Allegheny Conference asking that going to war or making preparation for war be made a disqualification for church membership; from the St. Lawrence Conference, ditto."[10]

Neither the *Minutes* nor *The True Wesleyan* reports on the debate or discussion these suggested amendments generated. The *Minutes* simply state that "These were…referred to the Committee on Revisals." Since the article "On Peace" remained identical in the next edition of the *Discipline,* it seems clear that the Committee on Revisals believed the General Conference discussion required no change.

While most of the articles opposing war and promoting peace which appeared in *The True Wesleyan* had biblical and theological roots, *The True Wesleyan* was a lively periodical which also provided extensive news coverage. Special emphasis was given to "reform issues," such as abolition, prohibition, and rights of women. Thus it is not surprising that articles reporting on more secular efforts to promote peace were also reported in its pages.

Accordingly in 1849 Wesleyans were urged to circulate, sign, and mail to their congressmen and representatives a Petition for peace which stated "the undersigned inhabitants (or citizens or legal

---

[9]"War Illumination," *The True Wesleyan,* July 10, 1847, 109.

[10]*The Wesleyan Methodist General Conference Book of Minutes*, Second General Conference, October 4–13, 1848, 78.

voters) of _____ in the state _____ deploring the manifold evils of war and believing it possible to supersede in most cases of alleged necessity by the timely adoption of wise and feasible substitutes, respectfully request your honorable body to take such action as you may deem best in favor of stipulated arbitration or a congress of nations for the accomplishment of this most desirable end."[11]

On other occasions *The True Wesleyan* reported on various state, national, and international peace conferences. In February of 1851 Wesleyans were urged to participate in the next Peace Congress scheduled to be held in London in July of that same year.[12] Even the advertisements carried in the periodical attempted to be consistent with the periodical's intentions to be "a journal of intelligence, instruction, and reform." An advertisement entitled "Wesleyan Tracts" was typical: "These tracts," it declared, "embrace a series on slavery, intemperance, war, licentiousness, and true piety to be circulated gratuitously.[13]

In 1853 the Wesleyan Methodist Church changed the name of its periodical from *The True Wesleyan* to *The Wesleyan.* The first edition to bear this new title summarizes the purposes and beliefs of the Wesleyan Church and its periodical. Included in that summary was the statement: "The doctrine that the gospel of Christ is opposed to war in all its forms, and the duty of refraining from those customs which tend to foster and perpetuate the war spirit." The editorial goes on to comment: "Christianity has suffered sadly in the world's esteem from the bad conduct of the church....The church early in its history forfeited its hold on the sympathies and affections of the masses by its glaring violation of the law of love in 'having respect' to the persons of the rich and in coveting the favor and patronage of the kingdoms of this world and the glory of them."[14]

The peace position of the Wesleyan Church was not limited to its periodical and General Conferences. At least some district conferences of the Wesleyan Methodist Church included peace studies in the preparation of their ministers. In a letter to the editor, Pastor E. Brookshire wrote, "Dear Brother Lee, Among the books the Miami (Ohio) annual conference required me to study was the Bible and J. Dymond on war. The following are some of the things I have learned from some of these books which I send for publication in *The True Wesleyan* if you think them worthy." Pastor Brookshire then quotes numerous biblical passages on peace and adds these quotations from Dymond: "Of all the Christian writers of the second century there is not one who notices the subject [of war] who does not hold it to be unlawful for a Christian to bear arms." "And says Clarkson, 'It was not until Christianity became corrupt that the Christians became soldiers.' There are more quotations in the apostolic fathers which relate to these points [on war and peace] than of any others; and to what did they apply these specific precepts of the New Testament which had been delivered? They applied them to war. They were assured that the precept absolutely forbade it."[15]

---

[11]*The True Wesleyan,* November 24, 1849, 186. This "Petition for Peace" was developed by the Executive Committee of the American Peace Society, George C. Beckwith, Corresponding Secretary.

[12]"The Next Peace Congress," *The True Wesleyan,* February 15, 1851, 26.

[13]*The Wesleyan,* November 7, 1855, 181.

[14]*The Wesleyan,* January 6, 1853, 2.

[15]E. Brookshire, letter to the editor, *The True Wesleyan,* January 8, 1848, 41.

While the Mexican War had produced special outrage and opposition among Wesleyans, their periodical continued to print many peace-related articles in the following years. These included book reviews, editorials, news reports, and articles reprinted from other periodicals. Such items appeared every month or two, thus keeping the issue and the Wesleyan position on peace before the church and its wider readership.

Even though the official position of the Wesleyan Church in opposition to war predominated in the pages of the church periodical, occasional objections were expressed about the position or about its frequent presentation. Just three months after *The True Wesleyan* began publication, the editor, Orange Scott, received a letter from a reader who opposed several references that had already been made to the peace position. Scott responded by insisting that the issue was an important one which deserved the attention it had already received; he went on to state his intention that *The True Wesleyan* would continue to present articles on peace as well as on all other relevant "reform issues."[16]

In 1845, Scott retired as the chief editor and the role was assumed by Luther Lee. In the years that followed, it became clear that Luther Lee was less committed to the peace position than his predecessor. This difference was first noticeable in an exchange between him and a Wesleyan by the name of L. King, who asked the question, "Can a member of the Wesleyan Methodist Connection, perform what is called 'military duty,' by attending 'military drills' etc., without violating the thirty-second section of the *Discipline* [the Article "On Peace"]? And would not such a person make himself liable to censure and even to expulsion if

he gave no signs of repentance? Yours for the right, L. King."[17] In response, the editor made a less than categorical response, as follows:

It is our opinion that members should not be expelled from the church for simply attending military drills, without reference to the motives, temper and spirit with which they do it.

It is our opinion that this section was not intended to be enforced as a condition of membership, but was placed there as a declaration of sentiment on the great question of war, which it condemns, with whatever fosters the war spirit. We were aware at the time of its introduction, that someone made this application of it, and hence, we opposed it, and obtained a modification of what was first proposed [an apparent reference to the action of the first General Conference which modified the report from the Committee on Peace by deleting the sentences which would have denied membership to any person who participated in the military].

The thing itself is too indefinite to justify its application to the expulsion of members. It affirms what "we believe"; we the members of the last general conference, but there is nothing in it requiring all members of the church to believe the same. It unequivocally condemns the practice of war, but to practice war and to attend a militia drill are not quite the same things....It is a question of conscience, and if a man's own conscience forbids him to do military duty, then let him refuse, be the consequences what they may to himself, but we should be careful how we

---

[16]Orange Scott, in *The True Wesleyan*, March 11, 1843, 39.

[17]L. King, "Doing Military Duty," *The True Wesleyan,* July 17, 1847, 115.

judge another man's conscience, not ourselves being liable to the same circumstances."[18]

Not surprisingly, King objected strongly to what he believed were the dangers and demerits of the editor's response. To his credit, Editor Lee printed King's response on the front page of the paper. King observes,

> You seem to think, that paying a tax in money to support fleets and armies, tends as much to foster the war spirit, as a reluctant attendance on a militia drill.

> No man pays a money tax for the express purpose of supporting fleets and armies; he pays it to the common treasury, and the offices of government appropriate it as they please—not as he wishes. Does paying a tax to support the pauperism etc., produced by intemperance—tend to promote intemperance? Does paying tax money into the U.S. Treasury, exert the same influence upon the minds of youth and children and even wives, mothers and sisters, that a military parade, the imposing uniform, waving plumes, glistening bayonets and music would? … And now allow me to inquire, if it can be reasonably expected by any reflecting mind, that a religion that will tolerate, or sanction military drills, and military parades, will ever succeed in converting "swords into plowshares" — and "spears into pruning hooks"— and that under its influence, nations will war no more....To me, it appears, that the *Friend Quakers* have a better religion in this respect, than the Wesleyan Methodists. Let us improve

ours or embrace *theirs.* Yours for the right, L. King."[19]

When the Civil War began, Cyrus Pringle was editor of *The American Wesleyan* (the name of the periodical from 1861 to 1883) and he had reservations about the historic peace position of the church and its periodical. He wrote the following in a May 1861 issue:

> We have never been what might be called an ultra peace man; yet we deprecate war as an evil fraught with untold calamities and sorrows. But as great a calamity as war is, as deep as it impresses its vices, and as wide as it spreads its devastations, it is not necessarily an unmitigated evil. There is often incidental good attendant on great public calamities as there are also incidental evils often attendant on great public blessings.

> As great a calamity as we conceive war to be, there may be a greater calamity than war. That greater calamity is the loss of liberty. Liberty is before life in importance and may not rightfully be sacrificed to save life.[20]

But it was not editorials nor biblical and theological debates which dramatically changed the position and practice of the Wesleyan Church on the issue of peace; rather it was that watershed of American history, the Civil War. As early as April 24, 1861, *The American Wesleyan* carried a quotation from another periodical, *The Independent:* "Fort Sumter scattered to the winds the theories of the Peace Society. From that moment war became a duty, a necessity," The same article went on to assert, "God may be answering the prayers of the past 20 years.

---

[18]Luther Lee, in *The True Wesleyan*, July 17, 1847.

[19]L. King, in *The True Wesleyan*, August 14, 1847, 129.

[20]Cyrus Pringle, editorial, *The American Wesleyan*, May 29, 1861, 86.

...Let our motto be: 'Justice and Liberty, God and Country!'"[21]

Editor Pringle was not alone in his sentiments. That same issue of *The American Wesleyan* carried a comprehensive report on the Allegheny Conference of the Wesleyan Methodist Church which was held near Meadville, Pennsylvania. The author of the report added this P.S.:

> The seat of the conference being remote from any of the great lines of early intelligence, we were all in ignorance of the attack upon Fort Sumter until sabbath p.m., the fourteenth instant, when the news reached us and produced a profound sensation. The insult to the national flag, the injustice and recklessness of the rebel party gave birth to high and holy resolve such as became the *good* and *true* and all along our journey homeward, but one sentiment was expressed by all we met and heard which was unmingled execration of traitorism and a hope that the most vigorous measures would be adopted by the government to crush the Rebellion. Amen; *so let it be.*[22]

The same paper carried an editorial entitled "The Great Crisis—War Is upon Us." The editorial begins as follows:

> Events have culminated; and as we have expected hostilities have commenced. The mad rebels of the south have put in deadly activity the engines of war— a war that is the most causeless and unprovoked that ever stained the history of human civilization against the best government, all things considered, that ever existed....
>
> But what a change has come over the hearts of twenty millions of free people in the last ten days. The storm of fire and the iron hail that the rebel forces poured upon Fort Sumter and her noble guard has had the grand result for which we give glory to God most High; it has burned up the mass of party prejudice and hatred that had embittered our political relations and united us as we were never united before, not even in the period of the Revolution....We believe that over all the wicked purposes devised by the rebels the overruling agency of God will be exerted to settle the future policy of our government upon the basis of right and justice, equity and freedom....Let our motto be "justice and liberty, God and our country."[23]

For the next sixteen months, *The American Wesleyan* devoted more space to the Civil War than to any other topic or issue. An overwhelming majority of the items endorsed the war and rejoiced whenever the North won victories. There were feature stories about Wesleyan ministers who had become chaplains and laymen who had become war heroes. If the readers of the church periodical opposed this sudden change of directions, it was not generally obvious in the letters to the editor. A few objections were received and printed, but the editors and subsequent letter writers clearly had little patience with their conclusions. One of the early letters of protest was written by H.R. Will, who asked in May of 1861, "Would any person reading *The American Wesleyan* have the least idea that it was the organ of a denomination having the following language in their book of *Discipline:* We believe the gospel of Christ to be every way opposed to the practice of war in all its forms, etc.?"

[21] *The American Wesleyan*, April 24, 1861, 66.
[22] Ibid., 68.
[23] Ibid.

The letter continued in the same spirit by a call to an examination of where the church stood on the issue:

> If *The Wesleyan* represents the principle of the body, we had better call a specific General Conference and have the *Discipline* so revised as to place us in a proper light before the world. We should have but little to say about other denominations passing resolutions simply to appear before the public eye while so much of our *Discipline* is but a dead letter.[24]

The editor responded with a strong defense of the Civil War as well as the policies of *The American Wesleyan,* in it using some facile reasoning or some obscure definitions. He asserted, "We are not now in the practice of war, nor are we employed in fostering the war spirit by any means. The whole North and West is aroused up as by a magic baptism from on high to put down *treason* and *rebellion,* the most causeless and unprovoked that ever existed in civilized society."[25]

In spite of the editor's clear preferences, additional objections were expressed. *The American Wesleyan* of July 17, 1861, carried a lengthy letter of objection to the war spirit that had characterized recent editions of the paper. The writer observed the following:

> One of our distinguishing features before the world was, opposition to war. We have reiterated a thousand and a thousand times until the world was well nigh ready to believe that we were not only anti-slavery but anti-war. But scarcely had the smoke of the first gun fired at Fort Sumter blown away until

our organ was crowded with war news. Dissertations and a writer defending ourselves by the force of arms, claiming that the only alternative was to fight—and anecdotes of ministers that declared themselves ready to leave the pulpit for the battlefield, etc., etc.[26]

Such comprehensive coverage eventually led the editor to produce a brief editorial in 1862 which stated:

> We are receiving strong remonstrations to further controversy upon the war question in the present state of public affairs; and we feel the propriety of deferring to this request. Nor is it necessary to say more upon this subject, since the main arguments have been employed that can be; and to say more would be a repetition. When the Rebellion is put down and peace is restored then if it would be thought necessary, brethren may use our columns to debate the question; but as we are now situated we must decline publishing anymore upon the subject for the present.[27]

At the next General Conference in 1864 enough delegates were uncomfortable with the article on peace which appeared in the *Discipline* that it was changed to read as follows: "We believe the Gospel of Christ to be intended to extirpate the practice of war and hence we cannot but deprecate those customs which needlessly foster and perpetuate the war spirit. We will not cease to pray and labor that the period may soon arrive, when 'Nation shall learn war no more.'"[28] (This modified section remained unchanged until the General Conference of 1935.)

---

[24] *The American Wesleyan,* May 22, 1861, 82.

[25] Ibid.

[26] *The American Wesleyan,* July 17, 1861, 114.

[27] "The War Controversy," *The American Wesleyan,* August 13, 1862, 126.

[28] *The Wesleyan Discipline,* Article XXI, 1867.

The new statement lacked the clarity and the power of the one it replaced. While some professed not to understand the meaning of "we believe the gospel of Christ to be every way opposed to the practice of war in all its forms," one could make the new statement mean almost anything. The statements "We believe the gospel of Christ to be *intended* [emphasis added] to extirpate the practice of war"; and "We will not cease to pray and labor that the period may soon arrive, when 'Nations shall learn war no more'" present high principles that no one was likely to oppose. At the same time their demands were so modest and ambiguous that they imposed no genuine behavioral expectations on church members.

The General Conference of 1864 also adopted the following resolution: "Resolved—That in the spirit of patriots and Christians, we affirm for ourselves and our churches, our unqualified loyalty to the government, and our readiness to endure and make all sacrifices necessary to the overthrow of the rebellion, and the destruction of slavery, its guilty cause."[29]

The promise to renew the discussion of the peace issue after the Civil War was never kept. Instead it became the practice and the policy of the Wesleyan Methodist Church to make participation in war a matter of individual conscience instead of denominational directive.

It is futile to speculate about what position the Wesleyan Methodist Church would now hold on peace had the Civil War not occurred. Only seventeen years elapsed between the founding of the denomination and the beginning of the Civil War. Such a short span apparently provided too little opportunity for the official peace position of the denomination to become a part of the warp and woof of its members, most of whom came from a denomination which did not share the Wesleyans' position on war and peace.

The Civil War presented the opportunity to abolish the hated institution of slavery. Since opposition to human bondage had been *the* major factor in the formation of the Wesleyan Methodist Church, it is probably not surprising that a war to eliminate this evil quickly gained wide support among the leaders and members of the denomination. A majority of Wesleyans seemed to support the idea that purity required purging the nation of the evil of slavery by any, or all means necessary, including war. As a result, "first pure" took precedence in principle and in practice over "peaceable."

---

[29]"Proceedings of the Sixth General Conference of the Wesleyan Methodist Connection of America," 1864 (microfilm copy of handwritten minutes, Wesleyan Church Archives), 195.

On the Worship of God

John E. Zercher

Born into a peace church, John Zercher nevertheless became a military officer in World War II. (He later explained that he had not heard much teaching on peace before the war.) However, in time he became one of strongest spokespersons for peace in the Brethren in Christ Church. He also became editor of his denomination's paper, the *Evangelical Visitor*, for which he wrote many insightful editorials, some of which were printed in *Lantern in the Dawn* following his death.

In this selection Zercher's editorial speaks to the growing practice of displaying the nation's flag in our churches. He explains why this practice is becoming increasingly popular, points out that the flag as a symbol carries a strong message, and presents various arguments against placing it in churches.

What arguments against displaying flags in churches might be added to Zercher's? How would one proceed to remove a flag that has had a place in the church building? How may one show respect to the country's flag without placing it in the church, assuming that you accept Zercher's thesis that in the right time and place the flag is to be honored by all, including peace people? How do you answer Zercher's question in the end: "Does the placing of the Stars and Stripes in the sanctuary contribute to the worship of God?"

Recently I had the occasion to talk with a young man....In our conversation he shared the observation—and his surprise—that in so many churches the United States flag is a part of the sanctuary furnishings. This confirmed an observation that I too had made.

The appearance of the national flag in our churches is a relatively recent phenomenon. It was not a part of the early meeting house furnishings. I believe that it has become a part of our worship symbols by two avenues.

In some instances the Brethren in Christ have taken over existing church buildings or provided pastoral leadership to a group whose roots were in another tradition. The national flag was a part of the sanctuary furnishings and continued to be after the change of ownership or leadership. The decision to retain the flag was not deliberate. The matter was not

---

This chapter originally appeared as John E. Zercher, "On the Worship of God," *Lantern in the Dawn: Selections from the Writings of John E. Zercher*, eds. E. Morris Sider and Paul Hostetler (Nappanee, Ind.: Evangel Press, 1980), 59–61.

tested theologically. The flag was there; it just remained.

The flag may have found its way into the sanctuary by means of a gift or by a decision to make the decor more contemporary. It is very possible that the biblical or theological basis for the addition of this symbol to our worship was not the prime consideration. The practice of peer groups rather than biblical urgency dictated the change.

It would be appropriate to ask what the biblical basis of authority is for including the national flag as one of the symbols of worship. If it is not a symbol of worship or an aid to worship, what is its purpose in the house of worship?

Symbols are powerful teaching instruments. Christ recognized this in instituting the Lord's Supper. The open Bible, the cross, the central pulpit, the communion table are symbols which quietly but effectively teach and aid in our worship.

Let me highlight biblical teachings which, I believe, bear upon the practice of including the national flag in our church furnishings.

Christ's teaching of the two kingdoms. At the beginning of his ministry Christ announced that "The Kingdom of God is at hand." At the close of his ministry he clearly stated that his kingdom was not of this world, else his disciples would have fought (John 18:36).

Are we not in danger of blurring Christ's teaching of the two kingdoms when we incorporate into our worship the symbol of the kingdom of this world? Even if we recognize the need for government and the biblical provision for it, one must admit that the values of the state are many times in radical opposition to the teachings of Christ. The church is a manifestation of this new kingdom with its own symbols—the cross, the Bible, the bread and the cup.

Separation of church and state. This principle is a concrete expression of the teaching concerning the two kingdoms. The state has its functions. The church has her mission. This principle of separation, which we take so much for granted, was purchased for us at great price. As Brethren in Christ, we are the direct descendants of those who paid by life and fortune for their understanding that the church and the state were separate.

I must ask if we are not betraying our heritage and those who suffered for this truth as we bring into our sanctuaries the high symbol of the state and seek to join what Christ has put asunder.

The transnational character of the church. Jesus was concerned about the activities in the house of God. He took some radical measures to correct the situation in the incident we refer to as "the cleansing of the Temple" (Mark 11:15–19). In the process he quoted Isaiah's statement, "My house will be called a house of prayer for all the nations" (Isa. 56:7).

Jesus affirmed a truth the Jews found difficult to accept: the house of God was for *all nations.* God is not a tribal deity nor a national god; nor is his church a national church. Do we not tamper with the biblical truth that the church of Jesus Christ is above nation and race when we include the national symbol among our worship symbols?

The teaching of peace and nonresistance. Symbols have a quiet but effective way of teaching. One could well ask the question of what the presence of a national flag will do to our church's commitment to peace and nonresistance.

Obviously a national flag has other meanings than warfare. But it is so closely identified with the military that it is difficult to separate the two. I seriously question if our peace witness can long be maintained if each time the congregation gathers, the nation's flag is part of the symbols in the sanctuary.

This relation of the flag to the military is symbolized frequently in most of our communities. It is in ours. The raising of the flag is a traditional part of our local high school's home football games. Just before the teams come onto the field the band moves into formation, the crowd faces the north end of the field, and a color guard from the local post of Veterans of Foreign Wars, armed with rifles, escorts the flag to the pole. The flag is raised to the playing of our national anthem with its distinct military overtones. I wonder if our youth seeing this relationship on Friday night can separate it on Sunday morning.

It is understandable that a government unit would find it appropriate to give prominence to the nation's symbol: our public schools are part of the state structure. The flag belongs over our post offices and government buildings. With this I have no problem.

The question which we as a church need to ask is this: Does the placing of the Stars and Stripes in the sanctuary contribute to the worship of God?

Chapter Eleven

A Statement on Militarism

1992 General Conference of the Brethren in Christ Church

The following statement, adopted by the General Conference of the Brethren in Christ Church in its 1992 meeting, lays out that denomination's strong official peace position, while at the same time recognizing that some members of the church differ from the normative statement. The statement argues that a spirit of militarism pervades our societies and has implications for our culture beyond strictly military considerations. The document provides a biblical examination of this spirit and suggests practical ways to combat it.

Do you agree that militarism is a pervasive influence in our countries? If so, what other evidences support that view? Can a case be made against that view? Are the measures for attacking the problem as found under "A Call to Peacemaking" practical? Are there other ways that could be added? Do you think that there is a connection between your personal lifestyle and militarism? How careful should we be to avoid employment with businesses, agencies, and other organizations that relate to the military program of our countries?

The purpose of this statement is to examine the nature of the use of military force in the world today and to determine our response as Christians committed to peacemaking. The statement not only looks at what military force and war do, but also considers how we can help to make peace in Christ's name.

For the sake of brevity, a number of related ideas are included in the term, "the use of military force": the belief that the use of military force is necessary and acceptable, the preparations to use military force, the threats to use military force, and the actual use of military force. In order to determine our response to the use of military force, we need to consider the following:

1. The reasons for the use of military force

2. The effects

3. Some biblical perspectives on the use of military force

4. What the Brethren in Christ Church has said

The Reasons for the Use of Military Force

Most nations (whether democracies, monarchies, or dictatorships) view the use of military force as a means by which they defend their national boundaries and interests, and protect their right to self-determination. Military force is also used to preserve freedom and human rights, to stop aggression, to overthrow oppressive governments, and to maintain or establish preferred forms of government.

As nations identify perceived threats to their security from within and without, other more negative factors also emerge. These include the use of military force to protect a nation's share of and access to the world's resources, to take desired land or other resources from less powerful people or nations, to institute a particular ideology or religion, or to repress dissent.

The Effects of the Use of Military Force in our Contemporary Setting

Many Christians believe that the use of military force is a legitimate means of national defense. Many also believe that God uses military force to punish evil and establish justice, and note that military force has often succeeded in achieving its desired ends. Other Christians, however, while recognizing the reality of war in the Old Testament and the likelihood that governments will always use military force, believe that they ought not participate in the use of military force. To support their conviction, they point not only to varying interpretations of Scripture but also to some of the wider implications or effects of the use of military force.

1. *Reliance on the use of military force can result in militarism:* When a nation regards military superiority as a major national priority, the result can be militarism—"the predominance of the military in the administration or policy of the state." When the military is predominant, reality is often defined in terms of military strength, and military force is seen to determine the course of history. National strength tends to be equated with military superiority, and loyalty to the nation is demanded above other values and commitments. Military spending consumes a significant portion of the national budget. Military force too readily becomes the method of choice by politicians for resolving internal and international disputes.

2. *Military images are common in everyday life:* In the United States, military images abound: for example, in the recruitment offices and Reserve Officer Training Corps programs in U.S. public schools and colleges, on television and in movies, in the abundance of military-style toys and video games, in our employment and investments, and in our national spending priorities. These images are not usually balanced by parallel images and models of nonmilitary and nonviolent solutions to conflict.

3. *The use of military force diverts valuable resources away from human need:* World military expenditures from 1950 to 1990 totaled $US21 trillion; in 1990, expenditures were $US880 billion—a slight decrease from the previous high of one trillion dollars annually (a result of the changing political climate in Eastern Europe). World military spending has equaled the income of 2.6 billion people in the 44 poorest nations. Military spending by poor countries has quadrupled since 1960 and accounts for 20% of the world's total military budget.[1]

In 1953, U.S. President Dwight Eisenhower, who served as Supreme Allied Commander in Europe during World

---

[1] Facts about worldwide military spending are compiled annually by World Priorities, Inc. The statistics used here are taken from Ruth Leger Sivard, *World Military and Social Expenditures*, 13th and 14th eds. (Washington, D.C.: World Priorities, 1989, 1991). Several international organizations are co-sponsors of the publication, including Project Ploughshares in Canada.

War II, said, "Every gun that is made, every warship launched, every rocket fired signifies, in the final sense, a theft from those who hunger and are not fed, those who are cold and are not clothed." His words are still true today.

Resources used for the military are not available worldwide to 14 million children annually who die before their fifth birthday, 3.5 million children annually who die of dehydration, 10 million women annually who bear malnourished babies, 1.5 billion people who do not have access to basic health services, one billion people who live in poverty, or 1.5 billion people who do not have safe drinking water.[2] We don't know whether money not spent on the military would in fact be spent on these and other human needs, but we do know that money spent on the military cannot also be spent on human needs.

Since World War II, the use of military force has created an entire industry. In the United States, many of the best scientists and engineers and the majority of research and development funding are devoted to the military. While other countries lead in technology and education, the U.S. ranks high among industrialized countries in infant mortality and child poverty rates. Scaling down the military-industrial complex and converting to a non-military economy is difficult because the livelihood of many people depends on the military. Doing so, however, could contribute to the development of other things which are also important for national security, such as programs to eliminate hunger, empower the poor, and educate our children and train them for life-affirming vocations.

4. *War is destructive:* When wars happen, no matter what positive ends may be achieved, they also kill and maim people, damage the environment, destroy or damage infrastructures, contribute to the spread of hunger and disease, create large numbers of refugees, and often cause general instability. In the twentieth century alone, there have been 227 wars and 107,800,000 deaths in war, most of them unarmed civilians. Over the past decade, more than 75% of war deaths have been of civilians, reversing the pattern of past centuries.[3]

5. *The use of military force affects us morally and spiritually:*

a. The use of military force helps to desensitize us to violence and human suffering. Not only is killing done impersonally (bombs are dropped from the sky at the push of a button), but dead and wounded people—civilian and military—are seen as regrettable but inevitable results of war.

b. It may short circuit the process of negotiation and reconciliation.

c. It encourages excessive nationalism and discourages sincere and informed dissent from the majority's approval of national military policies.

d. For Christians, the use of military force encourages trust in human and military strength rather than God's providence.

e. It teaches hate rather than love for enemies, making national enemies appear inhuman and deserving of destruction.

---

[2]Sivard, *World Military and Social Expenditures*, 1991, 9.

[3]Sivard, *World Military and Social Expenditures*, 1991, 21.

f. It compromises the unity of the global Christian community, causing Christians to kill other Christians across national boundaries, and hinders evangelism.

There are undoubtedly many interpretations of the profound changes that have occurred in the past several years. Many people are rejoicing at the end of the Cold War, the fall of communist and totalitarian systems, and the increase in freedom and democracy in many parts of the world. The verdict is not yet in on what these changes will ultimately mean, although there is reason to hope that resources previously devoted to the military will be used to improve social conditions in various places, including the United States. Whatever the outcome, we know that wars will continue and that the world still needs the gospel message of peace with God and between people. In the midst of violence, war, and the use of military force, Christians are called to offer peaceful and nonviolent alternatives.

Biblical Perspectives on the Use of Military Force

Because the Bible has always been our starting point for moral and spiritual discussions, we need to respond to the use of military force in light of biblical truth. Brethren in Christ theology has held that the general movement of Scripture is against the use of military methods of resolving conflict. The wars of the Old Testament are best seen as examples of God's deliverance of his people. In the New Testament, Jesus modeled and the disciples taught how Christians are to respond to enemies, including those who threaten our security.

The Old Testament

God is the one who determines the outcome of war: "The LORD your God is the one who goes with you to fight for you against your enemies to give you victory" (Deut. 20:4; see also 1 Sam. 17:47; 2 Chron. 20:15–17; Ps. 4:8; 20:7–8; 44:7–8; 81:13–14; Zech. 4:6). The stories of Joshua and Gideon illustrate that neither the size of armed forces nor the sophistication of weaponry is decisive in the outcome of war (see also Ps. 33:16–17).

When the Israelites wanted a king so that they could be like other nations, God allowed it but warned that having a king would result in the increasing militarization of their society (1 Sam. 8:11–22). David was not permitted to build the temple because he had shed too much blood (1 Chron. 22:6–10). God condemned Israel in part because of her trust in military strength rather than God (Ps. 146:3–4; Isa. 31:1; Jer. 17:5–7) and pronounced judgment because the poor were neglected (Isa. 10:1–2; Amos 2:6–7; 4:1; 5:11–12). Prophets such as Isaiah called the people of Israel to a "suffering servanthood" which modeled meekness, absorption of violence, and sacrificial suffering (Isa. 42:14; 53:1–12). God also set limits on retaliation, declared that revenge should be left to God (Deut. 32:35), pointed to a new way to respond to enemies (Prov. 25:21–22), and commanded love for neighbor (Lev. 19:18).

Other readings of the Old Testament—held by some Brethren in Christ as well as many other Christians—seem to suggest that war is commanded by God, people are ordered to kill, God uses people to wage war, and victory in war is celebrated; however, even this needs to be understood in light of God's revelation, culminated in the life and teachings of Jesus Christ.

The New Testament

Through His life, death and resurrection, Jesus Christ taught and modeled the way God was working in the world to bring salvation and make disciples of all nations. In His major sermon on the shape of salvation in the new kingdom (Matt. 5–7), Jesus Christ told His disciples that we are to love our enemies (5:38–48). On the cross, Christ paid the penalty for our sins, reconciling us to God while we were still his enemies (Rom. 5:8–11). Christ fulfilled Isaiah's vision of the suffering servant, continuing His mission to an unsaved world, and demonstrated how we are to respond to enemies (Luke 23:34; 2 Cor. 5:18–20). His resurrection was God's victory over the forces of sin and death (Matt. 28:18–20).

Jesus Christ refused the devil's offer of the kingdoms of this world (Matt. 4:8–10) and said that his disciples don't fight because they belong to another kingdom (John 18:36). He did not identify with the Zealots, who were Jewish revolutionaries committed to overthrowing their political oppressors by brutal force. Jesus and the apostles did not condemn soldiers or condone their occupation; rather, they met them at their point of immediate need (Matt. 8:5–13; Acts 10). There are no examples of Jesus or his followers using lethal violence on anyone who threatened or opposed them. When Peter used a sword in the garden, Jesus rebuked him and healed the man's ear.

The early church intentionally modeled itself after the life and teachings of Christ. The apostles taught that Christians are to follow the example of Jesus Christ, to overcome evil with good, to love all people, to be people of peace, and, within the limits of primary allegiance to God and love for others, to respect the state as God's means of keeping order in society (Rom. 12:14–13:10; 2 Cor. 10:3–4; Eph. 2:11–18; Phil. 2:5–11; 1 Thess. 5:13–15; 1 Pet. 2:13–25;1 Pet. 3:8–12). Both Jesus and the apostles also vigorously confronted evil, rather than passively acquiescing (Matt. 23; Mark 11:15–17; Acts 8:18–24). They consistently demonstrated care for the poor and needy (e.g., the parable of the Good Samaritan and the story of the rich young ruler, Matt. 25:31–46; Luke 4:18–19; Acts 4:34; 2 Cor. 8 and 9).

In the Revelation, the imagery of a transnational body of Christ is indicated (Rev. 5:9; 7:9). Martyrdom, patient endurance, and faithfulness on the part of the saints is the call of the Sovereign Lord (Rev. 6:9–11; 13:10). It is the "Lamb who was slain," not armies or nations, who overcomes evil.

The Brethren in Christ and the Use of Military Force

The Brethren in Christ have officially rejected participation in the use of military force as contrary to the teachings and example of Jesus. This conforms to the tradition of the early church and our own Anabaptist heritage. The original confession of faith of the early Brethren in Christ said that "it is completely forbidden to bear the sword for revenge or defense." The 1961 edition of the *Manual of Doctrine and Government,* the 1984 bylaws, and the proposed new doctrinal statement all reaffirm that basic position, the last-mentioned stating that "preparation for or participation in war is inconsistent with the teachings of Christ." General Conference, as recently as 1976, 1980, and 1982, adopted statements or resolutions which reaffirmed the church's opposition to the use of military force.

At the same time, however, there is not unanimous agreement in the church on matters of war and peace, and, as in other historic peace churches, there are some who sincerely hold to scriptural interpretations which permit participation in war. In recent years especially, there has been room in the church for people of varying persuasions. That has been comfortable for some, disquieting to others, but certainly a reality in the church. Another area of discomfort has been between those holding to separatist nonresistance and those who have become politically active in their opposition to war and the use of military force.

While we respect differing opinions in the Brethren in Christ Church, this statement affirms that the Bible calls us to a kind of peacemaking that does not include the use of military force, war, and violence. In a world where violence abounds and the use of military force causes much human suffering and death, we challenge those who disagree with the church's historic position to study the Scriptures from the context of peace. We invite all to prayerfully and conscientiously consider, in light of Scripture, what Jesus Christ would have us do to be his agents of peace and reconciliation.

A Call to Peacemaking

Individual and Family Responses to the Use of Military Force:

1. *Study:* In the spirit of the old gospel song, "Ain't Gonna Study War No More," we will read and study books on biblical understandings of peace. When so much of the information we receive affirms the use of military force, we need to be able to present a cogent explanation of biblical teachings on peace.

2. *Teach our children:* We commit ourselves to the practice of reconciliation in all our relationships, beginning with our families. We will teach and model to our children that there are alternatives to violence, military force, and war. These include a peacemaking spirit, appropriate confrontation of evil and wrongdoing, cooperation, compassion, forgiveness, generosity and servanthood.

3. *Set lifestyle priorities:* We will seek to observe lifestyle priorities which demonstrate our belief that the quality of life is not measured by the abundance of our possessions. A commitment to simplicity in lifestyle recognizes that military force is often thought necessary to protect what we have and contributes to the further destruction of our fragile environment.

4. *Examine our jobs and finances:* We will be alert to the possible connections between military force and our employment (e.g., manufacture of weapons parts, or other indirect support of the arms industry) and of the investment policies of companies in which we invest our money. Recognizing that a purist position is rarely possible, we will prayerfully consider what we ought to do to avoid direct or indirect support of military force.

5. *Be informed and involved:* We will be informed about issues related to the use of military force by studying current events in the light of the Scriptures. As citizens of democracies, we will respectfully make our views known to our elected officials. We will encourage them to pursue peaceful policies, and we will pray for them.

6. *Support the Peace Tax Fund:* We continue to endorse political efforts to establish a Peace Tax Fund in the United States and Canada which will provide a legal means for directing to peaceful purposes tax monies otherwise intended for military purposes.[4]

---

[4]In 1982, the General Conference of the Brethren in Christ Church endorsed the United States Peace Tax Fund bill, and from that time has continued to be listed as one of the sponsoring organizations of the National Campaign for a Peace Tax Fund. There are similar legislative efforts in other countries, including Canada.

7. *Register conscientious objection to war:* In the spirit of our forebears who rejected all participation in war and the use of military force, we encourage contemporary expressions of conscientious objection to war. These include registering as a conscientious objector with the U.S. Selective Service and supporting a peace perspective in our national legislatures.

8. *Pray and seek renewal:* Finally, we commit ourselves to ongoing prayer for peace between people and nations. We will also seek regular spiritual renewal as a means of confirming our dependence on God for our security.

Corporate Responses to the Use of Military Force

1. *Understand our purpose:* We are first and foremost citizens of God's kingdom who happen to live in particular nations. Our most important purpose as Christians is to make disciples of Jesus Christ. To do that, we are called to engage in spiritual warfare for redemption against the evil powers and to avoid entanglement in the darkness of the world. We commit ourselves to testing all our living by this purpose.

2. *Make peace with each other:* We pledge to work at peaceful and loving relationships with each other in the church, recognizing that it is inconsistent to fight among ourselves in the church or to misuse, abuse, and exploit others who are close to us while we condemn violence elsewhere.

3. *Teach peace and service:* We call the Brethren in Christ Church to a renewed commitment to peace education, i.e., teaching our historic biblical understandings about war and peace and the way of Jesus Christ. We

affirm that evangelism is an important form of peacemaking because it calls all people to be reconciled to God and to become brothers and sisters in Christ. We also affirm the sanctity of life for all human beings.

We call for pastors and others to preach peace in times of peace and to challenge us to a loyalty to Christ and His kingdom which is not compromised by competing loyalties and which engages us in acts of loving and vulnerable service toward even our enemies. We encourage church members to consider voluntary service in other parts of the world or in subcultures within our own nations as a way of learning how others live and of witnessing to the way of peace.

4. *Talk with those who disagree:* We call for open dialogue in our congregations on the more difficult issues related to the use of military force, including the differences between and implications of various types of nonresistance and nonviolence. We challenge individuals who disagree on matters of war and peace to talk to each other and to examine differing convictions in light of biblical teaching.

5. *Talk with Christians in other places:* We call for dialogue with our sister churches in the National Association of Evangelicals, the Christian Holiness Association, the Evangelical Fellowship of Canada, and the Canadian Holiness Federation on the relationship between evangelism/missions and a commitment to nonviolence in resisting evil. We also challenge individuals and congregations to learn from the worldwide experience of volunteers with Brethren in Christ Missions and the Mennonite Central Committee who

have worked in many places ravaged by war and violence.

6. *Join the global community:* We join with our Christian sisters and brothers around the world in a commitment to the church as a global community of God's holy people which is not divided by national, ideological, racial, or cultural boundaries. We covenant not to kill our Christian sisters and brothers in nations toward which our nations are hostile.

7. *Support alternatives to military force:* We recognize that military force is often used because of genuine desires for peace and self-determination; therefore, we will support initiatives which study, propose, and test nonviolent and nonmilitary means of achieving the same ends.

8. *Pray and witness:* In our corporate and private worship, we will pray regularly for peace. We will witness to the world that salvation in Jesus can free us from fear of enemies and that the power of the resurrection enables us to absorb the violence of an evil world and to work at peacemaking by the way of the cross.

Approved by the Board for Brotherhood Concerns February 28, 1992

Chapter Twelve

The
Military Chaplaincy

Martin H. Schrag

Views on the military chaplaincy vary widely. Some people hold that a peace denomination that approves its clergy for the chaplaincy opens the door to accepting other aspects of military life, and eventually to abandoning altogether its position on peace. A differing view maintains that God is with the men and women at the front, and thus that is where God's ministers should be also.

Martin H. Schrag holds the former view. For many years Professor of History of Christianity at Messiah College, he taught, wrote, and spoke widely and frequently on the historic peace position of Anabaptist-related groups. In the following article he examines how chaplains are chosen by the Canadian and United States governments and discusses the relationship between chaplains and the armed forces.

Do you agree with the author that state and church should be clearly separated and that to be a military chaplain is seriously to cross the line of demarcation? What case could be made on biblical grounds for a minister from a peace church becoming an army chaplain? Do you accept the author's assumption that the armed forces probably could not accept a chaplain from a peace church?

Requirements and Procedures in Becoming a Military Chaplain

*C*anada: To become a military chaplain in the Canadian armed forces it is necessary to have "an Arts degree or equivalent; have a degree or title in Theology from a college or seminary recognized by the denomination" of the applicant.[1] Also essential is an endorsement from the applicant's denomination, ordination by the same body, and two years of pastoral experience. The endorsement means that in the understanding of the sponsoring denomination, the applicant has the qualities to be a military chaplain, including having a theology compatible with the position. Formal ap-

---

[1] *Prospectus on the Canadian Forces Chaplain Branch (P)* (September 1988), 4.

This chapter originally appeared as Martin H. Schrag, "The Military Chaplaincy: An Evaluation from the Brethren in Christ Understanding of the Christian Faith," *Brethren in Christ History and Life* 13, no. 3 (1990):375–96.

plication to be a chaplain is made by a denomination that is a member of the Canadian Council of Churches' Committee on Chaplain Service in the Armed Forces.

Chaplains are recruited into the Canadian armed forces on the basis of statistical representation in the forces, that is to say, if fifteen percent of the soldiers are Baptists, fifteen percent of the chaplains are to be Baptists. With the Brethren in Christ having few, if any, of its members in the forces, there is no statistical basis for a Brethren in Christ clergy person becoming a military chaplain. On the basis of statistical representation, the Committee on Chaplain Service in the Armed Forces recognizes five Protestant denominations—Anglican, Baptist, Lutheran, Presbyterian, and the United Church—as bodies who can make formal applications as sponsoring denominations for clergy persons to become military chaplains. As of 1988 there were 101 Protestant chaplains, the spread of denominations being thirty-nine Anglican, nine Baptist, five Lutheran, seven Presbyterian, and forty-one United Church chaplains."[2] Of interest is that the Evangelical Fellowship of Canada is not related to the Committee on Chaplain Service in the Forces and is not seeking such a relationship. (No Information was gathered regarding the Roman Catholic chaplaincy program.)

After having been approved by the Committee on Chaplain Services in the Forces, the applicant must be approved by the Chaplain General (chief of chaplains) and accepted by the military. The decision on the latter is made by the directorate of Recruiting and Selection.

United States: Someone wanting to be a military chaplain in the United States armed forces must have a degree from an accredited college or university (a school listed in the *Educational Directory, College and Universities*) and a three-year seminary degree from an accredited seminary (a seminary listed in the *Directory, American Association of Theological Schools*).[3] Further, the prospective chaplain must be endorsed by his or her denomination as a person who has been ordained, and has the understanding and adaptability needed to be a good chaplain. In addition, the endorsing denomination must be approved by the Armed Forces Chaplaincy Board (AFCB) as an "Endorsing Agency." (The AFCB is the coordinating office of military chaplaincy in the United States armed forces, for each of the three services—the army, navy, and the air force, which has its own chaplaincy program.) At the time a denomination seeks approval by the AFCB, it needs to have a minister ready to become a military chaplain.

The major denominations, such as the Catholics and the United Methodists, have been approved by the AFCB as endorsing agencies. Some denominations, especially smaller ones, rather than each seeking approval directly by the AFCB, work together under one endorsing agency, such as the National Association of Evangelicals (NAE). (As of 1988 there were forty-seven endorsing agencies representing 120 denominations. Presently there are about 3,500 military chaplains in the United States Armed forces.)[4] Within the NAE, the Military Commission serves as the contact point with the AFCB.

When an endorsing agency, working in behalf of several churches, receives denominational approval for a person wanting to be a chaplain, that agency in-

---

[2]Ibid., 3.

[3]*Chaplain Corps, NAVY* (September 1, 1988), publicity piece.

[4]*Dictionary of Christianity in America* (1990), s.v. "Chaplain, Military," by C. B. Currey.

forms the branch of the service that the prospective chaplain has chosen. Concurrently, the chaplain-to-be applies directly to the service of his or her choice. Next, the chosen service interviews and evaluates the applicant, deciding for or against the person on the basis of evaluative criteria. When a person is rejected (or accepted), the reasons for the rejection or acceptance are not made public. When pressed as to whether the AFCB would approve a peace church as an endorsing agency, a high ranking officer (related to the AFCB) stated that he could think of no reason for such a church wanting (with integrity) to be an endorsing agency or to place chaplains in the military.

Several factors are taken into account in placing persons into the United States military chaplaincy. One factor is that each of the three services want to have approximately the same percentage of chaplains in its chaplaincy corps as there are soldiers from that denomination, or what is called "faith group" (the three major faith groups are Roman Catholics, Jews, and Protestants). (The system is akin to the Canadian statistical representation approach but more flexible. Informally the pattern is called a "rough quota system," and officially, "goals.") The three military services seek for a spread within the Protestant chaplaincy in order to have chaplains from the major orientations within American Protestantism (e.g., liturgical, mainline, liberal, conservative).

Another concern of the services is to have enough chaplains from groups to whom the military chaplaincy is not attractive, such as women and some racial minorities. Not enough individuals volunteer or are recruited from some faith groups, such as the Roman Catholics, and more individuals than can be accepted come from other orientations, as is true of conservatives or evangelicals. Thus, a Roman Catholic clergyman will more

likely be accepted than a Southern Baptist minister. This is another way of saying that the three services seek for that range of chaplains needed to meet the religious needs of the soldiers.

Above it was stated, in regard to the American armed forces, that consideration is given to the "understandings and adaptability" of those wanting to become chaplains. One of the understandings assumed when a denomination endorses a prospective chaplain is that such a person has an orientation, including a theology, that is basically consonant or can live with the aims and life within the military. A second understanding is that the applicant has a flexibility that enables him or her to respect and work cooperatively with chaplains from a variety of religious persuasions. This means working together with Roman Catholics, Jews, and Protestants, the last with a rather wide range of beliefs. Plans are underway to provide Buddhist chaplains, and, if needed, Muslim chaplains. This is not to imply any inherent compromising of beliefs, but it does mean working with a wide spread of fellow chaplains. Some evangelical chaplains have at times found themselves in settings not conducive to the evangelical understanding of conversion and personal piety.

The wide spectrum of chaplains explains why the military chaplaincy has no doctrinal or theological statement. The free exercise of religion implies the equality of all genuine religions.

A third understanding that a person brings to the military chaplaincy is that he or she may work in many different settings and situations—from settled base installations to the battlefield. The free exercise of religion, given the pluralistic context, calls for chaplains willing not only to cooperate with chaplains and military commanders having diverse understandings about religious ideas and practices, but also to work in many and varied contexts.

The Task of the Chaplain and Its Implications

The responsibilities of military chaplains have implications in two areas. The first concerns the establishment of religion by the government. In the United States, the constitutional basis for the chaplaincy is the first amendment guaranteeing the free exercise of religion. The first sentence in that amendment reads, "Congress shall make no law respecting an establishment of religion or prohibiting the free exercise thereof." The issue is whether the military chaplaincy program is a governmental establishment of religion. Because the chaplaincy is funded by federal taxes (to provide for chaplaincy pay, the building and maintaining of chapels, supplies and equipment) and is administered by a governmental department—the Department of Defense—many believe that the military chaplaincy is a church established by the government, and thus contrary to the principle of the separation of church and state. Those who disagree with this view say that chaplains are on loan from the churches to the government. It is true that military chaplains continue to be ministers in their denomination and that their denomination can withdraw endorsement. When the latter is done the individual is no longer a military chaplain.

At the same time, ministers who become chaplains become an integral part of the military organization. Whatever one's theoretical interpretation, on the practical level the chaplains and the military work together to actualize the military chaplaincy program. In this effort, church and state are not separate; the program comes together in one person—the military chaplain. The evidence supports those who regard military chaplaincy as a church established by the government.

The Canadian position on the military chaplaincy is outlined in *Prospectus on the Canadian Forces Chaplain Branch.* The statement does not mention the free exercise of religion in the Forces, but such freedom is a part of the Canadian heritage.

The second implication arises out of the major responsibility military chaplains have to assist the military in developing worship services, organizing religious educational programs, and providing pastoral care for the troops and their families when such families live on or near military bases. One aspect of such responsibility is counseling and advising soldiers regarding spirituality and morality. Counsel and advice can be meaningful for soldiers who have been uprooted from their homes and communities, and who in war are confronted with ultimate questions of life and death.

The concern regarding spirituality is understandable, but the problem is that the religious program led by the chaplain is inherently pro-military (the chaplain may believe he is neutral but the context is militarized) and thus suggests that Christian life and military service are compatible. Believers in a Christ who loved his enemies (Rom. 5:10; 2 Cor. 5:17–21) and calls his disciples to do the same thing, find discipleship and Christlike holy living incompatible with military participation. The Brethren in Christ have strongly emphasized that conversion will issue in discipleship and obedience, in those "good words" (Eph. 2:10) taught and modeled by Jesus Christ and the Apostles. Converted hearts are not to commit evil deeds; spirituality is not to be divorced from ethics. Jesus Christ is accepted both as Savior and Lord.

History of the United States Chaplaincy

Until the last decades of the nineteenth century, considerable variation existed as to model, purpose, and practice in the chaplaincy of the military units of the state and federal governments. There were appointed and volunteered, paid and unpaid, ranked and unranked, full-time and part-time chaplains. The question was debated whether the military chaplaincy was an establishment of religion, therefore unconstitutional, or a free exercise of religion, thus constitutional. A second question dealt with dress: should chaplains wear clerical garb (or nodistinctive dress) or the military uniform? Probably the most important question was whether the chaplain should be primarily a minister, a civilian volunteer financially supported by the church, or a man in the military—a commissioned officer financed by the government.

As the federal government became stronger and the nation became a world power, the military chaplaincy increasingly came under the control of the federal government. The result has been that the chaplaincy is seen as constitutionally legitimate; chaplains wear the military uniform (not required when leading a worship service), and are commissioned officers financed by the government. As the militarized chaplaincy developed, most churches on the whole did not seriously object to what was being fashioned, but rather cooperated with it. This suggests that churches have been less than alert to their spiritual and moral responsibilities.[5]

Also important for historical background is that both Canada and the United States subscribe to the Geneva Conventions. These conventions, first formulated in 1864 and revised several times since, have as their purpose the humane treatment of civilians, soldiers, and prisoners of war in wartime. The conventions also state that chaplains are to be unarmed noncombatants. In the United States Army, chaplain assistants (persons from the ranks) are to "provide armed security" for the chaplains.[6] Chaplains are of more than one mind as to the use of a gun should they be personally attacked by the enemy.

The Chaplaincy as an Integral Part of the Armed Forces

The military chaplaincy programs of Canada and the United States are "an integral part" of the armed forces of the two nations. Chaplains are inducted into the armed forces by taking the same oath as all other soldiers. As stated above, each of the chaplains remains a clergy person in his or her denomination, but in other regards, the chaplain is a part of the military. He is both a clergy person and a commissioned officer.

Except for the wearing of ecclesiastical vestments when leading worship services, as practiced in the liturgical churches, the only distinctively Christian piece of dress worn by the American chaplain is a small cross (if a Christian), often pinned on the coat lapel of the military uniform. Such dress identifies the chaplain more with the military than with the church. In the Canadian setting, the Christian distinctives for a chaplain (apart from leading worship services) are a hat band, a lapel cross, and, if the chaplain desires, the clerical collar.

In the United States, the chaplain as a commissioned officer has direct access to the military commander of his or her military unit and always serves as a member of the commander's staff. The chaplain is the advisor to the commander on moral and spiritual matters related to the command, and is "expected to 'speak with prophetic

---

[5]George H. Williams, "The Chaplaincy in the Armed Forces of the United States of America in Historical and Ecclesiastical Perspective," in *Military Chaplains*, ed. Harvey G. Cox Jr. (New York: American Report Press, 1973).

[6]*Chaplain Activities in the United States Army* (Washington, D.C.: Department of the Army, 1989), 9.

voice'" to the commander in behalf of the "religious rights of the soldiers."[7] Further, according to regulations, the commander can not tell the chaplain what to preach or teach in the chaplain's religious program (what if the chaplain in his ministry approved of homosexuality or preached pacifism?), or order chaplains into battle.

On the other hand, promotion is in part determined by the evaluations of the commanders, thus many chaplains want to be seen as good team players, not "troublemakers." The pay is good and retirement benefits are received after twenty years of service.[8]

Being an integral part of the armed forces, the chaplain operates in a program given to military objectives and is part of the needed military organization. Thus the military, not the church, determines the level of pay, the benefits received, the procedures in promotion, and the sociological context in which the chaplain operates. In short, chaplains live by the laws and regulations of the military.

Moreover, the religious program of a military unit or military base is the commander's program. The chaplain gives shape to and carries out that program and is accountable to the commander, as the following passages indicate:

> The Unit Ministry Team (UMT) [such a unit consists of at least one army chaplain and one enlisted chaplain assistant] is tasked by the commander to respond to the religious and spiritual needs of soldiers and their families.

> The chaplain is responsible to the commander for the religious educational program. [The reference is to Christian educational activities.]

> The UMT assists the commander by providing spiritual, moral, and religious support to the soldiers of the unit.

> Commanders will…provide, in coordination with the responsible chaplain, adequate time, facilities, and opportunity for the free exercise of religion (to the extent that such exercise is compatible with essential mission considerations and is otherwise in accordance with law and regulations).[9]

Commands are to provide programs of ministry in support of the free exercise of religion. The command religious program is an essential element of a command's total administration.[10]

The need for an administrative structure and accountability is understandable, but the role of the military commander is cause for concern. The relationship between the commander and the chaplain naturally varies according to personalities and context. The commander and the chaplain work together in actualizing the religious program. A safety factor is that the chaplain has recourse to the chief of chaplains should he have problems with the commander. At the same time, the chief of chaplains is subject to military superiors.

In addition to the chain of military command whereby the military is administered, chaplains have their own channel of authority. In the Canadian armed forces there are two chains of command, the second being that of the chaplains.

---

[7]Ibid., 5.

[8]It is significant to mention that the chaplain's commissioned status brings into play the psychological barrier that often separates commissioned officers from non-commissioned soldiers. That barrier is one reason some people think that chaplains should not be ranked officers.

[9]*Chaplain Activities*, 4–8.

[10]SECNAU Instruction 1730.7 (Washington, D.C.: Department of the Navy, 1983).

In the American system, in addition to the military chain of command, there is a "technical line of authority" consisting of chaplains attached to each of the echelons of the military command up to the chief of chaplains. Thus there is a chaplaincy line of authority but it does not stand independently of the military command structure; rather, it is tied to that military command at each of the echelons. Not being in the chain of military command the chaplain will not take command of a battle should all the officers of higher rank than the chaplain be killed in military action.

A description of the work of the military chaplaincy in the United States Navy implies a relationship between the work of the chaplain and the morale of the sailors. The Navy publication *Responsibilities for Religious Ministries* states that commanders are to "use all proper means to foster high morale, and to develop and strengthen the moral and spiritual well-being of the personnel under his/her command, and ensure that chaplains are provided the necessary logistic support for the carrying out of the command's religious program."[11] The United States Army publication *Chaplain Activities in the United States Army* states that the chaplain's program of "spiritual, moral, and religious support" carried out in assisting the commander is designed to help the soldier "achieve inner stability, calm and peace. Inner strength reinforces bonding among soldiers and enhances both individual and group spiritual awareness."[12]

Some people who oppose the military chaplaincy claim that the chaplain is a morale office. There may be some who directly seek that end but such is not the case with alert chaplains aware of the theological implications of their work. At the same time, chaplains work in contexts that are inherently pro-military. People inside and outside the armed forces know the task of the military is to fight battles. Further, any chaplain who overtly begins to denounce war as contrary to the Christian faith and to encourage troops to leave the forces would not be tolerated. In addition, any chaplain who helps soldiers "achieve inner stability" and aids the process of group bonding in a military context would enable the soldiers to fight more effectively, quite apart from any intention of the chaplain. A prayer helping soldiers to face death would contribute to morale. The point is that in an indirect way, given the military context of the military chaplaincy, chaplains can not escape being morale boosters. A professor of military history has written, "Chaplains [are]...responsible for religion, morale and morals."[13]

God, Chaplains, and War

The *Prospectus* mentioned above states that the "chaplain is seen by the Canadian Forces personnel as a symbol of God."[14] The chaplain is indeed a symbol of God. The highly deplorable element in this is that chaplains by their presence, especially in their being commissioned officers paid by the government and in military dress, identify God with the aims and purposes of their side of the conflict. In other words, military chaplains imply a divine legitimacy to war and that God is on the side to which the chaplain belongs.

People who believe war is sin and that God calls Christians to have no part in it

---

[11]Ibid., 1.

[12]*Chaplain Activities,* 4.

[13]*Dictionary of Christianity in America,* s.v. "Chaplain, Military."

[14]*Chaplain Activities,* p. 10.

find it particularly difficult to understand any chaplaincy that suggests war has God's blessing. Any verbalization on the part of the chaplains that they do not symbolize God's approval of war is contrary to the role they play. There are some 160 nations and only one God. None of these nations has a unique relationship to God. Care must be taken that in relating God to a given government, God is not reduced to a tribal or national deity. A very grave danger is that of a nation or a group of nations attempting to use or to manipulate God for selfish national purposes. Christ did not identify his work with the Roman government or with the Jewish religious establishment (neither did he politically undermine them); rather, he laid the foundation for a new option, the Kingdom of God to be visible in and central to the church. In the book of Acts we see the church becoming intercultural, interracial, and international. In the church, when it is true to God, we see the corporate aspect of God's plan of salvation.

It is true that God uses and allows wars as a means of punishing and judging nations and peoples. He does sometimes incorporate human evil into his ongoing plan for human existence. We mortals, however, do not know who is to be punished. The people of the Northern Kingdom of Israel could not believe that God would use the evil Assyrians to punish them, and the people of the Southern Kingdom were equally perplexed about the Babylonians. To act as if one's government is infallible in its declarations of war is not being responsible as Christians.

Moreover, God has indicated that vengeance is his task, not the Christians' work (Rom. 12:19). Billy Graham has written that God executes vengeance but His eternal positive purpose is redemption. Toward that end He sent His Son (or came as the Son) and through the life,

death, and resurrection of Christ and the outpouring of the Holy Spirit, he made provision for personal salvation, Christlike holy living, the harmonious community, the carrying out of the Great Commission, the ministering to the poor and needy, and the prophetic working against the evils of society. Recourse to military might in the furthering of the faith (or in its defense) is unknown in the New Testament.

It is also true that government is instituted by God and that Christians are to pray for the rulers, pay taxes, submit to governmental laws (when not contrary to God's will), and be thankful for the benefits received from governmental services. Moreover, some of the ideals and purposes of government and Christianity are similar in nature: freedom of religion, concern for justice and equality, the need for morality, freedom for human maturation, caring for the poor and needy, etc. In addition, we also need to be aware that we live in countries that provide many opportunities to work voluntarily for a better society, and to work with or in government for the same end. At the same time there are evils in society that we are to oppose. In all such activities the means are to be in keeping with the biblical ethic. But Christians are to have no part in means that are evil, such as war.

Spirituality and Morality

To this point some attention has been given to the divorce between spirituality and morality effected in war. Mention has been made of the chaplains having responsibilities in regard to the moral well-being of soldiers. Chaplains have discharged that responsibility in a number of ways and with varying intensity, including giving attention to immoral sex, excessive drinking, drugs, and gambling. Chaplains promote moral qualities such as honesty, racial equality, accepting responsibility, and respect for national ideals.[15] Important to the chaplain is the Uniform Code of Military Justice wherein is defined the crimes common to humankind and the military handling of such crimes. In short, the military chaplaincy is concerned about ethics.

In all such considerations of morality, however, there are blind spots related to the ethics of war because war is the business of the military forces. Tragically, the training of soldiers involves developing destruction skills, such as expertise in killing people, demolishing property, damaging the environment, and destroying societal infrastructures. The sad fact is that the governments of the world, given the international commitment to militarism, teach more people how to kill fellow human beings and how to engage in other forms of destruction than does any other human institution. If the taking of life is a justified method in war, justification can be found for other evils such as deception, dishonesty, stealing, and hatred. Thus it is not surprising that war fosters all kinds of evils. The means of war tend to undermine Christian ethics. It is true that some armies fight more humanely than other armies, yet all of them take life, personal and social.

Another aspect of ethics and war is the just war concept. The great majority of Christians have for most of the history of Christianity believed that wars may be participated in if they meet the criteria of the just war. The military chaplains of the United States and Canada do not attempt corporately to evaluate wars in terms of the just war criteria. Without evaluation and with very rare exceptions, military chaplains accept the decisions of their governments concerning whether wars are just or unjust.

(It is true that some chaplains do not accept the just war theory; within the chaplain ranks are those who see themselves as pacifists. Such chaplains are drawn by the evangelism and pastoral possibilities. Such motivation is highly commendable, but the problem is, as pointed out in this paper, that chaplains become a part of the military machine and, therefore, by their presence, inherently approve military means and military objectives. If such persons remained civilians, their context would be altered. The point of view raises the question as to whether such individuals would serve in any military force—including in Hitler's army.)

With the military chaplains not evaluating wars, the armed forces have a built-in approval for warfare from persons who have specialized expertise in knowing the will of God. In such a system we see the unethical fruit of the militarized chaplaincy.

The uncritical acceptance of governmental war decisions raises the question as to why the great majority of American Christians assume that the government always makes the right decision. Many people see the United States as a Christian country. Since the time of the Puritans many Americans have believed and continue to believe that the country is something like a promised land in which God will bring into being a type of new heaven and earth, or at least the best nation in the world. Behind the Puritan vision lies the medieval ideal of church and state together bringing into being the Christian civilization, with the church bestowing divine legitimacy on the state and the state ensuring that God would be worshipped aright. The Puritan worldview resulted in the conviction among churches that their task was to make the land a Christian nation; from this land would flow throughout the world the ideals of spiritual Christianity and democratic government. Thus the United States

---

[15]Richard G. Hutcheson Jr., *The Churches and the Chaplaincy* (Atlanta: John Knox, 1975), 129–61.

has a unique place in God's salvation history.

The resultant nationalism, or what could be called a type of civil religion, is one in which Christianity, nationalism, and militarism are uncritically mixed. Such a view sees no basic problem in the military chaplain being both a clergy person and a commissioned officer. Understandably, the individuals who are attracted to the military chaplaincy tend to be persons who are strongly patriotic. With such an orientation, chaplains can believe they are serving both God and country in the military chaplaincy. Such a view supports the belief that those who die in war give their lives for both God and country. In most instances the chief accent is not on God but on country. Coffins of the war dead are covered not with a Christian symbol but with the national flag (I do not know the Canadian practice).

In actuality, it is difficult not to give a religious coloration to a cause which calls for the giving and taking of life. The religious tendency is tied to the modern sovereign state which in self-interest is ready to call for almost any sacrifice. In this spirit, defense spending can reach astronomical levels. We need to be alert to the danger of turning nationalism into a religion.

In all of this, it must be pointed out, the nation has become the basic corporate entity, not the church. The place that the New Testament gives to the church many people of our age have given to the state.

Theological Concerns

There are two areas of Christian concern which point out the distinction between the mission of Christianity and the mission of the nation. One is how the in-group (the nation) perceives and understands outside groups that stand over

against and take a hostile attitude toward the in-group. Nations typically take a hostile and negative attitude to those who are hostile to them. This in-group/out-group division is not between the saved and the lost, but runs between political systems and along national boundaries. In this type of stand-off, security is seen in the size and sophistication of the military forces. If war comes, the aim is to defeat the enemy nation or nations through superior means of violence.

Such a situation places the military chaplain in a very difficult situation for he or she knows that in most wars the enemy has in its ranks both the saved and the lost. Military chaplains, given their knowledge of the Bible and theology, should be in the forefront of those who will not countenance the killing of the unsaved or the taking of the life of a fellow Christian.

In contrast to the nation's concept of the out-group, Christians (the church) see the basic division in the world as being between the saved and the lost, and thus see the out-group as in need of the gospel message. The aim is not to defeat the "enemy" but rather to work for the salvation of the lost and to bring the converts into the church.

A second distinction between the understanding of Christianity and the military is the way in which the two respond to violence. The military meets violence with violence. The solution to violence is having the superior means of violence. Such truth appears self-evident.

Over against such an approach, Jesus revealed a truth that is not self-evident. He was always very assertive in his servant ministry—preaching and teaching the gospel, healing the sick, feeding the hungry, ministering across ethnic and cultural divisions, outlining a new way of life for both the individual and the church, and expressing a love that went all the way to loving enemies. He also was vigorous in condemning and pointing out personal and societal evil. But when his enemies came to the end of their political and spiritual resources, they became violent. The response of Jesus was truth-telling and nonresistance. The result was the cross; it not only secured our salvation, it also is our ethical model. Christ told his disciples to expect persecution; some were put to death. When mistreated, Christians are to be patient and accept the cross as Christ accepted his. Rather than take life, Christians are to give their lives. The New Testament makes no reference to using violence in self-defense or to taking up of arms as the way to ensure the survival of the faith.

Summary

This study has shown that the military chaplaincy is dominated by the military. The nature of processing a minister into the military chaplaincy is largely determined by the military. Moreover, instead of serving as a civilian, wearing clergy or civilian dress, and being funded by the church, the chaplain is a ranked officer in the military, wears military dress (except in worship services), is financed by the military. All the costs of the program are covered by the military. Further, the chaplain is administratively under the military command, and the religious program of the military unit or military base is the military commander's program, the chaplain giving leadership to and administering the religious program. Also, the chaplain lives sociologically in the military context, governed as he or she is by the laws and resolutions of the military. The military chaplain, by being meshed into the military establishment and by his presence in a pro-military setting, in effect approves the military and its works.

This study has also pointed out some problems regarding the role and responsibilities of the chaplain. On the positive side, chaplains have direct access to the soldiers in terms of counseling and pas-

toral care. The military setting, however, does not have a place for that spiritual ministry to move into Christlike holy living modeled by Jesus in loving his enemies, who calls His followers to do likewise. In fact, the spirituality fostered by the chaplain is to a greater or lesser degree tied to the warmaking of the military forces. In the military, Christlike holy living and taking part in war are seen as compatible. Moreover, chaplains are symbols of God. Their presence as military officers in military dress implies a divine legitimacy to war, and strongly suggests that God is on the side to which the chaplain belongs. But Christians who believe that war is sin and that Christians should not participate in it, find it very difficult to believe that the war effort has God's blessing.

Further, because chaplains do not make ethical evaluations of war by the just war criteria, the armed forces have built-in approval of the justness of their wars from people with an expertise in the ways of God. The posture taken means that the chaplains have turned an ethical area over to the government.

Moreover, chaplains have less than a full opportunity to practice the Great Commission and to work harmoniously in the global church. In war the basic division runs between political systems and along national boundaries; in the Christian worldview it runs between Christians and non-Christians. Only in the latter division can the Great Commission be fully embraced.

Finally, the method of military violence is contrary to the example and teachings of Jesus Christ and the Apostles. They revealed a way of love and reconciliation which seeks to overcome evil with good. The cross issued in the resurrection, not death.

(NOTE: Nothing in this article is meant to suggest that military chaplains, by virtue of being chaplains, are not inherently Christians.)

Part III

❖

Applications
of Christian Peacemaking

❖

Chapter Thirteen

Peacemaking in the Family

Kathleen Leadley

An ordained minister in the Brethren in Christ Church and a past leader in the Women Alive movement, Kathleen Leadley reminds us that marriage and family both have a biblical base, that the rules for both are rooted in Scripture, especially in Jesus' teachings. Frequently human weaknesses threaten the institutions of marriage and family. The author shows how biblical principles can deal with such weaknesses and strengthen the family.

One of the principles Leadley suggests is sacrificial love. But how great should the sacrifice be? Does sacrificial love rule out divorce? On the other hand, has divorce become the easy way out, even for couples within the peace church tradition? How can a spouse truly forgive the partner who has been unfaithful? If money is the cause of much conflict between married couples, should partners have separate bank accounts? Finally, how can we do more to help people whose marriages are not peaceful? How would you resolve the conflicts in the marriage told in the story following the article?

It was a fresh fall morning as I sat at her table drinking a hot cup of coffee. Her three young children ran in and out of the kitchen, disrupting our serious conversation. Although marriage difficulties are never one-sided, the strain of long hours in beginning a new business, poor communication skills, and eventual infidelity had recently resulted in her husband leaving the family. Her dreams of a perfect marriage were shattered. But, in her words, "at least the screaming and fighting were over." As a pastor I have counseled many couples in similar circumstances and I knew that her struggle was far from over. Peace and harmony in family relationships do not begin with separation and divorce.

Most couples go into marriage with preconceived notions of what marriage and family will be. They think their lives will be perfect until they discover that there is no such thing as the perfect mate or the perfect family. When reality strikes and he isn't the man you thought he would be or she isn't the woman she pretended to be and the children aren't the children you both envisioned, a crisis sets in. This may be both a family crisis and a crisis of faith. The words most often used in these circumstances of divorce are "irreconcilable differences." I question, however, if such differences are a legitimate reason for ending a marriage; instead, they may be an excuse to avoid the hard work necessary to sustain a lifelong marital relationship. Certainly conflict is normal, but how we manage conflict brings either resolution to the problem or a stalemate of irreconcilable differences.

The Ordinance of Marriage

For this reason a man will leave his father and mother and be united to his wife, and they will become one flesh (Gen. 2:24).

Marriage is the most intimate relationship into which two human beings can enter, and it is the most complex of all relationships. While the parent-child relationship is also intense, it is one of increasing separation and growing independence. In contrast, increasing interdependence with a spouse is one of the hallmarks of the marriage relationship.[1] Any intimate relationship that has the potential for great joy also has the potential for great hurt and anguish. As Genesis states, it is a commitment and working out the union harmoniously takes commitment throughout life. No work is needed to have a bad marriage; all humans naturally demand their own way. We must live with the tension of our sin nature.

Causes of Family Conflict

Each one of you also must love his wife as he loves himself, and the wife must respect her husband (Eph 5:33).

Several years ago as a young wife and mother I decided to take a course at a nearby university. With my responsibilities as a stay-at-home mother, I needed a break from the demands of family life. Actually, I thought I really deserved a night away from our hectic home; I felt I had a right to some time to myself. In hindsight, I recognize that I had an attitude problem.

In this section I could give a litany of causes of family conflict, all of them appearing plausible. This list might include such things as poor communication, fi-nancial difficulty, the strain of raising children, or even sexual incompatibility. Certainly, it is difficult to understand your mate when communication skills are lacking. Frustration and anger are the result. Whenever there is a shortage of financial resources, the temptation to grumble is always there. Children do require a lot of time and attention, and that leads to fatigue; it takes dedicated teamwork to raise a family to maturity. With work, family, and community involvement, many couples report that they have anything but a romantic sexual life when the day is done. It is no wonder that the marriage bond may be stretched to the point of breaking.

Still, though it may seem simplistic, many causes of conflict stem from lack of humility. The big "I" manifests itself in stubbornness, unforgiveness, and a rebellious spirit. Humility in marriage is loving your wife and respecting your husband in mutual submission one to the other. There is no place in marriage for a bad attitude.

Humility is the test of all relationships, and how you relate to your spouse is the true test of humility. God has revealed humbling truths about himself in the Bible and about us as humans. We are a flawed people, prone to sin. We fall very short of His ideal in our relationships. Fortunately, we have Jesus as our model in relationships, even the marital relationship.

Jesus, Our Model

Blessed are the peacemakers, for they will be called the children of God (Matt. 5:9, nrsv).

We need only look to the sayings of Jesus to understand that the way of harmonious relationships is the way of peace. This includes relationships within the fam-

---

[1]Nicky Lee and Sila Lee, *The Marriage Book* (London, U.K.: HTB Publications, 2000), 17.

ily. We need to experience Jesus' way of peaceful relating to others to understand the principle of harmony in families. It provides an alternative to the world's understanding of how to respond to the stresses and strains of normal family life.

Jesus described true love that supersedes the Old Testament teaching about an eye for an eye and a tooth for a tooth (Ex. 21:24). He calls us to show radical love to all. He teaches us to pray for, do good to, and bless others. Jesus demonstrated to us the way of love by loving those who were clearly considered unlovable. He loved the outcast Samaritan woman at the well in a way that even her own people were not able to do. He respected the hated Roman authorities when they persecuted the Jews. He touched the untouchables as when He reached out to the lepers. He did the unthinkable when He embraced those who were considered detestable—the tax collectors, the prostitutes, and the demon-possessed.

Jesus always chose the way of sacrificial love, which for Him was the way of the cross. He paid dearly for His relationship to all humanity by giving His life so that we might live. It is when we understand the concept of the cross that our whole way of relating to people changes. No longer are we able to justify demanding our rights; we belong to another kingdom, the kingdom of God. We relate on a higher level; the way of the cross becomes for us the way of peace. What does that look like today in marriage? We need some practical tools to be able to deal with the daily stresses and strains of family life.

Resolving Family Conflict

Let us love one another for love comes from God (1 John 4:7).

At a time when 50 percent of marriages are ending in divorce, a clear plan to succeed is needed. It is not that stress was not a problem twenty, fifty, or a hundred years ago. However, we now live in more complicated times. The family unit is no longer valued as the backbone of society and cohabitation has become fashionable. The nuclear family is no longer only defined as husband, wife, and children; alternative lifestyles have become the norm. Finally, divorce no longer bears the stigma that it once did. Never before have marriage and family life been held in so low regard. We need some principles by which to build strong marriages. For this the Bible is our standard. Unless there is abuse in the family, all couples are able to make their marriage work if they are committed to it. Marriage is still an important institution, one worth protecting. Following are some guidelines for a lasting marriage.

Communication

This step has been both overstated and undervalued as a key to good family life. Each of us brings to the marriage a set of ways of communicating that we learned from our family of origin. Rarely do a husband and wife bring to marriage a common understanding of how to communicate. Good communication involves active listening and good conflict resolution skills. All couples need to recognize that listening will diminish the need for conflict resolution, and conflict resolution will become easier with good listening skills.

Bill and Lynne Hybels in *Fit to be Tied,* speak of planning formal peace conferences to resolve their differences.[2] Rather than reacting impulsively to perceived hurts, plan to have regular times to both affirm each other and air differences. Come to the table in a spirit of humility,

[2]Bill Hybels and Lynne Hybels, *Fit To Be Tied* (Grand Rapids: Zondervan, 1991), 130.

recognizing that perhaps you don't have all the facts. Talk openly but don't blame ("You always..."). Use "I" messages instead ("When you do that, I feel..."). Be ready to apologize for any misperceptions because emotional maturity is about putting yourself in the place of another to understand the other's views. It goes without saying that fair fighting includes the willingness to keep talking an issue out until it is resolved. This may take more than one "peace conference"! The goal is not to have a winner and loser but to effect compromise. Don't be ashamed to seek professional help if you are mired down in conflict.

Money, Sex, and Power

Recognize that these three issues are likely the source of many conflicts. Whoever controls the money has power. Whoever dominates the sexual relationship is more powerful. The abuse of power will always kill any relationship. Knowing that many conflicts can be traced to financial and sexual problems will help couples find their way to true intimacy.

The most intimate of relationships is the marital union. Sexual intimacy is closely aligned to spiritual intimacy and is the bond that cements the marital relationship. It is a form of communication that cannot be neglected but must be nurtured. Conversely, couples may emotionally leave the marriage bond and enter into sexual infidelity. The depth of betrayal in such situations is beyond compare. Heightened communication skills may be needed for a marriage to survive the affair, and the skills of a trained counselor will likely be required. However, there is hope even for couples seeking to rebuild their marriage following infidelity.

Money problems can drive a wedge between couples. Today it is common for couples to have separate bank accounts. Admittedly, it is far easier to share most anything than it is to share a joint bank account. Couples who are able to communicate openly about financial matters from the beginning of their marriage are able to learn the art of negotiation in other areas of marriage as well. It is not wise to get into the habit of relegating money as "his" and "hers" or to keep secrets about spending. A spirit of openness and cooperation in financial matters spills over into other areas of marital bliss.

Loyalty

Couples who have strong marriages are loyal to each other in every way. They do not talk about their spouses to others in a derogatory manner. They defend each other in the face of adversity and stand together in matters of raising the children. They seek to enjoy each other's interests, show kindness to each other, and overlook petty issues. They have an attitude of "It's you and I together." Loyalty is a virtue that includes keeping one's word. When a promise is made, it is kept; when discretion is important, it is honored; when agreements are made, they are respected. Good marriage is about honoring the marriage vows to love, honor, and respect each other from the beginning of the marriage to the end of the covenant.

Forgiveness

God demonstrated the ultimate act of forgiveness in sending His Son, Jesus Christ, to die for us. He who forgave us is ready and willing to help us forgive one another. There will be times of disappointment and disagreement in marriage. When those times come, there should be a plan of forgiveness in place. The person in need of forgiveness must ask for it with a pure heart. The party that has the power to forgive must extend forgiveness with grace and without continuing to be angry and resentful. Sometimes we require an extra measure of grace to be able to deal with hurt and disappointment with such aplomb. It is best to begin early in marriage to practice forgiveness in the little things so the pattern of forgiveness is well established before major life issues threaten to destroy the fabric of the marriage. Don't hold grudges. Do practice those three little words "I am sorry" on a regular basis. Get into the habit of forgiving readily, remembering the lavish love that God has extended to us in forgiveness.

To be sure, some disappointments may be more difficult to forgive than others. An example is the pain of betrayal. Betrayal may involve physical, emotional, mental, or sexual abuse. While any marriage is salvageable, realistically it requires the commitment of both spouses to the marriage union to begin the healing process. When infidelity is the cause of strife, a special measure of grace and forgiveness is required to restore the marriage to a place of health and wholeness.

Certainly, issues of abuse are the most difficult to deal with and may require temporary separation and possibly divorce. I say this not to give an easy out for warring couples but because we must recognize the existence of evil, even in marriage.

While separation and divorce may be a reality, our focus should be on the biblical permanency of the marriage covenant. Divorce is not one of many options, but a last resort when all other options have been exhausted. It is a scriptural truth that God hates divorce (Mal. 2:16), because He knows the pain it causes His children. When couples practice forgiveness as a way of life, they help to solidify their marriage, thereby avoiding many of the pitfalls that lead to marital breakdown.

Prayer

An old saying goes, "The family that prays together, stays together." While it may seem trivial to repeat it, there *is* power in a praying family. Couples and families who pray together learn to work out their differences on a spiritual plane in a way that cannot be achieved on any other level. Couples who begin to pray together early in their marriages build a foundation of reliance on God as their strength and their source of encouragement. This kind of family cannot easily be destroyed, for it is almost impossible to remain angry when prayer is the foundation resolving conflict. Usually the life of the one doing the praying is changed and softened in the process, which opens the door to peace and reconciliation in the family.

The Role of the Church

Be patient, bearing with one another in love (Eph. 4: 2).

The church has a key role to play in helping families overcome the pitfalls of marriage and family life. As the body of Christ, the church is able to surround families and nurture them to maturity. This may be a lifelong process because transitions are always taking place in family life. Just when you think you have the marriage thing figured out, along comes the family. When the physical demands of raising young children are over, the emotional demands of rearing teenagers begins. When it seems that the children will never mature, the empty nest years arrive. Each life transition needs to be negotiated with love and grace. As the church, we need to be patient and bear with one another in love.

The church has a responsibility to promote the permanency of marriage by proclaiming biblical principles, actively supporting couples in crisis, and at times admonishing couples who refuse to remain faithful to the marriage covenant. This is not to suggest that the sole responsibility rests with the church. Every couple must submit to the body of Christ and its teachings. Practically, this may require being part of a small group with other couples who are together seeking the same goals for their marriages.

Every church should have mentor couples who have been through the various stages of married life and can be good role models to newly married couples. All couples should be encouraged to find others who have raised their children well; their successes can become models. Other help can come from couples who have had some difficulties in their marriage or family life but have successfully negotiated the challenges together. Finally, couples who are serious about keeping their marriage vows may need to make themselves accountable to the leadership of the church. There are myriad traps that any couple may fall into and that seem impossible to overcome. The church is a place to receive help, and there is no shame is seeking it. Marriage is worth it.

Summary

My purpose is that they may be encouraged in heart and united in love (Col. 2:2).

In *The Case for Marriage,* Linda Waite and Maggie Gallagher state that there are five myths of the post-marriage culture.[3] For each of the myths, they debunk the idea that marriage is bad for us, and they reveal the benefits of marriage emotionally, physically, economically, and sexually to individuals and society as a whole. It's interesting that these secular findings concur with biblical principles. The authors conclude that successful family relationships are good for us.

Peacemaking efforts begin in the home, where love, affirmation, and cooperation are intricately twined together. As husbands and wives mutually submit to one another, the children begin to practice the way of peace and harmony in their own relationships. As the church surrounds the family with solid teaching and practical tools, the family is supported and strengthened. Just as each person needs to find God's purpose in life, so each couple needs to discover God's purpose for marriage. The best way to find God's purpose for your family is to humbly submit to each other through peace and reconciliation.

The following is a list of resources that may assist you in strengthening your marriage. This list is by no means exhaustive. May God be honored as you bear witness to the world with a lifestyle of peace and reconciliation within your marriage and family.

Reading List

Chapman, Gary. *The Five Love Languages.* Chicago: Northfield, 1995.

Cloud, Henry, and John Townsend. *Boundaries in Marriage.* Grand Rapids: Zondervan, 1999.

Hybels, Bill, and Lynne Hybels, *Fit To Be Tied.* Grand Rapids: Zondervan, 1991.

Lee, Nicky, and Sila Lee, *The Marriage Book.* London, U.K.: HTB Publications, 2000.

Wheat, Ed, and Gaye Wheat. *Intended for Pleasure.* Old Tappan, N.J.: Fleming H. Revell, 1981.

Gillian and Rod's Story

Gillian was a bright young wife and the mother of two beautiful girls. By all appearances she had gone into marriage well prepared for whatever came her way. She was in her late twenties when Rod proposed to her, and they eagerly planned for their wedding day some ten months later. Gillian was uni-

---

[3]Linda J. Waite and Maggie Gallagher, *the Case for Marriage* (New York: Doubleday, 2000).

versity educated and well along in her career aspirations. Rod was gainfully employed in industry. After marriage, they waited two years before starting a family and eagerly anticipated welcoming their first child into their lives. Gillian worked after the baby was born and managed well until their second child was born. Then things began to unravel for them.

With the arrival of the new baby, Gillian was no longer able to work, even part-time. The demands of raising two children began to overwhelm her. There seemed to be no end to bottles, diapers, and toys strewn all over the house. Rod began to complain that Gillian ignored him and his need for some special time with her. Gillian went on the defensive, screaming that her life was not the same either. If only he would help out, she would have more time for the things they used to do.

Complicating matters was a shortage of funds now that they no longer had Gillian s income to provide for the extras they were accustomed to. Gillian complained that Rod kept tight control over the money and that she didn t have any discretionary funds for herself. In the meantime, Rod kept up his usual golfing dates with his friends. "After all," he said, "I need a day out once in a while." Naturally, they both agreed, babysitters were out of the question; there were hardly enough funds for the necessities, let alone a night out together. Their relationship was reduced to shouts, commands. and constant arguing.

In frustration, Gillian approached her pastor. The only solution in her mind was to separate to let Rod know that she was not going to live like this anymore. Rod was so discouraged that he no longer cared. Complicating the issue was the fact that both Gillian and Rod came from divorced homes. Separation and divorce was the only model of resolving conflict they had known. Both of them saw no other solution than to call it quits.

Can this marriage be saved? How?

Teaching Peace to Children Who Play War

Harriet Bicksler

Should people who believe in peace allow their children to play with toys that resemble objects used in war? Harriet Bicksler, chairperson of Mennonite Central Committee (U.S.) and editor of *Shalom!*, examines both sides of this question. On the one hand, she points to studies that seem to show that the damage resulting from playing with war toys is minimal, that such play is part of children's normal fantasy world from which they eventually graduate. On the other hand, she makes a case that playing with war toys and watching cartoons that show violence can have long-ranging negative consequences. She also suggests that by allowing such play and the viewing of such cartoons, parents may condone their parallel in real life.

Several questions immediately come to mind from this thought-provoking article. First, on which side of the war toys issue do you find yourself? Why? How have you dealt with the issue of toys that encourage war or violent play in your family?

Think of games you played and the toys that appealed to you when you were a child. To what extent did they affect you or do they bear a relationship to the kind of person you are today?

Is it less problematic to read a book about war than to watch movies about war or to play violent video games?

The article states that the central question under consideration is this: "Is it possible to teach nonviolent peacemaking skills to children who are allowed to play with toys which are based on the assumption that force and violence are acceptable means of overcoming evil?" What is your answer to that question?

I wrote the following article when my children were still young, and my son was enamored with action figures and other toys that seemed to promote violence and war. My children are young adults now, and I don't yet have grandchildren, so most of what I know about toys these days I see on television. The specific information about toys in the article may be a little outdated, but the concerns and the issues remain the same.

Harriet Sider Bicksler, February 2002

Toys and play are important to children. For many children, going to the toy store is like a trip to fantasyland with a vast array of toys to choose from to satisfy any childish fantasy. One category of toy that has always been popular with children is the "war toy." In 1986, at the height of my own son's fascination with war toys, for example, the best-seller was the G.I. Joe toy system, including action figures, battle vehicles, weapons, and other accessories. In December 2001, the G.I. Joe doll enjoyed another resurgence in popularity, as children's fascination with the military increased in light of the new war in Afghanistan. Today's G.I. Joe toy is a high-tech version of a doll that was popularized during World War II but fell into disrepute during the Vietman War. Its popularity says something about American attitudes toward the military and the common belief in war and violence as legitimate methods of conflict resolution. It also creates a problem for pacifist parents.

G.I. Joe is not the only problem, however. In addition to G.I. Joe, the toy market is flooded with many other action toy systems, which include a variety of characters, weapons, battle vehicles, and a story line. Many of them have parallel video games, as well as television cartoons that are shown daily. The proliferation of these toys poses a dilemma for parents. Are they good for our children? What values do they teach? Why are children attracted to them? The dilemma is accentuated for parents who are Christian pacifists, who want to teach peaceful and nonviolent resolution of conflict. Is it possible to teach nonviolent peacemaking skills to children who are allowed to play with toys which are based on the assumption that force and violence are acceptable means of overcoming evil?

That is the central question under consideration in this article. I do not propose to answer the question directly because for me that is presumptuous. As a Christian pacifist parent heavily involved in real-life situations that require sorting through the dilemma in question, my thinking on the subject was very much in process when my children were young. I looked for validation of the parenting choices I made, and found affirmation and contradiction—both of which are reflected in this article. On the one hand then, this is a highly personal article, but on the other hand, it is one that explores a topic which is relevant for all Christian pacifists. How do we teach peace to children? More specifically, how do we deal with the issue of war toys and pacifist teaching?[1]

---

[1]In this article, belief in pacifism is assumed and I make no effort to argue the case for it. I define pacifism as the belief that conflicts and disputes between individuals and nations can and should be resolved nonviolently and I believe that the Bible supports that view.

The term "war toy" also requires clarification. Traditionally, war toys were guns, tanks, and toy soldiers. In the current toy market, however, the issue is clouded because of all the fantasy and superhero toy systems which include many variations of weapons, combat vehicles, and people to use them.

In some sense, these also are "war toys." For ease in reference, therefore, I have decided to use the term "war toy" generically to refer to all toys which include weapons and assume the use of lethal force and violence.

This chapter is an update of Harriet Sider Bicksler, "Teaching Peace to Children Who Play War," *Within the Perfection of Christ; Essays on Peace and the Nature of the Church*, eds. Terry L. Brensinger and E. Morris Sider (Nappanee, Ind.: Evangel Press and the Brethren in Christ Historical Society, 1990), 179–90.

In order to work toward a solution to the dilemma, I begin by describing more fully the toy market and its context at the time this article was first written. With that setting in mind, I will review the debate that goes on between those who argue either for or against the acceptability of these kinds of toys for children. I conclude with some suggestions for balancing creatively between extreme points of view.

Understanding the Context

Unless one makes a deliberate and radical choice to separate oneself entirely from the surrounding culture, it is difficult for parents of young children to avoid the issue of war toys. A visit to any toy store immediately confronts both parent and child with an impressive display of war toys. Writing in the December, 1986, issue of *The Other Side*, Barbara Oehlberg describes her local toy store as "a procurement center for the Pentagon": "There I was, a Christian peacemaker and educator, looking at toys that would encourage my young relatives to make nuclear war in our family living room!"[2]

Because the toy market changes rapidly, the specific toys are not as important as the assumptions they embody. It is, however, helpful to be aware of the types of toys to which our children are attracted and to look at a few specific examples.

In addition to the traditional toy soldiers, guns, and tanks, and the reincarnated versions of "G.I. Joe, the Great American Hero," there are many superhero toy systems. (When my son was young, they were Transformers, MASK, Centurions, Masters of the Universe, Rambo, StarCom and other lesser known versions.) Each line of toys is self-contained, with its own story line (reinforced daily by television cartoons), weapons, and combat vehicles. Toy manufacturers count on children getting hooked by one or more lines of toys and prey on that addiction by creating new and more intriguing additions to each collection. Each system has a set of "good guys" and "bad guys"—the story line, then, pits the two sides against each other. Each toy, including the following examples from the 1980s, comes with a job description: Jake Rockwell (a Centurion) is a "Land Operations Expert and Fireforce Assault Weapon System with Firing Plasma Missile"; Strafe (a Transformer) "shoots everywhere—since that's where the enemies are"; Peacemaker (another Transformer) "transforms into Pointblank's weapon."

These toys are in many ways merely a reflection of our society. The world is frequently divided into good and bad guys, with both the good and the bad arming themselves to the hilt to protect themselves from the other. The military-industrial complex that Eisenhower warned us about in 1960 shows no sign of disappearing. War is big business. Those who promote non-military solutions have generally been in the minority and are often considered out of step with reality. Pacifists do not often get very good press in today's world, especially since September 11, 2001. It is not hard to understand why war toys proliferate.

Yet the societal themes that war toys reflect are not limited to the twentieth century. In fact, as an article in *Time* magazine pointed out, most of today's toys are reincarnations of classic myths, "manifestations of ancient lore, the oral and written history of the human race."[3] The article goes on to describe categories of those ancient myths that have counterparts in modern toys: the knight, the mechanical marvel, the miracle power, the little people.[4] Further, the human history

---

[2]Barhara Oehlberg, "Beyond the Three Stooges," *The Other Side,* November 1986, 38.
[3]Stefan Kanfer. "In All Seasons, Toys Are Us," *Time,* December 22, 1986, 64.
[4]Ibid., 66–67.

that these toys have paralleled throughout the years has included many wars and much violence.

Concurrent with the violence and war of human history, however, have been people who have resisted those methods of conflict resolution. For them—many of whom are Christian pacifists—the argument that war toys are simply a reflection of society is not an adequate defense of them. If pacifists resist the wars and violence of their culture, then it seems natural and right that they should also resist the playthings that reflect the culture's bent toward violence. Many of them do, responding to the issue with strong arguments against allowing children to play with toys that are miniature versions of the instruments of the violence and death that they abhor and citing studies that show the relationship between pretend and real violence. Unfortunately, it is not always as simple as that.

An Ongoing Debate

To begin, the studies of the relationship between playing with war toys or watching violent cartoons on television and real-life aggression, violence, or a bent toward war making are not necessarily conclusive and are often debated. In addition, often the issue focused by a child's attraction to so-called war toys is not war and violence but the normal psychological development of the child. Various child psychologists argue that the appeal of fantasy toys, which often have warlike manifestations, has more to do with the child's psychological needs than it does with what those toys seem to represent to adults. Hence the dilemma for many parents, especially Christian paci-

fist parents: we want nothing to do with the violence and wars of our culture and we want to prohibit our children from playing with toys that reflect that aspect of the culture. At the same time, we are not sure that our children's attraction to these toys will turn them into warmongers or violent people, and we see evidence that certain kinds of childish needs are fulfilled by these toys. We search for some kind of balance.

The Case against War Toys

Lorne Peachey, former editor of *Christian Living*, a Mennonite family magazine, and author of *How to Teach Peace to Children*, asserts, "In short, with reference to parents in peace churches buying war toys for children, the sources agree: don't."[5] That would seem to be sufficiently clear-cut, yet other parents with pacifist sympathies do not fully agree. Recommending that parents "hold the line on toy guns as long as possible," Michael True nevertheless says that simple solutions are inevitably undermined in other ways and that parents always face the dilemma.[6] James and Kathy McGinnis, in their book *Parenting for Peace and Justice*, also describe how they clearly told their children that "we do not think it is fun to pretend to kill people," but still ended up giving in a bit on the war toy issue.[7] My own experience, although I am a deeply committed pacifist, was with similar ambivalence and being unable to maintain a hard line against all war-related toys.

The debate goes beyond pacifists, however. While many of the studies relating to violence in children have been focused on the effects of television violence and not war toys per se, it is easy to extrapo-

---

[5]J. Lorne Peachey, *How to Teach Peace to Children* (Scottdale, Pa.: Herald, 1981), 14.

[6]Michael True, *Homemade Social Justice* (Chicago: Fides/Claretian, 1982), 21.

[7]James McGuinnis and Kathy McGinnis, *Parenting for Peace and Justice* (Maryknoll, N.Y.: Orbis Books, 1981), 46.

late from those studies to the issue of war toys because the line between toys and television is frequently blurred. (Many toy systems intentionally parallel television cartoons.) Citing statistics that say that the average four- to eight-year-old child viewed 250 episodes of war cartoons and 1,000 commercials for war toys in 1986, religious syndicated columnist Michael McManus also refers to studies showing that 46 percent of adolescent boys exposed to television violence had committed at least one serious violent crime.[8] He implies that there is a direct connection. The organization Handgun Control Incorporated advocates a ban on the manufacture and sale of toy guns.[9] Marjorie Kostelnik, associate professor and program supervisor at the Child Development Laboratories at Michigan State University, argues that weapon play "allows children to practice and become more accepting of violence."[10]

Tracing the connection between toys and games and war in postwar Germany, Alan Keele says, "Even the most skeptical might grant that some kind of connection does seem to obtain between war, war games, and war toys; between battle and violent athletic contests; between the strategy of war and such strategic games as chess."[11] He then ponders why there is a connection, and notes that both wars and games suspend the normal rules of behavior, and when the player is unable to shift back to reality, he or she acts violently in real life.[12] Further, all games require polarization between opposing sides (the us-them mentality), and thus, "the psychological seeds of chauvinism...can [be] and often are sown ...through sports and games."[13]

The Case for Understanding the Appeal of War Toys

The opinions, the debate, and the documentation go on, and if they were all one read, there would not be much of a dilemma. But while there is significant evidence of a connection between war toys and games, and war and violence, it is not uncontested. One author, by way of example, tells of a teacher who tried to forbid all gunplay. When she finally gave in, accepted its inevitability and the children's apparent need for gunplay, they played at guns for a while but then the need dissipated within a few weeks.[14]

The scenario does not seem to be isolated. One experiment cited showed that children who were not naturally fighters did not act aggressively after watching television violence, even though naturally bellicose individuals did seem to become more aggressive.[15] The authors concluded that fantasy play (happening to some extent in the course of television viewing) often results in a decrease in hostile aggression. On the other hand, they agree

---

[8]Michael McManus, "War Toys Are Totally Unsuitable for Christmas," *The Patriot,* December 20, 1986, 47.

[9]Brian Sutton-Smith, *Toys as Culture* (New York: Gardner Press, 1986), 6.

[10]Quoted in Betty Holcomb, "Why Children Are Hooked on Superheroes," *Working Mother,* July 1987, 98.

[11]Alan Frank Keele, "Childhood Toys, Sporting Games, and the Seeds of War: A View from Postwar German Literature," *Soundings* 65 (Summer 1982): 158.

[12]Ibid.

[13]Ibid., 162.

[14]Maria W. Piers and Genevieve Millet Landau, *The Gift of Play: And Why Young Children Cannot Survive without It* (New York: Walker and Co., 1980), 83.

[15]Ibid., 99–100.

that television violence is "an exacerbating factor" in children who are already prone to violence.[16]

While it is important for parents to be aware of the possible effects of television cartoons and war toys on their children's propensity toward violence, and to consider those effects when selecting toys, it seems to be equally important to consider what needs those toys are meeting. The well-known child psychiatrist, Bruno Bettelheim, analyzes the appeal and value of fairy tales in *The Uses of Enchantment*.[17] Bettelheim says that "the fairy tale confronts the child squarely with the basic human predicament" and that though struggle against evil is inevitable, it is part of being human and one can overcome if one persists.[18]

The stark contrasts between good and evil that adults may find bothersome are, according to Bettelheim, helpful to children because they need to be able to clearly see the difference. At a later stage in their development, they will be ready to understand ambiguities. Fairy tales also help children come to terms with the monsters within them, and to know that they are not the only ones to think awful thoughts. And, "despite all the angry, anxious thoughts in his mind to which the fairy tale gives specific content—these stories always result in a happy outcome, which the child cannot imagine on his own."[19] That happy ending, which often includes the punishment of the wicked, is important because it helps the child to feel secure.[20]

Bettelheim extends the argument in favor of fairy tales to the issue of war toys in a more recent book, *A Good Enough Parent*. To parents who want to forbid all war toys, he says, "While these feelings toward violence are most understandable, when a parent prohibits or severely criticizes his child's gunplay, whatever his conscious reasons for doing so, he is not acting for his child's benefit, but solely out of adult concerns or anxieties."[21] He goes on to say that the child's need to discharge aggression through gunplay does not have as much to do with violence or war as it has to do with what is going on in the child's immediate environment, such as arguments with siblings or tensions with parents. Toy guns often represent a desire for self-protection, and playing "Superman" allows the child the "vicarious satisfaction" of being in control.[22]

Others also note that war toys and superhero play provide children with an opportunity to exercise the power and control that they generally lack: "Superheroes [and the toys that go with them] give kids access to power that is absent in their everyday experiences."[23] Even one who is appalled by the messages that accompany many war toys acknowledges that "kids do need symbols of good ver-

---

[16]Ibid., 108.

[17]Bruno Bettelheim, *The Uses of Enchantment* (New York: Alfred Knopf, 1976). This is not as large a leap from war toys as one might think. As the *Time* article indicates, many of today's toys are quite similar to traditional fairy tales. Many of the elements of fairy tales—for example, a struggle between good and evil resulting in the happy ending of good conquering evil—are present in the story lines behind these toy systems.

[18]Ibid., 8.

[19]Ibid., 123.

[20]Ibid., 147.

[21]Bruno Bettelheim, *A Good Enough Parent* (New York: Alfred Knopf, 1987), 215.

[22]Ibid., 216.

[23]Quoted in Holcomb, "Why Children Are Hooked on Superheroes," 95.

sus bad, powerful versus powerless. These symbols assist them as they 'work' their way through the meaning of these opposing words and the mental images that accompany them. Such learning is carried out through the child's fantasy play."[24] In addition, some note that because injustice, violence, and struggle are common themes in fairy tales, children are introduced to those themes early in life. Parents should not protect their children from the hard things of life, and fairy tales provide children with the opportunity to ask questions about violence and aggression rather than suppress them.[25]

But can children distinguish between real life and the superhero and fantasy play they experience with toys and on television? Does one's fantasy life carry over into reality? Another child psychologist, while arguing that war toys and fantasy play are acceptable outlets for children, claims that "your child knows well the difference between violence in fantasy on a TV or movie screen, and violence in action when he hits another child, is cruel to an animal, or destroys property."[26] A study by Robert Hodge and David Tripp, using a short, original stereotypical superhero cartoon with a group of children, showed that the children had no difficulty distinguishing what was appropriate in real life.[27]

I too think that healthy children know the difference between fantasy and real life. Occasionally, I would remind my son that just because he saw someone on television doing something did not mean he should do it too. His usual response was some form of, "Oh Mom, I'm not stupid, you know!" Likewise, when we had one of our frequent discussions on why I did not like war toys, he seemed genuinely unable to understand the connections that I made between his play and his attitudes toward war and violence. Even though I respected his intelligence, however, I still worried about the subtle influences that he and I were not conscious of at the time. In most cases, the problem with war toys and superhero play seems to be when the child does not develop beyond that stage or when he or she uses fantasy to escape dealing with the real world.[28] I was concerned about that possibility.

The Call for Balance

To summarize briefly before moving on to suggest some ways to deal with the war toy dilemma: many child development experts are concerned about the effects of superhero cartoon violence and aggressive fantasy play on children. The results of those studies concern me as well, both as a parent and as a Christian pacifist. Not only do I worry about the long-lasting effects of fantasy war play, but I am also offended by the rather explicit message of war toys that lethal force and violence are acceptable and even patriotic. At the same time, however, I tend to agree with some experts who claim that within limits and in otherwise emotionally healthy children, these toys and the play that is associated with them provide children with much-needed outlets for certain feelings. Again, some kind of balance seems to be indicated.

Balancing, though, involves dealing with contradiction. The International Playground Association, for example, maintains a position against war toys,

---

[24]Oehlberg, "Beyond the Three Stooges," 39.

[25]True, *Homemade Social Justice*, 65.

[26]Fitzhugh Dodson, *How to Parent* (New York: Signet Books, 1970), 252.

[27]Robert Hodge and David Tripp, *Children and Television: A Semiotic Approach* (Stanford, Calif.: Stanford University Press, 1986).

[28]Holcomb, "Why Children Are Hooked on Superheroes," 98.

arguing that "children are not given toys to help them become thieves, or drug addicts, or pimps, and they should not, therefore, be given toys, which, at the very least, sanction the notion that war at some level (even the toy level) is acceptable."[29] On the other side, Bettelheim maintains that playing with guns does not say anything about the child's future life, just as playing with blocks does not mean the child will be a carpenter or playing with cars does not mean the child will become a mechanic or race car driver.[30] Separately, both views make sense, but putting them together makes it difficult to arrive at consistent conclusions.

Some Practical Suggestions
Acknowledge the Dilemma

Given the contradictory messages parents get from the culture and the experts, and given our commitment to teaching pacifism to our children, I think that there are several ways for pacifist parents to work their way through the dilemma presented by war toys. First, it is important that we admit there is a dilemma. It will always be there—unless we choose to separate ourselves entirely from the culture in which we live. We will always have to sort through conflicting information and our own conflicting emotions—not to mention the pressure to conform to the values around us. We will have to distinguish between what is legitimate concern about the values our children are picking up and what is a projection of adult anxieties and perceptions onto our children.

Implied in the admission of the dilemma and its constant presence is the importance of accepting ambiguity and learning to balance between extremes. Both those involved in formal peace education programs and child psychologists acknowledge that a hard-line approach against war toys is often self-defeating. If such toys are forbidden, they seem all the more appealing, or the child will go to the neighbors to play without the benefit of parental counsel and limits on the kind of play,[31] or children will fashion their own guns out of whatever materials are available.[32] The McGinnises sometimes allowed battle toys like outer space battleships. Not knowing whether it was the right thing to do, they nonetheless did not want war toys to become an obsession with their children and "take on much more importance than they would otherwise."[33]

Choose a Comfortable Balance

A normal child will, in all probability, play with guns and other war toys or devise his or her own—whether the parent likes it or not. But that does not mean that it is acceptable to allow the child to have whatever he or she wants. There is a long continuum between total prohibition of all war toys and acceptance of anything. After arguing that "children need socially acceptable fantasy outlets for their hostile and violent feelings,"[34] Dodson goes on to warn against allowing toy guns that actually shoot something or other toys that are simply in bad taste.[35]

Part of our responsibility as parents is choosing the point on the continuum where we feel comfortable. Some families may legitimately choose to prohibit all

[29]Sutton-Smith, *Toys as Culture,* 6.

[30]Bettelheim, *A Good Enough Parent,* 216.

[31]Oehlberg, "Beyond the Three Stooges," 39.

[32] Dodson, *How to Parent,* 249.

[33]McGinnis, *Parenting,* 46.

[34]Dodson, *How to Parent,* 248.

[35]Ibid., 250.

war toys and games. Others may allow a squirt gun but little else. Still others may choose to distinguish between war toys that are more like "science fiction" and those that are more like reality. For example, in our family we allowed such fantasy toy systems as Masters of the Universe, Star Wars, and the Transformers, but we refused to buy G.I. Joe and Rambo toys because the latter were more closely connected to the American military system and the line between fantasy and reality was much less clear. That was not an easy balance to maintain or defend, but it helped to place limits and to provide opportunity for discussion of our values and beliefs. Along with the McGinnises, we thought that rather than forbid all war toys, it was more important in the long run "to let our children know how we feel about guns and war toys, and why we prefer other kinds of toys."[36]

Tell Your Children What You Believe

Consequently, besides acknowledging the dilemma and choosing a comfortable balance, parents also need to clearly articulate to their children their own pacifist values. Ultimately, of course, our children are free to make their own choices of values and lifestyle. However, whether one follows the biblical advice to "train children in the right way" or contemporary psychological advice, parental influence is extremely important. Noting that children who watch television shows which idealize the military score no higher than others on a War Acceptance Scale, Howard Tolley nonetheless goes on to point out that "children's perspectives on war in general...share a close relationship to opinions reportedly heard from parents."[37]

Parental influence on issues of war and peace is particularly crucial in light of prevailing cultural opinion. Defining play as "the primitive communication through which you can express and communicate all the longings, furtive wishes, glorious dreams, hopeless fears, that cannot be expressed in everyday arrangements," Sutton-Smith says that there have always been arguments about what is proper and improper play.[38] "That which is approved," he says, "is that which imitates the customs or the beliefs of those who would control the society."[39] It would seem reasonable to conclude, therefore, that unless parents make a concerted effort to counteract prevailing customs and beliefs, our children will assume what their culture and nation tell them about the military and war—which for Americans is that a strong military system is vital for our nation's survival. It is up to pacifist parents to teach our children that there are other, nonviolent means of ensuring national strength and survival.

Conclusion

My son is a young adult now, and seems to have lost his fascination with war toys. He doesn't even hunt! He went through a video game phase, but even that has faded. So in some sense, I feel vindicated by our decision to allow some toys in our home that, strictly speaking, would be considered war toys.

On the other hand, since I originally wrote this article, the United States has "won"one high-tech war against Iraq and is in the middle of another one against ter-

---

[36]Howard Tolley Jr., *Children and War: Political Socialization to International Conflict* (New York: Teachers College Press, 1973), 112.

[37]Ibid.

[38]Sutton-Smith, *Toys as Culture*, 252.

[39]Ibid., 251.

rorism. In addition, there have been many incidents of school violence in which children and adolescents have shot and killed teachers and classmates. While I think that other factors were probably more influential than war toys in these kids' decisions to resort to such horrific violence to settle their problems, I am still concerned that the accessibility of violent entertainment may have contributed to a greater acceptance of violence as means of resolving problems. Certainly the world has not become a more peaceful place, and one can't help wondering how that might be different if children were not conditioned in so many ways, including the toys they play with, to accept violence and war as appropriate and legitimate.

The oft-quoted remark of General Omar Bradley offers food for thought for pacifist parents: "We know more about war than we do about peace—more about killing than we know about living."[40] The alliance that I and many other parents have made with war toys in any or all of their varieties is an uneasy one, precisely because we want to teach our children about pacifism and about the value of human life, rather than about war and killing. When our children are enamored with superheroes and mechanical robots that transform into battle stations, we parents are responsible to teach them peace as well. We may not choose to do as Keele asks, to "say NO to everything even remotely conducive to war,"[41] but our children still need to hear us say repeatedly that war, lethal force, and violence are incongruent with our understanding of our calling as Christian peacemakers. Then, if we have been clear with our children about what we believe and reasonably consistent in the way we live, we can trust that their childhood preoccupation with war toys and superhero play will eventually fade and be replaced with an adult commitment to peace and nonviolence.

---

[40]Quoted in *True, Homemade Social Justice,* 65.
[41]Keele, "Childhood Toys," 165.

Chapter Fifteen

Ideas for Teaching Peace to Children in the Church

Julie Weatherford

In the previous article, Harriet Bicksler concentrates on teaching peace in the home, with reference to war toys and videos that depict violence. In the following article, Julie Weatherford of California, who pursues her interest in peace issues in part by serving on the Board for Brotherhood Concerns of the Pacific Conference of the Brethren in Christ Church, takes the reader to the Sunday school. After discussing the biblical aspect of teaching children about peace, she suggests practical ways to carry out biblical principles on a relational level, even in the physical qualities of a room.

Do you agree with such suggestions as eliminating competitive games and awards? How can the teacher practice peace in dealing with unruly children? Can children receive an overabundance of teaching on peace and thus be turned away from what the teacher wants them to accept? Do you agree with those who say that peace is best taught to children by example?

Children of today need to know and experience Jesus' ways of peace. Living in a world that is on the brink of self-destruction, in a culture that condones and often encourages violence, and in home situations too frequently torn apart by "irreconcilable differences," children need to hear and answer Jesus' call to peace and love. How can we as adult believers in the church help children grow to be peacemakers in the face of great pressure to conform to the world's ways of war, violence and conflict?

The church that desires to foster a peacemaking mentality in its children must include biblical and practical teaching on peacemaking as an integral part of children's learning within the church. This article will offer suggestions for accomplishing this.

I will start with the biblical aspect of teaching children about peace. The theme of peace clearly runs throughout the Bible. From Genesis' peaceful garden through Revelation's worship of the Prince of Peace, God's Word is replete with references to peace and accounts from the lives of peacemakers. Any child who grows up in the church without clearly understanding that our God is a God of peace and His people are to be people of peace is lacking fundamental aspects of biblical truth and of the Christian faith.

This article originally appeared as Julie Weatherford, "Ideas for Teaching Peace to Children in the Church," *Shalom!*, Fall 1987, 4–5.

For those of you who have chosen to make use of commercial children's Bible curricula, it is probably clear that the majority of curricula available on the market today reflects little or no peace emphasis per se. However, the lessons are almost always designed around Bible stories, so lessons which may not reflect any peace emphasis can often be adapted or added to in order to illustrate a truth concerning peace.

For example, one could easily use a unit on the life of Stephen to teach children about peace. Point the children to the disciples' answer to the Grecian and Aramaic widows' dilemma about food distribution as an example of nonviolent conflict resolution. Help the children see that Stephen, "a man full of God's grace and power," used that power lovingly and peacefully. Show how Stephen's last words at his stoning were words of forgiveness and peace toward those who were bringing his life to a violent end.

For those of you who design your own Bible lessons instead of using commercial curricula, decide whether your children would benefit more from a whole unit on peace, peace lessons interjected periodically, or a few minutes devoted weekly to a topic concerning peace. Having decided this, be creative. Consider designing lessons on Jesus' statements and actions concerning peace. Or plan specific peace lessons, using accounts from the lives of Paul, Peter, Stephen and other New Testament peace heroes. Study peace as the Psalms portray it. Look to Isaiah's prophecies concerning future and everlasting peace. Study the book of Philemon as an encouragement to two men to be reconciled. Follow the early church's struggle toward attitudes of ac-

ceptance between believing Jews and Gentiles.

Whether adapting prepared curriculum or designing your own Bible lessons to teach children about peace, you will find the results in terms of children's biblical knowledge and understanding to be well worth your efforts. But teaching the biblical basis for our peace position is only part of our responsibility, for children of today desperately need practical teaching about peacemaking.

Practical teaching about peace and peacemaking skills will not only enhance biblical understanding, but will help children develop peacemaking mentalities as they face the real world of street bullies, bothersome siblings, and selfish schoolmates, not to mention prejudice, violence and war. Peacemaking ideals should permeate every aspect of your teaching, from the way you set up the children's rooms to your discipline techniques. You are limited only by your imagination as to ways to teach practical aspects of peacemaking, but if you're like me, you would benefit greatly by reading these two excellent books: *The Friendly Classroom for a Small Planet,* by Priscilla Prutzman, and *A Manual on Nonviolence and Children,* by Stephanie Judson. J. Lorne Peachey's booklet, *How to Teach Peace to Children,* offers many excellent suggestions also.[1] Here are a few ideas, some original and some gleaned from these books and others, to get you thinking about practical ways to teach children about peace.

First, take a look at your relationships with your children. Do the children feel that they are loved and accepted by you in spite of their faults? Do your words, your tone of voice, and your actions show respect for their unique personhood? Do you work to find ways to affirm them, to

---

[1]Priscilla Prutzman, *The Friendly Classroom for a Small Planet* (Philadelphia: New Society, 1988); Stephanie Judson, ed., *A Manual on Nonviolence and Children* (Philadelphia: Nonviolence and Children Program, Friends Peace Committee, 1977); J. Lorne Peachey, *How to Teach Peace to Children* (Scottdale, Pa: Herald Press, 1981).

build their self-esteem? If your answers to these questions are negative or unsure, then pray that God will help you to be a better example of a peacemaker to your children. Remember that your example as teacher is a very powerful one.

Next, examine how your children relate to one another. As teacher, you cannot enforce loving and selfless behavior in your children at all times, but you can set the tone for cooperating, helping one another, and working together on projects and problems. Encourage sharing of feelings, information, and experiences. Try brainstorming with the children on solutions to conflict other than by physical or verbal violence.

Examine your standards of conduct and your discipline of children. Prime offenses in the group should reflect value placed more strongly on people than on things. Check yourself and what you discipline children for. Does a child get in more trouble with you for knocking over the easel or for calling another child a mean name?

How about the way you dole out praise? Do you praise the child who memorized the Bible verse more highly than the one who shared the crayons?

Check your reward system. Typical "Sunday school" practices such as giving awards or starring charts for attendance, verse memorization, or completed work usually encourage competition instead of cooperation.

Try to weed out competitive games from children's play times by introducing cooperative games instead. See Prutzman's and Judson's books for numerous examples.

Plan for children to learn from people who are or have been involved in peacemaking efforts. Look to your congregation and community for people who

have served God as conscientious objectors, peace marchers/protesters, writers of peace letters to political leaders, etc. Ask them to visit your group to share their experiences.

Involve children at age-appropriate levels in peacemaking efforts. For young ones, this might mean walking with you to drop a peace letter to the president in the church mailbox; older ones might write their own letters. Brainstorm ways that the children can help to promote worldwide peace. I recommend Jim and Kathy McGinnis' *Parenting for Peace and Justice*[2] for ideas on involving children in peace efforts.

Check your church and community libraries for age-appropriate books on the lives of famous peacemakers: Martin Luther King, Johnny Appleseed, Gandhi, etc. Allow for reading time during your session or let the children take the books home to read during the week.

Check the atmosphere created by the physical appearance and set-up of your room. It goes without saying that war toys should be banished from children's rooms. See that the furniture and its arrangement are not conflict-producers. (If the preschool room set-up has the blockbuilding area in a trafficked passageway, you are asking for conflict and you need to rearrange the room.) Decorate with peace-oriented art, photographs, and posters.

I hope you will find these ideas helpful in including biblical and practical teaching on peace as an integral part of children's learning within your church. May the Spirit and your own creativity guide you to develop ideas best suited to the needs of your children. Peace be with you as you teach Jesus' ways of peace to children much in need of them!

[2]James McGinnis and Kathleen McGinnis, *Parenting for Peace and Justice* (Maryknoll, N.Y.: Orbis, 1990).

Chapter Sixteen

Biblical Faith
and the Unborn

Ronald J. Sider

Ronald J. Sider has been one of the leading voices in North America on issues of peace and social justice. His many books—*Rich Christians in an Age of Hunger*[1] being perhaps his signature work—have reflected his passionate devotion to carrying out Christ's agenda for a more just society. He consistently argues that one should use Christ's method of peacemaking while working to achieve justice.

One of the founders of Evangelicals for Social Action, Sider has been a professor at Eastern Baptist Theological Seminary for more than twenty-five years. From his early years as a professor at Messiah College's Philadelphia campus, he has been personally involved in activities to affect Christian change in urban places. His writings aim to arouse Christian conscience in areas where many would prefer to be left uninformed. The next two articles demonstrate his extension of peace concerns to the questions of abortion and economic justice.

In this first selection, he speaks to the question of abortion, which has taxed the American conscience since the *Roe* v. *Wade* decision by the U.S. Supreme Court in 1973. The author acknowledges that the abortion question is emotional. He also admits that he has changed his own stance over time as the implications of the pro-choice position become more recognizably wrong.[2] Finding one's way through this issue is not easy, but in the end it comes down to a question of how people made in the image of God are to be treated.

The article triggers many questions. How should we assess the biblical discussion about abortion? Do hard cases justify the taking of vulnerable life? If the Christian community opposes abortion, then what is it prepared to do to care for the "unwanted and the burdensome" members of the human family? Is not "dehumanizing the other," as abortion advocates do in arguing that the fetus is not a person, the first step in all forms of genocide because it allows

---

[1] Ronald J. Sider, *Rich Christians in an Age of Hunger*, 3rd ed. (Dallas: Word), 1990. The first edition of *Rich Christians* was published in 1974 by InterVarsity Press.

[2] Consult Jean Staker Garton, *Who Broke the Baby?* (Minneapolis: Bethany House, 1998). Garton began her personal journey on this question as a pro-choice advocate. Gradually she came to realize the moral deception in the language and arguments of the movement. She now devotes her energies to helping people see through the language games abortion proponents are using to keep the public from asking the all-important question: Is the fetus human?

people to kill without calling it murder? If so, how will the deformed American conscience on this issue deal with questions about fetal research; infanticide; people who are severely handicapped, mentally ill, elderly, or terminally ill; and the enemies in the time of war?[3]

We can no longer base our ethics on the idea that human beings are a special form of creation, singled out from all other animals, and alone possessing an immortal soul.[4]
—Peter Singer

So God created man in his own image, in the image of God he created him; male and female he created them. Genesis 1:27, RSV.

Two contradictory views about persons struggle for dominance today. For some contemporaries, people are merely complex animals, an accidental product of blind materialistic processes. Self-fulfillment and usefulness to society determine dignity and value. For others, every person is the conscious creation of a loving God and reflects the very image of the Creator of the galaxies. Human dignity, value and worth come not primarily from the state, society or self-actualization but from God as a sheer gift.

The struggle to maintain the historic Christian belief in the inestimable value of every person rages on many fronts —genetic engineering, euthanasia, infanticide, abortion. Here, I focus on abortion.

Protecting the Sancity of the Human Life

For many American Protestants awareness of the abortion issue began in 1973 with the historic decision of the U.S. Supreme Court *Roe* v. *Wade*. This ruling swept aside laws in fifty states limiting the availability of abortions. The court decreed that the state had no "compelling interest" in protecting the unborn child until it was "viable" or "capable of meaningful human life"—in other words, for the first six months or "usually" (according to the court's reckoning) for the first seven months of pregnancy.

Even after "viability," the ruling went, the fetus is not a human being "in the whole sense," and the Fourteenth Amendment's guarantee that life shall not be taken without due process does not apply. A state may not prohibit abortion even at this late stage if the health of the mother is at risk. And the court defined *health* very broadly: health is a medical judgment "exercised in the light of all factors—physical, emotional, familial, and the woman's age—relevant to the well-being of the patient." Even a nine-

---

[3]See the very helpful article by Peter Kreeft, "Human Personhood Begins at Conception," *Journal of Biblical Ethics*, 4, no. 1, (1990): 8–13. Kreeft argues persuasively that Western society went wrong on the issue of abortion because it substituted a functional definition of personhood for the biblical one rooted in the image of God. Once the individual's legal rights in society are based upon a relative judgment of worth rather than a God-conferred status of personhood, no vulnerable person or group is safe in that society.

[4]Peter Singer, "Sanctity of Life or Quality of Life?" *Pediatrics* 72, no. 1 (1983): 129.

This chapter originally appeared as chapter 2 in Ronald J. Sider, *Completely Pro-Life: Building a Consistent Stance on Abortion, the Family, Nuclear Weapons, the Poor* (Downers Grove, Ill.: InterVarsity Press, 1987).

month-old fetus can be sacrificed for the "emotional" health of the mother.[5]

As a result of this ruling, abortion on demand became legal. Each year since then, about 1.5 million abortions have occurred in the United States. How are Christians to respond? First, it is imperative that those of us who feel abortion is a travesty and an affront to God still demonstrate genuine empathy for the dilemmas and anguish of the millions of women who have sought abortions. For any Christian discussion of the topic, we must understand the tormenting options facing the fifteen-year-old whose mistaken choices have produced an unwanted pregnancy that seems to threaten her entire future. Anyone who has sympathetically observed the burdens placed on a family struggling for decades to care for a seriously handicapped child understands how tempting abortion may seem to a couple informed that the fetus may be severely handicapped. How does one tell the victim of rape or incest that she must sacrifice herself for nine long months to nurture the unwanted seed of a vicious aggressor?

Honest struggle with the strength of pro-abortion arguments is also essential for those of us who wish to persuade those who adhere to these arguments. Women have experienced widespread discrimination and oppression for centuries. Their demand, however strident and overstated it may sometimes be, for the freedom to choose whether or not to give birth to a child which will probably impact her life more than that of the (frequently irresponsible) father is understandable. There is a global population problem today. Those overcrowded countries (Japan and China, for example) that have been most successful in quickly slowing their population explosions have adopted abortion as one measure. Whether in America's inner cities or in the slums of Latin America, some poor women already burdened with poverty and several children do seek abortions regardless of what the law or the church says. Many ask, Should we add to their trauma with laws that guarantee that their abortionists will be unqualified hacks in dirty back rooms rather than trained physicians in sanitary settings?

What also seems confusing to many is to notice that religious people, including evangelical Christians, cannot agree on whether the fetus is a fully human being. According to Kenneth Kantzer, former editor of *Christianity Today,* "No Biblical passage speaks of man or fully human life before birth or condemns abortion as murder."[6] A major consultation of evangelicals—including Harold Lindsell, Carl Henry and Harold J. Ockenga—in 1968 issued an Affirmation that said: "As to whether or not the performance of an individual abortion is always sinful, we are not agreed, but about the necessity and permissibility for it under certain circumstances, we are in accord."[7] The Affirmation included "individual health, family welfare, and social responsibility" among values that might warrant an induced abortion.[8] Today many of those at this conference would put the matter differently. But the conference certainly demonstrates the point that there has

---

[5]John T. Noonan Jr., "Raw Judicial Power," *National Review,* March 2, 1973, 261.

[6]Kenneth Kantzer, "The Origin of the Soul as Related to the Abortion Question," in Walter O. Spitzer and Carlyle L. Saylor, *Birth Control and the Christian* (Wheaton, Ill.: Tyndale, 1969), 553.

[7]Walter O. Spitzer and Carlyle L. Saylor, *Birth Control and the Christian,* (Wheaton, Ill.: Tyndale, 1969), xxv.

[8]Ibid., xxvi.

been major disagreement among evangelical Protestants.[9] Carl Henry still considers abortion morally justified in the case of rape, incest and "extreme deformity" of the fetus.[10]

On the other hand, no one except extreme male chauvinists doubt that the pregnant mother is truly a person with full human rights. In light of the uncertainty and disagreement about the status of the fetus as well as the strength of the arguments for abortion, one can understand why many compassionate people of goodwill consider abortion morally acceptable.

A decade ago, I found these arguments conclusive. But troubling doubts and disturbing questions have caused me to change my thinking: Does not the swift, easy transition from abortion to experimentation on fetuses to inappropriately withholding treatment to promotion of euthanasia suggest a dangerous assault on the sacredness of human life? Does not the level of trauma experienced after abortions suggest greater caution? Is the witness of church history irrelevant? And do not both individuals and society frequently support abortion for selfish, irresponsible reasons?

A Slippery Slope?

Is it not likely that permitting abortions also encourages experimenting on fetuses and growing acceptance of policies that withhold treatment from deformed children? Using federal money, a medical school in Los Angeles has conducted experiments on unborn fetuses scheduled for abortion.[11] Others have experimented on live fetuses *after* abortion, placing them in tanks of saline solution.[12] In Europe, according to a report by a research committee of the European Parliament, living aborted fetuses are dissected for research by the cosmetics industry to improve beauty aids.[13]

In a powerful article in the January 1985 issue of the *Atlantic Monthly*, civil libertarian Nat Hentoff reported on examples of what he called "infanticide." Even though many of them can live successful lives, "it is common in the United States to withhold routine surgery and medical care from infants with Down's syndrome [or spina bifida] for the explicit purpose of hastening death."[14] In the October 25, 1973, issue of *The New England Journal of Medicine*, two Yale doctors reported on forty-three babies who died because the doctors withheld treatment. Since these handicapped babies would have placed long-term emotional and financial stress on the parents, parents and doctors chose not to provide available treatment. So they died.[15] Deciding not to undertake extraordinary measures in cases where there is no hope of recovery is one thing. Failing to perform operations that

---

[9]For a recent evangelical defense of abortion in very limited situations, see D. Gareth Jones, *Brave New People* (Grand Rapids: Eerdmans, 1985), chap. 7. See also Lewis Penhall Bird, "Dilemmas in Biomedical Ethics," *Horizons of Science*, ed. Carl F. H. Henry (New York: Harper & Row, 1978), 139ff.

[10]Carl F. H. Henry, *The Christian Mindset in a Secular Society* (Portland, Ore.: Multnomah, 1984), 103.

[11]Curt Young, *The Least of These* (Chicago: Moody Press, 1983), 105; documentation in nn. 8–10.

[12]Maggie Scarf, "The Fetus as Guinea Pig," *New York Times Magazine* 19 (October 1975): 92.

[13]Val Dorgan, "Foetuses Experiments," *Cork Examiner*, August 25, 1983.

[14]Nat Hentoff, "Awful Privacy of Baby Doe," *Atlantic Monthly*, January 1985, 55. See also his "How Can the Left Be against List?" *The Village Voice*, July 16, 1985, 18, 20.

[15]See too the report of a similar situation in Oklahoma in "Early Management and Decision Making for the Treatment of Myefomeningocele," *Pediatrics,* October 1983.

would enable babies to live and enjoy life in spite of severe handicaps is quite another. It is infanticide. Fortunately President Reagan moved to protect handicapped infants in 1983. And the 1984 amendments to the Child Abuse Prevention and Treatment Act require all states receiving federal grants to combat child abuse to make certain that handicapped infants receive available treatment.

Widespread encouragement of euthanasia may not be far away.[16] Some folk call attention to the fact that eleven percent of all Medicare funds support people in the last forty days of their lives and twenty-five percent go to elderly folk in the last year of their lives.[17] On March 27, 1984, Governor Richard Lamm of Colorado suggested in a public speech that terminally ill elderly persons have "a duty to die and get out of the way."[18]

With growing frequency prominent people defend these developments with statements explicitly rejecting the historic Judeo-Christian respect for human life. Nobel prize winner Francis Crick has said: "No newborn infant should be declared human until it has passed certain tests regarding its genetic endowment and...if it fails these tests, it forfeits the right to live."[19] *Newsweek* reported in 1985 that Dr. Virginia Abernathy of Vanderbilt's school of medicine claims that an individual becomes a person only

when he or she becomes a "responsible moral agent—around age three or four in Abernathy's judgement."[20]

To be sure, slippery-slope arguments are treacherous. We dare not reject something good merely because it might theoretically encourage or lead to some danger or abuse. But in light of current practice and far more radical proposals, is it neurotic and irresponsible to ask with civil libertarian Nat Hentoff: "If fetuses have no rights, handicapped infants have no rights, can the aged and infirm be far behind?"[21]

Emotional Cost

Wrenching personal stories and scholarly studies of abortion's psychological costs also urge caution. A study reported in the *Scientific American* found that ninety-two percent of mothers who had abortions on medical grounds later suffered depression.[22] Eighty-two percent of the fathers also experienced depression.[23] In a stream of articles in pro-choice magazines like *Glamour, Mademoiselle* and *Redbook*, women have shared their anguish and guilt.[24]

I am angry at Billie Jean King and Gloria Steinem and every woman who ever had an abortion and didn't tell me about this kind of pain. There is a conspiracy among the sisterhood not to tell each other about guilt and self-hatred

---

[16]See its defense by Joseph Fletcher, *Morals and Medicine* (Princeton, N.J.: Princeton University Press, 1954), 172– 210.

[17]Young, *Least of These,* 132–33.

[18]*Denver Post,* March 28, 1984.

[19]Quoted in Hentoff, "Awful Privacy of Baby Doe," 55.

[20]"American Abortion Dilemma," *Newsweek,* January 14, 1985, 29.

[21]Quoted in ibid.

[22]*Scientific Americans,* June 1980, 42.

[23]Ibid. See also the studies by Arthur Shastak of Drexel University mentioned in Young, *Least of These,* 65–66.

[24]See the references in Young, *Least of These,* 64,. nn. 19–25.

and terror. Having an abortion is not like having a wart removed or your nails done or your hair cut, and anyone who tells you it is is a liar or worse. To decide to have an abortion is to make a life-and-death decision. A part of me is dying too."[25]

In Japan, Buddhist temples attempt to alleviate the pain of grieving mothers. At a cost of $340 to $640 each, they have erected over 10,000 small statues for the aborted. For a fee of $40 to $120, temple priests also contract to pray for the aborted. "We will give the best possible care to the soul of your unborn child." In the first seven years of the program, women paid the temple to pray for 120,000 aborted children.[26]

In a recent article in *Child Psychiatry and Human Development*, Dr. Philip Ney cited a number of studies showing that living children whose mothers had also had abortions suffer trauma. They fear that parental love is conditional: 'The haunted child survives to live in distrust of what may be in store for him."[27] Dr. Ney also found that child abuse is more frequent among mothers who have previously had an abortion.[28] Stanley Hauerwas's poignant question is surely relevant: "How do we tell our children what we are

doing and still make them glad that they are our children?"[29]

Christian History

Christian witness over two millennia presents a third reason for caution. In an important book published by Harvard University Press, John T. Noonan concludes from his survey of church history that fetal life has enjoyed "an almost absolute value in Christian history."[30] Unfortunately, as feminists point out, this historical rejection of abortion was often mixed with an extremely negative attitude toward sex itself. Theologians like St. Augustine attacked both abortion and contraception, insisting that unless the purpose of sexual activity was procreation, it was sinful.[31]

The earliest Christian condemnation of abortion, however, arose for a different reason. In his excellent overview of the early church's unanimous rejection of abortion, *Abortion and the Early Church*, Michael Gorman shows that the reason for this stand was a concern for the fetus. It is true that by the end of the second century, Christians generally believed that contraception was wrong because they thought procreation was the sole purpose of sex. Gorman, however, shows that the church's antiabortion stand came earlier

---

[25]"An anonymous article entitled, "An Apology to a Little Boy I Won't Ever See," *Providence Evening Bulletin,* April 23, 1980. Women Exploited by Abortion (12310 Flamingo Lane, Bowie, MD 20715) is an organization dealing honestly with this trauma.

[26]"Young, *Least of These,* 65.

[27]"Philip G. Ney, "A Consideration of Abortion Survivors," *Child Psychiatry and Human Development* 13, no. 3 (1983): 170. See similar findings in Anita H. and Eugene C. Weiner, "The Aborted Sibling Factor," *Clinical Social Work Journal* 12, no. 3 (1984): 209–15.

[28]Ney, "Abortion Survivors," 172.

[29]Stanley Hauerwas, *A Community of Character* (Notre Dame, Ind.: University of Notre Dame Press, 1981), 211.

[30]"John T. Noonan Jr., "An Almost Absolute Value in History," in John T. Noonan, ed., *The Morality of Abortion: Legal and Historical Perspectives* (Cambridge: Harvard University Press, 1970), 1–59.

[31]"See Beverly Wilding Harrison's fascinating revision of the historical material in *Our Right to Choose: Toward a New Ethic of Abortion* (Boston: Beacon, 1983), 119–86.

than this position on contraception. It is significant that the earliest Christian opposition to abortion arose in Jewish Christian churches with a strong Jewish heritage which did not oppose contraception. Furthermore, they discussed the two issues—contraception and abortion—in different contexts. Early Christian writers usually condemned abortion in sections dealing with violence, murder and infanticide. Contraception, on the other hand, they usually discussed in their treatment of marriage. "Early Christian opposition to abortion, then, did not arise because abortion was seen as a means of interrupting the natural course of sexual relations but because it was viewed as murder."[32] From the early Christian writers on, most Christians over the centuries have condemned abortion.[33] One cannot lightly reject twenty centuries of Christian conviction.

Selfish Motivations

Finally, the selfish, even trivial motivations that lead to some (not all) abortions strengthen growing doubts. Nat Hentoff says he knows women who have chosen to abort because they disliked their fetus's gender![34] The study of sociologist Kristin Luker suggests that economic considerations play a significant role. The typical pro-life activist is a married woman who has three or more children. She does not work outside the home and the family income is $30,000.

The typical pro-choice activist, on the other hand, is a married woman with two children. She works outside the home and the family income is over $50,000.[35] Is abortion justified if a major motivation is the desire to continue enjoying the affluence made possible by two incomes in the family?

In the larger society, too, economic concerns are important. Quietly it is hinted that it is cheaper for society to permit poor women to abort than to expand the welfare rolls. Materials on abortion produced by Planned Parenthood and similar organizations frequently present this argument.[36] Similarly, aborting potentially handicapped fetuses is more convenient than increasing societal funding for services for the handicapped. What some only whisper, an editorial in *The New Republic* was candid enough to say clearly. This editorial admits that abortion is no different from euthanasia, but insists that the social cost of caring for all the aborted fetuses is too high.[37] To what extent is the issue really affluence versus respect for the sanctity of human life?

One can hardly avoid remembering the Nazi defense of genocide, enunciated in 1935 by Arthur Gueth, director of public health in Nazi Germany:

> The ill-conceived "love of thy neighbor" has to disappear, especially in relation to inferior or asocial creatures. It is the supreme duty of a national state

---

[32]Michael J. Gorman, *Abortion and the Early Church: Christian, Jewish, and Pagan Attitudes* (Downers Grove, Ill.: InterVarsity Press, 1982).

[33]Noonan, *Morality of Abortion*, 1–59.

[34]*Newsweek*, January 14, 1985, 29.

[35]Kristin Luker, *Abortion and the Politics of Motherhood* (Berkeley: University of California Press, 1984), 194–97.

[36]See, for example, *Abortion and the Poor: Private Morality, Public Responsibility* (New York: The Alan Guttmacher Institute, 1979), 32.

[37]Norman B. Bendroth, "Abortion and the Third Way of the Kingdom," in *The High Cost of Indifference*, ed. Richard Cizik (Ventura, Calif.: Regal Books, 1953), 58. See the same kind of argument exposed in Hentoff, "Awful Privacy of Baby Doe," 58.

to grant life and livelihood only to the healthy and hereditarily sound portion of the people to secure the maintenance of a hereditarily sound and racially pure folk for all eternity. The life of an individual has meaning only in the light of that ultimate aim, that is in the light of his meaning to his family and to his national state.[38]

Is concern for one's affluent lifestyle any more defendable than purity of the race? Is abortion justified to preserve one's affluence?

Male sexual irresponsibility is also a significant factor in abortions. Linda Bird Francke has shown that the most significant factor in the decision to abort is the relationship with the male partner.[39] According to demographer Judith Blake, the strongest support for legal abortion comes from affluent white men. Feminist theologian Beverly Harrison is probably correct in concluding that this male preference is because many men "value women's greater sexual availability when abortion is legal."[40] But do women make progress by demanding the "freedom" to imitate this selfish male irresponsibility and frivolous approach to sexuality? This is precisely what Harrison does when she argues that apart from elective abortion, women have no moral choice with regard to pregnancy.[41] Vernie Dale rightly debunks the underlying assumption that a woman has no "control over her own body until after a male partner is finished

with it."[42] As Dale insists, female sexual irresponsibility is also a problem. Abstention from intercourse outside marriage is always a possibility—albeit one that Harrison never advocates! Might it not be better to challenge men to fidelity rather than to facilitate their flight from responsibility?

Even more disturbing is the suggestion of Beverly Harrison that "the well-being of a woman and the value of her life plan" matter more than the life of the unborn regardless of the status of the unborn.[43] Harrison postpones her discussion of whether the fetus is truly human until near the end of her book. She does that precisely because she thinks that question—however one answers it!—is less important than the "well-being" and "life plan" of the mother. But what if the fetus is truly a person? Does a woman's "life plan" justify murder?

At its core, as Ginny Earnest Soley points out in a superb article in *Sojourners*, the problem is a secular individualism that makes the self-interest of the individual the highest value."[44] By their sexual irresponsibility and failure to share fairly in the burdens of child care and parenting, many men have placed their individual selfish concerns above the rights of children, women and the larger community. Now in the name of the same destructive, individualistic selfishness, secular feminists demand abortion as part of their right to "reproductive freedom," appealing to that very individualism which has long led

[38]Quoted in James T. Burtchaell, *Rachel Weeping (San* Francisco: Harper & Row, 1984), 159.

[39]Linda Bird Franke, *The Ambivalence of Abortion* (New York: Random House, 1978).

[40]Harrison, *Our Right to Choose*, 163. See p. 256, n. 23 for the research of Judith Blake. Her data come from the sixties and early seventies. See also the discussion of male pressure in *Sojourners,* November 1980, 4–8.

[41]Harrison, *Our Right to Choose*. 195.

[42]*National Catholic Reporter*, February 22, 1985, 10 (italics in original).

[43]Harrison, *Our Right to Choose*, 16.

[44]Ginny Earnest Soley, "To Preserve and Protect Life: A Christian Feminist Perspective on Abortion," *Sojourners*, October 1986, 34–37.

many men to trample on the needs of children and the larger community. The solution surely is for both men and women to abandon secular individualism and refuse to place self above others.

Biblical Teaching

The dignity and worth of every human being flows from divine decree, not human decision.[45] Our essential humanity does not come from government, social interaction or self-actualization. It comes from the Creator of the galaxies who selected human beings alone out of all the created order to bear the divine image (Gen. 1:27). God prohibits murder. It is precisely because the neighbor bears this unique divine stamp that murder is wrong (Gen. 9:6). So precious, indeed, is every person that the Sovereign of history suffered the hell of Roman crucifixion so that whoever believes may live forever in the presence of the living God.

Christians therefore ought to reject every notion that makes human dignity and value depend on some humanly defined quality of life, some individually chosen level of self-fulfillment, or some societally determined level of social usefulness. No matter how poor and defenseless, old and weak, crippled and deformed, young and helpless, human beings enjoy God-given worth and dignity that sets them apart from the rest of creation.

This crucial foundation, however, does not settle the question of abortion. Abortion is wrong only if we ought to act on the assumption that the fetus is truly human. Is that the case?

The Scriptures nowhere explicitly teach that the fetus is a person. At the same time,

there are signs which point in that direction. The Bible very often uses words for the fetus that are normally applied to persons already born (Gen. 25:22; 38:27–30; Job 1:21; 3:3, 11–19; 10:18–19; 31:15; Isa. 44:2, 24; 49:5; Jer. 20:14–18; Hos. 12:3). Thus Luke calls Elizabeth's unborn child a "baby" (*brephos*) (Lk 1:41, 44).

Biblical passages frequently assume significant personal continuity between the unborn and the child after birth (for instance, Ps. 51:5; Jer. 1:5). Psalm 139:13–16 is perhaps the most striking example:

For thou didst form my inward parts,
thou didst knit me together in my mother's womb.
I praise thee, for thou art fearful and wonderful.
Wonderful are thy works!
Thou knowest me right well;
my frame was not hidden from thee,
when I was being made in secret,
intricately wrought in the depths of the earth.
Thy eyes beheld my unformed substance;
in thy book were written, every one of them,
the days that were formed for me,
when as yet there was none of them. (RSV)

The personal pronouns ("Thou didst knit *me* together in *my* mother's womb") indicate that the psalmist assumed that there was a direct link between himself as an adult and the tiny being that God had lovingly watched over in his mother's womb.

We need to be careful, however, not to press the biblical material beyond what it clearly says. Although strongly opposed to abortion, the careful study by the Orthodox Presbyterian Church (OPC) wisely insists that "there is *no way to demonstrate*, either from Scripture or from

---

[45]"If value is something that only human beings confer then the pro-choice point of view must ultimately prevail"—John Garvey, "Who Confers Value?" (*Commonwealth*, August 9, 1985, 424).

[46]"Report of the Committee to Study the Matter of Abortion," in Minutes of the Thirty-Eighth General Assembly, The Orthodox Presbyterian Church (7401 Old York Road, Philadelphia, PA 19126), May 24–29, 1971, 146 (italics in the original). The report will hereafter be cited as OPC Study (1971). So similarly, John Jefferson Davis, *Abortion and the Christian* (Phillipsburg, N.J.: Presbyterian & Reformed, 1984), 61.

science or from some combination of the two, that the unborn child *is* a human person from the point of conception."[46] This study points out that Jeremiah 1:5 uses a personal pronoun for Jeremiah even before conception: "Before I formed you in the womb, I knew you." No one would want to argue that Jeremiah was a person even before his conception![47] Furthermore, as my colleague Professor Tom McDaniel has pointed out to me, the ancient Near East tended to see all reality as personal. Therefore one dare not place too much weight on the personal pronouns here. The OPC document goes on to reject arguments adduced to prove that the fetus is a person based on John the Baptist's leaping in the womb, the Incarnation and Psalm 51:5.[48] We dare not claim that the Bible explicitly teaches that the fetus from conception is a person.

Does the Bible ever suggest the opposite? Does the Bible provide any hint that the unborn child is less than a human being? Some have found this suggestion in Exodus 21:22–24:

> When men strive together, and hurt a woman with child, so that there is a miscarriage, and yet no harm follows, the one who hurt her shall be fined, according as the woman's husband shall lay upon him; and he shall pay as the judges determine. If any harm follows, then you shall give life for life, eye for eye, tooth for tooth, hand for hand, foot for foot, burn for burn, wound for wound, stripe for stripe. (RSV)

This RSV translation (and a majority of commentators) understands this difficult text to mean that if the fetus is killed and a miscarriage follows, the penalty is a mere fine. On the other hand, if the mother is hurt or killed, then the penalty is an eye for eye or a life for a life. Many consequently conclude that the fetus has less value than the mother. Therefore, the fetus is not yet a person and abortion is permissible.[49]

Such an inference does not follow, however, even if one accepts the RSV translation. The text talks only about accidental killing. Furthermore, even accidental killing of the unborn is punished. Surely intentional destruction of the unborn would merit more severe punishment. "How can we defend the *intentional* destruction of the unborn on the basis of a passage which condemns even its *accidental* destruction?[50]

Furthermore, the absence of the death penalty for the accidental killing of the fetus does not mean the fetus is not seen as a person. The Mosaic Law did not normally prescribe a mandatory death penalty for accidental killing (Ex. 21:13–14, 20–21).

Substantial considerations, furthermore, suggest that the RSV translation may be wrong. There is no linguistic basis for arguing that Exodus 21:22 refers to a miscarriage. The literal meaning of the Hebrew is simply, "Her children came out." The noun in the singular is *yeled*, which is the normal word for "child." The

---

[47]OPC Study (1971), 146.

[48]Ibid., 146–48.

[49]See, for instance, Bruce Waltke, "The Old Testament and Birth Control," *Christianity Today,* November 8, 1963, 3. (Waltke has subsequently revised his position); and the many commentaries and translations mentioned in Jack Cottrell, "Abortion and the Mosaic Law," *Christianity Today,* March 16, 1973, 7. Also Harrison, *Our Right to Choose,* 68–69. Extrabiblical material from the Code of Hammurabi has influenced the RSV translation. Sections 209–14 discuss the penalty for striking a pregnant woman and assign a modest fine when a miscarriage results and a heavy fine when death to the mother occurs. See James Bennett Pritchard, *Ancient Near Eastern Texts Relating to the Old Testament,* 2nd ed. (Princeton, N.J.: Princeton University Press, 1955), 175.

[50]OPC Study (1971), 141 (italics in original).

verb (*yatza'*) means "to go out." This verb is very often employed to refer to the ordinary birth of a normal child and is not used elsewhere in the Bible to refer to a miscarriage.[51]

The translation in the New International Version is probably better:

> If men who are fighting hit a pregnant woman and she gives birth prematurely but there is no serious injury, the offender must be fined whatever the woman's husband demands and the court allows. But if there is serious injury, you are to take life for life, eye for eye, tooth for tooth, hand for hand, foot for foot. (Ex. 21:22–24)

In the first case the physical contact results in a premature birth, but baby and mother live. The fine is for the trauma of the dangerous, premature birth.[52] In the second case, if either the baby or the mother suffers harm, an equivalent penalty is exacted.

Neither this nor the previous reading of Exodus 21:22–24 suggests that the fetus is less than a person. In fact, nowhere in the Bible is there any hint that the unborn child is less than a human person from the moment of conception.

One other consideration is important. We need to ask about the relevance of the scientific fact that from the moment of conception a genetically distinct human being exists.[53] Nowhere has this fact been put more bluntly than in a pro-abortion editorial in *California Medicine*, the official journal of the California Medical Association:

> Since the old ethic [the traditional Christian viewpoint] has not been fully displaced, it has been necessary to separate the idea of abortion from the idea of killing, which continues to be socially abhorrent. The result has been a curious avoidance of the scientific fact, which everyone really knows, that human life begins at conception and is continuous whether intra- or extrauterine until death. The very considerable semantic gymnastics which are required to rationalize abortion as anything but taking human life would be ludicrous if they were not often put forth under socially impeccable auspices.[54]

Mere biological continuity by itself, of course, tells us nothing about whether the *imago dei* is truly present. But it does become relevant and significant when one remembers the scriptural understanding of the person as a body-soul unity. The prestigious German scholar Gerhard von Rad points out that the biblical teaching that persons possess the image (*tselem*) and likeness (*demuth*) of God "refers to the whole man and do[es] not relate solely to his spiritual and intellectual being."[55] Oliver O'Donovan, now Regius Professor at Ox-

[51]See the argument in Cottrell, "Abortion and the Mosaic Law," 8; the OPC Study (1971), 142–43; and Davis, *Abortion and the Christian,* 49–52; John Warwick Montgomery, *Slaughter of the Innocents* (Westchester. Ill.: Crossway , 1981), 98–101; C. F. Deil and Franz Delitsch, *Biblical Commentary on the Old Testament: The Pentateuch,* vol. 2, trans. James Martin (Grand Rapids: Eerdmans, n.d.), 134–35; and the Jewish scholar Umberto Cassuto, *Commentary on the Book of Exodus,* trans. Israel Abrahams (Jerusalem: Magnes Press, Hebrew University, 1967), 275.

[52]It should be noted, however, that the word *prematurely* in the NIV translation is not in the Hebrew text of Exodus 21:22. Both the NIV and the RSV are, to some extent, interpretations.

[53]See Oliver O'Donovan's discussion of the exception, namely, identical twins, in *The Christian and the Unborn Child,* 2nd ed. (Bramcote, Nottinghamshire, England: Grove Books, 1975), 12–13.

[54]*California Medicine* 113, no. 3 (1979), quoted in Davis. *Abortion and the Christian,* 22.

[55]Gerhard von Rad, *Old Testament Theology,* vol. 1, trans. D. Stalker (New York: Harper & Row, 1962), 145. See the discussion in Davis, 52–54.

154 A Peace Reader

ford, rightly objects to the way this body-soul unity is ignored when the question of abortion arises: "In a period when the most orthodox of current orthodoxies in theological anthropology has been that the Bible teaches 'body-soul unity,' it is ironical that Christians should have allowed their view of the fetal soul to drift upon a sea of speculation without seeking anchorage in any account of the fetal body."[56]

The Bible teaches that each person is a body-soul unity. Science tells us that from conception there exists a genetically distinct human being with a continuous biological development. Surely the most responsible conclusion is that we ought to act on the assumption that from conception the developing fetus is truly a human being made in the image of the Creator.

To be sure, there is no explicit biblical teaching that unambiguously asserts such a view. But not a word in the Scriptures suggests the contrary. Much in the Bible tends to point in this direction. If we remain agnostic, uncertain when the developing fetus becomes truly human, we have no choice but to adopt this working assumption. If there is any serious possibility that we are dealing with human beings, we must reject abortion. To do otherwise would be like shooting blindly into a darkened theater with the justification that we cannot know whether we will hit empty seats or murder innocent people.[57]

Christians then should conclude that from the moment of conception we must act on the assumption that we are dealing with persons created in God's image. Choosing to end the life of innocent persons is wrong. It is murder. Abortion, therefore, is wrong except when the physical life of the mother is threatened (for instance, tubal pregnancy or cancer of the uterus).

But that conclusion involves some wrenching, problematic cases. What about the population explosion or the mental health of the mother? Or the much harder cases of serious deformity, rape and incest?

Hard Cases

Although sometimes exaggerated, overpopulation is a genuine problem today. It is essential that countries like Mexico and India slow down their population explosions. Abortion has played a significant role in the reduced growth rates already achieved in places like China and Japan.

But murder is not an acceptable way to solve population problems. If abortion is acceptable as a policy for population control, so is killing young children. Surely Paul Ramsey is correct that any argument for abortion that also justifies infanticide is clearly wrong.[58] Abortion is an unacceptable form of birth control.[59] Increased research on nonabortive birth-control techniques is therefore essential.

Would an apparent danger to the mental life of the mother justify abortion? As a matter of fact, the scientific evidence seems to suggest that abortion seldom if

---

[56]O'Donovan, *Christian and the Unborn Child,* 11.

[57]See O'Donovan's comment on this in ibid., 5. Albert Outler echoes this opinion: "If it is only *probable* that a fetus is a human being...then we would do better to recognize abortion as a moral evil in every case and thus, even when chosen, a tragic option of what has been judged to be the lesser of two real evils."—"The Beginning of Personhood," *Perkins School of Theology Journal* 68 (June 1971): 32 (italics in original).

[58]Paul Ramsey, "Abortion, a Review Article," *Thomist* 37 (1973): 174ff.

[59]See Harrison's insistence that it is and ought to be a major method of birth control in, for example, *Right to Choose,* 42, 162.

[60]See Davis, *Abortion and the Christian,* 30–31 and studies cited in nn. 22–27.

ever improves the mental health of the mother.[60]

But if it did, would it be morally justified? Not if the unborn is treated as truly human. We would not endorse killing a one-year-old child or an elderly parent merely because caring for either created severe emotional strain or even the threat of suicide.

> Let us imagine a daughter caring for a difficult, but not senile, mother in an area where neither Social Services nor neighbors were available to help her bear the load. The doctor judges that the daughter is heading for a major, and permanent, breakdown, and sees no way of avoiding it short of killing the mother. If we valued mental health equivalently to human life we might feel able to advise him to take that drastic step (provided that he could get away with it). This is a conclusion from which most of us would shrink. In the last resort it is hard to accept that mental health or physical health or any *social* good is a value quite equivalent to human life.[61]

Christian ethics cannot accept abortion for reasons of "psychological health."

What about deformed fetuses? That wrenching dilemmas lie behind this question is painfully clear to anyone who has observed parents with severely deformed children. Nor are the social costs of care for the handicapped negligible. But can a society morally decide to eliminate persons because their care would be inconvenient or costly? Does greater affluence matter more than human beings?

And if it is permissible to kill deformed fetuses, why is it not equally acceptable to kill those who are normal at birth but subsequently become seriously handicapped? "And what will prevent us from enlarging our definition of 'deformity' as a pretext for eliminating all 'undesirables' from society?"[62] Nazi-type social experiments and genocide lurk down this road.

Pregnancies resulting from rape and incest pose perhaps the most wrenching dilemmas of all. Anyone with a beloved daughter senses the agony of nine months of pregnancy for a rapist's vicious violation. Anyone sensitive to the long history of male abuse of women in both rape and incest feels the strength of the case for abortion in such situations. On the other hand, one dare not forget cases like that of the famous gospel singer Ethel Waters, whose life resulted from the rape of her mother at the age of thirteen.[63]

Most crucial, however, is the fact that the unborn child is also a human being created in God's image. When we weigh the shame, pain and inconvenience of the mother against the life of the unborn, how can abortion be acceptable? We dare not kill one human being because someone else has done wrong. Certainly redoubled efforts to provide loving care for women in such agonizing dilemmas is essential. So is a much more vigorous attack on male exploitation and abuse. But murder of the innocent is not the solution.

I conclude that abortion is morally acceptable only in the very exceptional cases when the physical life of the mother is threatened. What programs and policies in church and society should we then promote?

---

[61]O'Donovan, *Christian and the Unborn Child*, 19.

[62]OPC Study (1971), 153.

[63]Ethel Waters with Charles Samuels, *His Eye Is on the Sparrow* (Garden City, N.Y.: Doubleday, 1951), 3–4.

Peacemaking and Economics

Ronald J. Sider

In this second article Ronald Sider seeks to make North Americans aware of how their government's foreign policy, especially in supporting American business, often injures the poor in underdeveloped countries. One does not need to shoulder a gun to betray Christ's message of peace. One can harm and kill simply by allowing agents of his/her country to pursue profits while neglecting the welfare of those who supply them goods in overseas markets. A theology of peace must include many issues beyond the narrow scope of military service.

While the statistics and illustrations reflect the article's publication a generation ago, the basic issues still remain the same. What responsibility rests upon the Christian community to be informed about justice issues that they are implicated in by virtue of national policy? How might the church be involved in addressing such issues? And what alternatives are there for Christian action when their political leaders do not heed the voice of Christian concern?

Probably few people reading this book will have killed another person. Many would choose going to jail rather than going to war. But joining the army is not the only way to participate in murder. Established economic structures can destroy people by the millions. Slavery did that. Child labor did that. Both were as legal as they were lethal. Legal structures can be violent. Therefore we must face a very painful question: Do we participate in economic structures that help destroy millions of people each year?

The story of the sugar we stir into our coffee or tea suggests an answer. The largest sugar mill in the world is in the Dominican Republic.[1] A U.S.-based multinational corporation, Gulf and Western, bought that sugar plant and huge sugar plantations shortly after

---

[1]See the extensive supporting documentation for the superb twenty-minute filmstrip, "Guess Who's Coming to Breakfast," available from the Packard Manse Media Project, Box 150, Stoughton, MA 02072.

This chapter originally appeared as chapter 3 in *Christ and Violence*, by Ronald J. Sider (Scottdale, Pa.: Herald, 1979). It summarizes sections from chapters 6–9 in *Rich Christians in an Age of Hunger: A Biblical Study* (Downers Gover, Ill.: InterVarsity Press, 1977). The statistical material cited here is documented in those chapters.

President Johnson sent the U.S. marines into the Dominican Republic in 1965 to protect U.S. investments there. In the last twenty years, the amount of land used for growing sugar cane has doubled. But almost all of that sugar goes for export to us and other rich nations. In the last twenty years, the per capita production of food, excluding sugar, in the Dominican Republic has decreased. Over 50 percent of the people in the Dominican Republic are starving or malnourished, and 50 percent of the children die before they reach the age of five largely because they do not have enough food.

Not even the Dominicans who work on the sugar plantations have profited. The sugar plantation workers earned less in real wages in 1978 than they did in 1968—in part because the Dominican government installed by U.S. marines has destroyed the cane cutters' labor union. The U.S. has invested more money per capita for police training in the Dominican Republic than in any other Latin American country. And those police have made widespread use of torture to suppress any opposition to the dictatorship which ruled for over a decade. Fortunately that government was replaced in 1978, thanks in part to President Carter's vigorous support of the results of an election which the armed forces wanted to annul. But that former government has made it possible for Gulf and Western to use a vast part of the country's best land to grow sugar for you and me at a handsome profit to the company.

Now who is responsible for the thousands of Dominican children who die each year of malnutrition? Just the top leaders at Gulf and Western? Just the Dominican Republic's elite who profit by cooperating with Gulf and Western? Or are you and I also implicated?

Jacques Ellul has pointed out that unjust economic systems can be as violent as rampaging armies: "I maintain that all kinds of violence are the same...the violence of the soldier who kills, the revolutionary who assassinates; it is true also of economic violence—the violence of the privileged proprietor against his workers, of the 'haves' against the 'have-nots'; the violence done in international economic relations between our societies and those of the third world; the violence done through powerful corporations which exploit the resources of a country that is unable to defend itself."[2] One can only agree with James Douglass:

> In the contemporary world of affluence and poverty, where man's major crime is murder by privilege, revolution against the established order is the criterion of a living faith....Truly I say to you, as you did it not to one of the least of these, you did it not to me (Matt. 25:45). The murder of Christ continues. Great societies build on dying men.[3]

In the last 50 years, especially the last 20, the Brethren in Christ, the Church of the Brethren, and the Mennonites have moved more and more into the economic mainstream of our society. Therefore, if we look carefully at present economic structures, we are forced to the conclusion that we are involved in murder by privilege. Unfortunately it is not true that our society's wealth is simply the result of God's blessing and hard work. To a significant extent, our affluence depends on unjust economic structures that make us rich and Latin Americans hungry. Fully *one-half* of all the cultivable land in Central America is used to grow export

---

[2] Jacques Ellul, *Violence* (New York: Seabury, 1969), 97.

[3] James Douglass, *The Non-Violent Cross: A Theology of Revolution and Peace* (New York: Macmillan, 1966), 285.

crops (sugar, coffee, bananas, flowers, and the like) to sell to the U.S., Canada, and other rich nations. That land ought to be used to grow food for the masses in Central America where 60 percent of the children die of malnutrition before they are five years old. But it is used to grow sugar and coffee and bananas for North Americans because we can pay for it and the starving children's parents cannot.

By the economic lifestyles we adopt, the economic structures that support those lifestyles and the politicians we elect (either by our votes or nonparticipation) to protect those structures, we participate in murder by privilege.

For Historic Peace Churches, that is a very painful situation to face. But if we are serious about our heritage of peacemaking, then we must explore more carefully than we have thus far how economic systems kill people just as surely as do guns and bombs.

I will explore the problem of institutionalized violence or structural sin in three steps. First, what is the biblical teaching on institutionalized violence? Second, how are we involved in it today? And third, what can we do about it?

There is an important difference between consciously willed, individual acts (like lying to a friend or committing an act of adultery) and participation in evil social structures. Slavery is an example of the latter. So is the Victorian factory system where ten-year-old children worked twelve to sixteen hours a day. Although both slavery and child labor were legal, they destroyed people by the millions. They represent institutionalized violence or structural evil. Tragically, most Christians seem to be more concerned with individual sinful acts than with participation in violent social structures.

But the Bible condemns both. Speaking through His prophet Amos, the Lord declared,

> For three transgressions of Israel,
> > and for four, I will not revoke the punishment;
> because they sell the righteous for silver,
> > and the needy for a pair of shoes—
> they that trample the head of the poor into the dust of the earth,
> > and turn aside the way of the afflicted;
> a man and his father go in to the same maiden,
> > so that my holy name is profaned.
> > > *(Amos 2:6–7, RSV)*

Biblical scholars have shown that some kind of legal fiction underlies the phrase "selling the needy for a pair of shoes." This mistreatment of the poor was *legal!* In one breath God condemns both adultery and legalized oppression of the poor. Sexual sins and economic injustice are equally displeasing to God.

Some young activists have supposed that as long as they were fighting for the rights of minorities and opposing militarism, they were morally righteous regardless of how often they shacked up for the night with a guy or a girl in the movement. Some of their elders, on the other hand, have supposed that because they did not lie, steal, and fornicate, they were morally upright even though they lived in segregated communities and owned stock in companies that exploit the poor of the earth. God, however, has shown that robbing one's workers of a fair wage is just as sinful as robbing a bank.

God clearly revealed that laws themselves are sometimes an abomination to him.

> Can wicked rulers be allied with thee,
> > who frame mischief by statute?
> They band together against the life of the righteous,
> > and condemn the innocent to death.
> But the LORD has become my stronghold,
> > and my God the rock of my refuge.
> He will bring back on them their iniquity
> > and wipe them out for their wickedness;
> the LORD our God will wipe them out.
> > > *(Psa. 94:20–23, RSV)*

The Jerusalem Bible translates verse 20 this way: 'You never consent to that corrupt tribunal that imposes disorder as law." God wants us to know that wicked governments "frame mischief by statute." Or, as the New English Bible puts it, they contrive evil "under cover of law."

God proclaims the same word through the prophet Isaiah:

Woe to those who decree iniquitous decrees,
*   and the writers who keep writing oppression,*
to turn aside the needy from justice
*   and to rob the poor of my people of their right*
                    (Isa. 10:1–4)

It is quite possible to make oppression legal. But legalized oppression is an abomination to our God. Therefore, He commands His people to oppose it.

There is one other aspect to institutionalized violence or structural evil which makes it especially pernicious. It is so subtle that one can be ensnared almost without realizing it.

God inspired His prophet Amos to utter some of the harshest words in Scripture against the cultured, kind, upper-class women of his day:

Hear this word, you cows of Bashan…
who oppress the poor, who crush the needy,
*   who say to…[your] husbands, "Bring, that we*
*   may drink!"*
The LORD God has sworn by his holiness
*   that, behold, the days are coming upon you,*
when they shall take you away with hooks,
*   even the last of you with fishhooks.*
                    (Amos 4:1–2)

The women involved probably had no contact with the impoverished peasants. They may never have realized clearly that their gorgeous clothes and spirited parties were possible only because of the sweat and tears of toiling peasants. In fact, they may even have been kind to individual peasants they met. (Perhaps they gave them "Christmas baskets"—once a year.) But God called these privileged women cows because they profited from structural evil. Hence they were personally and individually guilty before God.

We must conclude, I think, that if we are members of a privileged class that profits from structural violence and if we do nothing to try to change things, then we stand guilty before God. Structural evil is just as sinful as personal evil. And it hurts more people and is more subtle.

With this biblical teaching on structural evil or institutionalized violence in mind, we can now ask the second question: Are we involved in structural violence today? Three areas deserve attention: international trade, our consumption of nonrenewable natural resources, and our eating patterns.

First, the patterns of international trade. The industrialized nations have carefully shaped the patterns of international trade for their own economic advantage. Tariff and other import restrictions are one part of the injustice in international trade. The United States charges the highest tariffs on processed and manufactured goods from poor countries. The less manufacturing and processing done by the poor country, the lower the tariff. The reason is simple. Entrenched processing and manufacturing interests (both labor and management) want the United States to be able to buy cheap raw materials and profit from processing and manufacturing them here. The result, unfortunately, is to deprive poor countries of millions of extra jobs and billions of extra dollars from increased exports.

Even more serious is the fact that for decades the prices of primary products sold by developing nations have been declining relative to the prices of manufactured products and other high technology items which poor countries must buy from developed nations. The following examples illustrate the effect.

The government of Tanzania reports that one tractor cost five tons of sisal in 1963. In 1970 the same tractor cost 10 tons of sisal. In 1960 a rubber exporting country could purchase six tractors with twenty-five tons of rubber. In 1975 the same amount of rubber would only buy two tractors. One could present many more examples that the present patterns of international trade are fundamentally unjust.

Second, we are involved in structural violence in our consumption of nonrenewable natural resources. Is it just for 5 percent of the world's people living in the United States to consume approximately 33 percent of the world's limited, nonrenewable energy and minerals each year?

Third, our eating patterns. At first glance our eating patterns may seem very personal and private. But they are tightly interlocked with complex economic structures—national and international agricultural policies and decisions of multinational corporations engaged in agribusiness.

The rich nations import far more food from poor nations than they export to them. Poor developing nations are feeding the affluent minority! Astonishingly, since 1955, every year the rich, developed nations imported approximately twice as many dollars' worth of food from poor, developing nations as they exported to them.

But what about us? The U.S. exports more than it imports. But the situation looks startlingly different when one examines only U.S. food imports from and exports to poor, developing nations. Every year the United States imports more food from poor nations than it exports to hungry lands!

The United States imports about twice as much fish (most of it primarily for feed for livestock) as do all the poor countries combined. Two-thirds of the total world catch of tuna comes to the United States—and we feed one-third of that to our cats.

Cowboys and beef cattle are part of our national self-identity. Surely our beef at least is all grown at home. By no means! The United States is the world's largest importer of beef! Imported beef comes not just from Australia and New Zealand, but also from many countries in Latin America, where at least 40 percent of the people are seriously malnourished. Nor is the problem merely that we consume beef that hungry Latin American children need. Our demand for beef also encourages unjust structures in Latin America.

Take the example of Honduras. Honduras is a poor Central American country where one-third of the people earn less than thirty dollars a year. In spite of widespread poverty they export some 34.8 million pounds of beef to the United States each year. Beef for export is grown largely by a tiny wealthy elite of 667 families (.3 percent of the total population) who own 27.4 percent of all cultivable land.

In the last few years an intense struggle has raged in Honduras. The poor peasants want more land while predictably the powerful Honduran Cattle Farmers' Federation, which represents the wealthy farmers, objects. The wealthy farmers want to continue growing beef for Americans.

The infant mortality rate in Honduras is six times that of the United States. The World Bank indicates that malnutrition is either the primary cause or a major contributor to the death of 50–75 percent of all one-to-four-year-old children who die in Latin America. Who is responsible for those dying children? The wealthy Hondurans who want to protect their affluence? The American companies and the U.S. government that work closely with the Honduran elite? We who eat the beef needed by hundreds of thousands of hungry children in Honduras?

We dare not, of course, make the simplistic assumption that if we merely stop eating beef, hungry Hondurans will promptly enjoy it. Complex economic and political changes are required. The point here is that our eating patterns are interlocked with destructive social and economic structures that leave millions hungry and starving.

We are all implicated in structural evil. The patterns of international trade are unjust. An affluent minority devours most of the earth's nonrenewable natural resources. And the food consumption patterns in the world are grossly lopsided. Every North American benefits from these structural injustices. Unless you have retreated to some isolated valley and grow or make everything you use, you participate in unjust structures which contribute directly to the hunger of a billion unhappy neighbors.

But that is not God's last word to us. If there were no hope of forgiveness, admission of our complicity in guilt of this magnitude would be an act of despair. But there is hope—if we repent.

Thus far I have analyzed the problem and suggested that we need to repent of our sinful involvement in the institutionalized violence in our international economic order. But biblical repentance is not just a liturgical confession or a hasty fear. It is a whole new outlook and a radically new way of living. How then should we change?

We need change at three levels: (1) our personal lifestyles, (2) the church, and (3) secular society. In each case, the goal is peacemaking. More simple personal lifestyles will help us consume a less unfair share of the world's resources. More simple personal lifestyles will also free up time and resources to help end hunger and injustice in the world. Dramatic new forms of sharing in the one worldwide body of Christ would provide a new model for our global village dangerously divided between rich and poor. And structural change that would eliminate some of the systemic causes of hunger and poverty would also improve the chances of peace in our world. Senator Mark Hatfield has said: "The greatest threat to the stability of the entire world is hunger. It's more explosive than all the atomic weaponry possessed by the big powers. Desperate people do desperate things." If he is correct, then peacemaking through economic change in ourselves, the church, and secular society is one of the most pressing tasks today. Three areas call for attention.

First we need to pursue simpler personal lifestyles. As the Catholic saint Elizabeth Seton has said, "The rich must live more simply that the poor may simply live." But that is very hard in our consumer-oriented, materialistic society. We have been enticed by unprecedented material luxury. Advertising constantly convinces us that we really need one unnecessary luxury after another.

The standard of living is the god of twentieth-century America, and the ad man is its prophet. We Christians need to make some dramatic, concrete moves to escape the materialism that seeps into our minds via the diabolically clever and incessant radio and television commercials.

The graduated tithe is one very modest proposal which can help break this materialistic stranglehold. I share it because it has proved helpful in our family.

When Arbutus and I decided to adopt a graduated scale for our giving in 1969, we started by sitting down and trying to calculate honestly what we would need to live for a year. We wanted a figure that would permit reasonable comfort but not all the luxuries. Somehow we arrived at a figure of $7,000. (Two growing boys and a new daughter have recently raised it to $8,000.) We decided to continue giving a tithe of 10 percent on this basic amount. Then for every additional thousand dollars of income above that basic amount, we decided to increase our giving by 5 percent on that $1000.

The graduated tithe is only one model. There are many others such as communal living and living at the level of welfare recipients. They all raise tough theoretical questions and even tougher practical questions when you try to implement them. But the basic question is really whether we will dare to measure our lifestyles by the needs of the poor rather than by the practices of our affluent neighbors.

My second set of proposals pertains to the church. I want to suggest two theses: (1) without new forms which help us recapture the early church's powerful experience of community in Christ's body, it will be impossible to implement biblical teaching on our relationship toward the poor; and (2) it is a farce to ask Washington to legislate what the church refuses to live.

The church should consist of communities of loving defiance. Instead it consists largely of comfortable clubs of conformity. A far-reaching reformation of the church is a prerequisite if the church today is to commit itself to Jesus' mission of liberating the oppressed.

The God of the Bible is calling Christians today to live in fundamental nonconformity to contemporary society. Affluent North American society is obsessed with materialism, sex, economic success, and military might. Things are more important than persons. Job security and an annual salary increase matter more than starving children and oppressed peasants. Paul's warning to the Romans is especially pertinent today: "Don't let the world around you squeeze you into its own mold (Rom. 12:2; PHILLIPS). Biblical revelation summons us to defy many of the basic values of our materialistic, adulterous society.

But that is impossible! At least for isolated individuals. It is simply not possible for isolated believers to resist the anti-Christian values which pour forth from our radios, TVs, and billboards. Tragically, affluent church buildings and ecclesiastical lifestyles subtly reinforce the same sinful values of our secular society. The values of our affluent society seep slowly and subtly into our hearts and minds. The only way to defy them is to immerse ourselves so deeply in Christian fellowship that God can fundamentally remold our thinking as we find our primary identity with other brothers and sisters in Christ who are also unconditionally committed to biblical values.

Christian fellowship means unconditional availability to and unlimited liability for the other sisters and brothers—emotionally, financially, and spiritually. In the early church, when one member suffered, they all suffered. When one rejoiced, they all rejoiced (1 Cor. 12:26). When a person or church experienced economic trouble, the others shared without reservation. And when a brother or sister fell into sin, the others gently restored the straying person. The sisters and brothers were available to each other, liable for each other, and accountable to each other.

According to the New Testament, being part of Christ's body means being unconditionally available and totally liable for the other sisters and brothers. The problem is that churches in North America are not structured to help us do that.

I think we need to break down large congregations of more than 100 persons into small weekly home meetings of 15–25 people. All the small groups should still come together once a week for a common service of teaching, celebration, and worship, but the heart of the church should be the small home meetings.

It is in that kind of setting—and perhaps only in that kind of setting—that the church today will be able to forge a faithful lifestyle for Christians in an Age of Hunger. In small house-church settings, brothers and sisters can challenge each others' affluent lifestyles. They can discuss family finances and evaluate each others' annual budgets. Larger purchases (like houses, cars, and long vacations) can be evaluated honestly in terms of the needs of both the individuals involved and God's poor around the world. Tips for simple living can be shared. Voting patterns that liberate the poor, jobs that are ecologically responsible, charitable donations that build self-reliance among the oppressed and direct action campaigns that successfully challenge unjust multinational corporations—these and many other issues can be discussed openly and honestly by persons who have pledged themselves to be brothers and sisters in Christ to each other.

My second proposal on the church begins with the assumption that it is a tragic farce for the church to ask Washington to legislate what it cannot persuade Christians to live.

If we had time to examine what the Bible says about economic relationships among the people of God, we would discover that over and over again God specifically commanded His people to live together in community in such a way that they would avoid extremes of wealth and poverty—that is the point of the Old Testament legislation on the Jubilee, the Sabbatical Year, tithing, gleaning, and loans. Jesus, our only perfect model, shared a common purse with the new community of His disciples. The first church in Jerusalem and Paul in his collection were implementing what the Old Testament and Jesus had commanded. Compare that with the contemporary church.

Present economic relationships in the worldwide body of Christ are unbiblical, sinful, a hindrance to evangelism, and a desecration of the body and blood of Jesus Christ. The dollar value of the food North Americans throw in the garbage each year equals about one-fifth of the total annual income of Africa's 120 million Christians. It is a sinful abomination for a small fraction of the world's Christians living in the Northern Hemisphere to grow richer year by year while our brothers and sisters in Christ in the Third World ache and suffer for lack of minimal health care, minimal education, and even—in thousands and thousands of cases—just enough food to escape starvation.

We are like the rich Corinthian Christians who feasted without sharing their food with the poor members of the church (1 Cor. 11:20–29). Like them we fail today to discern the reality of the one worldwide body of Christ. The tragic consequence is that we profane the body and blood of the Lord Jesus we worship. Christians in the United States spent $5.7 billion on new church construction alone in the six years from 1967 to 1972. Would we go on building lavishly furnished expensive church plants and adding air conditioning, new rugs, and organs if members of our congregation were starving?

Churches need to adopt more simple corporate lifestyles. Virtually all church construction today is unnecessary. Four large congregations could share every church building if one group would worship on Friday evening, two on Sunday morning, and one on Sunday evening (the four congregations of Dallas' Fellowship Bible Church do that). Significantly simpler personal and ecclesiastical lifestyles would make assistance for economic development possible on an astonishingly increased scale.

We have seen that an Age of Hunger demands simplicity both in our personal lives and in our churches. But compassion and simple living apart from structural change in secular society may be little more than a gloriously irrelevant ego-trip or the proud pursuit of personal purity.

Eating less beef or even becoming a vegetarian will not necessarily feed one starving child. If millions of Americans reduce their beef consumption, but do not act politically to change public policy, the result will not necessarily be less starvation in the Third World.

Now, of course, if Christian churches live more simply and give some of the money saved to agencies promoting rural development in poor nations, then the result will be significantly less hunger. But at the same time that we change the lifestyle of our families and our churches, we must also seek justice in the public arena. Our Age of Hunger demands structural change.

I am aware that this is an exceedingly complex subject, and I don't pretend to be an expert in international economics. But a few things are becoming rather clear. Present patterns of international trade need to be changed. Industrialized nations should lower import restrictions on manufactured goods from poor nations. The U.S. ought to take the lead in establishing a large international grain reserve. The U.S. ought to expand its economic assistance (given through multilateral channels like the U.N.) for agricultural development among the poorest billion in our world. In 1949 at the height of the Marshall plan, the U.S. gave 2.79 percent of GNP in foreign aid. Today we are twice as rich but we give only .25 percent—only one-eleventh as large a percentage!

Who would profit from such changes? Tragically, many Third World countries are ruled by wealthy elites who use their limited foreign exchange to buy luxury goods from the developed world. But that does not mean that we can wash our hands of the whole problem. Many of these governments remain in power because they receive massive military aid and diplomatic support from the United States and other industrial nations. The United States has trained large numbers of police who have tortured thousands of people working for social justice in countries like Chile and Brazil. Multinational corporations in the United States work very closely with the repressive governments. Events in Brazil and Chile demonstrate that the United States will support dictatorships that use torture and do little for the poorest one-half as long as these regimes are friendly to U.S. investments.

What can be done? U.S. citizens must demand a drastic reorientation of U.S. foreign policy. We must demand a foreign policy that unequivocally sides with the poor. If we believe that "all men are created equal," then our foreign policy must be redesigned to promote the interests of all people and not just the wealthy elites in developing countries and our own multinational corporations. We should use our economic and diplomatic power to push for change in Third World dictatorships, especially those like Brazil and Chile that make widespread use of torture. We should insist that foreign aid go only to countries seriously committed to improving the lot of the poorest portions of the population. We should openly encourage nonviolent movements working for structural change in developing countries. U.S. foreign policy ought to encourage justice rather than injustice. Only then will proposed changes in international trade and foreign aid actually improve the lot of the poorest billion.

These questions are uncomfortable and upsetting. I sometimes wish that discipleship and peacemaking had less to do with my economic lifestyle and the economics of affluent Western nations. But they do intersect. So I am forced to make up my mind on two simple interrelated questions: Do I really believe that Jesus is Lord? Do I want to fall into theological liberalism?

Our most fundamental Christian confession is that Jesus is Lord. But He won't be Lord of our family life and allow radio and TV commercials to be Lord of our family budget and multinational corporations to be Lord of our business practices. If Jesus is our Lord, then He must be Lord of our business practices, our economic lifestyle, Lord of our entire life.

The Historic Peace Churches are a biblical people who have opposed theological liberalism. But still I'm afraid that we are in danger of falling into theological liberalism today. We usually think of theological liberalism in connection with issues like the bodily resurrection and the deity of Jesus Christ. And that is correct. Theological liberals have fallen into terrible heresy in recent times by rejecting those basic doctrines of historic Christianity. But notice why that happened. Modern people became so impressed with modern science that they thought they could no longer believe in the miraculous. So they discarded the supernatural aspects of Christianity and abandoned the resurrection and the divinity of Christ.[4] They allowed the values of surrounding society rather than biblical truth to shape their thinking and acting. That is the essence of theological liberalism. In our time, we are in desperate danger of repeating exactly the same mistake in the whole area of justice and the poor. We are allowing surrounding society rather than Scripture to shape our values and life. Have not our economic lifestyles and our attitudes toward the poor been shaped more by our affluent materialistic society than by Scripture—even though the Bible

says as much about this set of issues as it does about the atonement or Christology?

If we want to escape theological liberalism, if our confession that Jesus is Lord is genuine, then we must cast aside the secular economic values of our materialistic society. Now I know many of the people in our churches don't want to do that. They don't want to hear the Bible's radical call to costly discipleship. But that simply raises in a more painful way for every church leader the basic question: Is Jesus really our Lord?

Many pastors, Sunday school superintendents, and other church leaders agree that we should be concerned with the poor and work for peace via justice. They are willing to talk carefully about these things as long as the message is not too upsetting to the congregation, as long as it does not offend potential new members and hinder church growth. But they don't make it clear, as Jesus did, that we really have to choose between Jesus and Mammon. They are afraid to teach and preach the clear biblical word that economic systems perpetrate institutionalized violence and murder because that would offend business people. One wonders whether it is Jesus or church growth, whether it is Jesus or vocational security, whether it is Jesus or social acceptance who finally is our Lord.

There are very few church traditions as helpful as that of the Historic Peace Churches for enabling us to understand and live out the proper relationship between peacemaking and economics. Simplicity in both personal lifestyles and church life has been a part of our heritage for centuries. We of all people ought to be able to hear the God of the poor calling us today to more simple lifestyles. But one only needs to look at the vast wealth and

---

[4]See my article, "The Historian, the Miraculous, and Post-Newtonian Man," *Scottish Journal of Theology* 25 (1972): 309–19; and "St. Paul's Understanding of the Nature and Significance of the Resurrection," Novum Testamentum 19 (1977): 124–41.

affluent lifestyles among our people to see that this generation is abandoning that heritage at an incredibly rapid pace. Our parents and grandparents still understood the basic biblical call for separation from the sinful materialistic values of surrounding society even though at times they applied it in a superficial, legalistic way. But will there be any heritage of simplicity left to pass on to our children?

The following story illustrates the problem. Last summer a Presbyterian couple came to a Families for Justice Retreat I was leading. During the course of the weekend, they shared their agonizing difficulty in communicating their concern for a simple lifestyle with their teenage son. They explained that he went to a Christian high school where all his friends had their own cars with nicely remodeled interiors and cassette players. Naturally he wanted a car for himself. Each family drove two or three cars to church on Sunday. Rather than helping them communicate biblical values to their son, the Christian high school and even the church were subtly instilling the materialistic values of surrounding society.

Then the couple explained that their son was attending a Mennonite high school. They explained that they had left the Presbyterian Church and joined a Mennonite church in order to find support for their commitment to simple living. To their dismay, they discovered that most of the Mennonites there were rushing madly in the other direction. I have reflected a lot about that couple. Does that story provide the basic clue about where we are going?

Is Jesus or surrounding society our Lord? If we intend to follow the risen One, then I think we will discover that He calls us to be peacemakers through economic change—through more simple personal economic lifestyles, through more simple church lifestyles, and through action designed to change economic systems that produce violence by statute.

Chapter Eighteen

Racial Reconciliation: From Anger and Guilt to Passion and Conviction

Spencer Perkins and Chris Rice

Spencer Perkins was the son of John M. Perkins,[1] founder of the Voice of Calvary Ministries. VOC is a ministry aimed at African-American development in Mississippi and racial reconciliation with white Christians. For seventeen years Spencer and Chris Rice, his white co-author, worked together at VOC to achieve reconciliation between the races in the church and in the community.

This honest chapter reflects the tone of their whole book, *More Than Equals.* Racial reconciliation is the will of God, especially in the church, but it is a difficult task to accomplish, as the authors acknowledge as they discuss their church and the journey each of them had to undertake for reconciliation to occur. It is a spiritual process that involves pain and change. God's grace must make the process work or it will break down under human strain and frustration.

The chapter forces us to ask what it takes for both black and white Americans to give reconciliation a chance. What are the obstacles to reconciliation? Since we like to follow the path of least resistance, how can we experience the grace of God that motivates us to engage the hard, long process toward racial reconciliation?

Understanding some of the pain caused by our stormy racial history is only the first in the reconciliation process. This second section of the book is devoted to the step of submitting, which involves two things. First, as with all the difficult problems that face us individually and corporately, we need to turn racial separation over to God. Second, we need to submit to one another, white to black and black to white.

There will be little hope for genuine healing and trust unless we seek contact with our racially different neighbor. Voice of Calvary's racial reconciliation meetings in 1983 were a turning point in our

---

[1]Consult the books written or edited by John M. Perkins: *Let Justice Roll Down: John Perkins Tells His Own Story* (Glendale, Calif.: Regal, 1976); *A Quiet Revolution: The Christian Response to Human Need: A Strategy for Today* (Waco, Tex.: Word, 1976); *With Justice For All* (Ventura, Calif.: Regal, 1982); *Beyond Charity: A Call to Christian Community Development* (Grand Rapids, Mich.: Baker, 1993); *Restoring At-Risk Communities: Doing It Together and Doing It Right* (Grand Rapids, Mich.: Baker, 1995).

This chapter originally appeared as "From Anger and Guilt to Passion and Conviction," *More Than Equals: Racial Healing for the Sake of the Gospel*, by Spencer Perkins and Chris Rice, rev. ed. (Downers Grove, Ill.: InterVarsity Press, 2000), 131–42.

168 ·❖· *A Peace Reader*

efforts to submit to one another. The meetings affected us differently. So each of us will give his perspective on the aftermath of that tumultuous summer, which was when we really began to get to know each other.

Spencer: The Showdown

The racial reconciliation meetings marked yet another showdown in a long personal history of dealing with race. Up until 1983, although I understood what following Jesus meant, I took it seriously only once in a while. Now I was twenty-eight years old and had begun to give serious thought to how much I really believed in the teachings of Jesus that had been drilled into me as a child. That summer the reality of all those ideals was put to the test in a series of meetings that shook our church and ministry to the core.

The racial reconciliation meetings were the stuff that church and denominational splits are made of. Hardly ever do black and white Christians discuss their true feelings about race. It was explosive. Even today many VOC old-timers, when recalling an event or a person in our history, speak of "before the meetings" or "after the meetings." The meetings were a test of the strength of our Christian commitment—much as teenagers test the soundness of their parents' beliefs to determine if they warrant personal sacrifice.

I saw these encounters as a showdown between two of the most powerful forces in the universe: God and Race. Thirteen years earlier I had watched intently as my father struggled between these two foes after his beating in the Brandon jail. But up to this point I had never seen Jesus win over Race on a large scale. Was Jesus Christ the one superhero who had the power to defeat the shrewd, powerful villain called Race? A racial split that had occurred at Circle Church in Chicago a few years earlier was a haunting reminder that others had fought and lost.

Relationships between blacks and whites in America have been so strained that the trust needed to begin and sustain a relationship does not always come easily. Some blacks, whether consciously or unconsciously, will throw up a defensive obstacle course for whites to overcome before they will open up and begin to trust. A white woman attending one of our Christian community development workshops commented, "There is no way I could tolerate this type of game-playing. I would just give up, assuming that the black person didn't want a relationship." It's unfortunate that sometimes blacks carry such excess baggage when whites attempt to reach out. But as we've already shown, as we try to sit down at the "table of brotherhood" together, we all bring racial residue. Many blacks and whites, like this woman, are not willing to tolerate the inconveniences that come with trying to break through the ice of suspicion and mistrust in crosscultural relationships.

In the months following the racial reconciliation meetings, there was a slow exodus of people, both black and white, from our church. Though it saddened me to see people go, I was encouraged by the strong contingent of people who emerged from the battle with the look of determination that said, *We will stay and fight.* Before the meetings I hadn't been secure enough to climb into the same foxhole with the people of the church—especially my white sisters and brothers. After the meetings, I saw many of these people through different eyes. Not only my faith in them but also my faith in Christianity had been strengthened because of their commitment.

In some ways the shrinking of our fellowship reminded me of the process Gideon had to go through before God would let Israel go into battle. Gideon had gathered an army of thirty-two thousand soldiers. But the Lord said to Gideon, "You have too many men for me to deliver Midian into their hands" (Judg. 7:2). God didn't want Israel to assume that its own strength had been its salvation. So by the time the Israelites went into battle, God had dwindled their number to just three hundred—the most determined few. At VOC, maybe God was saying that the only witness to racial reconciliation that he would allow us to make would be a small one; otherwise we might think we'd done it ourselves.

I've always been a team player and have never been able to understand how you could follow Jesus alone. The people who emerged from this battle had, I felt, been tried by fire. For me, these were the brothers and sisters who had "the right stuff." I had finally found the people I could trust enough to fight with—who would not turn tail and run in the heat of a conflict. Together we would take up our cross and follow Jesus, even against a villain as formidable as Race. These were the people who could help me deal with my hurt and anger—and who finally helped me turn my anger into a passion for reconciliation.

Voice of Calvary Fellowship is broken into small groups that meet in homes one night a week to pray, study the Bible and support one another. That winter my wife, Nancy, and I started a new small group that solidified the direction I would take in following Jesus. It was in this small group that I got to know Chris and I began to see that he and I, like most blacks and whites in our church at the time, had experienced the reconciliation meetings totally differently: in the aftermath of the meetings he faced the decision of joining the exodus or staying.

Chris: Holding Up the Mirror

The atmosphere of blunt truth in Voice of Calvary's reconciliation meetings in the summer of 1983 confronted me with uncomfortable challenges. Even if I denied that racism had tainted me, there was something deep here that I couldn't quite grasp. I contemplated packing up and joining the slow trickle of church members who were leaving for greener pastures.

As I wavered that winter, I was asked to join Spencer and Nancy's new small group. I had some reservations. I didn't know either Spencer or Nancy very well. When I thought back to Spencer's question from a couple of years earlier—"Why are all you white people here?"—I feared that the new group might bring more of the same old truth-sharing, and I was reluctant to try again.

But if there was any possibility for hope, this was it. The new group was solidly biracial, many of its members were veterans of the battle for reconciliation at VOC, and all had committed themselves to be in Jackson for the long haul. I wasn't sure why Spencer's brother Derek and a white friend, Donna Wheeler (whom I married four years later), had taken a chance and invited me to join, but just the fact that I was asked was affirming and gave me hope. I decided to give it another try.

Every week we gathered in Spencer and Nancy's living room. We started by sharing our life stories. Each person took about an hour to tell us about his or her family, growing up and formative experiences. This took several weeks, but the testimonies began to draw us closer together. While I had not developed a single close black friend in my previous two years at Voice of Calvary, now I was getting closer to black brothers and sisters like Spencer, Gloria, Joanie, Lue, Derek, Karyn, Perry and Billy Ray. I began to see that Spencer was not the black terrorist I'd thought. In fact, I saw that he had a gentle spirit, hard on truth but soft on people. People I found difficult, he seemed to relate to easily, yet without sacrificing his honesty.

Through these friendships, God slowly knit a safe place of acceptance where I could assess my racial baggage more objectively. These secure relationships provided the context in which I could face the truth of the reconciliation meetings. It was one thing to be told that my skin color was not a stigma. It was quite another to become friends with a black sister like Gloria and hear her tell how her five-year-old son, Kortney, had come home from his Christian school telling her he didn't want to be black because his teacher said that when God washed away your sin it made you "white as snow." I wanted to wipe away the destructiveness of a society that confused children about race, because I wanted to wipe it away for Kortney and his mother.

The relationships in our Bible-study group also gave me the courage to examine my deepest motives. I began to ask myself, *Why am I here?* Some of my reasons were good and pure. After all, I had stepped out of my world and come to Mississippi because I wanted to follow God and help lift poor people up. I was motivated by compassion, to meet a need, to accomplish a task that would glorify God. My skills and resources were needed. God had blessed me so that I could give something back to him. I felt the satisfaction of giving and helping.

But there was another side to my "do-good" motives. My life was all mapped out: I would offer my skills to the black community for a while and then leave and get on with my real life. Maybe I would even use what I'd learned in a political career. Subconsciously, I had struck a deal with God: I'll do some good for the poor, but don't mess with my mind, my lifestyle or my life plans.

I realized that I was a kind of case-worker. People in need could, so to speak, come into my office, sit down in front of my desk and outline their problems and needs, and I would do whatever I could to help them. I would be the giver; they would be recipients. But when the recipients started saying that maybe the desk needed to be turned around and I needed to learn from them, I had begun packing up. I became aware that my real, deep-down motivation to leave during the reconciliation meetings was that I didn't want to go through the pain of looking into a clearer mirror, especially if it meant my potential for leadership and exercising my gifts might be limited.

God began showing me that he wanted me to move from giving to receiving, from leading to being led. God reminded me that when I made a commitment to Jesus, I put all of my life under his lordship. But there was still lots of unconquered territory, and one of the major terrains was marked "racial." God controlled some of it, but he wanted it all.

My motive for racial reconciliation needed to be for my own sake. Do-goodism wasn't good enough. It put the focus on what I was doing for others rather than on what God wanted to do in me. As God purified my motives, I found myself becoming not only a more effective soldier of reconciliation but also a more mature disciple of Christ.

Side by Side

My racial conversion process had been birthed with my arrival into the black community at Voice of Calvary in 1981. The racial reconciliation meetings of 1983 had brought the issue into turbulent adolescence. I had been tempted to rebel and go my own way. Now I decided to stay, and new friendships with blacks offered an opportunity for my commitment to mature another step.

The fact that the black people of our small group were reaching out to me created a tension. Hadn't blacks made it clear that we whites were getting in the way of their development? Despite their anger, despite the focus on "black," they were opening up their lives to me. *Why*?

An event in the fall of 1985 solidified my move toward racial conversion. A group of us from VOC Ministries staff had been meeting regularly on Thursday mornings. We had decided to spend more time together outside of work hours struggling with the muddy issues that were so much a part of our daily ministry.

One morning Lem Tucker, VOCM's president at the time, reminded the group that when he had asked me to step in a year earlier as acting fundraising director, it had been with the understanding that a search for a black replacement would begin immediately. But now, said Lem, he and I had met, and he had asked me to accept the full responsibility of being the ministry's development director. "This morning," continued Lem, "I want to discuss the role of white people at VOC—and Chris is our guinea pig!"

I was taken off guard. I fidgeted in my seat. Sweat began to drip under my arms. I enjoyed friendly relationships with everybody in the room. But I knew that the members of the group—which was mostly black—would speak their feelings honestly. All of them put a high priority on developing black leadership.

Nearly everyone in the room responded. And through it all, the message was clear: "Chris, we accept you as part of us. We appreciate the gifts you bring to this ministry. We've seen you up close over the last four years, we've seen your struggle with your racial prejudice. We affirm your being in a leadership position." Melvin Anderson's words encouraged me the most: "You know, I don't think of Chris as being white. He just seems like one of us."

It was as if God had reached out through my black friends, put his hands on my shoulders and said, "This is where I want you." I flashed back to one of my mental arguments for leaving VOC: I'm not wanted here. I'm not needed here. Now I understood: The blacks hadn't rejected me. I'd been the one to think I should leave. When they said, "You need to be willing to step to the side," I had heard "Step back." When they said "mutual submission," I'd heard "black domination." When they mentioned the importance of black leadership, I'd heard "No room for white leadership."

What the black brothers and sisters were saying throughout the reconciliation process was "Stay here with us. Stay and serve. Let's show the world that when black and white Christians come together, we can work as equals." Finally I understood that the reconciliation meetings had not been a purge, or a coup that would elevate black over white. We were *partners*, moving ahead side by side.

Just exactly how the newfound ideal of partnership should be expressed in the practical life of our church still had to be worked out. One important question was how our church should be led. Spencer was deeply involved in facing that challenge, so I'll let him tell you how we began to work it out.

Spencer: Our Tiny Witness

One of the results of the racial reconciliation meetings was a renewed resolve to develop black leadership. Although our church was about 50-50 black to white and our surrounding community was nearly 90 percent black, the church leadership was made up of five whites and two blacks, and the pastor was white. There had never been any overt plan for whites to have a majority in leadership; it just happened that way. In an all-black church setting blacks have no problem taking leadership. But we realized that when blacks and whites come together for a common cause, the whites tend to feel more secure taking on the leadership roles—whether it's volunteering to lead in a church project or being willing to be considered for eldership. So we decided to make an intentional effort to affirm black culture and encourage black leadership. This was an attempt not to put blacks over whites but only to balance the scales—especially since we lived and worshiped in a black neighborhood.

In the fall of 1983 four people—three blacks and one white—were confirmed as elders in our church, and I was one of them. As a result of the racial reconciliation meetings, we decided to return to interracial pastoral leadership. When our church was born in 1977, we had appointed biracial copastors, Phil Reed and Romas McLain. But Romas served only a few months before leaving for seminary. Because we all loved and trusted Phil, we allowed him to continue as pastor even though we didn't think it ideal for an interracial church in a black neighborhood to have a white pastor. (Sometimes, though, your ideal seems so clear to you, God will not give it to you. Struggling to reconcile ideals with reality has been a way of life for VOC ever since I can remember.)

After the racial reconciliation meetings, the elders and congregation felt the best form of leadership would be a three-person pastoral team. Only a few weeks before this decision was reached, Phil had offered to step down in favor of a black pastor. But the black members of the body had affirmed him, insisting that he stay.

Over the next couple of years the church's leadership stumbled around, trying to find the right combination of pastors. Then in 1985 the Reverend Donald Govan (known as Mr. G) and I joined Phil to form the pastoral team for Voice of Calvary Fellowship.

Even though Phil is white, he chaired the team. He was the one paid by the church and who did the day-to-day administration and most of the preaching.

He served in this fashion even though the authority is shared by the pastoral team. Not many people would be willing to work in such a structure. I praise the Lord for Phil. In my opinion, he is an unsung hero—one of the few pastors in this country to be a part of a truly interracial body of believers with interracial pastoral leadership.

Any plural leadership, and especially when it is interracial, has special risks. As the unity of the pastors goes, so goes the unity of the church. Since we became a team, Phil, Mr. G and I have had to fight for our unity. My relationship with Phil has been the toughest. We are both more opinionated than Mr. G, and therefore we have had to struggle harder to maintain our unity. Several people have commented that our relationship reminds them of a marriage. If we don't spend time together, our relationship deteriorates, and when it deteriorates, it's much harder to attain unity in decision-making. Marcia, Phil's wife, marvels at how we are able to remain committed to each other. It has been said that the first and most important rule in a marriage is "Never mention divorce as an option." In the same way, in order to maintain unity among ourselves as copastors, each of us must be confident that the other two will not decide on their own to walk away. This confidence is essential for survival.

Voice of Calvary Fellowship still struggles with how to live out our witness of racial reconciliation. Even though our church has many people coming and going, our membership still runs about 60 percent black and 40 percent white. I often wish that every member had to experience something like the racial reconciliation meetings. Many new members are attracted by our witness and lifestyle but were not part of the fellowship during this trying time. Sometimes newcomers take our interracial character for granted without understanding the blood, sweat and tears it took to reach this point.

God told Israel that he would bless them so that they could in turn bless the other peoples of the world. Over the years God blessed us greatly at Voice of Calvary, and the evidence to me is that the faith of many people around the country and world has been strengthened because of our tiny witness here in Mississippi—a witness to the power of a God who can bring together and reconcile those who have been most divided.

Chris: Autopsy versus Recovery

Beneath the surface of the racial harmony that was a marvel to VOC visitors before 1983, a volcano was sizzling. When it erupted, explosive emotions spewed forth. Blacks and whites who had worked and worshiped and lived side by side were suddenly at odds. We realized how little we really knew each other. Past incidents had ignited sparks that should have been immediately extinguished. Instead, later problems had fanned the flames of mistrust and misunderstanding. It seemed that a raging fire was out of control.

Yet if you visit Voice of Calvary today, you will see many of the same people who endured the fires of 1983 now sharing genuine, deep friendships. You'll see us worshiping together, living on the same streets, reaching out to our neighbors in ministry. You'll see our children enjoying friendships together. You'll see us continuing to talk about and work through racial struggles.

What happened? Why didn't we blacks and whites go our separate ways?

The story of another group that attempted to reconcile the races might illuminate the issues. The Student Nonviolent Coordinating Committee, called SNCC (or Snick, for short), was arguably

the most creative and idealistic civil rights organization of the 1960s. SNCC's student leaders adopted radical grassroots methods and constantly butted heads with their more traditional counterparts at the NAACP and Martin Luther King's Southern Christian Leadership Conference (SCLC). SNCC's staff lived in the poor communities where they worked. Their vision was not only to fight injustice but also to show how black and white could live and work in harmony. This caused great disturbances in Southern towns. Their dangerous ventures—voter registration, community organizing, sit-ins and marches—paved the way for some of the more well-known political gains of the civil rights movement. SNCC's bold goal? To rid America of racial segregation and discrimination in every arena of life.

SNCC's efforts helped to break down tremendous legal and political obstacles. In town after town, enemies like Alabama sheriff Bull Connor were defeated. On the national level Congress passed the Civil Rights Bill of 1965.

But in the aftermath of these victories SNCC found that its dream for racial harmony was dying. The conflict hit boiling point at a staff retreat in May 1966 when SNCC debated asking whites to leave the staff. Mary King, a white SNCC worker, recalls the divisive mood of the debate: "[Some blacks argued that] white people ...were inherently incapable of comprehending the black experience. For SNCC to become the type of organization they desired, it would have to rid itself of white staff members and become 'black-staffed, black-controlled, and black-financed.'"[2]

In the months afterward white SNCC staff and blacks who were supportive of interracial cooperation trickled away. By the following year only one white staff worker remained.

---

[2]Mary King, *Freedom Song* (New York: Morrow, 1987), 500.

[3]Nicholas Lehmann, *Promised Land* (New York: Knopf, 1991), 177–78.

Bob Zellner...hung on until a meeting in Atlanta in 1967, where he was planning to propose a new organizing campaign. "I was in one room, and the executive committee was in another," he says. "They offered me a compromise: you can do the project, but you can't come to meetings. I wouldn't accept that because SNCC never required second-class citizenship of anyone. Then they said, 'Okay, you can come to meetings, but you can't vote.' I said no. They finally said, 'Okay, good luck.'"[3]

Only two years after the landmark civil rights bill, SNCC was a blacks-only organization. The racial unity that SNCC had dared to proclaim, and had pursued at great risk, ended in divorce—"separated due to irreconcilable differences." SNCC's political victories had been considerable, but the relationships between individual blacks and whites had not been strong enough to hold the organization together.

The same challenges that split SNCC in 1967 were faced by VOC in 1983: mistrust between the races, whites' tendency to dominate the leadership of an interracial group, unresolved residue from growing up in an unequal society. Yet VOC's confrontation did not result in a racial split. Why?

In the difference between SNCC and VOC lies our only hope: *Reconciliation is ultimately a spiritual issue.*

SNCC had the weapons to win a political war but not a spiritual one. Like SNCC, VOC reached a point of painful conflict that looked impossible to transcend. But a deeper motivation enabled us to persevere and make the sacrifices necessary to stay together. Even after 1983's racial confrontation, blacks at VOC didn't ask whites to be second-class citizens. None of the white church leaders or ministry staff were asked to leave. In fact, when the church picked new elders, a white was added along with three blacks. During that same time Derek, a black brother, asked me to join the new small group. Then Lem, another black brother, asked me to take a key leadership position, directing the ministry's fundraising efforts. Black friends as well as white encouraged me to accept the position. The actions of VOC's blacks proved that they desired not to separate from whites, or to be our superiors, but to be partners in a shared mission.

The powerful lesson in these two stories is that the gulf between black and white can be crossed only on a bridge built by the hands of God. This is what SNCC lacked and—by the grace of God—what VOC grasped. This is what sustained us through the racial reconciliation meetings. Without God at the center, there is no basis for reconciliation.

The Peace Witness in Criminal Justice

Marlin Jeschke

Marlin Jeschke, Professor Emeritus of Philosophy and Religion at Goshen College, describes our criminal justice system as being parallel to war—both represent violence and the breakdown of law. Peace churches, he maintains, accept a dual approach: opposition to international war but acceptance of the current state of criminal justice as justifiable, indeed necessary. We too often assume, he adds, that punishment will make bad people good. But, he insists, there is no strong statistical support for that view. For Christians it is grace, not punishment, that makes people good. We need to insist on reconciliation and restitution because the redemption, not the punishment, of sinners is the church's business. He concedes that there will always be the need for prisons, but the treatment of inmates must be compatible with Christian love and nonviolence.

Jeschke's thought-provoking article raises many different kinds of questions. Should denominations and congregations be engaged in prison ministries that help bring about reconciliation and redemption? What is the responsibility of the church to help bring reconciliation of prisoners with victims and their families? Do you agree with the author that punishment is not effective? Would we be likely to agree wholeheartedly with the author if we or our family members were victimized by a drunk driver, by someone stealing our identity through credit card theft, by an arsonist destroying our house? Would you take someone to court if you knew that conviction meant incarceration of the offender and hardship for his family?

Since the time of the Reformation, Anabaptists, members of other historic peace churches, and more recently many Christians of other denominations have refused to go along with those who use war as a means of dealing with fellow human beings whom our society considers enemies. However, many Christians, including evangelicals, go along with our society in dealing with offenders by means of violence and force. Politicians promise to wage war on crime, which usually translates into acquiring more guns and other hardware as well as building more prisons. It usually also encourages stereotyping and even demonizing of criminals or lawbreakers, as often happens to enemies in war. Above all, dealing with criminals usually means retribution, punishment. That, as we again see in war, is retaliation.

It is often said, rightly, that war is the result of a breakdown of law. In a sense that is also true in the case of criminal justice. Too often people regard the apprehension and conviction and sentencing of offenders as a success of the law. But in a truer sense it is a failure of the law, because the real purpose of law is its observance. On that accounting crime is a breakdown of law, which results in the resort to force, to police action to deter unlawful conduct.

Many Christians have trouble relating their faith with the world of criminal justice. These worlds are far apart. In fact, this should not be so. In the classic cadences of the church's liturgy, Christians confess before God that they have offended against his holy laws. They further confess that, although guilty, they have not been condemned, but are justified by faith. When we stop to think about it, we realize that both the gospel and criminal justice concern themselves with common problems of ethical conduct, the confrontation of offenders, justice, and human community. The Bible is not unrealistic about the intrusion of evil into God's good world. From the murder of Abel to the sins that Paul addresses in the Corinthian church, God has made provision for dealing with sinners, those who disobey his will, his gracious law; that provision is salvation, not condemnation. There is condemnation, to be sure, but only *after* offenders against God's law have been offered and have rejected his grace.

Court procedures may still include an oath upon the Bible or an oath before God, but the language and spirit of the Christian faith is notably absent from the sphere of American law and criminal justice. If we heard of a judge who pronounced sentence by saying, "Go and sin no more," we would expect him to immediately be relieved of his office, unless we thought we were hearing lines from another sacrilegious TV comedy. Even though many police officers, lawyers, and judges are members of Christian churches, the message of the church about sin, salvation, forgiveness, grace,

faith, and regeneration rarely if ever penetrates the everyday world of our police stations, court chambers, jails, and prisons. That world employs another language—law, crime, charges, arraignment, trial, sentencing, prison. It also, unfortunately, manifests another spirit. Christian faith and criminal justice seem to have gone their separate ways in the modern world. Christian thought has been pushed out of the world of law and criminal justice by modern secular developments, but the fault may all too possibly be that of a growing irrelevance of the church.

Many people in our society, Christians included, accept a dual system. The church deals with sins that are nonissues in secular law, such as adultery and promiscuity, maybe greed and pride. Criminal justice deals with shoplifting, burglary, drunk driving, assault, and homicide. Most Christians in the United States are content with such a two-track system. They consider the criminal justice system to be part of our Christian America and uncritically accept its spirit and its methods, ignoring the wide gulf that separates it from the gospel.

In our application of the peace message we may have developed a blind spot in the realm of criminal justice. Missing in the secular criminal justice system of our state and federal governments is a concern, and indeed provision for, offering offenders the gospel—that is, presenting them with the invitation to repent, receive forgiveness, be reconciled, make restitution where that is called for, and be regenerated and transformed into ethical conduct by the spirit of Christ.

In that light, reflect for a moment upon the standard practice in our current criminal justice system's treatment of an offender. The system asks only two questions. First, is the accused guilty as charged? This is a most appropriate question. We must avoid false charges against innocent people. Recent serious research has uncovered numerous cases of wrongful imprisonment of people in Los Angeles and Illinois, to cite only two examples. Second, if an accused person is found guilty the system asks: What is the punishment? No lawyer or judge asks whether the offender wants, by the grace of God, to receive the gospel, repent, be born again, make restitution to the extent that such is possible, and be reconciled with the victim.

Our criminal justice system does include a Christian, or at least a religious, component: chaplaincy service. But please note: chaplaincy service comes into the picture only after the offender is in jail or prison, and when it does it collides head-on with the criminal justice system's basic method and message. The chaplaincy ministry, if it is genuinely true to the gospel, tells offenders they can repent and be forgiven, receive remission of sins. But with too few exceptions the criminal justice system says: You will be punished for your offenses regardless of whether or not you repent and ask for forgiveness.

The world of criminal justice assumes that punishment will change behavior, that if fines or prison will not make people good, they will at least deter them from criminal conduct. Our criminal justice system thus places an inordinate confidence in punishment to deal with crime. This is ironic because Christians rightly claim that the New Testament teaches us that grace, not law, is the way to deal with offenders. Most Christians tend to think of law in the religious sense as doing good works in order to merit God's favor and salvation. But as we can see from the New Testament, in Judaism law meant the use of punitive coercion to deter undesirable behavior. That is why the unconverted Saul tried to bring Jewish Christians to Jerusalem in chains. And that is why the Jews flogged the converted Paul five times to get him to quit preaching the gospel. But Paul contended that the law does not have the power to make people good. Only grace can do that. Yet still today our criminal justice system is committed to punishment as the way to make people good or at least to make them stop their bad conduct, whether that is shoplifting or armed robbery. In this respect, criminal justice, like an army in war, resorts to punitive action to force an "enemy" into ceasing what is considered unacceptable conduct.

Now we can concede that societies will find it necessary to have some organization and procedure for stopping wrongdoers in order change their behavior and to protect society. We need not, however, take for granted the connection between what a given body of law identifies as crime and what it prescribes to deal with an instance of crime. For example, we can surely agree that stealing is wrong, but we need not concede that the penalty for theft should be cutting off the right hand of a thief. It is very hard, though, to get some conservative Muslims to make this distinction. So also it is most difficult to get some people in our society to call in question the penalty of imprisonment prescribed for violation of many laws. To question the penalty seems to imply a questioning of the morality of the law itself. It suggests that the questioner is soft on crime. Conversely, to endorse a law on theft seems to imply an endorsement of the most common penalty our society imposes, jail or prison.

In an earlier era British society made excessive use of the penalty of death by hanging, and that for a wide array of crimes, including pickpocket theft. Several Southern states imposed the death penalty for rape until the Supreme Court prohibited the death penalty for that crime on the grounds that it constituted cruel and unusual punishment. Those who first wrote those laws prescribing the death penalty for theft and rape were for the most part professing Christians, and they considered that penalty justifiable and right. We now see the matter differently. But we do not seem to be more willing or able than people of a former time to make an impartial review of whether our present customary punishment of prison for most offenses is justifiable or even effective.

We should remember that our modern Western prison system is not even two centuries old. Penitentiaries were begun by the Quakers about 200 years ago to provide an alternative to the way of retribution, to provide offenders with the solitude that might bring them to penitence. The primary intention of the penitentiary was the rehabilitation of the offender. But in the course of time the intention became punishment. As Charles Colson has said: "The very fact that in public discussion, at least in America, the two terms 'imprisonment' and 'punishment' tend to be used interchangeably suggests how bankrupt our thinking is in this field. If someone breaks the law, society says, 'send him to prison.' Any punishment other than prison is met with a howl of protest because society believes the offender has escaped punishment. Unfortunately, this is the way people have been conditioned to think."[1]

Prison does punish. It inflicts intense suffering in the form of loneliness and, above all, loss of freedom. Isn't it interesting that those people who say prisons have become "country clubs" or "Hiltons" (and they are the people who have never been in prison) are the ones who in other contexts seem to be the first to claim that they would die rather than lose their freedom?

The infliction of punishment, though it is an unquestioned axiom of our society, is precisely where our existing criminal justice system fails most pathetically. One of the phenomenal illusions of our society is this: while we think we will make offenders pay and we continue to escalate prison sentences, our prison system is an organized, structured, institutionalized, systematic way of letting offenders off. This may seem to contradict what I have just claimed about prisons as punishment. Let me therefore explain.

The popular myth has it that convicts who are "doing time" are paying their debt to society. In fact, punishment is a substitute for offenders making right what they did wrong. It creates or reinforces in them the illusion that their punishment somehow makes up for their offense. Those who have visited people in prison have likely noticed how inmates have internalized this idea. Like the society that has sentenced them to long terms in prison, convicts often are conned into thinking that with their punishment they are paying their debt to society.

What happens in the punishment of imprisonment is not unlike what often happens in the case alcoholism. Alcoholics sometimes try to punish themselves for their addiction, but this punishment does not have the power to change their behavior. On the contrary, it becomes an attempted trade-off and thus an evasion of the real need to cease the undesirable behavior.

The problem with the punishment of imprisonment is not only the illusion it fosters that offenders are paying for their crime. Prison actually prevents the possibility of achieving what is really needed, namely, for offenders to make restitution and seek reconciliation. It prevents this goal in two effective ways. First, prison physically removes offenders from society, making it impossible for them to go

---

[1]John Stott and Nicholas Miller, eds., *Crime and the Responsible Community* (Grand Rapids: Eerdmans, 1980), 152.

to the people they have wronged to find reconciliation and, if needed, to make restitution. Second, prison economically removes offenders from gainful employment, making it impossible for them to earn the money to make restitution.

Someone who stops to reflect upon our prevailing system cannot help but see the absurdity of it. In what sense is a burglar paying his debt by serving his prison term? In a sense he is incurring more debt in that the citizen he robbed must pay taxes to maintain him in prison and often to put his family on welfare. In another sense society incurs a debt to him if its sentence is unjust and if for a theft of only a few hundred dollars it robs him of thousands of dollars of income that he could make if he held a job. If, for example, a burglar is imprisoned for six months for stealing tires from a store, he loses over five thousand dollars in earnings at minimum wage levels, but the storeowner remains resentful because his losses are never repaid.

There is also the injustice of robbing an imprisoned offender of his marriage, home, and family. So often imprisonment leads to divorce, breaking up marriages and families. Prisoners are justifiably outraged because they know this injustice of robbing them of a marriage and family is often out of proportion to the offense they perpetrated. We may say, "That's tough! That's the cost of criminal behavior." But that does not alter the fact that before God the scales have been reversed. Thus we may be guilty of a more egregious injustice than the offender committed, and God will hold us accountable for such an injustice.

Another evil of the prison system is that it reinforces an offender's behavior by confirming the practice of inflicting suffering as a means to power. In this respect it is again like war. And it is also like a parent striking a child who has just struck another child, saying, "This will teach you not to hit other kids!" Natu-

rally, the real message the child gets is that hitting is the way to power, the means to control and domination. It is also the lesson people take from war: violent coercion is the way to domination. Prison too often simply reinforces the violent mentality offenders have already developed. One cannot easily resist the impression that punishment represents the moral bankruptcy of a society that cannot think of an alternative way of dealing with offenders, that is deceiving itself about the failure of punishment.

What is wrong with this all too familiar picture? There is none of what the Bible calls expiation, the removal of sin and wrong, of a barrier between two parties. Unless a wrong, an offense, is removed by the act of reconciliation and restitution, there is no restoration of community, of what the Bible calls shalom. Incarceration discourages and can even prevent reconciliation and the restoration of community.

Let us never forget that Christianity makes the mission of the expiation of wrong the heart of its message. And Christians should make the effecting of such restoration of offenders their area of expertise, their ministry. The redemption of offenders has historically been the church's business. This answer is given already in Mosaic Law, which is often considered pre-Christian or even sub-Christian. Yet Mosaic Law calls for restitution and reconciliation in case after case, as we see in Exodus 21–23. The teachings of Jesus and the whole New Testament reinforce the principle. In all our dealings with offenders we should begin with the urgent and serious summons (*invitation* is almost too mild a word) to such offenders to seek reconciliation with the persons they have wronged, to make right what they did wrong, and to make restitution where it is called for and to the extent that it is possible. There is even justification for the use of a measure of constraint in thus summoning offenders to make right their wrong.

Because removal of wrong—the elimination of the obstacle between people created by an offense—is indispensable to the restoration of offenders, several implications follow. First, regardless of the protestations of leaders in our society that they would like to do away with the problem of crime, as long as the criminal justice process is formally and officially structured to prevent the rehabilitation of offenders rather than to effect it, we can never have real rehabilitation. Indeed, a society that thus hinders the opportunities for, rather than encouraging, the removal of wrong will continue to be plagued by crime and will deserve to be.

The present criminal justice system does not always demand prison. We have provisions for probation, but it is mostly used without requiring the offender to make things right and without an adequate support system to help the offender find a new way. Reporting once a month to a probation officer is not adequate. As a result, probation too often ends up fostering in offenders' minds the idea that they were simply let off.

I have been drawing illustrations for the most part from property offenses, because up to 90 percent of all offenses are property crimes. Moreover, it is easiest to show the redemptive principle of restitution for such offenses. Though many people are rightly upset by crimes such as burglary, they may be more ready to entertain the idea of an alternative to prison in the case of theft than in cases of violent crimes such as assault, especially if they recognize that imprisonment adds to the loss entailed by the theft whereas restitution offers the possibility of compensation. This is not to say that

we cannot also find redemptive ways of dealing with violent crime. Many Christians have found reconciliation and forgiveness even in cases of homicide. But we will already have come a long way once we have accepted the nonpunitive way in the high proportion of all offenses involving property.

The protection of society from crime is also important. For Christians fidelity to the gospel comes before security, and it happens that the Christian way of dealing with offenders according to the gospel offers far more protection from crime than our present criminal justice approach. We must remember that incarcerating offenders often gives us a false sense of security. For every one hundred convicted offenders who go into prison each day, ninety-eight or ninety-nine are being released. What kind of people are these ex-prisoners? As Charles Olson points out, "Society has spent millions of dollars over the years to create and maintain the proven failure of prisons. Incarceration has failed in its two essential purposes, correcting the offender and providing permanent protection to society. The recidivism rate of up to eighty percent is the evidence of both."[2] Where programs of victim-offender reconciliation and restitution are established, offenders' recidivism rate is only a fraction of that of ex-prisoners.

We will always have some dangerous offenders who need to be detained. As patients in psychiatric hospitals sometime require restraint, so we will need to restrain some violent persons for society's safety and for their own good. But such detention can be effected in a humane way that is compatible with Christian love and nonviolence.

Christians committed to peace and nonviolence have long recognized the implications of their faith for the problem of war. We have not sufficiently

---

[2]Ibid., 153.

recognized its implications for criminal justice. It is time for us to overcome this blind spot in our ethical vision.

Of course, criminal justice may not cut off as many people's lives as war does, though it does end lives in cases of capital punishment, and it did so also in the case of the Branch Davidians of Waco, Texas. Prison merely cuts big chunks out of the middle of people's lives—five, ten, or twenty years. Like war, the criminal justice system also destroys homes, but not necessarily houses, though sometimes it does that too, as in the Philadelphia tragedy of 1985, when a whole block of rowhouses was firebombed by Philadelphia's police force and burned to the ground. But even if the criminal justice system does not usually destroy houses, it often destroys the families living in them, as when an innocent family breaks up after the father is incarcerated.

It is time for people committed to peacemaking to apply the meaning of their faith to the treatment of offenders. We can, of course, try to infiltrate the system to make it better, by providing chaplains, for example. The danger of this, however, is that it can lead us to excuse or even bless the existing system by merely salving wounds, as a medical corps that tends to the wounded in war. Or we can speak prophetically about the system to criticize and improve it. Certainly we can discourage the building of more prisons. Best of all, we can set up models for dealing with offenders that show a new way other than the retaliation of punishment, that instead make the reconciling power of the cross a reality in the world of criminal justice. Victim Offender Reconciliation Programs (VORPs) that demonstrate this alternative model in criminal justice have been created in many parts of the country.[3]

---

[3]For material on Victim Offender Reconciliation Programs, contact Mennonite Central Committee, 21 S. 12th St., Akron, PA 17501 (in Canada: 134 Plaza Drive, Winnipeg, Manitoba R3T 5K9).

Accepting Immigrants: Casa el Norte

Lamar F. Fretz

How should Christians relate to refugees who come to our countries to escape the horrors of war and the debilitating effects of persecution and poverty? Lamar Fretz, who was formerly a member of the MCC Board and Executive Committee and who has had a lifelong interest in refugees, describes one attempt in the area of Fort Erie, Ontario, Canada. At Casa el Norte ("The House in the North"), various people and groups put aside the issues that normally divide them to meet the needs of newly arrived refugees. This program continues and has given inspiration and direction to a similar development for Tibetan refugees, also in the Fort Erie area.

Many of our communities contain refugees. What scriptural mandates encourage us to help them? If they are of another religion, should we expect them to attend our churches in return for our help, or even to become Christians? What should be the scope and duration of our support? Discover stories of how congregations have helped refugees and make the stories known to your congregation. How does aiding refugees promote peace?

Tears rolled down his cheeks and he spoke with great feeling: "Never in my life have I seen anything like it. I didn't know that kind of love existed." Tony, a refugee from Sri Lanka, was talking about his reception at "La Casa" in Buffalo, New York. "I come from a Buddhist and Christian background. But this experience brought me to a point of decision to a new commitment to Jesus."

Tony and a caring group of people in Fort Erie, Ontario, asked me to listen to them and carry a request to Mennonite Central Committee. For five years stranded refugees were being put up in motels, paid for by local people. They were weary.

The request was for MCC to buy a house and run a program like "La Casa" on the American side of the border.

I had to tell them that MCC, wherever in the world it works, tries to avoid putting money in buildings. Together we wrote a proposal and circulated it among interested agencies. From a group that was not even asked came a gift of $100,000. The Sisters of St. Joseph in Ottawa wanted to shift their ministry from a secluded one to something in the open where people were hurting.

So in September 1990, "Casa el Norte" (house in the north) began to host refugees in Fort Erie. The house

---

This chapter originally appeared as "Casa el Norte: The House in the North," *Shalom!*, Fall 1997, 10–11.

holds up to 16 people (even though the local health department says only four). The average stay is a week. On the American side, in "La Casa," which hosts one hundred, they often wait for a month for immigration formalities. In somewhat of an unusual move, MCC Canada is placing a volunteer worker in the United States—at "La Casa."

More refugees enter Canada at the Fort Erie–Buffalo Peace Bridge than at any other port of entry. One refugee produced a crumpled piece of paper on which was written a name. She showed the paper to Patricia, a leader in the reception group. "I was told to ask for this person." To her surprise, Patricia saw her own name. That information had come from Mexico City.

People come from Sri Lanka, El Salvador, Kuwait, and the Horn of Africa. Often they are stranded without food or lodging. A family of seven from El Salvador was so frightened that they all wanted to sleep in one room. When billeted to motels they were often terrorized by strange sounds or even a knock on the door. In a house they can prepare their own food and hear each other's stories.

Along with others, local Brethren in Christ people help at many levels. The Canadian Board for Brotherhood Concerns gives $500 each year for food costs. The Sherkston congregation is a model of support with an organized committee to meet all sorts of needs, including taking people into their homes. Of equal importance is the informal support from individuals who simply go to "Casa el Norte" and ask how they can help. The Christian Benefit Shop, which sends a lot of money overseas to MCC, helps to outfit the refugees with clothing to face the cold Canadian winters.

Expressions of thanks come from the Somali-Canadian Society in Toronto:

People often become too busy to thank others and to let them know what they did was noticed and appreciated. Particularly with refugees, we have so many pressures on us that we move from one disaster to another and we are too busy trying to stay afloat to remember what we went through last week.

In the last few years thousands of our people have passed through your area and church workers have helped them with everything from bus fare to accommodation. Here in Toronto, Somalis often speak of you with affection and appreciation as they tell their stories of how they came here and strangers treated them as if they were their brothers and sisters. One of my friends told it to me like this: "That dark house," he said, "was a bright light to me when I came."

Two hundred Spanish-speaking people have settled in Fort Erie. This should be seen as an opportunity for evangelism. How comforting it is to know that our missionaries go to Mexico to learn Spanish to give a witness. What about a witness in Fort Erie? The Jehovah's Witnesses are mobilizing themselves to move in and offer many of the practical services that these people desperately need. Shouldn't we be doing the same? Could these people be integrated into existing Brethren in Christ congregations? One ponders Matthew 25:37: "The righteous will reply, 'Lord, when did we see...?'"

Some people speak no English. Many are highly educated and speak several languages. Many are Muslim. There are a billion Muslims in the world and we know little about them. Could it be that our fear of communists will shift to the Muslims so that we see them as the next "dragon" to be slain? Should a Christian check the theology of others before getting involved, or just go ahead and minister to the need and care for theology later? Just because the world is a global village and we are close to people does not mean that we will be understanding.

Nobody in Fort Erie looks at the 17 million refugees in the world and says that they should come here. On the other hand, very few countries are as accepting as Canada is. For many years, the American view was that culture should be a "melting pot" and that people should be assimilated. But, according to the cover story in the July 8, 1991, issue of *Time,* "Gone, or going fast, is the concept of melting pot, of the United States as the paramount place in the world where immigrants shed their past in order to forge their future."

In Canada, the approach is more "stew" than "soup," and people are encouraged to keep their ethnic identities. A celebrated case is the request of a Sikh who wanted to become a Royal Canadian Mounted Police person but wear a turban instead of a hat. Most Canadians are unhappy that this is accepted. They feel that immigrants are allowed to practice their religious beliefs while traditional Christian customs are being denied.

They also fear that Sikhs are coming to evangelize—the very kind of motivation for a Canadian to go to another country. What Canadian Christians ought to see is that there are still people in the world who are true to their convictions and beliefs. Further, because it will not be too many years until white-skinned people will be a minority, it is important to work at understanding rather than lash out. This is an immediate challenge for Canadians, especially Christians, and for immigrants. Somehow, at "Casa el Norte," Fort Erie, Christians have been able to set aside some of these larger issues and concentrate on meeting present human need. (In fact, their work has been seen as a model by a group in Windsor, Ontario, wanting to copy the program.) The "house in the north" is a means by which they respond to Scripture: "Just as you did it to one of the least of these who are members of my family, you did to me" (Matt. 25:40, NRSV).

Chapter Twenty-One

Transforming Conflict in the Congregation

John A. Byers

When I (E. Morris Sider) was pursuing graduate studies at a Canadian university, my adviser, a former army officer, once said to me: "I know your kind of people. They don't take guns and shoot the enemy with bullets. They get up in council meeting and shoot each other with words." Who could deny that there is an element of truth in what he said? John A. Byers, bishop of the Central Conference of the Brethren in Christ Church, does not deny that conflict occurs in congregations. If it is not present, the potential for it to develop is real. Conflict in the congregation, he shows, can be damaging, but the main issue is how conflict is handled—how it is transformed into something positive. Byers identifies the causes of conflict and shows how conflict can be resolved so we may fulfill the biblical mandate to live as peaceably together as possible.

What are the points of conflict in your congregation? Have the author's suggestions for resolving conflict been applied? Can all conflicts be resolved? If not, what should the action of the congregation be? How would you proceed to resolve the conflict in the story that the author tells at the end of his article?

In the midst of the turmoil of September 11, 2001, news networks reported that New Yorkers turned to churches. They were seeking a place of peacefulness. It is natural to expect the church to be a place of peace and its people to be the most peace-loving people on earth. Their leader is the Prince of Peace. They teach the gospel of peace. Their call is to the way of peace. Yet the church is no stranger to turmoil: just read the book of Acts or listen to the news. Conflict is present in the church.

The reality of that conflict is more good news than bad. It is good news because it testifies to the authenticity of relationships within the church. It is good news because it demonstrates that conflict can be a positive force for the mission of the church when its powerful energy is appropriately channeled. The challenge is to transform that energy to accomplish the specific mission of a church rather than destroy it: to transform it from something destructive to something constructive.

Paul's conversion story (Acts 9:1–19) is one of conflict transformed. Paul saw the gospel conflicting with the Law. He was determined that the Law should win. It is likely that Paul's encounters with people like Stephen began to raise questions in his mind, thus creating an intrapersonal conflict. Then God struck him down and blinded him with a great light. Out of that conflict, Paul became a positive force for the kingdom of God and no longer sought its demise.

The church is not always so effective in transforming conflict. It tends to over-react in one of two directions: either it seeks to avoid conflict at any cost (flight), or it gets caught up in aggressive behavior (fight).

The flight approach is represented in an e-mail communication I received noting the ten characteristics of a healthy congregation. One of the ten was "avoid conflict." The fight stance is demonstrated by a church that had to call the police to bring calm to a council meeting.

If conflict can be positive, why is it so often negative? First, it is messy and unpredictable. We cannot be sure of how others will respond. Neither is it predictable how *we* will respond. Second, as David Loft says, "It leaves us all feeling soiled and dirty."[1] That is true for onlookers as well as for participants.

Conflict is a natural part of any interaction. Where there are people, regardless of their commitment to Christ, there will be tension. In fact, without tension things collapse. Conflict, or what Richard Hobgood refers to as resistance, is "response to changes in an effort to keep equilibrium where the ebbs and flows of living seek a point of balance."[2]

Conflict is innate in the church. The church is commissioned to go into enemy territory. God told Jeremiah he would minister "in the midst of deceit" (Jer. 9:6). The passion of Paul and Barnabas for reaching the lost resulted in a sharp contention (Acts 15:39). Forward progress creates friction.

The church is also conflictive by nature. The church's incarnational mission gives birth to a ministry team that comprises persons from many backgrounds. Lydia, a businesswoman; the Philippi jailer; and the converted slave girl were all part of the Philippian church. Those different perspectives necessitated Paul's admonition in Philippians 4:2 to "agree with each other in the Lord" (NIV). Ministry needs, gift mix, and levels of spiritual development create some messy situations. The turbulence of these conditions tends to create chaos, which invites conflict. Even though there is love, the work of melding everyone into the body is stressful. It is like two porcupines seeking to warm each other on a winter night. If they get too close, they prick each other. If they are too far apart, there is no warmth. When conflict erupts in the church, people are usually surprised. Feelings of fear and helplessness tend to feed the conflict. Understanding the types of conflict, the causes of conflict, and ways to respond to conflict reduces the sense of helplessness and helps to turn the conflict into positive energy.

Types of Conflict

Conflicts are rooted in several basic conditions. Some are due to struggles within a person, some come from tensions between persons, and others are caused by substantive issues.

Intrapersonal conflict is the turbulence inside an individual. But internal struggles have a rippling effect on other relationships. A person frustrated at work becomes surly at church. The cause is unrelated to the situation at church. A transformational approach to conflict responds by seeking to identify the intrapersonal cause before addressing the immediate issue over which conflict is occurring.

Interpersonal conflict is more about personality than issues. It occurs when two individuals have a different view about the same thing. One congregation encountered conflict when a relational pastor and a task-oriented lay person differed on how to remodel the church building.

---

[1]David Loft, ed., *Conflict Management in Congregations* (Bethesda, Md.: Alban Institute, 2001).

[2]William Hobgood, *Welcoming Resistance* (Bethesda, Md.: Alban Institute, 2001).

The Myers Briggs Type Indicator identifies four basic elements of personality that cause people to view life from different perspectives and that flavor how each person makes decisions, accepts changes, and relates to other people when under tension.[3] Paul and Barnabas are good examples. Paul's personality made him hit the ground running to carry out his plan. Barnabas was the encourager; relationships were his focus. He was there for the good of others. Their dispute had more to do with their personalities than with John Mark's performance.

Substantive conflict is issue-focused. The differences are over facts, methods, goals, and values. Issues can range from changing the time for worship to changing the style of worship. This type of conflict is more difficult to keep healthy because it frequently involves people's convictions. It brings a much higher level of emotional energy and a greatly decreased ability to listen. Suggested changes in this context are seen as departures from truth, not just changes in method.

Causes of Conflict

Sin is the easy thing to blame for conflict. While it is important to check one's own heart for any indication of sin, to simply label conflict as sin is not only damaging but unbiblical. The early church was divided over circumcision. Rather than labeling each other, they talked through the issues and found a way to grow through the conflict. Their willingness and ability to work out the differences indicated that their hearts were right, not sinful.

One's spiritual condition does impact whether conflict transforms or deforms. But there are other issues that might be termed "the little foxes" (Song 2:15) that

can spoil the vine, things that cannot be ignored or they may become sin.

Poor communication is a culprit in much conflict. Congregations tend to take it for granted that everyone knows what they need to know, but not all do. Uninformed people feel left out. Sometimes people create waves by taking inappropriate actions because they simply do not know protocol. Communication involves connecting all parts of the body in an informed manner. It cannot be assumed that everyone understands "how it is done around here." Commitment to good communication does much to keep conflict positive.

Leadership styles can cause conflict. Some leaders are aggressive while others are passive. Nehemiah and Ezra provide good examples of the two styles. Some people are process-oriented, some are take-charge persons. The temptation is to label a person and relate accordingly. A pastor was in conflict with a lay businessperson. He stereotyped all businesspersons as wanting power. He was surprised to discover that the issue was his own assertiveness rather than the lay person's desire for power. The layperson said, "Because the pastor is used to thinking on his feet, he can out-talk me on any issue, and that intimidates me."

Control and power are what got Adam and Eve into conflict with God. It is human to want to feel important and have a sense of control. James and John were no exception (Matt. 20:20–23). Leaders who desire power and control tend to intimidate. They also lean toward being insensitive. Because power is viewed as a status symbol, communication is difficult for the other person, and the leader sees counsel with others as unnecessary. This sort of leader seeks honor of position rather than exercising servant leadership.

---

[3]David Kiersey and Marilyn Bates, *Please Understand Me* (Del Mar, Calif.: Prometheus Nemesis, 1984).

Failure to recognize the systemic nature of the church is a basic cause of conflict. Christians should readily acknowledge that we are members of the body of Christ. As members of that body, we are parts of a greater whole. Nothing happens to one part that does not affect the entire body. Neither is a conflictual action an indication of a problem of one member alone: it could be a disease of the body. Most of the time in conflict we act like there is no connection between the action of a member and the attitude of the body. Thus, when someone causes a disturbance, scapegoat theology comes into play. Persons with responsibility to manage the issue look for the cause and usually find it in an individual. That person is disciplined or dismissed and once again there is peace. Yet later another conflict arises. Why? The congregation did not look at the possibility that the entire body may have failed to disciple or love or warn, and the leaven of disruption is still active in the life of the church. In conflict the church needs to examine the entire body or there will continue to be harmful conflict.

Understanding its types and causes is the first step in moving conflict toward transformation. The second step in transforming conflict is developing skills for managing dynamic relationships.

Managing Conflict

The management of conflict is similar to composing music. The sound of the tenor line alone becomes monotonous and unpleasant to listen to. Put that part in right relationship with the other parts and there is harmony.

Conflict management has the same goal. A single point of view is overbearing. Coordinated with other views it brings harmony. The blending of views requires skill in managing conflict. Therefore, it is important to have some basic understanding and skills to use in creating harmonious relationships.

The Life Cycle of Groups

Life is dynamic and its experiences move us through a series of cycles. Each group has a *forming stage*. It is the birth stage that occurs when a church is planted, a new ministry is started, or there is a significant change in leadership. It is a time when expectations and assumptions tend to be ignored. Formation is followed by the *storming stage*. This is the time when expectations and assumptions make their presence known. It is named the storming stage not to call for aggressive behavior, but to acknowledge that the blending of expectations and the working out of assumptions will produce tensions that need to be dealt with.

Once through this stage the church can move to the *norming stage*. Although the church seeks to avoid falling into a rut, effective management of energy calls for a pattern of ministry. In the norming stage a pattern develops that is based on the input from the storming stage. Then the church is ready for the *performing stage;* when gifts have been identified and roles accepted, then mission can be accomplished.

Congregations are always in one of these four stages. They will go through these stages more than once, and the sequence of cycling is dependent on what is taking place in the life of the congregation. With the gaining of new people or a change in the functions of individuals, the church moves into the forming or storming stage, and the situation must be normalized. If a congregation understands the life cycle, in times of stress it can look to see why it is in the storming cycle and then respond appropriately.

---

[4]Speed Leas, *Moving Your Church through Conflict* (unpublished class notes, 1987).

Levels of Conflict

There are five levels of conflict.[4] Each level represents a deepening of tensions. The deeper the level, the more difficult transformation becomes. Identifying these levels and recognizing their nature helps to stop the downward slide.

LEVEL ONE

Here there is a *problem to be solved.* Two persons disagree over what to cut from the budget. The disagreement is treated as a true difference of opinion. The focus is on solving the problem using clear and concise language. Relational issues are not involved at this level.

LEVEL TWO

An unsolved problem turns into a *personal disagreement.* A subtle shift in emphasis occurs from the problem to personal interests. The parties give more energy to being right than to working out the disagreement. The conversation turns from discussion of specific solutions to more general and emotional comments.

LEVEL THREE

This is *contest* territory. It is the level where conflict goes public and is noticed by noninvolved persons. The focus is on winning. The language becomes distorted, exaggerated, and divisive. At this level others begin to take sides or form teams. They appeal to what "everyone knows" but everyone knows that those things are not written down. Therefore, confusion grows.

LEVEL FOUR

This is *the fight/flight* level. At this level, people often emotionally and physically detach themselves from others so they do not feel the pain their actions are creating. They decide that it is no longer possible to relate to "those people"; after all, "they" will not change. Each side is concerned about the good of their subgroup, those who agree with them, rather than about that of the entire congregation. Nonverbal language is more important than verbal.

LEVEL FIVE

Here conflict is fully out of control, and many really don't want it to be controlled because the object is to prove those on the other side wrong and destroy them. People on each side have a personal sense that they have been called by God to clean up the mess. They intend to see that "those people" are never involved in the church again.

In some groups conflict is not allowed. Even though it exists, it is not to be recognized. Groups often come to this after there has been major unrest. People do not want to wrestle with any more disagreement. This also happens in congregations that deny that conflict is a part of church life. In either case, the congregation will eventually find itself in level five conflict.

Conflict that is not transformed by level three is very difficult to transform. Even when transformation takes place, deep scars remain. On levels four and five, conflict cannot be undone by the church itself. Outside consultation is necessary.

Steps for Transforming Conflict

The following eight suggestions for keeping tensions healthy and for restoring relationships can be considered a recipe for transforming conflict.[5]

1. KNOW YOUR HEART

Motives are very subtle. Unacknowledged ones are often the reason that conflict moves beyond level one. A vital

---

[5]Douglas C. Lewis, *Resolving Church Conflicts* (New York: Harper & Row, 1981).

step in the midst of a conflictive situation is to ask God to show us our true heart. Right attitudes are a prerequisite for getting in touch with what is driving a person.

2. HELP OTHERS FEEL BETTER ABOUT THEMSELVES

Genuinely affirm the other person. Persons who feel good about themselves are able to be more vulnerable, flexible, and open. They listen better. Paul consistently practiced this principle. Most of his letters begin with a word of commendation, even when he had to correct his hearers. Serious efforts at conflict management are focused as much on the other as on the self.

3. STRIVE FOR EFFECTIVE COMMUNICATION

Communication involves both sending and receiving. Frequently the message is distorted by the perceptions of the sender or the hearing of the receiver. The sender must realize that the message is being received by the other through the filters of past relationships and present perceptions. In-depth and reflective listening are necessary, therefore, to provide for message clarification. The fact that one has spoken is no indication that one has communicated. Unless there is clear communication, transformation will not take place.

4. EXAMINE AND FILTER ASSUMPTIONS

Assumptions are opinions that have not been verified. They often are based on impressions instead of solid information. As Douglas Lewis suggests, "In times of conflict participants make assumptions that have no basis in reality but determine their actions and their perceptions of other people's behavior in the situation."[6] The way to prevent assumptions from derailing the process is to check out the assumptions with the other person in the interest of eliminating those that are not valid.

5. IDENTIFY THE GOALS: KNOW WHAT IS WANTED

Conflict means there are at least two persons with differing ideas. We are people with goals. If there were no goals, there would be no conflict. Both parties need to know what they and the other want in order to work toward an agreement. That will identify why there is a conflict. In this process, try asking "what" instead of "why" questions. "Why" questions have a negative connotation, while "what" seems more positive and therefore invites openness.

6. IDENTIFY THE PRIMARY ISSUE

Most conflicts involve a number of issues but one is primary. Both parties need to agree on what the primary issue is. Often this is the hardest issue to deal with; thus the parties are tempted to focus on lesser ones. However, until the primary issue is identified and owned by both parties, reconciliation cannot progress. Only after it is managed can the other issues be dealt with. Solutions that are offered need to address the main issue; otherwise the solution will be ineffective.

7. DEVELOP ALTERNATIVE GOALS

Once the primary issue is established, it is important to spend time looking for alternative goals—goals that accomplish the purpose but are different from the ones proposed by either group. Give time to brainstorming on other ways that the goal can be achieved to the satisfaction of both groups. This is proof positive that the groups can work together. Hope is critical in working with conflict. Parties must believe there is a way to reach goals and to work cooperatively toward achieving them.

---

[6]Ibid., 59.

8. DEVELOP A CONFLICT MANAGEMENT PLAN

The sense of relief over working through conflict can be so euphoric that groups tend to stop with finding the solution. That can be fatal. The hard work of conflict transformation is only as good as the keeping of the agreement. Phil McGraw affirms the need for managing conflict in a chapter titled, "Relationships Are Managed, Not Cured."[7] A prescribed plan is needed to manage rumors or discomfort that arises after the parties have worked through the conflict. A way needs to be built into the relational process to keep movement on the agreement on target and to provide early detection of a rekindling of the conflict. One strategy is to create a conflict transformation team to which people can go when they hear rumors, feel slighted, or sense dissatisfaction with the agreement.

Conclusion

When we understand conflict in a way that enables us to respond to relational tensions in a healthy manner, we can make conflict a positive force and keep relationships healthy. But conflicts are like wildfires: they may be contained in one area and then erupt in another place. Understanding conflict, recognizing its causes, and having a plan to manage it will help congregations to attain the goal of reconciliation.

What worked in one conflictual situation may not work in another. The important thing is to be flexible, to try a variety of approaches. Remember that the process takes us to the goal. A businessperson submitted a major dispute to arbitration and lost millions of dollars. However, he gave the arbitrators a good rating, saying that while he lost the case, the process was fair.

It will not always be possible to help two parties to continue a relationship. But a good conflict management process enables them to come to the place where they are able release the baggage of the conflict and relate to others with a free conscience and a pure heart. Then they have met the biblical mandate to live as peaceably as possible with others (Rom. 12:18).

The Triangle: A Story

Wally Pugh[8] was pastor of Riverview Church. This was his first church, and he was young, inexperienced, and ambitious. He came to this assignment fully expecting to make a difference.

Wally s call to the church came through a rather unusual procedure. There was no face-to-face interview. The church s call and the pastor s acceptance were based primarily on the recommendation of a mutual acquaintance. Both parties relied on the insights and information of one individual. The pastor did not know of past conflicts in the church. The committee did not know the pastor tended to shy away from conflict.

Pastor Wally was a strong but caring leader. He was in frequent contact with the people of the congregation and sought to listen to what they had to say. It was not long before the pastor learned that one lay leader, Jane Brown, who had several influential positions in the church, was seen as a controlling person. Frequently people would express consternation at the way Jane insisted on setting the standards for who got involved in ministry and how things were done.

At the same time Jane informed Pastor Wally that she was fully committed to what was best for the church. If anyone felt intimi-

---

[7]P.H. McGraw, *Relationship Rescue* (New York: Hyperion, 2000).

[8]All of the names in this story have been changed.

dated by her actions, she wanted to know. She would rather step aside than be a hindrance.

Pastor Wally and Jane did not feel any high level of tension between them. There was no indication from either person of dissatisfaction with their ministry relationship.

When future comments came to the pastor, he reported them to Jane. His assumption was that she would accept them and respond appropriately. Unknown to the pastor, Jane went to the people who criticized her and asked them if they had said what the pastor reported. Unfortunately, they replied that they had not.

Soon Jane confronted the pastor, saying he wanted to get rid of her. That was her explanation of why he had made up such stories.

Pastor Wally knew that he did not want Jane to go. In fact, she and her family were important to the congregation. He sensed, however, that the way Jane s opponents had responded to her indicated the presence of a conflict that he did not fully understand.

Jane demanded an apology from the pastor for trying to get rid of her. She began looking for additional evidence to support her claim that the pastor was against her.

The pastor had learned from early relational experiences to avoid tension if at all possible. In fact, he believed that having a major disagreement that created discomfort with another believer was unacceptable. Yet he also understood the scriptural teaching on the need for reconciliation. He knew that he had no desire for Jane and her family to leave, but if he apologized for being against her, he would only be placating her, not bringing about reconciliation. Furthermore it was not true that he opposed her. Without their reconciliation, the church would suffer and its effectiveness diminish. They needed help to work through their relationship.

Create an ending to the story by suggesting how reconciliation could occur.

Part IV

Stories of
Christian Peacemaking

The War Prayer

Mark Twain

Mark Twain's place in American literature is recognized, but few know his satire on politically sanctioned attacks by dominant countries upon peoples of weaker nations. When America planned to attack insurgents in the Philippines in 1905 as part of the aftermath Spanish-American War, he penned this "war prayer" to express his outrage. After reading it to his daughter Jean and close friends, he decided not to publish it, saying that such unvarnished truth could be uttered only by the dead. Thus the piece was not published until 1923, more than a decade after the author's death.[1]

Mark Twain challenges us to analyze our war prayers concerning the safety of "our combatants" and the success of "our cause." What are we implying that God should do to the "enemy"? Does Twain's satire approach the truth of James 4:1–3 concerning prayer spoken from wrong motives? How should Christians pray when their nation is involved in an international conflict?

It was a time of great and exalting excitement. The country was up in arms, the war was on, in every breast burned the holy fire of patriotism; the drums were beating, the bands playing, the toy pistols popping, the bunched firecrackers hissing and sputtering; on every hand and far down the receding and fading spreads of roofs and balconies a fluttering wilderness of flags flashed in the sun; daily the young volunteers marched down the wide avenue, gay and fine in their new uniforms, the proud fathers and mothers and sisters and sweethearts cheering them with voices choked with happy emotion as they swung by; nightly the packed mass meetings listened, panting, to patriot oratory which stirred the deepest deeps of

---

[1]These details are reported by Albert Bigelow Paine, Mark Twain's official biographer and custodian of his papers until 1937. See his biography, *Mark Twain* (1912; reprint, Broomall, Pa.: Chelsea House, 1997), 3:1232–34.

Reprinted by permission from *The Plough Reader*, Winter 2001. *The Plough Reader* is published by The Bruderhof Foundation of Farmington, Pa. The Bruderhof movement was begun in Germany in 1920 by Eberhard Arnold, who wanted to recapture the spirit of early Christianity as exhibited in Acts 2 and 4 and in the writings of the early Christian fathers. He admired the Anabaptist group known as the Hutterites, though there is no formal union between the two groups. There are currently Bruderhof communities in England and the United States.

their hearts and which they interrupted at briefest intervals with cyclones of applause, the tears running down their cheeks the while; in the churches the pastors preached devotion to flag and country and invoked the God of Battles, beseeching His aid in our good cause in outpouring of fervid eloquence which moved every listener.

It was indeed a glad and gracious time, and the half-dozen rash spirits that ventured to disapprove of the war and cast a doubt upon its righteousness straightway got such a stern and angry warning that for their personal safety's sake they quickly shrank out of sight and offended no more in that way.

Sunday morning came—next day the battalions would leave for the front; the church was filled; the volunteers were there, their faces alight with material dreams—visions of a stern advance, the gathering momentum, the rushing charge, the flashing sabers, the flight of the foe, the tumult, the enveloping smoke, the fierce pursuit, the surrender! —then home from the war, bronzed heros, welcomed, adored, submerged in golden seas of glory! With the volunteers sat their dear ones, proud, happy, and envied by the neighbors and friends who had no sons and brothers to send forth to the field of honor, there to win for the flag or, failing, die the noblest of noble deaths. The service proceeded; a war chapter from the Old Testament was read; the first prayer was said; it was followed by an organ burst that shook the building, and with one impulse the house rose, with glowing eyes and beating hearts, and poured out that tremendous invocation—"God the all-terrible! Thou who ordainest, Thunder thy clarion and lightning thy sword!"

Then came the "long" prayer. None could remember the like of it for passionate pleading and moving and beautiful language. The burden of its supplication was that an ever-merciful and benignant Father of us all would watch over our noble young soldiers and aid, comfort, and encourage them in their patriotic work; bless them, shield them in His mighty hand, make them strong and confident, invincible in the bloody onset; help them to crush the foe, grant to them and to their flag and country imperishable honor and glory.

An aged stranger entered and moved with slow and noiseless step up the main aisle, his eyes fixed upon the minister, his long body clothed in a robe that reached to his feet, his head bare, his white hair descending in a frothy cataract to his shoulders, his seamy face unnaturally pale, pale even to ghostliness. With all eyes following him and wondering, he made his silent way; without pausing, he ascended to the preacher's side and stood there, waiting.

With shut lids the preacher, unconscious of his presence, continued his moving prayer, and at last finished it with the words, uttered in fervent appeal, "Bless our arms, grant us the victory, O Lord our God, Father and Protector of our land and flag!"

The stranger touched his arm, motioned him to step aside—which the startled minister did—and took his place. During some moments he surveyed the spellbound audience with solemn eyes in which burned an uncanny light; then in a deep voice he said:

"I come from the Throne—bearing a message from Almighty God!" The words smote the house with a shock; if the stranger perceived it he gave no attention. "He has heard the prayer of His servant your shepherd and shall grant it if such shall be your desire after I, His messenger, shall have explained to you its import—that is to say, its full import. For it is like unto many of the prayers of men, in that it asks for more than he who utters it is aware of—except he pause and think.

"God's servant and yours has prayed his prayer. Has he paused and taken thought? Is it one prayer? No, it is two—one uttered, the other not. Both have reached the ear of Him Who heareth all supplications, the spoken and the unspoken. Ponder this—keep it in mind. If you beseech a blessing upon yourself, beware! lest without intent you invoke a curse upon a neighbor at the same time. If you pray for the blessing of rain upon your crop which needs it, by that act you are possibly praying for a curse upon some neighbor's crop which may not need rain and can be injured by it.

"You have heard your servant's prayer—the uttered part of it. I am commissioned by God to put into words the other part of it—that part which the pastor, and also you in your hearts, fervently prayed silently. And ignorantly and unthinkingly? God grant that it was so! You heard these words: 'Grant us the victory, O Lord our God!' That is sufficient. The whole of the uttered prayer is compact into those pregnant words. Elaborations were not necessary. When you have prayed for victory you have prayed for many unmentioned results which follow victory—must follow it, cannot help but follow it. Upon the listening spirit of God the Father fell also the unspoken part of the prayer. He commandeth me to put it into words. Listen!

"O Lord our Father, our young patriots, idols of our hearts, go forth to battle—be Thou near them! With them, in spirit, we also go forth from the sweet peace of our beloved firesides to smite the foe. O Lord our God, help us to tear their soldiers to bloody shreds with our shells; help us to cover their smiling fields with the pale forms of their patriot dead; help us to drown the thunder of the guns with the shrieks of their wounded, writhing in pain; help us to lay waste their humble homes with a hurricane of fire; help us to wring the hearts of their unoffending widows with unavailing grief; help us to turn them out roofless with their little children to wander unbefriended the wastes of their desolated land in rags and hunger and thirst, sports of the sun flames of summer and the icy winds of winter, broken in spirit, worn with travail, imploring Thee for the refuge of the grave and denied it—for our sakes who adore Thee, Lord, blast their hopes, blight their lives, protract their bitter pilgrimage, make heavy their steps, water their way with their tears, stain the white snow with the blood of their wounded feet! We ask it, in the spirit of love, of Him Who is the Source of Love, and Who is ever-faithful refuge and friend of all that are sore beset and seek His aid with humble and contrite hearts. Amen."

(After a pause) "Ye have prayed it; if ye still desire it, speak! The messenger of the Most High waits."

It was believed afterward that the man was a lunatic, because there was no sense in what he said.

Nonresistance under Test

E.J. Swalm

For many years a bishop in the Brethren in Christ Church in Canada, E. J. Swalm was a leading peace advocate. In World War II, he was a forceful leader in helping to obtain concessions from the Canadian government for conscientious objectors, including alternate service. During and following the war he was for a number of years chairman of the Canadian Historic Peace Churches. As a young man he was conscripted into the army in World War I. In the following story, he relates what happened when he took his peace position. Note the support that he received from home and church, the strength of his convictions, and the witness that he and others became to army personnel.

Given similar circumstances, would most peace people hold to their convictions with the same tenacity as Swalm did? Is it possible for the peace position to be a convenient stance until strongly tested? How does one explain the large number of peace church members who went into the army in World War II? Were Swalm's actions foolhardy or noble? Should he have taken, if available, some kind of noncombatant service, such as joining the army's medical corps, an action to which he remained strongly opposed? How supportive of a conscientious objector would your congregation and denomination be?

We shall never forget the day, August 6, 1914, while on our way to a prayer meeting in the evening, we stopped at a foundry where one of our ministers passed us and informed us that Germany and Britain were in a state of war. He also told us of the other European nations that had declared war and we immediately had a strange intuition that before this war would be ended, we would be called upon to take our stand for the convictions we had along this line.

Months rolled on! The war continued with greater interest and became more serious. Nineteen fifteen, sixteen and seventeen came and went, but in the fall of seventeen, the Canadian government instituted what they called the "Selective Draft" in which they drafted every unmarried man from eighteen to thirty-four inclusive. They gave privilege of appeal-

---

This chapter is an abridgment of E.J. Swalm, "The War Clouds Gather for the First World War," *Nonresistance under Test: A Compilation of Experiences of Conscientious Objectors as Encountered in Two World Wars*, comp. E.J. Swalm (Nappanee, Ind.: E.V. Publishing House, 1949).

ing to tribunals and applying for exemption under one of six heads. Among them was that you conscientiously opposed the bearing of arms and belonged to a religious denomination whose tenets of faith forbade the same.

We applied for exemption under this ruling and it was granted. More particularly did they give it to us for agricultural reasons, as our father had only one arm and we were needed on the farm. We were very pleased about this and yet, we seemed to feel that this was not all, and that sometime before it would be over, we would face a more stern crisis than that we had yet faced.

In March of 1918, the war intensified to the point that the Allies were becoming alarmed on account of their weakening position and needed more recruits. The day was past when enough recruits could be found by voluntary enlistments. Consequently, a more rigid type of conscription had to be inaugurated; and the Canadian government, by an Order in Council at a midnight session, passed what they called "the Man Power bill" which drafted every man from twenty to twenty-three inclusive, without exception.

When we were apprised of this law, we felt that the moment was drawing near when we would have to take our stand, as we were right in the middle of this draft. It was only a few weeks later that we went to the mail box one Monday morning and drew from the mail box a piece of mail that was different from any we had ever received, and yet we were all too conscious of what it contained. It was a draft informing us that our number was D-3109171, that we were to report for duty at the first Depot Battalion, Second C.O.R., Hamilton, on May 7, 1918, without fail.

We were made to realize that that which we had feared and anticipated for such a long time was just about at our door. This brought a cloud over our family life. I showed the draft to my parents and my sister, and we felt very sorrowful. It was just one week until we were expected to report. We ate and slept poorly because of the solemn situation that was facing us. We knew that the Nonresistant Relief Organization—an organization composed of representatives from various nonresistant churches—was already working on our exemption status and representatives had been to Ottawa to see what could be done for us.

My father left immediately on the morning train to interview this Committee to see what might be offered to us from our government by way of exemption. He returned the next day saying nothing could be offered, and that he feared that even the exemption privileges enjoyed in the past may have been abrogated. We sought every available place for information that might give us something by way of governmental privileges whereby we might not be forced to take up arms and thus honour our convictions in the matter.

Every avenue we sought failed us, and we came down to the close of the week with nothing to offer except to stand on our own convictions. We received a letter on Saturday from one of our staunch ministers, who encouraged us and said that our position should be that of one of the early church. We should take our stand and say, "We cannot fight because we're a Christian. We cannot fight though we die."

My parents received another letter from a man who had heard I was soon to be drafted, and he dropped a very encouraging word in the course of his letter and said, "Tell Ernie we are praying for him." Just how much this encouraged our hearts we are not able to put in words.

The Friday morning, previous to our leaving home on Tuesday, we went to the barn early to feed the horses. While we were feeding the horses, my father came to the barn. He watched me in silence mix the feed for a little while, and then he said to me, "My boy, I'd like to have a few words with you." He said, "The days are very dark and they seem to be getting darker, and I realize that it will be only a few days until you're going to be forced away from your home and we won't have the pleasure of associating together as we do now." He said, "I'd like to ask you something. Suppose that the worst comes to the worst? How is it with your soul?"

I realize that it was very difficult for my father to ask this question, and yet I deeply appreciated his approaching this matter as it is the most vital aspect of the whole affair. I took a brief and rapid retrospect of my Christian life. I said to him, "You remember the night that I knelt at the altar of prayer in the old brick church and gave my heart to God?" to which he said he remembered, and told how the burden was lifted off his heart when he saw his children seek God. Then I said, "You remember some years later while seeking God for a deeper experience, I knelt in this very barn and consecrated my life to God and sought Him for sanctifying power." This he also remembered. Then I said in a few words, "I want you to know that it still holds good this morning."

My father then said, putting his arm around my neck and weeping, "I would far rather get word that you were shot, that I should never see you again after you leave home, than to have you come home again, knowing that you compromised and failed to live up to the convictions that you had. Though it would be very hard for me to lose my only son, and it would mean a lot, I'd rather know that you honoured your convictions if it cost you your life, and I must spend the rest of my days without you."

This courageous attitude on the part of my father stimulated my faith and was a great help, and put a buoyancy in my soul that I cannot describe.

Then he said, "The Word of God says that 'whatsoever two or three agree upon respecting anything, it shall be done.' Let us go up in the granary and pray." I consented, and we went up in the granary, where we knelt in prayer together and God visited us in that granary in an unusual manner. It was there that I prayed through, and God was pleased to let me see the firing squad with all that it means. There I faced it and was willing, if needs be, to die for Jesus.

We left the granary that morning with such victory and such confidence and such a determination that the devil was defeated on that point from that day on, and when in the actual fray and the thickest of the conflict, while taking our stand for right, we would turn our thoughts back with a great deal of satisfaction and remember the granary experience and how God marvelously visited us there, determination was renewed in our soul.

We began to make preparations for leaving home under conditions that were unusual as we expected never to return again. As my father planned to accompany me to the army to help me in whatever way he could, we had asked the Lord to help us to sell our cattle that we had been feeding. The Lord was pleased to answer prayer and sent us a buyer that very morning and gave us our price, the cattle to be delivered just before we left home.

I want to refer to a touching incident. We drove those cattle to town together—a privilege we had very much enjoyed annually for years. This day as we were delivering a herd of very good cattle, sold for wartime prices, we suddenly discovered we had driven the cattle two miles and never exchanged a word. At the end of two miles my father broke the silence and said, "These cattle do not mean much to me. My farm this last week looks the smallest that it ever has. I'm realizing that it means something to part with my son."

While he needed the money and could make good use if it, yet he was deeply conscious there were things that money cannot buy.

How vividly we recall the last Sunday spent at home. We went as usual to the House of God to enjoy what we thought was the last service in the old brick church where we had been carried as a child, where we had been brought up and first attended Sunday School, where we heard the Gospel preached while in sin, where we had been brought to know the Lord.

We taught our Sunday School class as usual with a great deal of emotion. When the class was dismissed, saying good-bye to the boys was almost more than we could stand. As one young fellow, who didn't make any profession, said good-bye, it touched our hearts deeply. He said, "Goodbye, Mr. Swalm, I hope you'll come back again safely."

We heard old Bro. Alex McTaggart preach the sermon. He spoke about Daniel in the Lions' Den. We knew that sermon was being preached for our benefit. What a determination we had in our soul, by the grace of God to stand true, let it cost what it will.

After meeting came the farewell, which proved a touching scene. Many kind things were spoken, by many friends who wished us the very best. Ere we left the churchyard we went out to stand at our mother's grave and to just pause for a moment in brief silence and meditation. We thought, "Ere we stand by this grave again, we're going to see our mother in heaven."

This determination was born out of reality of conviction. We felt in our heart we were determined to obey God and to honour our convictions, letting the cost be what it would.

As we drove away from the old church, our feelings were again touched. We shed a few tears. Yet we turned away with that triumph and victory that comes as God helps folks in the hour of special need.

That Sunday afternoon a score of our friends came in to extend their best wishes, to pray with us and to offer kind words and assistance, which were all deeply appreciated. In fact, one never knows how many kind people there are until such an hour of need arises. We sang hymns, and finally my father asked me what was my selection for a hymn. Quick as a flash, something seemed to say, "Sing that old song, 'Would you live for Jesus and be always pure and good, let Him have His way with thee!'"

A Sad Farewell

We spent all day Monday in preparation to leave, arranging our few effects, distributing them among our loved ones, for we never expected to need them again. While walking around the field on the farm on Monday, which we thought was the last opportunity, father said to me, "Can you say in the language of Paul, 'none of these things move me, neither count I my life dear unto myself, that I might finish my course with joy.'" To which I replied, "I believe I can," for it did seem real in my own soul.

We had a peculiar feeling all day Monday. We rather wished it might have been possible for us in some honourable and mysterious way to have taken wings and flown away from our loved ones without being forced to bid them good-bye, for the thing we dreaded the worst was not facing the firing squad, but giving our loved ones good-bye for what we thought was the last time. We knew that it would be a tense moment, and our heartstrings would be pulled.

We went to bed Monday night, arising early Tuesday morning, making hasty preparations to leave home and go to the army. The Lord gave us a good night's rest. We ate breakfast and made all the final preparations, then approached the family altar.

How vividly we recall our father reaching up on the shelf and getting down the Bible for family worship for the last time. We had many times seen him do it, never remember of his missing purposely the occasion of family worship, regardless of who was in our home. This we felt would be the last time. He was providentially directed to read the Fourteenth Chapter of John, the first fourteen verses, and when he came to the fourteenth verse, which says, "If you ask any thing in my name, I will do it," he seemed to have a supernatural pause, almost a hesitancy between every word, which seemed to carry with it an unusual promise for us that morning of particular application. We knelt in prayer and asked God to sustain us and give the needed grace for the steps we were about to take. God graciously answered and never one moment did He fail us in all the experiences we were to go through in the next ten weeks.

And then came the awful moment of saying farewell—the last good-bye to our stepmother, then have the parting word with our only sister, whom we loved so dearly, who threw her arms around our neck, refusing to let go until we literally dragged her out on the lawn. Finally the dreaded moment of parting came. Amid the bitterness of blinding tears, we looked back several times going out the lane. Our hearts were broken as we saw her standing there sobbing as if her heart would break. We hope it shall please the Lord not to ask us to have our heartstrings stretched again like they were that morning.

It was just about daybreak as we turned from the lane to go up the road, past the orchard. At the corner of the orchard we took one last long look back at the old home where we were born. In our hearts we said farewell with a resignation to the will of God and a determination that if we never see it again, we intend to

be true and to wake in that home that's prepared for those who are faithful.

We were soon at the depot and though many incidents might be referred to, as well as to the friends we met on the train, we now come to our arrival at Hamilton and our coming to the C.O.R. where we expected to have the privilege of immediately taking our stand as a conscientious objector. In this we were disappointed as we were ushered into army routine and life so gradually and so slowly, that it became a question to decide just when and where we ought to take our stand.

Meeting the Test

After a couple of hours waiting in the canteen with all who reported that day, a captain who had charge of the medical history sheets came in and we, in turn, received our medical history sheet and informed him that we didn't intend to take service because we were a conscientious objector. To this he replied he had nothing to do with that and that I would have to conscientiously object to the captain of my company, but said, "I'll give you this tip. Don't try anything like that, my boy, for we've had two or three that tried that here. Until we got through with them, they were mighty glad to carry on and be a soldier. I'd advise you to profit by their mistakes."

At that, we asked for an interview with the captain of our company, which we were granted. We were paraded before Capt. Marshall. We laid our case before him and he referred us to Major Bennett of "A" company. We had a little interview with Major Bennett, who said that in all the search that he could make with reference to our exemption privileges in the past, he believed that they had been abrogated and that I would have to take service of some kind—noncombatant to say the least—to which I replied I would not.

First, he tried to flatter me; then he tried to scare me and said that there were no others in the army who were taking the stand I did. He said that there had been some, but after they were threatened and told what would happen to them, they all took service and carried on. He told me I had better take service or else I would be put in chains, taken overseas and placed in the front lines as a barricade and would be shot down first thing, with all the other cowards and despicable characters who would stop bullets to save better men who were coming up behind.

I replied, "Be that as it may. By the grace of God I am determined in my stand, and I will not take service because I intend to be a conscientious objector." To this he replied, "We won't force you to put on the uniform, but we'll just make you so glad to do it that you'll put it on."

At this we were turned over to the quartermaster's stores and ordered to take our uniform. At this point my father was ordered off the grounds and told by a sergeant-major that as long as he was there they couldn't get this boy to do anything. My father said, "Can I give him good-bye." They said "Yes, but don't be all day about it." So my father and I stepped outside the door. We embraced each other for what we thought was the last time, my father saying "I have done the last thing I can do for you, my boy. There is nothing left but put your hope and trust in God."

He left me and went out on the corner of the sidewalk to watch what might occur. I was again taken in and offered my uniform which I gracefully, yet positively declined. I was put between two soldiers with fixed bayonets and marched to my bunk room and given my uniform and ordered to put it on. I refused again and then an order—strangely as it may seem— came through, that they were not to force a uniform on that man, but to let him wear civilian clothes. I couldn't understand this at the time, but later I learned it was a direct answer to prayer and a confirmation of my father's faith, who was being attacked in an unusual way by Satan himself, as he stood on the sidewalk. Next day as he visited me and found me in civilian clothes, he knew his prayer was answered.

My father then went to visit Bishop S. F. Coffman of the Mennonite Church, who had charge of this work and was doing his very best to help the boys that were drafted. Since I was the first of the Brethren in Christ (Tunker) Church to be drafted, it was clearly evident that they were making a test case of mine. My father came back the next day, assuring me that Bro. Coffman and the Nonresistant Relief Organization were doing their very best to get an exemption and that we should stand true to God in any case.

Bro. Coffman said he would follow this case to the Privy Council in England, before he would be defeated. When I refused to put on the uniform, I was placed under arrest by Sergeant Hartley and taken to the Guard Room. To my surprise, contrary to what I had been told, I there met seven or eight other conscientious objectors who had taken the identical stand that I had.

When we met each other, we were so delighted, we thanked God and took courage. It was really a relief to realize that we had taken our stand, that we were now under arrest and our way seemed more clear. We want to thank God for the association we had with those splendid young men, representing many different Protestant denominations, who had a close walk with God and whose lives have made a contribution to ours which we shall never be able to appreciate fully.

Next morning, we were paraded before the Battalion Officer Commanding, Col. Belson. There again we were asked to take our stand, the charge being laid against us. We reaffirmed our faith and positively declared that we could take no branch of the service whatever, because we felt that no matter what branch of the service we were taking, we were a part of the military machine. We offered our services for any kind of medical or relief work, if we could do it as a civilian, but not as a soldier.

The Colonel said, "I suppose you have some Scripture for that," to which I replied, "Yes." I said that I considered Saul of Tarsus, as he held the clothes of those that stoned Stephen, was a noncombatant. We don't read that he threw any stones but he was thoroughly guilty of the crime because he was consenting unto his death. So we feel that it is not the branch of the service that we object to. It is the service. For this reason, we could not take any part of it, whether it be stretcher bearer, whether it be making munitions, or what. We would be just releasing another man to shoot the bullets and to take life.

At this we were remanded for a District Court-martial which we were informed would convene some time within a month. We were again taken to the guard-room and kept under close arrest and the District Court-martial sat in just one month's time.

During that time we were forced to put on the "fatigue" suit of the uniform. We refused to put it on but an officer ordered a man to strip us of our civilian clothes and put it on us, which he did without any objection on our part. We were promised our civilian clothes would be sent home, but instead someone either stole them or sold them. We never saw any of that suit again. We were given light duty around the camp, such as cleaning the yard, which afforded us a bit of exercise and passed the time.

One day, a young man by the name of John Reid, who was a conscientious objector, but not a member of a church whose tenets of faith upheld nonresistance, took a firm stand against bearing arms. His own pastor was ashamed of him. He came down and told the officers of the army that this man was not real and they should give no recognition to his profession or pacifism and even advised them to treat him roughly, calling him a coward.

We shall never forget the day on which he was refused even a court-martial, but was forced to go overseas. He refused to accept his kit and lay down on the ground, refusing to march. They actually carried him into a patrol wagon and took him away. We will always remember how sad it seemed, as he shoved a couple of dry bread crusts under his belt, in case they might try to starve him, and said he would have something to eat. We admired his courage and offered many prayers in his behalf.

He accepted a mild form of noncombatant service when he joined the Imperial Army, but was permitted to return home again and we had the privilege of entertaining him in our home after the war was over.

Many threats and scoffings were offered us during our confinement preceding the court-martial, in which they pretended to have arranged to shoot us to watch just what effect it had upon us. This did not have much of an intimidating effect because we had settled it all in the granary, ere we left home.

One day when Sergeant Hartley was taking us up to headquarters to give a summary of evidence, the boys were joking about shooting me, to which Sergeant Hartley replied, "What's the joke about the shooting?" We informed him they were running a bluff and had actually taken a paper off the file and read that they had purchased ammunition for my execution. He said, "This is nothing to joke about. I'll see that it is stopped," and we were never again threatened with anything like it. We mention this merely to show that Sergeant Hartley, with some other officers of the army, were the finest gentlemen we have ever met. Indeed, not all army men were corrupt. Some of the biggest and finest men we have ever met wore military uniform.

Court-Martialed

The day of court-martial arrived. We were paraded to the medical officer to be examined to see if we could stand hard labor. From there we were ordered to the court-martial tent. While standing outside, just waiting to be called in, the devil made a thrust at us with a sense of loneliness and even told us what a fool we were to take this stand, that we might be shot, while others were going forth and having a good time. We immediately asked God to rebuke the devil. Right in the midst of that season of loneliness and feeling so far away from all our loved ones, as we looked down the road, what should meet our gaze but one of the most encouraging sights we have ever seen. Who was coming up the road but Eld. D. W. Heise of Gormley, Ont.! He would have walked right past us only we drew his attention. He came over, and said, "What are you doing here?" We said, "We're just waiting for the court to assemble. We're going to be court-martialed." He said, "I read it in the Toronto Globe yesterday. I knew your father couldn't get here so I arose at three o'clock. I walked to Yonge Street (a distance of three miles), took the first radial to Toronto, caught the first boat out of Toronto, arrived in Niagara-on-the-Lake and walked up through the lines on my way to the Orderly Room in search of you." He got there just five minutes before I was court-martialed.

We have often said that he looked so good that if God had opened the skies and let an angel fall, it couldn't have looked any better to us than Bro. Heise did that morning. Immediately we were called in. The charge was read. We were tried as a conscientious objector; we were tried as a defaulter, for having disobeyed a lawful command given by a superior officer, in that while in active service we refused to put on our uniform when ordered to do so by Sergeant Hartley. To this we conscientiously had to plead guilty. They then asked us if anyone was there to plead for us and we said Bro. Heise was.

Bro. Heise came in with the solemnity of a funeral procession. After being asked a few preliminary questions, they asked him to testify in our behalf. Bro. Heise sought to tell them about our conversion, to which they objected or at least interrupted and said, "All we want you to do is to testify to his character." Bro. Heise very kindly said some beautiful things. We hope he didn't say anything that did violence to his conscience. It would be immodest for us to repeat what he said, but we have often thought if we can only be acquitted as well at the Judgment Seat of Christ as the Bro. Heise did it that day, we shall count ourselves very fortunate and be well satisfied.

We shall never forget the kindness of Bro. Heise in this respect and we herewith print a copy of a letter which he sent to my father after the court had closed and our sentence was pending, which shows his thoughtfulness and sacrificing spirit which indeed was appreciated by my father.

Toronto, May 31, 1918
Eld. Isaac Swalm
Duntroon, Ont.

Beloved Brother:
I trust you still find the sustaining grace of God sufficient in these days of sorrow and perplexity. I have just returned from Niagara where I was privileged to see Ernie and give evidence before the Military Court as to his character and standing in the church, and then just gave him good-bye and left.

His trial was ended when I left but no decision given. Poor boy! How our hearts go out

to him and others, but our God is sufficient.
Ernie knew nothing of his trial coming today
until yesterday. I saw it in the paper yesterday
and went over this morning. I am on the go
almost night and day this week on behalf of
our boys, but it is all—"inasmuch." No time
for anything more this time.

> *Look up and pray,*
> *Dave*

We also want to make mention of a young man we met in that court that day, whom we had never seen before—a man who has come into our lives and made a contribution for which we shall never cease to thank God. His name is David Nichols. He did not belong to any particular denomination. Because of this fact, he had no exemption privileges and was sentenced to two years, serving six or eight months of it in Kingston Federal Prison, and was released in March, 1919.

After his release he wrote us a letter, asking if he might spend his vacation with us, for he had secured a good position in Toronto as an accountant. We were glad to have him come and visit us, and from that day to this he has spent most of his annual vacations in our home and we regard his coming with great pleasure. In fact, we have a regular little camp meeting in our home when he is visiting us. We have exchanged letters once a month from that time to this.

At this military court this morning, the military officials sought to build up a supposed case in order to trap Mr. Nichols and create an argument in favor of war. They said, "Mr. Nichols, are you married?" He said, "No." They said, "Suppose that you were married and your wife died unsaved. What would become of her?" He replied, "Most decidedly

she'd go to hell." They pretended to be very much horrified at such a statement. Mr. Nichols re-emphasized that that would be her lot—the lot of all those who failed to accept Christ.

Then they said, "Now, Mr. Nichols, we're going to suppose a case. We will suppose that you are married and that your wife is unsaved, and that here is a regiment of the German army coming to kill your wife, and you know it. She knows it. Suppose that you, out of respect to your wife, take a gun and with a lone hand go out and fight against this regiment. We know it's impossible but just suppose that you were able to keep that regiment back for at least six months. Suppose that at the end of six months, or during that six months, your wife has gotten converted and when the six months were ended, you're not able to hold them back any longer. They break through and they kill your wife. Wouldn't you have been doing the Lord's will in holding back that regiment for six months, even though you slew a few of them? To think that your wife has been saved and will accompany you to Heaven."

We all wondered what Mr. Nichols would say, and quick as a flash, with hardly a moment's hesitancy, Mr. Nichols came back with a reply, and said, "Of course, in the first place, on your part it's only supposition. In the second place, I'm not married. In the third place if I ever do get married, I shall marry a Christian. Then nothing like you suppose will need to happen."[1]

This indeed clinched the argument. The men were very glad to change the conversation. This was a direct fulfillment of the promise of Jesus that in an hour of crisis we shall not even take thought of what we

---

[1] David J. Nichols passed to his eternal reward in February 1948. His homegoing was triumphant. His last words to his sister-in-law, who was at his bedside in the brief absence of his wife, were, "I am going. Tell Jennie [his wife] that I will meet her in the glory and the struggle has not been too hard after all." In a very few minutes he undoubtedly was with the Prince of Peace.

shall say, but He promised to put words in our mouths that would rebuke the offender; words that could not be gainsaid.

Just to show how wonderfully God sustains His children and helped the boys in their replies to officers, even though they were not trained men so far as education was concerned, we cite the following case of a young Irishman, a Christian, a very devoted young man, who when interrogated by one of the officers and was charged, laid hold of the Scriptures in a very effective manner. The officer said, "You conscientious objectors are a bunch of cowards. You're afraid to go to war. You're afraid to die. I consider you a bunch of weaklings, without any strength and no concern for your fellowmen. You want all the benefits for yourselves. You've no love for your friends, nor your dependents. And furthermore, I rather think you've gone wrong in your heads. You're just a little bit mentally deranged. I think you've got a spider on the ceiling."

All this was said to intimidate the young man, who was an artless young Christian, yet well acquainted with the Word of God. The young man, without much hesitation, said "No, sir, I beg your pardon. You're mistaken there. God's Word says that 'God has not given us the spirit of fear but of power and of love and of a sound mind'" (2 Tim. 1:7).

One would think that very Scripture was put in the Bible to answer that one question alone. How marvelously God makes His Word fit individual cases and silences men who do not know His Book.

After the Court was dismissed, we were paraded back to the Guard Tent to live our life of confinement until the day that the sentence should be read off. The sentence was promulgated from the military division at Toronto, by the Officer Commanding, and in three days all those who were court-martialed were paraded into what is called "a hollow square." The Battalion lined up in a hollow square. Those whose sentences were to be read off were paraded in with all the rest of the prisoners from the Guard Tent, and those who were courtmartialed, while their sentences were being read, the Battalion Sergeant-Major removed their caps and shoved them two paces forward. This was done to make a spectacle of them and to intimidate the rest of the soldiers that they do not pursue a similar course. We felt very happy in our own souls as this experience was being realized and had a profound feeling of sympathy for the boys who looked on and only wished they might have felt that consolation in their own heart, that we felt so keenly at that moment.

After the sentences were read out, we were again returned to the Guard House and told that evening we would begin our sentence, which was two years of hard labor. We would be taken to St. Catharine's to the Lincoln County Jail, to wait the arrival of the provincial sheriff who would take us to the Federal prison in Kingston in due time....

Guidance:
An Adventure in Failure

E. Stanley Jones

E. Stanley Jones was one of the leading missionary statesmen of the twenti-eth century. His long career in India brought him close to the independence movement led by Gandhi. Jones used interreligious dialogue as an evangelis-tic tool, believing the gospel freely shared would help many to discover for themselves that faith in Jesus Christ was superior to all religious systems.

He was a prolific author, and the sale of his books worldwide brought invita-tions for him to speak in many countries, where he met leading national Chris-tians, like the Christian pacifist and social activist Toyohiko Kagawa of Japan, and was granted audiences with heads of state. Like few Americans in his day, he was able to see global issues in non-Western ways without any loss of conviction that Jesus Christ is the savior of all peoples or any diminished zeal for evangelism as the supreme task of the church.

A Methodist minister who supported John Wesley's doctrine of entire sanctifi-cation, Jones was also a convinced Christian pacifist. This selection from his autobiography, *Song of Ascents*, tells how he worked with the Japanese peace envoys to Washington, D.C. in trying to avoid war in the Pacific. While Pearl Harbor and the declaration of war that followed seemed to say his peace mis-sion was futile, his stance on the issues gave him an open door for evangelism that few Christians had in post-war Japan.

This selection sheds light on long-standing criticisms of Christian pacifism. Many assert that the peace stance is too idealistic, suited only for a millennial kingdom but impractical in the real world of international competition and con-flict. It is argued that since pacifism cannot keep nations from fighting, it is irrelevant. One must opt for a more realistic Christian stance. Jones makes us ask whether we should take Jesus' way of peace because it works or because it is right. Or, maybe more importantly, we must ask whether it works immedi-ately or in the long-range triumph of Christ's kingdom. Would we say missions were a failure because hundreds of missionaries died from various causes before they ever founded a church among people of a native culture? The disciples of Jesus on Good Friday evening were ready to believe God's pro-gram of peace had perished on a Roman cross. Easter Sunday put things in a different light. Is Christian pacifism a decision to view life from the perspective of Easter Sunday and to reject the temptation to believe that things are what they seem to be on Good Friday evening?

After finishing the National Christian Missions, speaking from two to five times a day for a year, I was in Los Angeles in 1941 ready to go back to India. I was awakened in my hotel room about four o'clock with the inner voice saying: "I want you here." It persisted. I struggled with it: "Lord, I can't. The National Christian Mission is over. My work is done. My wife and daughter are in India. I haven't seen them for over a year (as it turned out, it was to be six years). The boat with my trunk is leaving San Francisco today (I was to pick it up in the Philippines). I do not see how I can stay." But the voice was persistent: "I want you here." After fighting with it for two hours I succumbed, said I would obey. I sent off five telegrams, one of them to take my trunk off the boat and leave it with the Methodist Publishing House in San Francisco. (The fact is I've never had time to pick up that trunk. After twenty-five years what I had in it is probably obsolete.)

But what was I here for, now that I had obeyed? "I want you here"—what for? I vaguely felt it was connected with the giving of my efforts to head off, if possible, the impending Japanese-American war. This was August, 1941. Dr. Kagawa and I, speaking at a conference in Lake Geneva, used to go out by the lakeside at daybreak to pray together for peace. One day he said: "You go to see Admiral Nomura, the Japanese ambassador at Washington. He wants peace." That gave me a clue. He also said: "Japan needs a place for her surplus population, warm enough to take off our

coats." He mentioned New Guinea. New Guinea, I found, was the second largest island of the world, after Greenland; was the one practically uninhabited country of the world with a population of a million and a quarter and could sustain forty to fifty million; belonged to Australia and to Holland, neither of whom needed it. That also gave me a clue.

So I went to Washington, going out, like Abraham, not knowing whither I was going. The doors began to open. The Japanese envoys at Washington began to trust me. I scarcely knew why, for I had written an "Open Letter to Japan" before the Chinese-Japanese war, begging them not to go to war with China. That letter was forbidden in Japan but was made a school subject in China. I still wondered why they trusted me. But they did. From September till December 7, Pearl Harbor day, I took off three days each week to go to Washington to see what we could do to head off the war. I would have evangelistic series in different parts of the country from Sunday to Wednesday then go to Washington from Thursday to Saturday. Dr. O.G. Robinson, a Methodist pastor, set up the interviews in my absence and sat in at all the interviews except those with the President. Some days we would have ten solid hours of interviews. The interviews were with senators, representatives, state department officials, supreme court judges, public men and religious leaders. We formed a continuous prayer vigil in an Episcopal church where, around the clock, night and day, for a week, people came to pray for peace. I cabled Australia, China, and Japan

---

This chapter is an abridgment of E. Stanley Jones, "Guidance: An Adventure in Failure," *A Song of Ascents: A Spiritual Autobiography* (Nashville: Abingdon, 1968), 188–207.

about the vigil of prayer and suggested they hold one for a week in their countries. Australia responded and said they would have a vigil. China did not. Dr. Kagawa cabled: "Japanese church leaders holding vigil for week. We are doing what we can at this end." Someone wrote me: "I am an atheist, but the vision of Christians on their knees praying night and day for peace has touched me deeply."

I went through those tense, tragic months and came away with a deep respect for democracy. I had dealt with governments in India and elsewhere in the East, and they were largely closed corporations. But here was democracy open and responsive, and it cared. I cannot remember a single snub, or a single refusal of a request for an interview during those three months. Here were busy men, very busy men, who would give a patient and sympathetic ear to a moral and spiritual appeal. I cannot remember a cynical remark or sneer, except one, and that from a prominent pastor, who, when he heard that I had said to Dr. Robinson as we stood beside the Potomac River waiting for the time of an interview; "I would be willing to throw myself into this river if it could help to bring peace," remarked: "That would be bad for sanitation." The only other cynical reply was by a state department official who, when I suggested giving New Guinea to Japan for her surplus population and also suggested that we inform the Japanese of our willingness to suggest this, replied: "If you told them that, I would have apoplexy." Apart from the above, there was nothing but courtesy and a willingness to listen to any feasible and sensible proposal.

Moreover, I believed then, and I believe more so now, that the Japanese at Washington were not playing a double game, pulling the wool over our eyes while the Japanese in Japan were getting ready to strike. They were of the peace party and were trying desperately to find a basis for peace and were brokenhearted when the negotiations broke down and war broke out. The fact that they were never hailed before the war guilt tribunal to be tried for war guilt shows that the military believed they were of the peace party. When I raised this question with General Douglas MacArthur at the close of the war, he replied: "I agree with you; they knew nothing of what was going to happen at Pearl Harbor." He sent a special messenger to the Japanese Washington envoys after the war at Karuizawa to assure them that they would not have to appear before the war guilt tribunal. Admiral Nomura told me personally, "We had no notion of Pearl Harbor. We thought the crisis meant that diplomatic relationships were going to be broken, or that the Japanese fleet was going to Southeast Asia, a crisis spot, but of Pearl Harbor we knew nothing." Mrs. Gwen Terasaki, American wife of the public relations man at the Japanese Embassy, said to me: "My husband called me up on the morning of Pearl Harbor and said excitedly: 'It's happened.' And when I asked, 'What's happened?' he replied: 'Turn on your radio.' And he was weeping."

So I was basically convinced all the way through that the Japanese at Washington wanted peace and that President Roosevelt wanted peace, at least in the Pacific; I'm not so sure about the Atlantic—a question mark. I was only concerned with the Pacific, and there he rang true in every move. If he was playing a part, acting as though he wanted peace in the Pacific when he really wanted war, as some have suggested, then he was a superb actor. All my contacts with him seemed real and only real. He seemed to be anxious for peace and responded to any appeal in that direction...

On November 29, Mr. Terasaki came to me at the Robinson home and said, "We're afraid the negotiations are going to break down at this 2:30 P.M. meeting with the President today. Could you see the President before 2:30 and explain to him our psychology?" We called up the President's secretary, Marvin H. McIntyre, and asked if it was possible for me to see the President before 2:30, as the Japanese wanted me to explain to the President the Japanese psychology. It was then 12:30 P.M. The secretary replied: "These are the President's engagements before 2:30—every minute is taken. But if you will dictate to my secretary over the phone a memorandum of what you want to say, I'll see that the President gets it before 2:30; so if you don't get to see him, you will have your message across to him. But I'll make the suggestion about the interview." "In that case," I replied, "I'll have to write it." I ran upstairs and wrote the memorandum, read it to Mr. Terasaki, got his approval, and dictated it over the phone. I was simply interpreting the Japanese viewpoint and psychology as Mr. Terasaki interpreted it to me. This is what I dictated: "The Japanese say, 'We've been four years at war in China. We are in a war mentality. In a war mentality men cannot think straight. The Allies were in a war mentality at Versailles, and they made a bad peace. You help us from a war mentality to a peace mentality. Don't compel us to do things, but make it possible for us to do them. If you treat with us this way, we will reciprocate doubly. If you stretch out one hand, we will stretch out two; and not only can we be friends, but also we can be allies.'"

An important memorandum, I felt, for the Japanese were offering to leave the Axis—"Not only can we be friends, but also we can be allies." That was a supreme offer of reversal, an offer to change sides.

But there was a condition: "Don't compel us to do things, but make it possible for us to do them." This referred to the communication which the American government gave to Japan on November 26, which was in substance: "Get out of the Axis, get out of Indo-China, get out of Indonesia, and have equality of trade." This was not quite an ultimatum, for it was in diplomatic language; but it bordered on it. It put Japan in a box: she had to knuckle or fight us. Terasaki was pleading that we make it possible for Japan to do these four things, to make it possible to save her face.

I was suggesting that New Guinea was the way to save Japan's face; that it really belonged to Japan's surplus population, cooped up in her little islands, only 18 percent of which are arable. The Western nations grabbed these islands in the Pacific when grabbing was good, before Japan woke up. New Guinea belonged to Australia and Holland, neither of whom needed it. So I went to the Australian minister at Washington, Richard Gardiner Casey, who was very sympathetic. His reply: "I agree that we must do something about Japan's surplus population. If we don't do it now, we will have to do it in ten years. Have you brought this up to your state department?" I replied that I had and that their reaction was that it is difficult for America to talk about giving away someone else's territory. So I suggested that America give a hundred million dollars each to Australia and to Holland as compensation. Then everyone would be doing something for peace—Australia, Holland, Britain through Australia, and America....

I found a good deal of sympathy before the war for the New Guinea proposal. A representative of the state department said to me: "We don't want to appear bureaucratic, but all we can say is that we are considering it." My reply: "But you can't consider it too long. You must do something dramatic for peace. Japan may strike." Alas, they considered it too long!...

But back to the account before Pearl Harbor. The next day after I dictated the memorandum over the phone, Mr. Terasaki came to us delighted. He said: "The President took very seriously the memorandum. The whole of the conversation was around it." Mr. Saburo Kurusu, the special envoy, sent his special thanks. Then Mr. Terasaki asked me if I could take a plane and go to Warm Springs, Georgia, and "say something by word of mouth to the President—there must be no record." (The President had gone to Warm Springs after the 2:30 P.M. interview with the Japanese envoys.) We called up the President's secretary and placed the matter before him. His reply: "Yes, I think you can see the President, but if the Japanese will allow you to write the substance of the suggestion, it can be brought over to me by Dr. Robinson tomorrow. It will be put into a special bag, be sealed in my presence; it will go down by special plane on Monday, and I will guarantee that no one will see it, not even a secretary, before it gets into the hands of the President." Mr. Terasaki agreed, but added: "You can give the substance of the suggestion, but one thing you must withhold, that you must say by word of mouth or not at all." The letter was taken over to the secretary the next day, but the secretary said: "The situation has grown worse so the President is returning to Washington Sunday night. So I will give it to him when he arrives at the railway station Monday morning, December 1."

In the meantime I had gone to Thomasville, North Carolina, for an evangelistic mission. I said to them: "You must let me off. The Japanese want me to say something to the President by word of mouth, or not at all. And if I do not say it and something should happen, I would feel forever condemned." So they let me cut off Wednesday night. I went back to Washington and arrived on December 3. I got in touch with the President's secretary, and

he told me that the President took a favorable attitude toward my letter, which was given to him at the railway station and was read on the way back to the White House. Then I said: "There is one thing I couldn't say in the letter. I must say it by word of mouth; can I see the President?" He came back in a few moments and said: "Can you get here in twenty minutes? Come to the East Gate, where someone will meet you, and you can go into a secret entrance to the President's office, so you won't have to run a barrage of reporters." The President said on my arrival: "I thought of sending the cable to the Emperor two days before I got your letter suggesting it. But I've hesitated to do it, for I don't want to hurt the Japanese envoys here at Washington by going over their heads to the Emperor." "That," I replied, "is the point on which I have come. This suggestion about sending the cable to the Emperor did not come from me; it came from the Japanese envoys here at Washington. They asked me to ask you to send the cable. But they also said that there could be no record, for if it were known that they had gone over the heads of the Japanese government to the Emperor, their own heads wouldn't be worth much." The President replied: "Well, that cleans my slate. I can do it." "But," I replied, "the Japanese envoys tell me you must not send it the way you sent the cable to the Emperor over the sinking of the *Panay* in the Yangtze River. You got no reply, because it never got to the Emperor. It was held up in their foreign office. This time, they tell me, you must send the cable directly to the Emperor, not through the foreign office. I don't know the mechanics of it, but this is what they tell me." He replied: "I'm just thinking out loud. I can't go down to the cable office and say I want to send a cable from the President of the United States to the Emperor of Japan. But I could send it to Grew, and as an ambassador he has the right of audience to the head of a state."

(Here he paused long enough to tell me the difference between an ambassador and a minister; the minister has no right of audience to the head of a state; the ambassador does.) "Grew can give it directly to the Emperor, and if I don't hear within twenty-four hours (I've learned how to do some things), I'll give it to the newspapers and force a reply.''...

This was December 3; the cable was sent on December 5, was given to the Emperor December 6, came out in the newspapers on December 7, the day that the attack on Pearl Harbor took place—too late.

When Mr. Kurusu, the Japanese Special Envoy for Peace, was repatriated from White Sulphur Springs, West Virginia, where the Japanese envoys were interned, he told me he had a luncheon with Tojo, the Prime Minister, and Tojo said to him: "If that cable had come a week sooner, this need not have happened.'' Mr. Terasaki became an advisor to the Emperor after the war, and he told me that the Emperor said to him: "If that cable had come one day sooner, this war need not have happened.'' (Leonard Mosley, in *Hirohito, Emperor of Japan,* in regard to the cable, says: "Whatever the method of delivery, we do know that it never got there.'' This statement of the Emperor—and that of the Prime Minister—seems to settle the matter—it did get there.)[1]

Whether we were within one week or one day of heading off the war I do not know. I sometimes wonder if we had not taken the President's secretary's suggestion that we send a letter to the President at Warm Springs, and had I gone personally and told the President then that the Japanese wanted him to send the cable, whether it would have saved a week, and might have saved the peace. It is easy to be wise after the event. "We did the best; we must leave the rest.'' But it is a haunting thought. Our best endeavors are often not good enough. In this case it was the easiest way out. I did not have to cancel an evangelistic series which I seldom or never do, and it was easier for the President's secretary to send a letter than to arrange a conference. But the harder way is often the right way.

I wrote it off as an adventure in failure. It is not ours to succeed or fail—it is ours to do the highest we know and leave results with God. For he has a way of rescuing some good out of apparent failure. "In everything God works for good with those who love him'' (Rom. 8:28, RSV). It was so in this case. The story of my attempting to head off the war got into the Japanese newspapers and gave me a hearing in Japan for the gospel during my nine visits to Japan since the war. I turned over to the Japanese pastors 147,000 decision cards signed mostly by non-Christians during those visits. Cut it in half and say that only half were serious enough to go through with it and become outer followers of Christ, and yet it is still impressive. Mr. Kurusu said to me after the war: "Japan will never become a democracy until Japan becomes Christian.'' I inquired: "What about you, Mr. Kurusu, are you a Christian?'' He replied that he was not. "Don't you want to be?'' I asked. And when he said he did, we went into his parlor; and we knelt and prayed, and he gave himself to Christ. When I left, I said: "When I return to Japan in two years, I want to find you in the Christian church.'' His reply: "You'll find me there.'' When I returned two years later and met him, the first thing he said: "I couldn't wait for you to baptize me. I've already been baptized.'' He mentioned his conversion to Christianity in his memoirs. His American wife, a stately

---

[1]Leonard Mosley, *Hirohito, Emperor of Japan* (Englewood Cliffs, N.J.: Prentice-Hall, 1966).

lady, after his death said: "His conversion lifted a great load of depression from him. It lighted up his whole life, and I'm so grateful for what you did for him." She leaned over and kissed my brow. That kiss lingers like a benediction. It was for both of us. Her husband and I both tried and we both failed, for both of us a heartbreaking failure, but God rescued out of that failure some good—for him it meant finding Christ and for me a greater opportunity to help others to find Christ. So the Christian always wins if he remains Christian. Even if he outwardly fails, he is a better man for having made the attempt. The payoff is in the person. It brought me a discovery of the Japanese people. Many after the war went to Japan prepared to swear at the Japanese. They came away ready to swear by them. They are a wonderful people, but were badly led. Now after the war the real qualities of the people have come out. They have an amazing capacity to recover from calamity. And an amazing capacity for friendship. In welcoming me back to Japan on one of these evangelistic tours, a Christian leader said: "Stanley Jones is one of us." I am. I believe it was at this welcome reception in the top story of a tall building that the building began to sway back and forth by an earthquake. I paused in my address and said: "Well, I've never had such an earth-shaking welcome before." But I was shaken inwardly more than outwardly by the Japanese people. They got me.

I have stood nine times at the place where the atomic bomb fell in Hiroshima and with a group of Japanese laymen and ministers have stood in a huddle like a football huddle, praying that no Hiroshima should ever happen again to anybody, anywhere in the world, and dedicating ourselves to peace. At a luncheon the mayor of Hiroshima in his welcoming speech said: "If the sufferings which the Hiroshima people have gone through will help to bring peace in the world, so that no Hiroshima should ever happen again to anyone, anywhere, then we welcome that suffering and are grateful that we have gone through it."

But to go back: On December 5, the Japanese asked me if I could stay in Washington over the weekend, as they were afraid something was going to happen. I told them I had an engagement to speak at the University of Illinois Convocation at Urbana on Sunday afternoon, December 7. But I would come back on Monday morning....

As I sat at breakfast with Mr. E.V. Moorman in Urbana on December 7, we read in the papers the cable President Roosevelt sent to the Emperor. Hope sprang up within us. Maybe this cable would head off the impending war. But some hours later, as I came down the steps of the hotel on my way to speak at the convocation, I heard an excited voice announcing over the radio the attack upon Pearl Harbor. Here I was on my way to speak on "Peace," and peace was gone! I announced to the several thousand students and others present what I had heard over the radio—news to most, a shock to all. I told them I could not speak on "peace," for peace was gone, but I would speak on "What Christ Means to Me." When that world of peace which we had tried to build up had crashed, was anything dependable and solid remaining, unshaken? Yes, the real values of my life were intact. I belonged to "a Kingdom which cannot be shaken"—the Kingdom of God. In success or failure, in peace or war Jesus Christ was "the same yesterday, today and forever," and his Kingdom was "unshakable." When I asked at the close of the address how many wanted to remain to find Christ and enter that unshakable kingdom, a thousand students stayed. They were going into a very shaken world and needed something unshakable. It was a moving service.

After an additional night meeting in a church two pastors volunteered to drive me to Chicago to get a plane out for Washington at 5 A.M., for I had promised the Japanese at Washington I would come back on Monday, the eighth. I would keep my promise. It was a slim hope, but I thought maybe that this attack on Pearl Harbor was a local affair and not real war. But on the plane I heard military officers talking, and I knew this was war. So I got off the plane at Pittsburgh, where I had an engagement in a couple of days. Dr. Robinson told me over the phone that the Japanese at Washington were interned, so there was no use to come on. While in Pittsburgh I wrote a letter to each of the Japanese envoys interned at White Sulphur Springs, not sure they would get it. It was this: "War has come, but I want to assure you that it has not been your fault. I believe that you tried honestly and sincerely to head off this war. I want to tell you of my gratitude for your endeavors. Also, that I will be with you in thought and prayer during the trying days ahead."

I did not know whether they had received my letter until about two years later, when they were about to be repatriated. Admiral Nomura wrote: "Before I leave your shores, I want to say good-bye to you and to thank you for your letter and the noble sentiments contained in it."

After the war, when in 1949 during my first visit to Japan I was in the waiting room of the Emperor's palace, waiting for my interview with the Emperor, Mr. Terasaki, now an adviser to the Emperor, took out of his pocket a letter and said: "Do you see that letter? It kept my soul alive during the war. To think that you believed in us when almost everyone thought we were playing a double game. It was dangerous for you to send that letter, for you see it is stamped 'Opened by Censor.'" "No," I replied, "it was not dangerous, for I sent a copy of this letter to the President, to the state department, and to Lord Halifax the British Ambassador.".…

Mr. Kurusu told me something after the war which throws some light on the fact that the Japanese envoys at Washington were desperately trying to find peace before Pearl Harbor and took risks to get it. Mr. Kurusu told me he sent a cable to Tojo, the Prime Minister, asking his approval for the request that they ask President Roosevelt to send the cable to the Emperor. Tojo cabled: "No time for this now." In spite of that Mr. Kurusu and the Japanese envoys at Washington asked me to ask the President verbally to send the cable. They actually disobeyed the Prime Minister and went over his head to the Emperor—in behalf of peace. They risked a good deal—their own necks.

Mr. Terasaki told the Emperor of our endeavors before Pearl Harbor and told him what I was now doing in Japan. The Emperor said, "I want to thank you for what you are doing for Japan. What our people need is moral and spiritual regeneration." I am not free to share what passed between us. But knowing me and my life mission, you can probably guess. He kept me three quarters of an hour and invited me back to see him when I came to Japan two years hence. He gave me a second interview, and the chamberlain said privately at the close: "That was a very interesting interview." He was a Christian. The Emperor gave me a third interview, but I was not able to take it; my plane left the day before.

As I was speaking to a group of businessmen at the YMCA, suddenly in the midst of my address the audience rose to its feet. I wondered what I had done to cause it. But Prince Makasa, brother of the Emperor, came in with an attendant, walked up to me, shook hands, and said: "Welcome to Japan." And walked out. In a later interview with the prince I said: "I'm grateful that you are teaching Old Testament history to the girls of the Union Christian College." I told him of a rabbi who once said to a friend: "Ours is a religion of frustration—we are looking for a Messiah who hasn't come and for a Kingdom that isn't here." So I suggested to the prince that he "move up from a religion of frustration to a religion of fulfillment." He took it good-humoredly. Of course, we talked of deeper things. Of this, too, I am not free to speak....

As I look back over this guidance which I received in the Los Angeles hotel at the close of the National Christian Mission, "I want you here," I now see in review that the guidance was right, although it failed in its immediate objective, namely, the attempt to head off the war between Japan and America. But it opened the doors for evangelism in Japan. Even if it had not opened those doors, I would do it over again. For it is not ours to succeed, but to be obedient to the highest we know.

Chapter Twenty-Five

From Pearl Harbor
to Calvary

Mitsuo Fuchida

Forty years ago I (Luke Keefer Jr.) heard Mitsuo Fuchida tell his conversion story at a public meeting in Harrisburg, Pennsylvania. Few stories have gripped my life as his did. His story is really two stories,[1] for God also was working dramatically in the life of an American soldier, Jake DeShazer.[2] Both men felt they were doing their patriotic duty, a task that involved them in harming their enemies. How God brought both men to saving faith in Jesus Christ, wove their lives together, and called them into evangelistic careers is miraculous.

When we stand in the midst of warfare, we are overwhelmed by the strength of human hatred. We ask, Is there any power stronger than hate? Can anything stop the killing once it begins? When hostilities cease, can anything change the heart attitudes that give birth to killing? Fuchida and DeShazer say there is such a power in the gospel of Jesus Christ.

I must admit I was more excited than usual as I awoke that morning at 3:00 A.M., Hawaii time, four days past my thirty-ninth birthday. Our six aircraft carriers were positioned 230 miles north of Oahu Island. As general commander of the air squadron, I made last-minute checks on the intelligence information reports in the operations room before going to warm up my single-engine, three-seater "97-type" plane used for level bombing and torpedo flying.

The sunrise in the east was magnificent above the white clouds as I led 360 planes towards Hawaii at an altitude of 3,000 meters. I knew my objective: to surprise and cripple the American naval force in the Pacific. But I fretted about being thwarted should some of the U.S. battleships not be there. I gave no thought of the possibility of this attack breaking

---

[1]You can read the stories in "From Pearl Harbor to Calvary," published by Bible Literature International, P.O. Box 477, Columbus, OH 43216. BLI has upgraded this pamphlet to a full-color piece useful for evangelism titled "Finding Forgiveness at Pearl Harbor." This chapter is a condensed version. Read also Elizabeth Sherrill's tribute "I'll Never Forget You...Mitsuo Fuchida," *Guideposts,* December 1991, 40–43.

[2]For Jake DeShazer's story, read the ninety-six-page paperback by C. Hoyt Watson, *DeShazer* (Coquitlam, B.C.: Galaxy Communications, 1998).

This abridgment appeared as "From Pearl Harbor to Calvary," by Matsuo Fuchida, *The High Calling*, Spring–Summer 2001, 15, 24. *The High Calling* is published by the Francis Asbury Society, a Wesleyan evangelistic organization.

open a mortal confrontation with the United States. I was only concerned about making a military success.

As we neared the Hawaiian Islands that bright Sunday morning, I made a preliminary check of the harbor, nearby Hickam Field and the other installations surrounding Honolulu. Viewing the entire American Pacific Fleet peacefully at anchor in the inlet below, I smiled as I reached for the mike and ordered, "All squadrons, plunge in to attack!" The time was 7:49 A.M.

Like a hurricane out of nowhere, my torpedo planes, dive bombers and fighters struck suddenly with indescribable fury. As smoke began to billow and the proud battleships, one by one, started tilting, my heart was almost ablaze with joy. During the next three hours, I directly commanded the fifty level bombers as they pelted not only Pearl Harbor, but the airfields, barracks and dry docks nearby. Then I circled at a higher altitude to accurately assess the damage and report it to my superiors.

Of the eight battleships in the harbor, five were mauled into total inactivity for the time being. The *Arizona* was scrapped for good; the *Oklahoma, California,* and *West Virginia* were sunk. The *Nevada* was beached in a sinking condition; only the *Pennsylvania, Maryland,* and *Tennessee* were able to be repaired. Of the eight, the *California, West Virginia,* and *Nevada* were salvaged much later, but the *Oklahoma,* after being raised, was resunk as worthless. Other smaller ships were damaged, but the sting of 3,077 U.S. Navy personnel killed or missing and 876 wounded, plus 266 Army killed and 396 wounded, was something which could never be repaired.

It was the most thrilling exploit of my career. Ever since I had heard of my country's winning the Russo-Japanese War in 1905, I had dreamed of becoming an admiral like Admiral Togo, our commander-in-chief in the decisive Battle of the Japan Sea.

Because my father was a primary school principal and a very patriotic nationalist, I was able to enroll in the Naval Academy when I was eighteen. Upon graduation three years later, I joined the Japanese Naval Air Force, and served mostly as an aircraft carrier pilot for the next fifteen years. So when the time came to choose the chief commander for the Pearl Harbor mission, I had logged over 10,000 hours, making me the most experienced pilot in the Japanese Navy.

During the next four years, I was determined to improve upon my Pearl Harbor feat. I saw action in the Solomon Islands, Java, the Indian Ocean; just before the Battle of Midway on June 4, 1942, I came down with an attack of appendicitis and was unable to fly. Lying in my bed, I grimaced at the sounds of the firing all about me. By the end of that day, we had suffered our first major defeat, losing ten warships altogether.

From that time on, things got worse. I did not want to surrender. I would rather have fought to the last man. However, when the Emperor announced that we would surrender, I acquiesced.

I was in Hiroshima the day before the atom bomb was dropped, attending a week-long military conference with the Army. Fortunately, I received a long distance call from my Navy Headquarters, asking me to return to Tokyo.

With the end of the war, my military career was over, since all Japanese forces were disbanded. I returned to my home village near Osaka and began farming, but it was a discouraging life. I became more and more unhappy, especially when the war crime trials opened in Tokyo. Though I was never accused, Gen. Douglas MacArthur summoned me to testify on several occasions.

As I got off the train one day in Tokyo's Shibuya Station, I saw an American distributing literature. When I passed him, he handed me a pamphlet entitled, "I was a Prisoner of Japan" (published by Bible Literature International, known then as the Bible Meditation League). Involved right then with the trials on atrocities committed against war prisoners, I put it in my pocket, determining to read the story later.

What I read was the fascinating episode which eventually changed my life. On that Sunday while I was in the air over Pearl Harbor, an American soldier named Jake DeShazer had been on K.P. duty in an Army camp in California. When the radio announced the sneak demolishing of Pearl Harbor, he hurled a potato at the wall and shouted, "Jap, just wait and see what we'll do to you!"

One month later he volunteered for a secret mission with the Jimmy Doolittle Squadron—a surprise raid on Tokyo from the carrier *Hornet*. On April 18, 1942, DeShazer was one of the bombardiers, and was filled with elation at getting his revenge. After the bombing raid, they flew on towards China, but ran out of fuel and were forced to parachute into Japanese-held territory. The next morning, DeShazer found himself a prisoner of Japan.

During the next forty long months in confinement, DeShazer was cruelly treated. He recalls that his violent hatred for the maltreating Japanese guards almost drove him insane at one point. But after twenty-five months there in Nanking, China, the U.S. prisoners were given a Bible to read. DeShazer, not being an officer, had to let the others use it first. Finally, it came his turn—for three weeks. There in the Japanese P.O.W. camp, he read and read—and eventually came to understand that the book was more than a historical classic. Its message became relevant to him right there in his cell.

The dynamic power of Christ which Jake DeShazer accepted into his life changed his entire attitude toward his captors. His hatred turned to love and concern, and he resolved that should his country win the war and he be liberated, he would someday return to Japan to introduce others to this life-changing book.

DeShazer did just that. After some training at Seattle Pacific College and Asbury Theological Seminary, he returned to Japan as a missionary. And his story, printed in pamphlet form, was something I could not explain.

Neither could I forget it. The peaceful motivation I had read about was exactly what I was seeking. Since the American had found it in the Bible, I decided to purchase one myself, despite my traditionally Buddhist heritage.

In the ensuing weeks, I read this book eagerly. I came to the climactic drama— the Crucifixion. I read in Luke 23:34 the prayer of Jesus Christ at His death: "Father, forgive them; for they know not what they do" (RSV.) I was impressed that I was certainly one of those for whom He had prayed. The many men I had killed had been slaughtered in the name of patriotism, for I did not understand the love which Christ wishes to implant within every heart.

Right at that moment, I seemed to meet Jesus for the first time. I understood the meaning of His death as a substitute for my wickedness, and so in prayer, I requested Him to forgive my sins and change me from a bitter, disillusioned ex-pilot into a well-balanced Christian with purpose in living.

That date, April 14, 1950, became the second "day to remember" of my life. On that day, I became a new person. My complete view on life was changed by the intervention of the Christ I had always hated and ignored before. Soon other friends beyond my close family learned of my decision to be a follower of Christ, and they could hardly understand it.

Big headlines appeared in the papers: "Pearl Harbor Hero Converts to Christianity." Old war buddies came to visit me, trying to persuade me to discard "this crazy idea." Others accused me of being an opportunist, embracing Christianity only for how it might impress our American victors.

But time has proven them wrong. As an evangelist, I have traveled across Japan and the Orient introducing others to the One Who changed my life. I believe with all my heart that those who will direct Japan—and all other nations—in the decades to come must not ignore the message of Jesus Christ. Youth must realize that He is the only hope for this troubled world.

Though my country has the highest literacy rate in the world, education has not brought salvation. Peace and freedom—both national and personal—come only through an encounter with Jesus Christ.

I would give anything to retract my actions of twenty-nine years ago at Pearl Harbor, but it is impossible. Instead, I now work at striking the deathblow to the basic hatred which infests the human heart and causes such tragedies. And that hatred cannot be uprooted without assistance from Jesus Christ.

He is the only One Who was powerful enough to change my life and inspire it with His thoughts. He was the only answer to Jake DeShazer's tormented life. He is the only answer for young people today.

Chapter Twenty-Six

Political Earthquake Rocks the Eastern Bloc

Barbara (von der Heydt) Elliott

The author was a journalist residing in West Germany when the Communist wall crumbled in Eastern Europe and Russia. She interviewed many refugees who fled the Communist countries just before the collapse occurred. Later, she traveled through these countries, talking with the Christians who played key roles in resisting state atheism and bringing about peaceful change. She wrote her book *Candles behind the Wall* to tell the stories of these people and to make the world aware that Christian faith played a major role in the defeat of Communism. Faith gave people the strength to confront the secular state in all its might and to overthrow it largely by peaceful means. Her book challenges the Western assumptions that democracy, capitalism, and military might overthrew Communism. She believes religion was the vital component in the revolution and that this analysis has been largely ignored in the press in the United States.

The chapter selected gives the account of the prayer meetings in Leipzig (in East Germany) that stilled the guns of the Communist army. It raises interesting questions. Are spiritual weapons alone sufficient for defeating military force? Or should Christians combine fighting and praying? Can quiet conviction expressed through peaceful protest actually arouse the conscience of those in power to do the right thing?

Since *Candles behind the Wall* was published, the author has returned to the United States. Now Barbara Elliot, she lives in Houston, Texas, where she is founder and president of the Center for Renewal. As overcoming Communism was the moral issue of the late twentieth century, she believes reclaiming the inner city to be the pressing moral agenda for the twenty-first century. Her Center for Renewal attempts to link churches with financial resources to inner-city ministries that are making a real difference in our society.

Many people in Leipzig were afraid. It was October 9, 1989, and no one had forgotten the blood-spattered deaths of the demonstrators in Tiananmen Square only four months earlier. Now tens of thousands of people were expected to come to the Nikolaikirche for the weekly *Friedensgebete,* or "Prayers for

This chapter is taken from chapter 8 of Barbara von der Heydt, *Candles behind the Wall: Heroes of the Peaceful Revolution that Shattered Communism* (Grand Rapids: Eerdmans, 1993).

Peace." Only three days earlier, a Leipzig newspaper had conveyed the threat: "We are ready and willing to...conclusively and effectively put an end to these counter-revolutionary actions. *If need be with a weapon in hand!*"[1] Live ammunition was distributed to the military.

A week earlier, 2,000 people had pressed into the overflowing Nikolaikirche for the Monday night *Friedensgebete,* with another 3,000 massing in the square outside the church. Leipzig resident Petra Seela witnessed the assault at the end of the evening: "It was [done with] brute force, with riot sticks, attack dogs, and walkie talkies, and we were shocked....We knew some of the people fleeing, and we saw the fear and terror in their eyes."[2]

Now, a week later, the city of Leipzig looked as if it were preparing for a civil war, an image that was not far from the truth. Army units, helmeted police in riot squads, reservists, and paramilitary squadrons were being trucked in, all having been put on alert. Armored vehicles, military transport vehicles, and water cannons lined the streets near the Nikolaikirche.

Other warlike preparations were being made. Thousands of pints of blood for transfusions were rushed to the hospitals, where staffs were rescheduled to treat the anticipated victims. Heart surgeons at the Karl-Marx University were on emergency call; surgeon and doctors working in intensive-care units throughout the city were told to be prepared to treat shooting victims. The Thomaskirche, one of the three churches in Leipzig that had agreed to hold *Friedensgebete* along with the Nikolaikirche in order to accommodate the expected overflow crowds, had been designated as an emergency first-aid center to treat wounded. When he heard that news, one doctor blurted to another, "My God, they're going to shoot us all!" Children in school were warned not to go into the center of town because there could be shooting. Parents were told to collect their children from kindergarten earlier than usual, so they would be safely home before the danger was acute.

Although the Prayers for Peace weren't scheduled to begin until five P.M., the troops were briefed in the morning before being posted. Some military personnel were asked to sign statements that they would obey orders to fire, even if members of their family were in the crowd. *Bereitschaftspolizisten,* the reserve police commonly called *Bepos,* had a chilling exchange with their chief officer:

> Comrades, from today on it is class war. The situation is like June 17, 1953. Today it will be decided, either for us or for them....If the truncheons aren't enough, then guns will be used." The *Bepos* asked: "People will be coming to the demonstration with children. What will happen to the children?" The officer's answer: "They have bad luck. We have guns, and we don't have them for nothing!" As indignation swelled in the room, the *Bepos* pressed the question, "Who will take the responsibility for that?" The prompt answer: "We take the responsibility!"[3]

---

[1]Commander Günter Lutz, from the Kampfgruppenhundertschaft "Hans Geiffert," *Leipziger Volkszeitung,* October 6, 1989, 2.

[2]Petra Seela, "2. Oktober bis 8. Oktober," in *Jetzt oder nie—Demokratie: Leipziger Herbst 89* (Leipzig: Forum Verlag, 1989), 51.

[3]The comparison of the situation to that of June 17 is a reference to the East German uprising against the Communists on June 17, 1953, which was put down with the help of Soviet tanks and bullets. The quotation is from Neues Forum Leipzig, *Jetzt oder nie—Demokratie,* 92–93.

After the briefing, the atmosphere in the barracks was as edgy as it was on the streets. Some of the reservists argued with each other about obeying an order to fire on the crowds in Leipzig's streets. "Many lay on their beds and cried. They knew that their own wife could be among the demonstrators."[4] Their brother or mother could be opposite them, their nearest friend. And yet they knew that if they refused to fire, they could end up in jail or be shot from behind.

However reluctantly, the *Bepos* took their place along with the paramilitary groups, special riot units, army soldiers, and members of the Stasi secret security forces. Armored vehicles rumbled through the streets, taking positions at critical intersections throughout downtown Leipzig. Stasi cameras mounted on tall buildings at six strategic points throughout the city recorded every movement on film. Thousands of military and security personnel flooded into the city in convoys. At the intersection of the *Runde Ecke* alone, where the Stasi building was located, there were thirteen military vehicles, six of which were manned by military police with machine guns. Some of these guns were filled with tear gas cartridges, others with bullets. Ten armored vehicles stood nearby with motors running. All of them carried live ammunition.[5]

Friedensgebete *in the Face of Threatened Violence*

Inside the offices of the Nikolaikirche, the phone was ringing off the hook. Numerous people, some choking back tears, were calling to warn Pastor Christian Führer not to hold the *Friedensgebete*. These individuals had reason to fear. State officials had already confronted Führer repeatedly and ordered him to

cancel the service. But he remained unwavering.

All over the city, families were having earnest discussions about who should go to the Nikolaikirche and who should stay at home. Those who would dare to go would risk arrest—and possibly their lives. Christoph and Maria Bormann were having just such a discussion. Both of them had been regular participants in the *Friedensgebete* for several years, and Maria was a long-standing member of the Nikolaikirche's vestry. Understandably, both of them wanted to attend—but when Maria looked at their small daughters, she said, "One of us has to be here for the children." So she decided to stay home. Did she think that her husband might be risking his life to go? "That was certainly a possibility," she admitted later.[6]

Christoph headed for downtown Leipzig without Maria, joining the sea of humanity streaming toward the church. Traffic was blocked everywhere, and people abandoned their cars to continue on foot. All public transportation was jammed to overflowing, and ultimately stopped running altogether. Nearly every face was ashen, and there was no idle chatter. The fear in the air was palpable. Those on foot were shocked to see the armored vehicles as they neared the church. The rows upon rows of helmeted and masked riot police armed with truncheons were a sobering sight, almost surrealistic figures with hidden faces.

Across town, Helga Wagner, a member of the Communist party and professor at Karl-Marx University in Leipzig, was in a meeting when the call came: "Five comrades should go to the Nikolaikirche!" Sensing something important was happening there, she answered spontaneously, "I'll go along." As a member of the party, she was supposed to shun

---

[4]Ibid., 93.
[5]Ibid.

the church, but now she was responding to an official request. At two P.M. she entered the Nikolaikirche, one of 500 members of the Communist party there under orders to take seats in the church.[7] Although the service wasn't supposed to begin until five P.M., the nave was already packed, and the rest of the church was filling rapidly. At 3:30 the doors had to be closed on the bursting crowd.

Lutz Ramson had worked his way through the crowds with the greatest difficulty. When he finally made it to the Nikolaikirche at 2:30 P.M., he was startled to see that the church was already almost full. Since he was a member of the vestry, he went to the front of the church and began to set up the microphone. When he took a second look at the crowd, it confirmed his gut feeling that something was very different. Because of his association with the *Friedensgebete* over the past six years, he recognized many of the people there. But the Communists in the church changed the composition. What Lutz saw everywhere was naked fear. "We were afraid—that was visible, but they were afraid too."[8] Catcalls, shouts, and boos floated inside the church. "We thought it was for us," Helga Wagner recalls, "because they knew who was sitting …inside." The party members wondered fearfully if word had spread that the Communists had infiltrated the church.

Meanwhile, the pilgrimage to the churches continued. Seventy thousand people were on foot and moving through the city. "It was unbelievable," Christoph Bormann recalls. "Everywhere you looked there were people." The forces that were supposed to put down this demonstration were every bit as nervous as the participants. Riot police held their shields with sweaty palms. The hour of the prayers drew nearer, and six thousand people pressed against one another in the Nikolaikirche and the three other churches participating in the *Friedensgebete*—the Reformierte Kirche, the Thomaskirche, and the Michaeliskirche. As the clock ticked toward five P.M., Leipzig was strung taut.

Even as Christian Führer began the *Friedensgebete* in the Nikolaikirche, his wife continued to take frantic phone calls from people begging him to cancel the service to avoid civil war. But the service was held in the usual way, as it had been every Monday. To open the service, he read from Isaiah 45; then the participants read the Beatitudes, as they did each week, letting the words ring out:

Blessed are those who hunger and thirst for righteousness,
for they will be filled....
Blessed are the peacemakers,
for they will be called sons of God.
Blessed are those who are persecuted because of righteousness,
for theirs is the kingdom of heaven.
(*Matt.5:6-10*)

The liturgy was kept deliberately simple. To create a feeling of familiarity, the same hymns and passages from the Bible had been read and sung again and again in the *Friedensgebete*. In the course of the service at the Nikolaikirche, two men from Dresden reported that first steps were taken toward a dialogue between their mayor and demonstrators. *Neues Forum* had issued a written appeal to those in Leipzig, urging them to remain peaceful.

Shortly after the service began, a very pale and bedraggled Peter Zimmermann, a theologian at Leipzig University,

---

[6]Drawn from the author's interview with Christoph and Maria Bormann in Leipzig on February 26, 1991.

[7]Neues Forum Leipzig, *Jetzt oder nie—Demokratie,* 88.

handed Christian Führer a message that he begged him to read over the microphone so that those in the church as well as those outside listening to the service via loudspeaker could hear. Zimmermann had spent the day frantically brokering a joint appeal from six well-known Leipzig personalities to the people of the city in an attempt to avoid brutal confrontation and seek peaceful change and dialogue. The document that he had brought with him was the result of harried negotiations with three secretaries of the Communist party and the unlikely coalition of the conductor Kurt Masur, the cabaret artist Bernd-Lutz Lange, and Zimmermann himself. Christian Führer took the paper from Zimmermann's shaking hand and read it to those assembled.

The effect was electrifying. Was there a way out of the seemingly certain shooting waiting in the streets outside? Susanne Rummel, a participant in the *Friedensgebete,* recalls that the entire church breathed a communal sigh of relief, and when the news went out over the loudspeakers, those outside experienced a brief flicker of joy. "But it didn't last," Susanne notes. From outside there came waves of chants, accompanied by whistles and boos and clapping: "Stasi out!" "Gorby, Gorby," and "We're staying here!" The atmosphere in the church was bursting with tension. "Somehow," Susanne recalls, "we all seemed to be ducking in expectation of a terrible blow.... No one wanted to say the words 'civil war' or 'spilled blood,' but it was all tangibly

near to each of us. The pastor offered to keep the church open for all who didn't want to go out."[9]

Bishop Werner Leich made a compelling appeal for nonviolence, which he personally delivered at each of the four churches holding the *Friedensgebete.* He hurried from one church to the next with his message. This was a familiar and recurrent theme. Nonviolence had been preached week after week at all the *Friedensgebete* gatherings. The Christians were determined not to return evil for evil. Tonight more than ever, the course of events might depend on whether they could act on that belief.

And then something remarkable happened. In the words of Protestant Superintendent Friedrich Magirius, "The spirit of peace and non-violence spread over those assembled. Everyone held his neighbor tightly, and this spirit went out with the people onto the square." Those who had been inside the church mingled among those assembled outside, bringing the spirit of peace with them. "The power was contagious," Magirius recalls.'[10]

Pastor Christian Führer remembers the moment this way: "The spirit of Christ, the spirit of non-violence and renewal fell on the masses, moved the people deeply and became a tangible force of peace....It was like the Book of Acts when the Holy Spirit fell on Cornelius and his household. This is something quite remarkable because these people were mostly not Christians. And yet these people behaved then as if they had grown up with the Sermon on the Mount."[11]

---

[8]Drawn from the author's interview with Lutz and Marianne Ramson in Leipzig on February 27, 1991.

[9]Neues Forum Leipzig, *Jetzt oder nie—Demokratie,* 83–84.

[10]Friedrich Magirius, "Wiege der Wende," *Leipziger Demontagebuch* (Leipzig: Gustav Kiepenheuer Verlag, 1990), 13.

[11]This and subsequent quotations are drawn from the author's interview with Christian Führer in Leipzig on February 28, 1991.

Nineteen-year-old Raphaela Russ recalls, "With an amazing composure the mass began to move, past the curious onlookers who hemmed the edges of the streets, past the mobilized security forces, past the barking dogs in the narrow streets and alleyways, past the heavily guarded Stasi building."[12]

An amorphous mass of 70,000 people assumed purpose and form, moving slowly through the city of Leipzig on the streets that ring the center of the city. Some people carried candles, each shielding the tiny flame with one hand. Others linked arms with each other in encouragement. Demonstrators saw the light glinting off the weapons, looked at the walls of shields and helmets and armed vehicles, and walked peacefully between them.

As the crowd moved through the streets of Leipzig, voices rang out. "We are the people!" and "No violence!" they repeated in chorus. As the procession neared the *Runde Ecke* where the Stasi headquarters were, the mood grew ugly, with some among the crowd hissing boos and catcalls. But others shouted even louder, "No violence! No violence!" When the word came that they must turn back, some went scrambling in wide-eyed panic onto the side streets, clambering over fences, fearing that the order to shoot had been given. But it was a false alarm; the attack had not come.

The soldiers, reservists, and paramilitary troops all stood tensely on guard, watching in near disbelief at the human flood flowing past them, people as far as the eye could see, and more coming. Those driving the military vehicles kept the motors running in readiness for the anticipated order to move in on the crowd. The young men on the front lines fixed their gaze on their feet when demonstrators tried to look them in the eye. They shifted their weapons uneasily.

In a tone both desperate and courageous, one among the crowd blurted out the question that thousands more wished they could articulate: "We are the people and you are the people. Are you really going to shoot us?" He aimed his question at a perplexed reservist.

Susanne Rummel and those with her did the same. "We walked together, hesitatingly at first, until we came to Karl-Marx Square and then we saw them—the wagons where the troops sat with their helmets and shields....We talked with them, asked them whether we looked like enemies of the state or anarchists and whether they really would beat us."[13]

Seventy thousand demonstrators moved through Leipzig's streets without offering a single provocation to the armed guards who were waiting for the order to shoot at them. No one hurled a stone through a window in frustration at the mute and fearful years. No one shouted defiantly at the massive display of police and military power. No one so much as knocked off a policeman's cap. The only fires that were lit were candles. Forty years of frustration, repression, and pent-up resentment were not expressed in any way that gave the armed forces reason to shoot. The order to open fire on the demonstrators never came.

Eventually the crowd dispersed in an orderly way. As they made their way home, the tension slowly left the city. Some uncorked a bottle of wine in celebration. By the next morning, the country had turned a corner. *Die Wende.* It was the showdown.

Reflecting on that night she experienced on Leipzig's streets, Raphaela Russ

---

[12]Raphaela Russ, "wenn es sein muss, mit der Waffe in der Hand!" *Die Revolution der Kerzen: Christen in den Umwälzungen der DDR,* ed. Jörg Swoboda (Wuppertal: Oncken Verlag, 1990), 144.

[13]Quoted in Neues Forum Leipzig, *Jetzt oder nie—Demokratie,* 83–84.

wrote, "With the bloodless end of the 9th of October a new era began. Who would have believed it before? The question still remains, who prevented the security forces from attacking? It's clear to me that God wrote history here."[14] The battle was fought not with the weapons of this world, but with the weapons of prayer and peaceful restraint.

Pastor Christian Führer sees the event as a powerful testament to God's spirit at work on earth:

> Non-violence is clearly the spirit of Jesus. With these people who grew up with pictures of class enemies, and whose parents grew up with the Nazis and violence and racial hatred, you can prove that it didn't come from here. It's not a question of one's upbringing. And the few Christians that there are in this unchristian country—they didn't do it either....That was the spirit of God at work. We few people couldn't have done it. God honored us by letting us play this part in His plan.

An Echo of Jericho: The Berlin Wall Falls

It is clear that during this critical time, Gorbachev withheld explicit approval for a bloodbath to put down the demonstration, and the East German regime may not have dared to give the order to fire on its own. But this was a radical change for the Soviets, in light of the Soviet response in 1953 in East Germany, in 1957 in Hungary, and in 1968 in Czechoslovakia. And the Soviets had threatened Poland with invasion as recently as 1981. There was nothing inevitable about a peaceful end, as Chinese demonstrators had found out in Tiananmen Square only months before. Had the Soviets themselves changed? Recent behavior gives no consistent

answer: they used violence again in Lithuania in January 1991. But for some reason, the situation in East Germany turned out differently.

The East German regime was now in disarray. In a tense politburo session on October 18, Erich Honecker was unceremoniously dumped and replaced by Egon Krenz. The number of demonstrators swelled to 200,000 in Leipzig, then 300,000. City after city followed Leipzig's example, with millions filling the streets. A nation was on its feet because the people had found their voice. The regime was scrambling to meet their pent-up demands to be able to speak freely, to travel, to organize, to reform. So many things were different, including the fresh creativity, wit, courage, and humor that people used to illustrate the banners they carried. It was as if they were negotiating by poster board, as their appetite for change was whetted by new victories.

The turning point in Berlin came on November 4, 1989. One million people assembled in the Alexanderplatz, with the "best and brightest" of the country addressing the huge crowd. The mass of people moved in procession to Unter den Linden, then to the Palace of the Republic, then back to the Alexanderplatz. The critical point came at the Palace of the Republic, where the street continues straight on to the Brandenburg Gate, the huge, well-known archway that is the gateway between East and West Berlin, and symbolically between the two parts of the divided country.

Anyone who could think militarily knew that if a million people continued marching straight ahead, the tanks would have to roll and the soldiers would have to intervene to stop them. But those in the procession also knew the Stasi and their methods. If the Stasi put a few hundred provocateurs into the crowd to keep

---

[14]Russ, "wenn es sein muss," 145.

marching ahead, to draw the crowd toward the Brandenburg Gate, that would provide the needed reason to attack. It was not discussed, but all the genuine participants knew that even if hundreds broke away, they must not.

As the crowd neared the curve, Werner Krätschell stood at that spot near the Brandenburg Gate with his wife. "We have to stand here and watch this," he told her. "It is unforgettable." What he remembers most is the silence: "Hundreds and thousands of people walked around this curve without saying a word. It was a silent march at this point. One heard only the soft sound of the feet of these people. Everyone knew this was the critical point."[15] There was no provocation, there was no attack. A million people silently signaled with their feet that they wanted change, but peaceful change.

Five days later, the Berlin Wall fell. Ironically, the regime hadn't intended that at all. In fact, they kicked it over by accident in a pratfall.

When the entire politburo resigned on November 8, a committee was charged with drafting a new law on travel. The draft they produced was given to staffers, who concluded that by logic it had to include anyone who wanted to travel to the West, and they amended it accordingly. Without further checks, the draft was given to the regime's spokesman, Günter Schabowski, in the middle of a press conference, who simply read it. As the message sunk in, an incredulous question came from a journalist: Did that mean that any East German could cross the border to the West? Schabowski admitted that it looked that way, judging by the text. The government had intended to control travel by issuing visas, but that went unnoticed in the hubbub that boiled over immediately.

The news reached the airwaves with lightning speed, and people swarmed to the cross-points in Berlin, some still in pajamas, mobbing the surprised border guards, who knew nothing about what had happened. When the people told them what they'd heard on the radio, the guards were unsure what to do. After trying to hold back the growing, jostling crowd, some guards in exasperation and confusion simply shoved back their caps and let the people charge through. The crowd became jubilant, and the people of a nation that had been divided fell into each other's arms. There were tears, flowers, and streams of uncorked champagne.

Shortly thereafter, on New Year's Day, young people danced on the Wall in exhilaration, and the nation wept in disbelief and joy. Reunification, which occurred on October 3, 1990, took place less than a year from the moment the Wall fell.

On the night that the Wall fell, people leaving the Nikolaikirche marched through the center of the city. Week after week during the fall of 1989, they had marched in a circle around Leipzig after the *Friedensgebete*. On November 9, they marched for the seventh time, this time straight through the city. It was a silent march commemorating the fifty-first anniversary of *Kristallnacht*, the beginning of violence against the Jews leading up to World War II. And on that night, people left the Nikolaikirche praying for their country. As they walked through Leipzig for the seventh time, they heard a crash as resounding as that once heard in Jericho: it was the sound of the Berlin Wall falling. The German Democratic Republic had been in existence for exactly forty years.

The biblical allusions are startling.

---

[15]Drawn from the author's interview with Werner Krätschell in Berlin on May 28, 1991.

Allegiance
and Rebellion

Miroslav Volf

Miroslav Volf of Yale University tells of his encounter with immigration officials who could not understand why he wanted to become a citizen of the United States but refused to bear arms for his adopted country. Volf's insistence on declaring his unwillingness to bear arms stemmed in part from his experiences in his native Yugoslavia and in part from his conviction that his first allegiance is to a higher power that rules by peaceful means, not by force.

Pacifists by law can no longer be prohibited from becoming citizens of the United States. But should the state retain the right to deny citizenship to anyone who refuses to defend the country? Should there be complementary obligations for citizens to perform if they refuse to bear arms, such as serving with a relief agency or in a social welfare program? Is it conceivable that the coveted possession of Canadian or United States citizenship might tempt a pacifist to abandon, if necessary, the peace position?

It was Good Friday 1997. There I was in the Los Angeles Convention Center with 5,000 other people hailing from every conceivable nation. No, it was not a multinational gathering of Christians assembled to worship the Crucified One. We were there to be sworn in as citizens of the United States of America. On the day when Christians all over the world confess allegiance to Jesus Christ, I was to swear my allegiance to a political power. The thought that the state was seeking symbolically to supplant faith and insinuate itself in the place of the master crept into my consciousness and I could not just dismiss it.

An urge came upon me to rebel against the state in the very moment of becoming its citizen. I did rebel, in a sense. When the whole crowd recited the "Oath of Allegiance to the United States," I kept silent as the others declared that they would "bear arms on behalf of the United States when required by the law."

On my application for naturalization I stated that I would not bear arms. To demonstrate the sincerity of my convictions I appended a brief statement explaining that in communist Yugoslavia I had been persecuted partly because of my pacifist stance. The explanation didn't help. In this country I had to be a member of a recognized religious body with an official pacifist position.

During the interview, my interlocutor tried to persuade me to change my mind.

This chapter originally appeared as Miroslav Volf, "Allegiance and Rebellion," *The Christian Century*, July 2–9, 1997, 663.

"A stapler is an 'arm,'" said the exasperated woman behind the counter.

"I use a stapler every day," I responded, "but not to kill people."

"We don't want you to kill people!"

"So we agree?"

"But would you not defend your wife and your children?"

"I will defend, but I will not kill."

"There are mean people out there, ruthless autocrats, you know."

"Yes, I know. I was born in former Yugoslavia."

"Then you should know better."

"Maybe I do," I said.

Later, another official listened for about ten minutes to a dozen ways of saying "I will defend, but not bear arms" and then suggested a compromise. At the place on the form where I had checked that I will not bear arms she drew a line and wrote, "Will defend." I initialed, and was granted permission to become a citizen—citizen Volf, who will defend without bearing arms...except staplers, of course.

It would not be accurate, however, to say that rebellion was in the forefront of my mind. But there was a struggle going on inside of me during the whole ceremony.

I had taken along an issue of the *Christian Century* to read during my unoccupied moments. It contained a review of Jimmy Carter's *Living Faith*. I read about a recent president who asserted that Christian faith "has always been at the core of my existence"; a public servant whose attempts to unite spirituality and social service were shaped profoundly by Koinonia Farms and Habitat for Humanity, particularly "by their concern for racial reconciliation and for alleviating poverty"; a politician who has done door-to-door evangelism with an Hispanic pastor.[1]

None of this was conceivable for a politician in the world I come from. I grew up under the totalitarian rule of communists whose declared goal was to stamp out Christian faith, if not today, then tomorrow. Along with many others, I was beaten up and jailed for the simple act of publicly proclaiming the gospel. Later the communists were replaced by democratically elected nationalists. There was a marked difference between them, but mainly in style, not substance. The politicians carefully nurtured the image of being good and loyal members of the church—as a weapon in political battles and as a screen for blatant disregard of Christian precepts about integrity and social justice. What would it take for a person the likes of Jimmy Carter to be elected as president of my native and still beloved Croatia?

My question was not born of naïveté. I am sufficiently suspicious of political power that I would want to peek behind Carter's words and look at the record. And I know that because national politics did not mix well with the prophetic activism, he was not re-elected. Yet his deeply Christian moral vision and pattern of social engagement remain singular among "Christian" politicians. And if it is true that democracies get the leaders they deserve, then for all its wrongs there is something profoundly right about the nation that would choose him as its president.

A day or so after I was naturalized, I received a congratulatory card from my in-laws. It featured not a patriotic slogan but this quotation:

> As citizens, Christians share all things with others, and yet endure all things as if foreigners. Every foreign land is to them as their native country, and every land of their birth as a land of strangers....They pass their days on

---

[1]Jimmy Carter, *Living Faith* (New York: Times Books, 1996).

earth, but they are citizens of heaven. They obey the prescribed laws, and at the same time surpass the laws by their lives.

The passage was from the early second-century Epistle of Mathetus to Diognetus. The words put in a memorable way the dialectic of distance and belonging, of strangeness and domesticity, of surpassing the laws and obeying them. A word of welcome appropriate to citizen Volf, who this year for the first time will be celebrating Independence Day as an American citizen—a citizen whose ultimate allegiance is to a polity whose ruler is the crucified Messiah.

Chapter Twenty-Eight

Working for Peace in Northern Ireland: The Christian Renewal Centre

Ronald A. Wells

Ronald A. Wells is a professor of history at Calvin College in Grand Rapids, Michigan. He is recognized in the field of church history as one interested in the interface of Christian faith and human history, epitomized by his book *History Through the Eyes of Faith.*[1]

When, more than a decade ago, he first thought of *People Behind the Peace*, the book from which this chapter is taken, there were several spots in the world where peace seemed unlikely: South Africa; Berlin, Germany; and Northern Ireland. He notes that significant progress has been made in all three cases. Apartheid has ended in South Africa; the Berlin Wall has fallen; and since 1998 a significant peace process has been underway in Northern Ireland.[2] These are signs of hope in our world; when Christians let their faith engage the "labor of love," change can occur in cases that seemed hopeless.

The author tells the stories of Christian groups who have made a difference for peace in Northern Ireland. This chapter focuses upon a charismatic community that emphasizes the role of prayer and the Holy Spirit in changing people's attitudes regarding the conflict in Northern Ireland.

The article leads us to ponder the role of intentional communities as change agents in areas of religious conflict. How do they serve as beacons of witness, places of refuge, and training schools for peace? How does "praying in the Holy Spirit" energize the peace process? Persistent trouble spots in the world possess long histories and often involve entrenched evils that have demonic power. How can we train people to pray for these places with persistence and discernment?

---

[1]Ronald A. Wells, *History through the Eyes of Faith: Western Civilization and the Kingdom of God* (San Francisco: Harper and Row, 1989).

[2] See chapter one of *People behind the Peace: Community and Reconciliation in Northern Ireland* (Grand Rapids: Eerdmans, 1999), which Dr. Wells devotes to "Religion as Cause and Cure of Conflict in Northern Ireland."

This chapter is an abridgment of "The Christian Renewal Centre," *People Behind the Peace: Community and Reconciliation in Northern Ireland*, by Ronald A. Wells (Grand Rapids: Eerdmans, 1999), 81–99.

The Christian Renewal Centre (CRC) is located outside the town of Rostrevor in County Down, about fifty miles south of Belfast....

The person who had the idea for the Centre, and who has been the moving force behind its work, is Cecil Kerr. He is a man of gentle spirit with sparkling, captivating eyes, a ready wit, and, above all, deep insight into the spiritual dimensions of "the troubles." Like Ray Davey at Corrymeela, Cecil Kerr would want our attention to be focused elsewhere, first on the Holy Spirit and then on the many people who have supported the work of the Christian Renewal Centre since its founding a quarter-century ago....

Cecil Kerr was born and raised in Enniskillen, County Fermanagh, in the southwestern part of what is now Northern Ireland. While the town was made up of equal proportions of Protestants and Catholics, the two communities lived apart as much as possible. Cecil, growing up in Enniskillen during World War II, had only one Catholic friend. Here was a young man whose British family had been in Ireland for about three centuries. That he had virtually no encounters with the native Irish says a great deal about the divided society in which he grew up.[3]

Cecil was raised in a conventional home and was associated with the (Anglican) Church of Ireland, as much for cultural as for religious reasons. But when he was a teenager, he experienced a powerful conversion that put him on the road to (what they call in evangelical circles) "full-time Christian work." After completing his secondary education at Portora Royal School, he enrolled in Trinity College, Dublin, to study Hebrew and Oriental languages....

Cecil's meeting of Myrtle, the woman who would become his wife, brought him both love and "a considerable challenge to my narrow northern upbringing."[4] Paradoxically, it was this woman, an evangelical from the Republic of Ireland, who began to broaden Cecil's horizons, a process that would culminate in this young man's becoming one of the leading Protestant activists in Irish reconciliation....

It is with a combination of deep love and mixed political orientations that Cecil and Myrtle began their life together in Northern Ireland. Having been ordained, Cecil had his first clerical appointment at St. Patrick's, a Church of Ireland parish in Coleraine.

The significant change came in the young Reverend Kerr's life in 1968, when he was appointed the Church of Ireland chaplain at Queen's University, and pastor of the Church of Ireland church on campus, the Church of the Resurrection. ...For the first time, Kerr had ecumenical colleagues, including the Catholic Father Tony Farquahar, the Methodist David Tuttle, and the Presbyterian Ray Davey, the most influential of the three. Ray Davey was the "senior" chaplain in every sense of the word, and the younger chaplains—especially Cecil Kerr—readily acknowledge their debt to him. Kerr offers this recollection:

> Ray Davey's vision of reconciliation was a constant challenge and inspiration to us. While working with the YMCA during the Second World War he was taken prisoner in North Africa. His experiences of sharing with Christians of other denominations in a prisoner of war camp taught him many

---

[3]These comments about Cecil Kerr's life and work are taken from interviews with the author conducted on January 15, 1991, and October 6, 1998, in Rostrevor, and from his book *The Way of Peace* (London: Hodder & Stoughton, 1990).

[4]Kerr, *Way of Peace*, 27.

important lessons about unity in Christ across the traditional barriers. In such a crucible of suffering ancient prejudices were melted. In many ways Ray foresaw the gathering storm in Ulster and in positive ways he and others who shared his vision prepared for it. Under his leadership the community of reconciliation which is now Corrymeela was born. I was privileged to be closely involved with him in some of the early projects in setting up that house of peace on the north Antrim coast. We used to take work parties of students to Corrymeela. Facing the challenge of working together to restore an old building forged lasting friendships across many inherited barriers. Ray and I presided over fervent discussions with the students late into the night. During such times, possibilities opened to us of finding new ways of living together in our divided land.[5]

The 1960s were a time of great turmoil in academic institutions, and Queen's was no exception....Cecil Kerr and Ray Davey believed that if Christianity was to be a vital force in Northern Ireland, it had to speak to the issues being forced into public attention, first by the legitimate protest of Queen's students and the Northern Ireland Civil Rights Association, and later by the terrorism of the Provisional wing of the IRA. As Kerr himself has admitted, he felt powerless in the developing circumstances. He faced something of a crisis in his calling. On one level, his ministry at Queen's was very successful. He was good with students, and with the help of his partner in the gospel, Myrtle, their home and the Church of the Resurrection were centers of good and much-appreciated activity. But Cecil was deeply concerned about

certain questions: Couldn't Christianity speak more positively to the desperate circumstances in West Belfast? Was there no power that could change this seemingly endless sectarian strife?...

In the spring of 1971, when Ulster was in deep turmoil because of violence and when Kerr was honestly casting about for his future direction, he happened to meet three Americans on the Queen's campus. They were from the Church of the Redeemer in Houston, Texas, a parish of the American Episcopal Church that had experienced a dramatic renewal. At first, Kerr did not know what to make of these visitors. "Their accounts of the miracles wrought through the Holy Spirit seemed to conservative ears rather unlikely, if not bizarre," he recalls. When asked why they had come to Belfast, the visitors replied, "The Holy Spirit sent us."[6] They further explained that they had no prior knowledge of Belfast other than what they called "a word of prophecy" they had received in a meeting in Houston which told them to go. Kerr ultimately was to warm to these strange Americans because their testimonies about the Word of God among them rang true. Later on, after he himself visited the church in Houston and had a good conversation with its rector, Graham Pulkingham, Kerr had a new vision of what might happen in Ireland if the whole church would be open to the Spirit. At that time Kerr read the J. B. Phillips version of Acts, and it showed him again what was possible with God:

> Here we are seeing the Church in its first youth, valiant and unspoiled—a body of ordinary men and women joined in an unconquerable fellowship never before seen on this earth. Yet we cannot help feeling disturbed as well as moved, for this surely is the Church

---

[5]Ibid., 24.
[6]Ibid., 26–27.

as it was meant to be....But if they were uncomplicated and naïve by modern standards we have ruefully to admit that they were open on the God-ward side in a way that is almost unknown today. No one can read this book without being convinced that there is Someone here at work besides mere human beings....[7]

In 1972 Kerr began a systematic inquiry into the whole notion of "baptism in the Holy Spirit." He wanted for his life and ministry the power promised to the New Testament church. But he did not want to rush after what some people thought of as a passing phase in the church. Cecil and Myrtle decided to go on a retreat with some Queen's students and with Roy Millar, a Belfast surgeon, and his wife, Rosemary. During that weekend, the Millars were to lead a Bible study and share their experiences of baptism in the Holy Spirit. On one occasion, other retreat participants prayed for Cecil with the laying on of hands. At the time, nothing discernible happened. But later on, while praying in his own room, he reports being "aware of the presence of God, like a loving Father offering me all the inheritance he had promised, and asking me to receive it as a gift."[8]

...After her own initial doubts and questions were answered, Myrtle joined her husband in a baptism of the Holy Spirit. Together the partners went forward with a renewed sense of purpose.

Northern Ireland has had many dark years since 1969. Perhaps 1973 was one of the worst....Many Christians felt powerless in the depths of the darkness. They had prayed about "the troubles" for many years, and to no apparent avail. Many non-Christians noted the religious roots of the conflict, and they either mocked Christians for still believing or gave up on the gospel altogether. For the latter group, it seemed like nonsense to say, "Religion has failed; give us more religion." Christians, for their part, agreed, or should have done so. Indeed, many Christians should have said something more like "Religion has failed; give us Christianity."

In truth, the Christian religion in Ireland had become compartmentalized in denominational boxes, divided by the social realities of ethnicity and social class.... Many Christians agreed with Cecil Kerr (as they did with Ray Davey) that there would be little progress toward a political solution in Ireland unless and until there was some progress in overcoming enmity and divisiveness among Christian groups.

During 1973 Kerr had several new experiences that underscored the continuing parallel of darkness and light. The occasion that was simultaneously the most exciting and the most unnerving for him was the time he was invited to come back to his hometown of Enniskillen to lead a youth outreach program, an annual event that required school presentations and open-air meetings. The invitation committee was composed of the three main Protestant churches—Presbyterian, Methodist, and Church of Ireland. Kerr accepted the invitation on the condition that he be allowed to bring along a group of Christian students from Belfast and Dublin, both Protestant and Roman Catholic. Still, he felt uneasy about this new course of ministry. He would be taking his new vision of Christians together back to his hometown, where the "normal" pattern of religious division was the rule. He knew what Protestant hardliners would say about a local man, who knew the rules of society, who came back to

---

[7]Ibid., 30.

[8]Ibid., 34.

Enniskillen with a "mixed" group of students.

During the time the team spent in Enniskillen, there was a short outdoor service that was led by a Catholic priest and several nuns. Kerr remembers the experience vividly, and its cost:

> As I stood there I suddenly began to feel a great fear coming over me. I sensed that as the cars drove past many of my friends and relatives were looking at me. In my mind...I could see them rolling down the windows of their cars and shouting "You are a traitor." Then I had an almost physical sensation of a bullet being shot into my back. It was all so frighteningly real to me that I had to ask my brothers and sisters from both traditions to pray that I would be delivered from that fear.[9]

Nevertheless, the group persisted, and prayed that those opposing the student team would be released from the prison houses of the heart and mind, where they were so sure they had God in their own boxes.

Kerr had another significant experience in 1973: the vision for the Christian Renewal Centre began to come clear to him. The CRC would be a place where Christians of all denominations could come to pray and work together for an Ireland united in Christ. Kerr believed that a community of men and women should live together to model this new way of worship, work, and service. Further, both he and his wife had the deep conviction that, just as they had learned from each other about "north and south," the CRC should be near the border in order to facilitate the meeting of Irish folk both from the United Kingdom province of Ulster and from the rest of the Republic of Ireland. The area outside the town of Rostrevor seemed ideal....

The community of like-minded people that Cecil and Myrtle Kerr gathered around them in Rostrevor was intentionally focused on Christian unity and reconciliation. As Cecil explains, "Our unity as brothers and sisters in Christ would have to demonstrate in practical ways the unity Christ desires for his people. That meant providing a place of welcome for all who came; an open house where people could find the Lord in each other."[10]

The community at Rostrevor has often been amused by the way weekend visitors think it a sort of heaven-on-earth to live in a lovely setting, in constant prayer and in fellowship. Happily for the Centre, one of its earliest members helped other members with their initial thinking along these lines. Walter Skelsey, who had a great deal of experience with the Scargill Community in Yorkshire, England, led other members of Rostrevor through Dietrich Bonhoeffer's writings about community. This kind of Christian realism was of great importance as the CRC began its mission. Kerr explains:

> Innumerable times a whole Christian community has broken down because it had sprung from a wish dream. The serious Christian, set down for the first time in a Christian community, is likely to bring with him a very definite idea of what Christian life together should be and try to realise it. But God's grace speedily shatters such dreams. Just as surely God desires to lead us to a knowledge of genuine Christian fellowship, so surely must we be overwhelmed by a great general disillusionment with others, with

---

[9]Ibid., 45.

[10]Ibid., 66.

Christians in general, and, if we are fortunate, with ourselves. By sheer grace God will not permit us to live even for a brief period in a dream world. He does not abandon us to those rapturous experiences and lofty moods that come over us like a dream. God is not a God of the emotions but the God of truth. Only that fellowship which faces such disillusionment, with all its unhappy and ugly aspects, begins to be what it should be in God's sight, begins to grasp in faith the promise that is given to it. The sooner this shock of disillusionment comes to an individual and to a community the better for both. A community which cannot bear and cannot survive such a crisis, which insists upon keeping its illusion when it should be shattered, permanently loses in that moment the promise of Christian community. Sooner or later it will collapse. Every human wish dream that is injected into the Christian community is a hindrance to genuine community and must be banished if genuine community is to survive.[11]

A further resource for the Christian Renewal Centre as it sought to develop an effective community of love and reconciliation was encouragement from leaders and lay people from other faith traditions. I have already mentioned Cahal Daly several times in this book. That Catholic prelate has been a source of enormous support for all peace-seeking Protestants. The community in Rostrevor found particularly welcome the cardinal's comments at a British church-leaders' conference on Northern Ireland:

The Church cannot identify itself with any political community. A Christian

preacher speaks to the whole people of God, and not to members of the unionist party or the nationalist party. The Gospel is for all men, and not just for a politically homogeneous group. The Kingdom of God is a universal kingdom, not a political faction. When Churchmen say "our people," they must not confine the phrase to people of one political persuasion. Indeed, I am convinced that our ministry of reconciliation summons all of us churchmen in our political situation in Northern Ireland to try to speak across the denominational divides and to address ourselves to both communities. We must never assert the rights of one community without also affirming the rights of the other community....[12]

With these sources of caution, inspiration, and support, the Christian Renewal Centre began, and over the years it has sustained a highly successful ministry of reconciliation and peace. A realist, however, might want to ask the visionaries at Rostrevor and elsewhere this question: Can people really change, and is religion the key to that change? Well, the reply comes, to the realist let us say this: No military solution to the Northern Ireland conflict could be found. In any case, now that The Agreement has provided a framework for peace, the main question in Northern Ireland has moved to the matter of reconciliation: Now that peace has come, can the former enemies be civil to each other, even friendly? Can the bitter enmities be broken down, and can there be forgiveness for past hurts? In this specific regard, Cecil Kerr values highly the words of Martin Luther King, who a few years before his death wrote, "He who is devoid of the power to forgive is devoid of the

---

[11]Ibid., 66–67.
[12]Ibid., 152.

power to love. Forgiveness is a catalyst creating the atmosphere necessary for a fresh start and a new beginning."[13]

The question of whether people can really change in response to the gospel is difficult to answer definitively. But, for supporters of the Christian Renewal Centre and other activists in reconciliation efforts in Northern Ireland, the testimonies of ordinary people are a significant witness to their belief. As Cecil Kerr often says, "rays of hope are piercing the darkness" in Northern Ireland. Let us look at some examples.

David Hamilton was a Loyalist prisoner in the Crumlin Road prison in Belfast, serving a sentence for armed robbery as a member of a terrorist organization. One day, when a team from the Renewal Centre was giving presentations and leading worship in the prison, Cecil Kerr sensed that he had "a word of knowledge" from God to share. Even though the surroundings made this all a bit strange, Kerr reluctantly said what he felt: "I believe that God is speaking to at least one man here who is going to become an evangelist, who will win many people to Christ."[14] Hamilton later wrote Kerr that someone else had expressed a similar view about him. Kerr's suggestion from God had confirmed the direction that Hamilton was already considering. When Hamilton was released from prison, his evangelical zeal and his ex-prisoner status made him a logical choice to work with the Irish branch of Prison Fellowship (an international organization founded by Chuck Colson in America). For several years thereafter, he worked with and ministered to prisoners and their families. And he worked with more than just Loyalist prisoners. He befriended an ex-Republican terrorist, Liam McCloskey, one of the hunger strikers of 1981 who did not die. McCloskey has since renounced violence and become a committed Christian. It is a remarkable witness for peace and reconciliation when two former sworn enemies—David Hamilton, a Protestant, and Liam McCloskey, a Catholic—share a platform together to give witness to the transforming possibilities of God's love in people's lives.

And then there are the stories of people who have been touched by the violence but yet have had the grace to forgive the perpetrators. One such story that largely escaped the notice of the press is that of the Travers family. Mr. Tom Travers, a resident magistrate, was attacked by an unknown gunman as he and his family left church after mass. The only apparent motive was that a Republican terrorist wanted to make an example to the Catholic community of "one of their own" who worked in the criminal justice system. Mr. Travers was shot but not killed. However, his daughter Mary, who was walking next to him, was shot dead. A little while after this tragedy, Mary's mother found the courage and the grace to write Cecil Kerr:

> Mary was a young woman full of compassion, forgiveness and love and we know that she forgives, and would want us to forgive, those who planned and carried out her murder and the attempted murder of her dad. We, in the name of the Saviour, would like you to remember Mary and our family in your prayers, and also those who were responsible for her death. We would also like you to pray that all men who have murder in their hearts will be overcome by the love of God so that they, like Mary, will one day be at peace with him.[15]

---

[13]Quoted in ibid., 186.

[14]Ibid., 163.

[15]Ibid., 177.

Harry McCann was also a person unknown to history until his tragic circumstances, and grace, thrust him into the spotlight. One morning Harry got into his car to go to work. When he turned on the ignition, a bomb went off, and he became the victim of another indiscriminate act of violence. He was rushed to the hospital, where he recalls hearing a doctor saying, "He's a bloody mess; he'll never be any use for anything." Well, Harry's legs may be gone —amputated at the thighs—but he is mightily useful. I was present at the Christian Renewal Centre when Harry spoke at a meeting. Though it was clearly difficult for him to use his artificial legs, he walked unaided and resolutely, using walking sticks. His cheerful spirit put all observers at ease. His story is quite dramatic, but Harry modestly underplayed the drama. In fact, the force of the blast that hurt him threw him up into the air, and he has had many difficult years following the major surgery he underwent. Harry dismissed all that when he spoke, saying, "Ah, it wasn't easy, but no need to tell blood-curdling stories." He told of the way in which he—not previously a committed Christian—found the grace to say, on the way to the hospital, "Father, forgive them." During his long hospital stay, his inherited Roman Catholic faith took on a new reality for him as he read the Bible and a Catholic prayer book. Today he travels frequently to all kinds of gatherings about forgiveness and reconciliation....Many people think of him as an "icon of grace."

One final testimony from ordinary people will conclude this answer to the question of whether forgiveness and reconciliation are truly possible in this context. At the CRC, on a day of renewal (a day when people from the community are welcome to share in song and testimony), I heard the testimonies of Bridie and Michael McGoldrick. This middle-aged Catholic couple was on vacation (ironically, at Warrenpoint, about two miles from Rostrevor) on July 8, 1996, when their lives changed forever.

When they turned on the TV news, they heard the report that a part-time taxi driver from Lurgan had been killed in Belfast in a sectarian shooting. This young man, also named Michael, was the only child of Bridie and Michael McGoldrick. He had just graduated from Queen's University and was making a little money over the summer as a taxi driver before beginning work. The senseless nature of this random killing of their only child shocked the McGoldricks to the core. All manner of terrible thoughts came to them in the aftermath. At the same time, their hometown of Portadown was the focal point of international media attention, since the marches at Drumcree were imminent. Yet somehow they found the grace to come through this dark time. The McGoldricks believe they received special grace from God, because they freely acknowledge they could not have made it on their own. In the months thereafter, the McGoldricks have found it in their hearts to forgive young Michael's murderers. They admit that their willingness to participate in reconciling work with Protestants at the Christian Renewal Centre has caused some in their Catholic community in Portadown to ostracize them. These ordinary folks are, however, sustained by and sometimes amazed at how their own deep tragedy has allowed them to become channels of God's peace. They are very active in United Christian Aid, a charity that, among other things, ministers to people who have lost children in tragic circumstances. They have gone to Chernobyl and Romania to help others and have pledged to continue to work for peace. When I was in the McGoldricks' presence, listening to their story, it seemed to me that there was less terrible darkness, and more light.

During one of my many visits to the Centre, as I engaged the scene and watched the joyful people, either in praise or in personal conversation, I wondered how they carried on so well in the face of continuing tragedies and atrocities. I asked Cecil Kerr to focus with me on this specific question. Of course he told me of God's sustaining grace that he and Myrtle daily receive. That was the answer I expected to hear. But then Cecil went on to admit that, of course, it was very difficult to come back again and again with confidence after experiencing repeated blows with the suffering people to whom he ministers. Yet, he pointed out, at the moment when news of yet another tragedy seems too heavy to bear, God seems to raise up a person—often a previously very ordinary one—to become an icon of grace. For example, when the Remembrance Day bombing occurred in Enniskillen in 1987, Cecil Kerr was particularly shaken because it was his hometown that was targeted. He led a team from the Centre to minister in Enniskillen. And, he reports, while he and his comrades ministered, they were also ministered to. This is a large part of what keeps Kerr and the people at the Centre going—that in the darkness they always find transcending evidence of God's grace....

At the end of his novel *Trinity,* Leon Uris wrote, "In Ireland there is no future, only the past happening over and over."[16] Cecil Kerr and his colleagues of the Christian Renewal Centre can understand such pessimism, but their profound conviction is that Uris is wrong. There is a new future for Ireland—a bright future whose signs are already apparent.

I want to conclude this discussion of the Christian Renewal Centre and the members' work for reconciliation and peace by discussing their understanding of their ministry of prayer. In the autumn of 1997, I sat in the meditation chapel of the Christian Renewal Centre with Harry Smith, a senior assistant to Cecil Kerr. Smith's particular calling is prayer. More specifically, he teaches people about the nature and function of prayer. Smith is a British Christian who has been at the CRC for seven years....His ministry of prayer at the Centre comprises several elements: publishing a prayer newsletter, holding "prayer schools" three or four weekends a year, and taking a prayer-teaching mission to communities where "renewed" Protestants and Catholics together would like to accomplish in their home areas what Smith does at Rostrevor. Smith organized one such prayer group—of Protestants and Catholics alike—in Carrickfergus one weekend in 1994. The group so enjoyed each other's support and fellowship there that they have stayed together to pray—but also to study British and Irish history.

Of particular interest...is the "prayer school" that Smith led at the Centre in November 1997 called "The Healing of the Nation." Here the regular "method" was employed—of modeling and teaching people how to pray and what to pray—but the focal point in this instance was the healing of the Irish nation. Smith knew that the weekend he chose, November 14–16, was crucial for two reasons: it was the weekend after Remembrance Day, when people stop to remember those who have given their lives for the nation; and it was the tenth anniversary of the bombing of Enniskillen, which had produced the witness of Gordon Wilson. Later, I asked Smith to tell me how that prayer school went. He reported that the diversity of the registrants, in terms of both locale and denomination, was quickly

---

[16]Leon Uris, *Trinity* (London: Corgi Books, 1976), 900.

overcome by their cooperative spirit. They experienced the sheer power of common prayer in the midst of a divided society. They learned how to pray for those in authority by using their names and mentioning their roles. They learned how to pray specifically for justice and righteousness in the nation. They learned how to pray for the peacemakers....

These folks doubtlessly joined many others over the next winter in praying for peace in Northern Ireland. When the breakthrough came on Good Friday 1998, and The Agreement was signed, people who had learned to pray at the Christian Renewal Centre were surely grateful, but they probably were not surprised. Those who pray with such purpose and inten-sity are more accustomed than most other Christians to having their prayers answered....

Kerr and the CRC have been a great encouragement to many clergy in both Roman Catholic and Protestant churches. Those clergy people who have caught a new vision of what the gospel can mean for reconciliation often face indifference or even opposition in their church communities. Kerr has received many of these folk at the Centre and has encouraged them not to give up but to remain in their churches. This is a role for which Cecil Kerr is largely unsung, as befits a man who is often the one leading others by the Holy Spirit, the most self-effacing person of the Trinity.[17]

---

[17]Author's conversation with Ken Newell, August 8, 1998.

Chapter Twenty-Nine

Peace Breaks Out in the Middle East

Sam Hine

We are conditioned by the news we hear from the Middle East. Modern Israel was born in war, and wars and violence have seldom been absent in the decades since 1948. Both sides have legitimate grievances. Both have indulged in violence, and, like most combatants, both find it virtually impossible to ask for or to grant forgiveness. To visit the region or to hear spokespersons from both sides leaves one with the vague but pervasive feeling that peace will never be achieved in the "Holy Land."

Sam Hine's article lights a candle in this dark scene of hopeless despair. There are those in Palestine who believe in and work for peace. Courageous people on both sides of the conflict are seeking reconciliation with people "on the other side." We need to hear their story if we are to be helped to believe that peace has a chance in Jerusalem. Can we dare to believe that small minorities can bring profound changes, that weak people can overcome the powerful, that quiet voices can silence the shrill voice of hate, that the leaven of peace can flavor the dough of nationalism?

Enough bad news. Ever since the outbreak of the recent Palestinian uprising, the media have flooded us with body counts, graphic images, dire predictions, and the inevitable biases and polarized opinions that only fuel the flames of anger, mistrust, and despair. Surely, we are farther than ever from the peace that so recently seemed so near.

So they say. True, if peace were merely the product of the political wrangling, coercion, and compromise called a "peace process," there would be little reason for hope. If peace in the Middle East depended on military leaders and politicians, then we might never see peace. But on the ground the people who should be making headlines—the little people quietly working for cooperation and understanding between Jews and Arabs, or working to change the hearts and minds of their own people—show us that despite the odds, the real peace process is alive and well.

It starts with little deeds that shatter stereotypes, like the Palestinian teens who came upon a Jewish settler who had strayed into the heart of Hebron. Weeping and shaking, the settler expected to share the fate of soldiers caught in Ramallah only days before. Instead, he was comforted and escorted to the nearest Israeli army roadblock.

This article first appeared as Sam Hine, "Peace Breaks Out in the Middle East," *The Plough Reader*, Winter 2001, 4–8.

Sometimes simple deeds make big waves. You may have heard of Omri Jadah, the young Palestinian who didn't weigh religion and nationality when he dove into the Sea of Galilee in August to rescue a drowning Israeli child. He heaved six-year-old Gosha Leftov safely into a friend's arms, only to be caught himself by the strong undertow and dragged to his death. He left behind a wife and two children, with a third on the way, but his sacrifice touched the hearts of Jews and Arabs alike. "He saw a kid drowning. It wasn't an Israeli kid or a Palestinian kid, it was just a kid," said Tim Rose, publisher of the *Jerusalem Post*. "We would all benefit if that kind of thinking could percolate up."

Hamas kidnapped and murdered Yitzhak Frankenthal's son, an Israeli soldier, in 1994. Today Yitzhak brings together bereaved Israeli and Palestinian parents to issue a joint call for peace. During the recent unrest he was unable to organize an emergency meeting in Israel because Palestinians cannot enter Israel and Israelis cannot enter Gaza. Undeterred, Yitzhak convened the meeting in London. As far as Yitzhak knows, this was the first time in the history of wars that bereaved parents from both sides—while their peoples continued fighting—came together to project a genuine, warm reconciliation. Their message was clear: We, who paid the dearest and most painful price of all, sit together discussing peace. We lost a child yet we do not seek revenge—only peace. If *we* can sit and talk, so can anyone."

As long as deaths on "our" side are tragedies while "their" deaths are merely statistics, the violence will continue. Thanks to Seeds of Peace, an American organization that brings Arab and Israeli youth together in a summer camp in Maine, one Arab death opened young Jewish eyes to the reality of the situation. Like other participants, Asel Asleh, a student at Elias Chacour's integrated high school in Ibillin, kept in touch with his new Jewish friends once he returned to Israel, e-mailing, phoning, and visiting regularly. When Asel was shot in the neck near his home in Arabeh, Galilee, his Jewish friends across Israel knew he hadn't been throwing stones.

When Noam Kuzar, a 19-year-old Israeli soldier, was called on to help repress the uprising, he took responsibility for his own actions. He simply refused to go, and was sentenced to 28 days in jail. Noam hopes others will follow his lead, and doesn't seem to mind scrubbing floors for the rest of his active duty. "People ask me why I'm there cleaning and why I'm not in my fighting unit. I get to talk to people in the army about it quite a bit."

Dalia Landau of Ramle offered to give her house back to the Arabs that were evicted in 1948, even though it had been her home since childhood. She and her husband Yehezkel agreed with the original Muslim owners, the Al-Khayri family, to make the house a daycare center for local Arab children, and Ramle's only Jewish-Arab community center. Open House now also offers a summer camp for Arab and Jewish children, a tutorial program, and classes in language, computers, parenting, swimming, and creative arts. With Michail Fanous, a Palestinian Christian, as co-director, Open House stands as a shining example of cooperation among the country's three religions. In the wake of the recent violence, Yehezkel says, there is much fear and hostility to overcome. "But at least there was no fighting in the streets between Ramle's two communities, as happened in other mixed cities. I'd like to think that what we've been doing in the last ten years helped to calm the atmosphere."

Yacoub Munayer, an Arab, experienced firsthand the eviction from Lod and Ramle in 1948. Josef Ben Eliezer was one of the Israeli soldiers who drove them out.

In the book *Why Forgive?* Josef tells how he was forced to flee Germany and then Poland as the Nazis advanced. He escaped to Palestine in 1943. Determined never to be trampled on again, he joined the Israeli army. Then unexpectedly, on that day in Lod, his childhood in wartime Poland flashed before his eyes, and he relived his own experience as a ten-year-old boy driven from his home. Recently, Yacoub heard Josef's story and extended his forgiveness, and the two reconciled in Lod.

Many Palestinians are Christians, firmly committed to the nonviolent gospel of their Prince of Peace. In some areas, they have effected a decidedly more nonviolent approach to liberation. Palestinians also bring to the table an age-old process of nonviolent conflict resolution called *sulha*. The goal of sulha is to restore honor to both the offender and the offended through a process of forgiveness and restitution, mediated by respected local leaders, that eventually brings both families together in a mutually beneficial final resolution. Elias Jabour, a respected mediator in his local community, says, "A civil court can only satisfy one side; somebody always loses. Making the Arab sulha satisfies all parties—all are happy in the end." Sulha can only be set in motion if the offender seeks it, and if the offended party promises not to seek revenge. Applying this wisdom on a daily basis to current conflicts is Zoughbi Zougbhi, Executive Director of the Bethlehem-based Wi'am Center for Conflict Resolution.

Shulti Regev, a Jewish Kibbutznik, has put together a proposal for a "Public National Committee for Sulha and Reconciliation in the State of Israel." Reminiscent of South Africa's Truth and Reconciliation Committee, the body would hear testimonies, appeals and complaints, offering a foundation on which to rebuild trust. Respected spiritual and civic leaders on both sides have expressed support and willingness to serve on the committee. "Politics is not always the most efficient means of addressing such a depth of hostility among people who must continue to live together after mutual hurt," Shulti says.

Peace will be born in places where all sides can come together safely on neutral ground. Tantur Ecumenical Institute in Jerusalem has filled such a role for over 25 years. Jonatan Peled, a Holocaust survivor, is spearheading another venture. He recently left a job directing the Re'ut-Sadaka (Friendship) Jewish-Arab youth organization, in order to establish a permanent "Friendship Village," an education center and farm available to multicultural youth groups throughout Israel as well as youth living in other areas of social and ethnic conflict. The Arab town of Shefa-Amer, between Haifa and Nazareth, has donated land to establish the center. "The basis for building trust is knowledge of the other," Jonatan says. "Such knowledge can only be achieved through acquaintance, dialogue, and learning. In other words, a vital precondition for the establishment of a real peace is mass education toward a culture of peace.

Another man who knows that tolerance and understanding must be learned is Nafez Assaily, a Sufi Moslem who runs the Library on Wheels for Nonviolence and Peace. The library serves children in villages throughout the West Bank who have no access to public libraries. Besides providing books that promote peace, coexistence, and nonviolence, it distributes educational materials to kindergartens lacking proper supplies, and even offers financial support to families unable to afford children's school fees. Although the uprising and border closures block his library from many Palestinian towns, Nafez is optimistic. "These violent demonstrations and the reactions of Israelis are signs that they will sit at the table in the near future to discuss peace in a serious way, because both sides understand the price they paid."

To achieve that elusive peace, we must start listening to those who haven't been heard. As elsewhere, women have been conspicuously underrepresented in negotiations determining their fate. One organization out to rectify that situation, Bat Shalom, has teamed up with its Palestinian counterpart, the Jerusalem Center for Women, and released a petition calling on Palestinian and Israeli women to lead the way:

> The men tell us not to be scared. They tell us to be strong. We are scared, and we want them to be scared too. We do not want to be "strong." We don't want them to think that they are strong enough to make the other nation disappear or go down in defeat and disgrace....There are too many men with too many egos involved in burning this piece of land. They talk of a security based in might. We know that security means being good neighbors. Without forgetting the wrongs of the past, nor the unequal distribution of power, we will focus an how to *live* here in peace. We do not want the next generation of children to wear uniforms, to go to war. We want them to know self-determination and dignity, without the need to fight for them.

Despite its "honest broker" pose at the negotiating table, America bears responsibility for the role its military aid plays in this confrontation. One of the few American Jews to speak frankly about his own guilt is Rabbi Michael Lerner of San Fransisco, editor of *Tikkun Magazine,* a bimonthly Jewish critique of politics, culture, and society. In a widely reprinted opinion piece, he wrote:

For every outrage on one side there is a story of outrage on the other. For me, that doesn't justify either side—both are wrong and both sides need to atone. I have to take responsibility for my side, my community, my people....To me, Israeli deaths are a personal tragedy. But have we not yet learned that in God's eyes every human being is equally treasured? As a religious Jew, I know that God and the Torah are served best when we insist that every human being, including our enemies, be seen as equally valuable to God and equally created as embodiments of the divine.

As a result of his stand, Rabbi Lerner has received death threats and had so many subscriptions cancelled that *Tikkun's* financial base is jeopardized. (To subscribe, call 415-575-1200.)

In Israel, too, a few religious leaders are showing the way. Rabbis for Human Rights, made up of ninety Reform, Orthodox, Conservative, and Reconstructionist rabbis, has been instrumental in blocking home demolitions and supporting displaced families. During the height of the recent unrest they accompanied Palestinians who had come under fire while trying to harvest their olives.

And every day, prayers for peace rise to the God of three religions, such as this one from a Palestinian pastor: "My brothers and sisters, it is my prayer that what we suffer as a nation will not harden our hearts, but keep them tender and ready to forgive. Lord, help us not to be preoccupied with our own present suffering and unable to see the suffering of people in the rest of the world, even the suffering of our enemies."

Wherever our allegiance or sympathy lies, and whatever our prescription for change, the fate of this very special piece of land concerns us all. Its suffering may be far from over. But next time your blood boils at the latest news, remember these peacemakers and many more like them, who reject the destructive urges of anger, tribalism, and fear. Remember their actions and words, which even in these difficult times are moving a violence-torn region slowly and surely toward peace. So can yours.

Part V

❖

Christian Reflections
on September 11, 2001

❖

Chapter Thirty

Reflecting on
Tragedy and Terror

Faculty, Department of Biblical and Religious Studies
Messiah College

In a previous generation the question, "Where were you when...," was understood by all to refer to the news report of the assassination of President John F. Kennedy. This same question for the current generation will automatically trigger images of planes crashing into the World Trade Center in New York City. Events like this tragedy grip the collective soul of a nation. Immediately one is rooted to the news sources, both horrified by and attracted to what they are reporting. Instant feelings surge to the surface, and questions still vaguely formed demand satisfying answers. People respond to tragedy by giving vent to feelings and by attempting to find a framework of meaning.

Thus, we should not be surprised that all of us felt a great need to talk about September 11, 2001, to tell others how we felt about the situation and to ask one another for perspectives that would help us to think and act like Christians. In private and in public much was said that was helpful; and some things were expressed that were not worthy of Christ. It takes time for us all to let instant emotions subside, to let the noise and confusion diminish so we can hear the gentle voice of the Lord.

What the Biblical and Religious Studies department wrote in the October 5 edition of the Messiah College student newspaper, *The Swinging Bridge*, is one of the more positive Christian perspectives. It is considerate and objective, recognizing diverse Christian positions while still indicating some clear Christian responses that all should embrace. A general Christian attitude seems much clearer for all of us than do questions of national policy in response to such events.

This college statement leads us to wrestle with certain questions. Does God have one ethical standard for individual behavior and another for national behavior? If so, why? If not, then how is evil to be overcome in society? What can Christians do when they cannot agree about national policy?

This chapter originally appeared as "Reflection on Tragedy and Terror: An Open Letter to the Messiah College Community from the Faculty of the Department of Biblical and Religious Studies," *The Swinging Bridge*, October 5, 2001.

The attacks on the World Trade Center in New York and on the Pentagon in Washington, D.C., shocked us and people all around the world. We realized in an instant that the United States was vulnerable to a terrorist attack in a way we had never imagined possible. We saw images of violence on TV unlike anything seen before. This was not the imitation violence of the theater or the distant violence of news being reported from a foreign land. This was a massive act of violence perpetrated against people in our own country. We were all numb with disbelief. The terrorists who planned these attacks did their work well. Our understanding of the world was altered in a moment and virtually all of us feel much less secure than we did a month ago.

It is hard to put words to events like those that took place on September 11; it is harder yet to make sense of such tragedies. As Christians, however, and especially as Christian scholars, we cannot avoid that task. We cannot presume to have answers for all the questions that have raced through all our minds and hearts over the last few weeks. Nor are we so wise that we can dictate to other Christians how they should think and act in light of what has happened. But we do hope this letter, and various follow-up opportunities to discuss it, will help the Messiah College community better understand the attack and our nation's emerging response to it.

One of the problems we face is simply how best to label the attack that took place on September 11. Was this an act of war? To call it that may predispose us to assume counter-violence has to be part of our necessary response. In a war you hit back and hit back hard. Or was this a massive and horrible crime? To describe the attack in that way predisposes us to view the claims of justice and punishment in a somewhat different light. Our point is that, from the very beginning of our discussion, we need to be very careful how we choose our words because the words we choose can shape the way we feel and think about the situation.

We know that many Christians are asking if this event was somehow part of God's historical plan for the world. Is this God's punishment of America? Are we viewing the beginning of the end of human history and the prelude to Christ's return? What is going to happen next? We think it is reasonable to ask such questions, but we also consider most of the answers we have heard to these kinds of questions inappropriate and irresponsible. We ourselves are quite convinced that the events of September 11 are not part of God's plan for the ages; this is not the beginning of "the End Times." We are also discouraged by speculation about why God may have "caused" this to happen. We do not believe God "causes" this kind of evil; people are responsible for these acts. What God does is help us and others cope with evil, including this tragedy.

Surely part of what we observed on September 11 was a demonstration of great hatred against America. If that is so, it is incumbent on us to try to understand where that hatred comes from. The magnitude of hatred displayed in the attacks on September 11 is difficult to fathom, and it in no way justifies the acts committed, but hatred has its causes. In this particular case, the hatred of the attackers was at least partly rooted in the perception that America has been an exporter of immorality to other parts of the world and that our nation has, at times, been a force for injustice and oppression. It is not just terrorists and extremists that view America in this way. Many people around the world, from many different faiths, are concerned about how America's cultural, military, and economic power impacts their societies negatively as well as positively.

In terms of how we should react as a nation to what has taken place, Christian leaders have said almost without exception that prayer and compassion should be the first response, and all of us have been heartened by the outpouring of prayer and aid from people across the nation and around the world. Christians have been almost unanimous in saying that revenge and hatred should not be part of our response, and political and church leaders alike have been very careful to say America should never become involved in any kind of crusade against Islam. Most would agree that the long range goal should be to build a safer and more just world and not merely to punish those who carried out these terrorist acts.

Of course, the potential for violent action does loom on the horizon, and it makes sense for Christians to begin to think now about how they might respond. Within the long history of Christian faith two bodies of opinion have coalesced regarding how to respond to acts of violence like we witnessed on September 11. Christian pacifists have argued that Christians should never respond with lethal violence to acts of violence committed against themselves and/or those they love; Christians who believe in "just war" theory have argued that sometimes people and/or nations need to use lethal violence to see that justice is carried out. Each of these groups has criticized the other. Just war Christians have often accused pacifists of being impractical and out of touch with reality. Pacifists have said that just war Christians have overestimated the effectiveness of violence, saying that violence even when used for just ends necessarily begets more violence and does not bring true peace. Both sides make valid points and sincere Christians can be found on both sides of this divide—including within our own department. We need to respect each other and listen to each other, and we also need to strive as much as possible to arrive at a common witness on the matter of violence.

Historically, Messiah College and its founding denomination have been committed to the pacifist position, arguing that Jesus' personal example requires individual Christians to reject the use of violence and that the witness of the biblical prophets calls us as a nation to make our policies as nonviolent and just as possible. In a world where violence is often seen as the only valid response to violence, we think it is imperative that everyone understand the logic of Christian nonviolence. In actuality, most proponents of the just war theory would agree. The classic just war position argues that violent action can only be considered after nonviolent means of dealing with a situation have been fully exhausted. It seems clear then that the first Christian response to any situation of violence has to be to explore and exhaust all nonviolent means of dealing with evil before the use of lethal violence becomes an option to consider.

What does all of this mean in the present situation? Obviously, we are not in a position to propose or to decide what US policy should be. We have insufficient access to information and political expertise to do so. Nonetheless, we believe it is our responsibility as Christians to encourage our national leaders to remember the claims of peace and to pursue justice with as much nonviolence as is possible. We also believe it is our duty to help Americans in general to understand better the global influence of our nation and why some people view us so negatively. As events unfold in the days and weeks ahead, we will be planning a variety of events where we can discuss these and other matters as we struggle together to understand our interrelated responsibilities as citizens of America and as disciples of Jesus who is the head of the church universal which transcends all national boundaries.

While we do think it is important for us to discuss and debate the situation we confront, we never want to forget our even more fundamental responsibility as Christians to pray for others in times of crisis. We need to pray for those who have been directly impacted by this disaster through personal harm or loss of loved ones. We need to pray for those who continue to work at the attack sites, recovering bodies and clearing the rubble. We need to pray for our national leaders and, indeed, for political leaders around the world as they grapple with how to respond. We need to pray for Muslims living in the United States that they will be spared from acts of vengeance at the hands of their neighbors. We need to pray for those in the military who might be ordered into action, and we simultaneously need to pray for peace activists who have already begun to rally against the use of force. Finally, and most difficultly, we need to pray honestly and caringly for our enemies. While we may disagree on other matters, we would all agree on the need for prayer. May God grant all of us peace in this tragic moment of human history.

September 11 and the Just War Theory

Duane K. Friesen

Duane Friesen, Professor of Bible and Religion at Bethel College, Kansas, has written widely on the relationship of Christians, including pacifists, to the state and the surrounding culture. He argues for a reasoned participation of even Anabaptist-related groups in these spheres.

Many Americans have failed to consider how a distinctive Christian identity should shape their response to terrorism. In the following article, while the author agrees that acts of terror are crimes that justify a response, he does not agree that the action should be military. Such action as has been taken by the United States mainly fails to fulfill the historic criteria of a just war.

Is the author's call for other means of defense, such as understanding and treating the reasons that lie behind the events of September 11, a practical response to acts of terror? Is the author correct in maintaining that just war criteria are largely not met in American action in Afghanistan (e.g., on proportionality)? Does the just war theory sound more plausible following September 11 because the acts of terror are so close to home rather than occurring in another part of the world? What action can peace proponents take in persuading governments to use other means than war to combat violence?

Before Christians can begin reflecting on September 11, we must be clear about the meaning of Christian identity. The most important question is what "story" or narrative describes the lives we ought to live.

Many American Christians uncritically combine their Christian identity and American identity. They conveniently relegate Jesus to the spiritual and personal realm. The most popular phrase to describe this position is "Christ died to save us from our sins" as an all-encompassing statement of Christ's work in the world. The prob-lem with this theological position is that it provides no framework for making moral judgments about politics. The ethical norms for politics for most American Christians come from the surrounding popular culture of Ameri-can patriotism. Their political position can be described with the sentence: "America was unjustifiably attacked, and we need to respond with violent force." The identity of the "we" is am-biguous. It is an American "we" that lacks clarity about what difference it makes for Christians to do moral reflec-tion on politics. American Christians

254 ✣ A Peace Reader

need a richer biblical narrative to define their identity, one that makes central to their identity the life, teachings, death, and resurrection of Jesus Christ.[1]

The story of Jesus must be understood in the light of God's call to Abraham and his descendants to be a distinctive people who bring God's blessing to all the nations. When God's people were carried into exile after the destruction of Jerusalem by the Babylonians, Jeremiah wrote to them to live and prosper in Babylon, and there in enemy territory to "seek the welfare [shalom] of the city where I have sent you into exile, for in its welfare you will find your welfare" (Jer. 29:7, NRSV).[2] Jeremiah's letter reflects a radical alternative to the politics of national identity tied to Davidic kingship. Jesus was in continuity with the letter of Jeremiah when, in the context of Roman imperial power, He became obedient to the cross and called His followers to love their enemies rather than to join the Zealot's cause of violent rebellion against Rome. In the Sermon on the Mount, Jesus teaches that we should "be like God" in loving our enemies.

The text of the New English Bible captures the meaning:

> Love your enemies and pray for your persecutors; only so can you be children of your heavenly Father, who makes his sun rise on good and bad alike, and sends the rain on the honest and the dishonest. If you love only those who love you, what reward can you expect? Surely the tax-gatherers do as much as that. And if you greet only your brothers, what is there extraordinary about that? Even the heathen do as much. There must be no limit to your goodness, as your heavenly Father's goodness knows no bounds. (Matt. 5:44-48)[3]

Paul is in continuity with Jesus' life and teachings when he states in Romans 12:17-21 that we are not to retaliate violently against evil, but to love our enemies and to overcome evil with good. Many Christians have taken Paul's discussion of submission to authorities in Romans 13: 1-7 out of the context of his larger argument about loving enemies. In Romans 13 Paul is not advising Christians to take up the sword to protect the good and punish the evil; rather, he is referring to the

---

[1]See John Howard Yoder, *The Politics of Jesus* (Grand Rapids: Eerdmans, 1972) for the best description of what it means to take Jesus seriously as an ethical norm for politics. Yoder explains the many ways Jesus has been interpreted so as effectively to dismiss Jesus from the political arena. These interpretations then lead to a justification for deriving our political norms from other sources.

[2]For a much fuller description of the implications of the letter of Jeremiah, see my description of an Anabaptist theology of culture in the book *Artists, Citizens, Philosophers: Seeking the Peace of the City* (Scottdale, Pa.: Herald Press, 2000).

[3]For a description of the many ways in which the Sermon on the Mount has been interpreted, see Harvey K. McArthur, *Understanding the Sermon on the Mount* (London: Epworth Press, 1961). Most of the interpretations that he describes have evaded applying love of enemies to the political sphere. One example of this evasion is the position of the well-known evangelical Carl F.H. Henry, who applies Jesus' teachings to interpersonal relationships and not to the larger social and political sphere. Henry states his position bluntly: "It does not bear on the questions of war or public oaths."— *Christian Personal Ethics* (Grand Rapids: Eerdmans, 1957), 323. For an alternative to these evasive readings of the Sermon on the Mount, see Glen Stassen, *Just Peacemaking: Transforming Initiatives for Justice and Peace* (Lousville, Ky.: Westminster John Knox Press, 1992). Stassen argues that the teachings of the Sermon, grounded in God's grace-filled deliverance, call for peacemaking and justice-making that are applicable to political realities.

judicial authority of the pagan Roman state.[4] However, in a fallen world of sin symbolized by the sword, Christian hope is grounded in the resurrection. Christians live in the presence of God's empowering grace that breaks the power of violence in our lives. Life can be transformed; violence is not inevitable. Our hope is grounded in God, who overcomes evil through the Lamb that was slain, not through violence and death.

The church, as the body of Christ in the world, is called to witness to this hope and to be a transnational community among the nations. As a body of people whose central symbol is the cross and who are united in the common meal of the Eucharist, the church transcends national boundaries and the national identity symbolized by the flag. The message of the church to the world is God's love for the whole cosmos (John 3:16). Even as Christ has reconciled the world to himself, so we have been entrusted with the ministry of reconciliation (2 Cor. 5:18). Love of enemies is integral to the good news of God's reconciling love to all people and is, therefore, centrally connected to the missionary calling of the church.

It is within the framework of this narrative that Christians are called to seek justice. Justice is the establishment of right relationships among people and among communities.[5] Justice requires that everyone live securely in the land, in safety without fear of violence. The brutally violent acts of September 11 that killed thousands of innocent persons who were engaged in the normal routine of daily life is a gross violation of the biblical meaning of shalom. But so is the U.S. war in Afghanistan, where since the bombing began in October 2001, it is estimated that more civilians have lost their lives than were killed on September 11.[6] In addition, the bombing in Afghanistan has devastated the infrastructure of that country and has created thousands of refugees, people who have been forced to flee their homes. The question is how we as Christians should seek justice. How do we protect people against terrorist violence without committing another wrong in using violent force that destroys other people's peace and security?

When Christians orient their lives by the story of Jesus and the church, then we will respond to September 11 in a way that is different from the dominant responses in our culture. The Christian

---

[4]For a more in-depth commentary on Romans 13:1–7, see John H. Yoder, *The Politics of Jesus.* In the book *Artists, Citizens, Philosophers,* I state: "What does Paul mean that government is a servant of God to protect the good and punish the evil? Paul is referring to the pagan Roman state. Just prior to this passage he has urged the believers to give food and drink to their enemies and to overcome evil with good (Rom. 12:20–21), so it would be a contradiction for him now to tell them to take up the sword to protect the good and punish the evil. In a world of sin, God providentially uses the pagan state to order human life. The sword symbolizes the judicial authority of government. This is a fact of governments: they have authority and exercise their authority through the use of coercive force. The sword is not a symbol for the approval of war or of capital punishment" (p. 234).

[5]Justice defined within a Christian narrative should be distinguished from secular liberalism. Justice is not primarily individual freedom in the pursuit of happiness, though the respect for the dignity of the person created in the image of God is an important element of a Christian view of justice. Justice is not primarily retribution against those who have committed acts of injustice, though God's judgment of sin is an element of justice. The emphasis is communal, not individualistic. The primary concern is the restoration of sinners to right relationship and to community, not punishment and retribution.

[6] See the documentation by Professor Marc W. Herold of the University of New Hampshire at http://pubpages.unh.edu/mwherold.

narrative subverts the call to pursue retaliation and vengeance because *our* enemies have violated *our* identity as a nation. The Christian narrative subverts the American story that we are justified in using force to preserve American self-interest. Self-interest to protect *our* security lacks the universal vision of shalom for all peoples that is central to the biblical story. Christ not Caesar, is Lord. God does not bless our nation at the expense of others. That absolute commitment to national self-interest is idolatry in the light of the Christian narrative of the one God revealed in Jesus Christ.

A Christian narrative stands in opposition to the rhetoric of holy war. Christians oppose such a war, which justifies using violent force to "...destroy evil..." in the name of God or freedom. The simplistic division of the world into forces of good and evil and the identification of *our* side with righteousness lacks a realistic view of the sin and blindness that extend to all sides in this conflict.

Though the terrorists are fully responsible for the acts they committed on September 11, and no amount of corruption and evil committed by the West against the Islamic world can justify what they did, the United States is partly responsible for creating the hatred in the Middle East that feeds terrorism. In the Gulf War, the United States aligned itself with the repressive regime of Saudi Arabia to protect its oil interests. The placement of U.S. troops on Saudi Arabian soil and the humiliation of the Gulf War fueled the anger that produced an Osama bin Laden. The United States appeals to international law when it is in its self-interest, but it extends lopsided support to the state of Israel, failing to adequately support United Nations Resolution 238, which calls for Israel to withdraw from the occupied territories of Palestine. The assumption that terrorism can be destroyed by violence is an illusion. We cannot humiliate our enemies and expect them not to seek revenge.

In the light of the Christian narrative, three morally rigorous ethical positions have been developed in the history of the church: those of pacifism, just war, and just peacemaking. The most recent of these, just peacemaking, builds its position around emphases in both the pacifist and just war traditions. The aim of pacifism is to make peace. In just war theory, the use of violent force must lead to peace, to a positive outcome, if the violence of war is to be justified. Just peacemaking asks a different question. What practices should be taken into account that can lead to more peaceful relationships between adversaries? The central question is not, Is war justified? To that question pacifists answer "no" and just war advocates say "yes, under certain conditions."[7]

The oldest Christian tradition is pacifism, a practice that was most prevalent in the first three hundred years of the church, prior to Constantine. It continues as the ethical position of a minority of Christians within most major denominational traditions (Roman Catholic, Protestant, Orthodox, Pentecostal),

---

[7]Glen Stassen, ed., *Just Peacemaking: Ten Practices for Abolishing War* (Cleveland: The Pilgrim Press, 1998). The ten criteria of just peacemaking are organized around three general categories: (A) Peacemaking Initiatives: (1) Support nonviolent direct action; (2) take independent initiatives to reduce threat; (3) use cooperative conflict resolution; (4) acknowledge responsibility for conflict and injustice, and seek repentance and forgiveness. (B) Justice: (5) Advance democracy, human rights, and religious liberty; (6) foster just and sustainable economic development. (C) Love and Community: (7) Work with emerging cooperative forces in the international system; (8) strengthen the United Nations and international efforts for cooperation and human rights; (9) reduce weapons of offense and weapons trade; (10) encourage grassroots peacemaking groups and voluntary associations.

among evangelicals outside the main-stream, and as the official position of the historic peace churches (Mennonite, Friends, and Church of the Brethren). Many Christian pacifists are committed both to the pursuit of justice and to nonviolence. The most common mis-understanding of pacifism is that pacifists commit themselves to nonviolence but ignore the concern for justice. Nonviolent resistance is not passivity or withdrawal from conflict, but engagement with evil powers through nonviolent means of transformation.[8]

The just war tradition began in the late fourth and early fifth centuries un-der the leadership of bishops Ambrose and Augustine. Given the Christian nar-rative is it possible for Christians under any circumstances to justify the use of violent force? Clearly there is a pre-sumption, given this narrative, against violence. The logic of the Christian faith is the practice of nonviolence and love of enemies. Therefore, it was necessary for Christians to develop criteria that might allow for exceptions to the rule of nonviolence. It is very important that Christians who use just war theory un-derstand this narrative framework. Many Christians use just war theory to easily justify war in the name of na-tional defense and national self-interest because they lack an adequate Christology and a view of the church that can generate an alternative ethical framework.

One example of the misuse of just war theory is that of the editors of *First Things*. They celebrate the resurgence of patriotism as a sign of "an overwhelm-ingly Christian nation rooted...in the Judeo-Christian moral tradition."[9] The editors frequently refer to the American "we." They do not indicate how the moral imperative to follow Christ and to embody Christ in the world in a trans-national community that transcends the nations provides an alternative normative political ethic. They simply bless the ac-tions of President Bush. In his critique of the editors' stance, Stanley Hauerwas states that they fail "to suggest how the Church can maintain its independence."[10]

The first question to consider is whether *war* is the appropriate response to the terrorist violence of September 11. Certainly, according to the criterion of just cause, the United States has the right to use military force. Since this was an attack on the people of the United States, the U.S. government also is a le-gitimate authority to respond to the attacks: the United States has the right to defend its citizens against attack.[11] These are probably the two just war cri-teria that can most easily be met. Acts of terrorist violence were committed against innocent people and killed over three thousand persons. These acts had

---

[8]For a description of the varieties of pacifism, see John H. Yoder, *Nevertheless: The Varieties of Religious Pacifism* (Scottdale, Pa.: Herald Press, 1992). For a more detailed account of the integral place of justice within Christian pacifism, see my article in the *Mennonite Quarterly Review* (January 2002), 63–71. The abstract reads: "Many nonpacifist Christians mistakenly believe that a commit-ment to nonviolence entails the neglect of justice. To the contrary, a biblically and theologically grounded pacifism regards seeking justice as central to a nonviolent philosophy of life. We can iden-tify a number of normative peacemaking practices for seeking justice in Christian pacifism that are an alternative to the assumption that the use of violent force as a last resort is the only way to achieve justice" (p. 63).

[9]"In a Time of War," *First Things* (December 2001).

[10]"In a Time of War: An Exchange," *First Things* (January 2002).

[11]This right to defend itself was legitimated shortly after the September 11 attacks, by the Security Council of the United Nations.

a negative ripple effect on thousands of others, upon the people of the United States as a whole, and upon the larger world community.

Many assume that if there is a just cause, then war is justified. However, because of the Christian presumption against violence, and given the difficulty of controlling violence in a war, a number of other just war criteria must also be met. The most important question is whether war is the appropriate response. Must the United States revert to war, the last resort, or are there other ways to respond? An October 2001 editorial in *America* says:

> We should ask if the use of the word *war* is apt. The use of the word by the President is rhetorically satisfying. But calling our response *war* gives the terrorists a stature that they do not deserve. It treats them like a government, when in fact they are more like organized criminals—mass murderers, not soldiers. The fact that the terrorists acted immorally, against every standard of military conduct, does not mean that we have the right to do the same in response. We must not become like what we hate. The just war theory emphasizes that waging war is a last resort, not a first option. Diplomatic efforts are to be preferred, not only because they are less violent, but also because in the long run, only with the cooperation of other nations will we make the world safe from terrorism.[12]

Shortly after September 11, I developed the following chart, in which I propose that it would be better to name what happened on that date a "crime against humanity." To call the event a crime elicits a very different type of response.

A third criteria of just war is that it must be made clear to the enemy what they must do to avoid war. Soon after the attacks on September 11, President Bush and Congress began using the rhetoric of war. No time was really given to considering other options.[13] The United States did state to the Taliban in Afghanistan that they could avoid war if they turned over Osama bin Laden to the United States. It is, however, evident that the United States was not patient enough to allow the process to unfold. The President, Congress, and the American people were angry and could not wait to retaliate.

The world did not ever get the chance to know whether Muslim clerics (even fundamentalist ones) had sufficient integrity as Muslims to eventually hand over bin Laden (assuming they had the power to do that).[14] Let us assume that the United States had good evidence to link bin Laden to the crime, and that this evidence could have been presented to the Taliban through intermediaries in the Muslim world. Bin Laden had clearly violated the fundamental ethical principles of Islam by directly attacking innocent civilians. The United States not only had the possibility of gaining wider support in the Muslim world,

---

[12] "A Just War?" editorial, *America* (October 8, 2001).

[13] I support other parallel strategies (other than war) that are being used to curb further terrorist actions, such as the investigation into the terrorist network, arrests of suspects based on evidence that can stand up in a court of law, identification of the flow of money and freezing of assets of organizations connected to these terrorist networks, and reasonable measures to increase security within the United States.

[14] The argument of the time was that only military action could lead to the capture of bin Laden, and that other approaches would be ineffective. As of this writing (over six months after the September 11 attacks), American leaders admit they do not know where bin Laden is, even after an aggressive military campaign.

Crime	War
1. A horrendous crime against humanity.	1. An attack on the United States and its identity.
2. We identify the event as an immoral act, contravening international law and prompting international support.	2. We accept the terms of the terrorists, who identify it as an attack against the United States.
3. Emphasis on justice: The objective is to identify the perpetrators, arrest them, and bring them to trial.	3. Emphasis on retaliation: The objective is to seek vengeance.
4. Actions are taken under the rule of law and are open to public scrutiny.	4. Actions are taken unilaterally ("national vigilantism") and are only subject to the rules of war (essentially secret, using propaganda to mobilize public opinion).
5. Pinpoint the doers of the crime and direct our anger to bringing them to justice. Actions are based on the principle of noncombatant immunity.	5. War inevitably leads to "collateral damage"—civilian casualties. We create new victims, the families of those who lose their loved ones, and we become like the evil we deplore.
6. Focuses on the causes and searches for motives for the crime. Asks questions such as, "Why do these people hate us? Are we partly responsible (through our actions in the Gulf War)? Can we stop the cycle of violence and counter-violence?" All of this requires that we look closely at history to put the conflict in a larger context.	6. Perpetuates the cycle of violence, seeing violence as redemptive. Runs the risk of breeding more anger and hatred, fostering the next generation of terrorists. Fails to get at the root causes of terrorism.
7. Requires long-term thinking, careful reflection, and patience. Resists finding a quick-fix solution.	7. Tends to favor short-term actions that make us feel better, but do not address the underlying causes of the conflict.

but it had world opinion on its side. What might have happened if the United States had eventually brought its case before the world in an international court that included Muslim jurists? We do not know, but it is not unreasonable to consider that in the long run such approaches might have a more enduring impact on reducing terrorism.

This leads to several other ethical considerations in determining whether a war is just. One cannot engage in war unless it is likely to be successful. One of the most important questions is: What is the goal the war is supposed to accomplish, and how will we know when we have been successful? To unleash the destructive power of war, and then not accomplish the goals one set out would lead to a far greater evil in the long run, and not meet the criteria of proportionality (i.e., that the overall good is greater than the evil that results from using military force). The aim of a war, according to just war theory, is to restore peace, to correct the injustice that was done. Clearly, President Bush's rhetoric to "eliminate evil" is absurd. But what about the goal to eliminate terrorism? How will we know when that has been done, and how will we know whether military actions are indeed accomplishing that goal?[15]

Most worrisome is whether the kind of military action the United States is using is really stopping terrorism. Is it not just as likely that the use of military force is preparing the soil to generate more terrorists? How does one measure the results? These are serious questions. The United States has a kind of utopian view of life, a

faith in the efficacy of military force to accomplish the elimination of terrorism that has some of the qualities of blind faith. It is ironic that pacifists are so often accused of utopianism. The confidence and trust in military force is astounding, equivalent to trust in God. The choice of war to respond to terrorism may well be a profound error in historical judgment. Retired General Wesley Clark, who commanded the war in Kosovo, states it well:

> The solution to terrorism is not going to be found in bullets. It's not going to be found in precision ordinance or targeted strikes. It's really going to be found in changing the conditions. It's going to be found in establishing a global safety net that starts with security and goes to economic development and political development.[16]

In addition to the criterion of *jus ad bellum* (whether resort to war is justified), a war is not justified if it does not meet the criterion of *jus in bello* (whether the means used in conducting the war are just). The two principles of *jus in bello* are proportionality and discrimination or noncombatant immunity. Civilians may never be directly targeted in order to win a war, even to save the lives of soldiers. No end can justify means that are evil in themselves. Though the United States claims the war in Afghanistan targets directly only suspected terrorist hideouts, it is estimated that the massive use of high-tech air strikes had killed by the end of 2001 (after less than three months of war) more civilians than were killed in the terrorist attacks on the World Trade Cen-

---

[15]In his response to the editors of *First Things*, Stanley Hauerwas makes this point: "If a war is to be just, the purpose—which is necessary so your enemy will know the conditions for surrender—must be stated at the beginning. Asking the Taliban to turn over Osama bin Laden comes close to naming such a purpose. A war on terrorism does not."

[16]Quoted by Robert Seeley ("Even Strategists Must Oppose This War"), an article on the website www.peaceresponse.org/resources/evenstrat.shtml.

[17]Professor Marc W. Herold, op. cit.

ter and the Pentagon.[17] A policy that protects United States soldiers from harm (only a handful have been killed as of this writing), yet puts in harm's way thousands of civilians, is grossly immoral. "Hightech strikes that destroy the infrastructure of already fragile or impoverished societies *de facto* attack its civil society."[18]

Finally, war does not help us address the underlying causes of terrorism. Choosing to respond to terrorism with the paradigm of war does not generate self-examination to determine what causes terrorism. We have not examined whether U.S. policy might be partly responsible for creating the conditions that generate terrorism. Though nothing can justify the terrorist acts of September 11, the placement of troops on Saudi Arabian soil during the Gulf War was one of the major factors that turned Osama bin Laden against the United States. One of the sources of hostility toward the U.S. is its

Middle East policy. The Bush policy is a dismal failure with its double standard of criticizing Palestinian violence without addressing the underlying cause of the Palestinian/Israeli conflict: Israel's illegal occupation of Palestinian land.[19] By putting the effort into a war, U.S. policymakers are not focusing their energy on how to address positively the underlying material, social, and political conditions within the Islamic world that cause despair and violence.

War may generate patriotic fervor and give Americans the feeling that *we* are really doing something about terrorism, but will it be successful in the long run? To return to themes we considered at the beginning of this essay, the issue is really a matter of the narrative that shapes our trust. Do we Christians put our faith in the paradigm of war, or in the story of God's victory over evil through the life, death, and resurrection of Jesus Christ?

[18]Statement by J. Bryan Hehir, Roman Catholic scholar, in *America* (October 8, 2001).

[19]For an instructive account of perceptions within the Islamic world of the West, particularly the United States, see the National Public Radio documentary, "Why Are They So Angry at Us?" (Http://americanradioworks.org/features/resentment/print.html). The respected Egyptian analyst Mohammed Sid-Ahmed says: "America sees itself otherwise than what it's seen by others....The fact is that America is powerful, rich, can be self-satisfied in those terms. It does not understand that other societies with very serious problems don't look at America the way America looks at itself."

Chapter Thirty-Two

Patriotism without Militarism

Paul Schrag

Paul Schrag is the editor of the *Mennonite Weekly Review*. This editorial from the October 11, 2001 edition was written as one of a series of reflections on the events of September 11.

The call to war inevitably forces the question of patriotism. The assumption is that people who love their country should be willing to fight for it. Those who refuse to fight, even on religious grounds, are often lumped together with others whose reasons for not supporting the war effort are considered dubious or even traitorous.

The editorial asks us to define what we mean by patriotism. Is patriotism so inherently connected with militarism that Christian peacemakers should shun the term? Or can those who truly love their country dissent from majority opinion when they feel an action of their country involves wrongdoing? At the level of political philosophy, is dissent compatible with patriotism? Why is it that Americans celebrate political diversity as a sign of healthy government during times of peace, but leave little room for diversity during times of war? Why is a country's decision to fight considered so free from error that any voice raised against the policy is interpreted as treason rather than as healthy dissent?

United we stand" implies an expectation of conformity that pervades American patriotism in a time of crisis. To disagree with any part of the slogan's assumed message would be, well, un-American.

What about those who are not united behind military action? We do stand united behind some of the slogan's meanings, such as sharing the nation's sorrow and a desire that the murderers be brought to justice. But we can't help but think that the most common meaning, the one by which true patriotism is judged, is support for military action.

We wish this were not so, because dissent can be patriotic.

If patriotism means wanting what is best for one's country, and if one firmly believes that waging war will neither make Americans safer nor create a more just world, then advocating for peace is an act of patriotism.

This chapter originally appeared as an editorial in the *Mennonite Weekly Review*, October 11, 2001.

Tolerance of dissent and respect for a diversity of beliefs are among America's most cherished ideals. America has not always lived up to these principles. But, in many ways throughout its history, it has moved closer to them. One example is the treatment of conscientious objectors, who were persecuted during World War I but gained recognition of their rights before the United States entered World War II.

Religious minorities, such as members of the historic peace churches, are grateful for these American ideals. These principles must be practiced more deliberately in a time of war, when Americans are tempted to pressure each other to conform.

Responsible patriotism is not blind patriotism. Loyal citizens can ask tough questions and sometimes raise troubling issues, recognizing that the country faces difficult choices.

Many Americans would acknowledge that the country has not always made good decisions about war and peace, Vietnam being a notable example. If a person can call for a stronger and quicker use of force and be considered a patriot, why cannot a person who believes restraint would be in the national interest also be so recognized?

We advocate the idea that peace is patriotic not because we desire to be acclaimed as patriots. In fact, some Mennonites would shun such a label, considering it too closely connected to militarism and a sense of national superiority and the idea that God uniquely blesses America.

Perhaps it is impossible to define the word "patriotism" in a way that separates it from these associations. But that is only because so many Americans have thought of patriotism in these terms for so long.

There is much to love about America and much to criticize. Everyone knows that a good citizen does both of these things. More people should know that dissent ought not to end when war begins. A strong nation, a nation whose actions match its ideals, tolerates minority voices. Even voices that express a patriotism without militarism.

Selected Bibliography on Peace and Peacemaking

Biblical Studies on Peacemaking

Alt, Franz. *Peace Is Possible: The Politics of the Sermon on the Mount.* New York: Schocken, 1985.

Atkinson, David John. *Peace in Our Time? Some Biblical Groundwork.* Grand Rapids: Eerdmans, 1985.

Barrett, Lois. *Doing What Is Right: What the Bible Says About Covenant and Justice.* Scottdale, Pa.: Herald, 1989.

Barrett, Lois. *The Way God Fights: War and Peace in the Old Testament.* Scottdale, Pa: Herald, 1987.

Barth, Markus. *Israel and the Church: Contribution to a Dialogue Vital for Peace.* Richmond: John Knox, 1969.

Bauman, Clarence. *The Sermon on the Mount: The Modern Quest for Its Meaning.* Macon, Ga: Mercer University 1985.

Clark, Robert E. D. *Does the Bible Teach Pacifism?* England: Fellowship of Reconciliation, 1976.

Craigie, Peter C. *The Problem of War in the Old Testament.* Grand Rapids: Eerdmans, 1978.

Cullmann, Oscar. *Jesus and Revolutionaries.* New York: Harper & Row, 1970.

———. *The State in the New Testament.* New York: Scribner, 1956.

Desjardins, Michael R. *Peace, Violence, and the New Testament.* Sheffield, U.K.: Sheffield Academic Press, 1997.

Eller, Vernard. *War and Peace, from Genesis to Revelation: King Jesus Manual of Arms for the Armless.* Scottdale, Pa: Herald, 1981.

Enz, Jacob. *The Christian and Warfare: The Roots of Pacifism in the Old Testament.* Scottdale, Pa: Herald, 1972.

Ferguson, John. *The Politics of Love: The New Testament and Nonviolent Revolution.* Nyack, N.Y.: Fellowship of Reconciliation, 1977.

Furnish, Victor Paul. *The Love Command in the New Testament.* Nashville: Abingdon, 1972.

Gerlach, Barbara. *The Things that Make for Peace: Biblical Meditations.* New York: Pilgrim, 1983.

Grimsrud, Ted, and Loren Johns, eds. *Peace and Justice Shall Embrace: Power and Theopolitics in the Bible; Essays in Honor of Millard Lind.* Telford, Pa: Pandora, 1999.

Guelich, Robert A. *The Sermon on the Mount: A Foundation for Understanding.* Waco, Texas: Word, 1982.

Harder, Helmut. *The Biblical Way of Peace.* Akron, Pa.: The International Mennonite Peace Commission, 1982.

Horsley, Richard A. *Jesus and the Spiral of Violence: Jewish Resistance in Roman Palestine.* San Francisco: Harper & Row, 1987.

————. *Sociology and the Jesus Movement.* New York: Crossroad, 1989.

Kraybill, Donald B. *The Upside-Down Kingdom.* Scottdale, Pa.: Herald, 1990.

Lapide, Pinchas. *The Sermon on the Mount: Utopia or Program for Action?* Translated by Arlene Swidler. Maryknoll, N.Y.: Orbis, 1986.

Lasserre, Jean. *War and Gospel.* Translated by Oliver Coburn. Scottdale, Pa.: Herald, 1962.

Lind, Millard. *Monotheism, Power, Justice: Collected Old Testament Essays.* Elkhart, Ind.: Institute of Mennonite Studies, 1990.

————. *Yahweh Is a Warrior.* Scottdale, Pa.: Herald, 1980.

Lohfink, Gerhard. *Jesus and Community: The Social Dimension of the Christian Faith.* Translated by J. P. Galvin. Philadelphia: Fortress, 1984.

MacGregor, George H. C. *The New Testament Basis of Pacifism and the Relevance of an Impossible Ideal.* New York: Fellowship of Reconciliation, 1954.

Mauser, Ulrich. *The Gospel of Peace: A Scriptural Message for Today s World.* Louisville, Ky.: Westminster/John Knox, 1992.

Maxwell, Kenneth L. *Seek Peace and Pursue It: Psalm 34:14.* Valley Forge, Pa.: Judson, 1983.

McSorley, Richard T. *New Testament Basis of Peacemaking.* Scottdale, Pa.: Herald, 1985.

Minear, Paul. *Commands of Christ: Authority and Implications.* Edinburgh: St. Andrews Press, 1972.

Moffatt, James. *Love in the New Testament.* London: Hodder & Stoughton, 1929.

Nygren, Anders. *Agape and Eros: A Study of the Christian Idea of Love.* Translated from the Swedish by Philip S. Watson. Philadelphia: Westminster, 1953.

Perkins, Pheme. *Love Commands in the New Testament.* Ramsey, N.J.: Paulist, 1982.

Rad, Gerhard von. *Holy War in Ancient Israel.* Translated by Marva J. Dawn and John H. Yoder. Grand Rapids: Eerdmans, 1990.

Rensberger, David. *Johannine Faith and Liberating Community.* Philadelphia: Westminster, 1988.

Russel, Chester. *Was Jesus a Pacifist?* Nashville: Broadman, 1971.

Schottroff, Luise, et al. *Essays on the Love Commandment.* Translated by Reginald and Ilse Fuller. Philadelphia: Fortress, 1978.

Schrage, Wolfgang. *The Ethics of the New Testament.* Translated by David E. Green. Philadelphia: Fortress, 1988.

Spicq, Ceslas. *Agape in the New Testament.* 3 vols. Translated by M. A. McNamara and M. H. Richter. St. Louis: B. Herder, 1966.

Swaim, J. Carter. *War, Peace, and the Bible.* Maryknoll, N.Y.: Orbis, 1982.

Swartley, Willard M. *War and Peace in the New Testament.* New York: de Gruyter, 1996.

Tambasco, Anthony J. *Blessed Are the Peacemakers: Biblical Perspectives on Peace and Its Social Foundation.* New York: Paulist, 1989.

Tannehill, Robert C. *The Sword of His Mouth: Forceful and Imaginative Language in Synoptic Sayings.* Philadelphia: Fortress; Missoula: Scholars Press, 1975.

Travis, Stephen. *Christ and the Judgment of God: Divine Revelation in the New Testament*. Basingstoke, U.K.: Marshall Pickering, 1986.

Trocmé, André. *Jesus and the Nonviolent Revolution*. Translated by M. H. Shank and M. E. Miller. Scottdale, Pa.: Herald, 1973.

Verhey, Allen. *The Great Reversal: Ethics and the New Testament*. Grand Rapids: Eerdmans, 1984.

Wenger, John C. *Pacifism and Biblical Nonresistance*. Scottdale, Pa.: Herald, 1968.

Yoder, John H. *He Came Preaching Peace*. Scottdale, Pa.: Herald, 1985.

————. *The Politics of Jesus: Vicit Agnus Noster*. Grand Rapids: Eerdmans, 2nd ed.,1994.

Yoder, Perry B., and Willard M. Swartley, eds. *The Meaning of Peace: Biblical Studies*. Louisville, Ky.: Westminster/John Knox, 1992.

Yoder, Peter B. *Shalom: The Bible s Word for Salvation, Justice, and Peace*. Newton, Kans.: Faith and Life, 1987.

Zerbe, Gordon. *Non-Retaliation in Early Jewish and New Testament Texts: Ethical Themes in Social Contexts*. Sheffield, Eng.: JSOT Press, 1993.

Historical Studies on Peacemaking

Anderson, Richard C. *Peace Was in Their Hearts: Conscientious Objectors in World War II*. Watsonville, Calif.: Correlan, 1994.

Bacon, Margaret Hope. *The Quiet Rebels: The Story of the Quakers in America*. New York: Basic Books, 1969.

Bainton, Roland. *Christian Attitudes toward War and Peace*. New York: Abingdon, 1960.

Barth, Emmy, ed. *He Is Our Peace: Meditations on Christian Nonviolence: From the Writings of Howard Goeringer, Eberhard Arnold, Christoph R. Blumhardt, and others*. Farmington: Plough, 1994.

Bender, Harold. *The Anabaptist Vision*. Scottdale, Pa.: Herald, 1944.

————. *Nonresistance in Colonial Pennsylvania*. Ephrata, Pa.: Eastern Mennonite Publishing, 1985.

Bowman, Rufus D. *The Church of the Brethren and War, 1708–1941*. Elgin, Ill.: Brethren Publishing House, 1944.

Braght, Thieleman J. van. *Martyrs Mirror*. Scottdale, Pa.: Herald, 1989.

Brock, Peter. *Freedom from Violence: Nonsectarian Pacifism, 1814–1914*. Toronto: University of Toronto Press, 1991.

————. *Freedom from Violence: Sectarian Nonresistance from the Middle Ages to the Great War*. Toronto: University of Toronto Press, 1991.

————. *Pioneers of the Peaceable Kingdom*. Princeton: Princeton University Press, 1970.

————. *The Quaker Peace Testimony, 1660–1914*. York, Eng.: W. Sessions, 1999.

————. *The Roots of War Resistance: Pacifism from the Early Church to Tolstoy*. Nyack, N.Y.: Fellowship of Reconciliation, 1981.

————. *Studies in Peace History*. York, Eng.: W. Sessions, 1999.

————. *Varieties of Pacifism: A Survey from Antiquity to the Outset of the Twentieth Century,* Syracuse: Syracuse University Press, 4th ed, 1998.

Brock, Peter, and Thomas P. Socknat, eds. *Challenge to Mars: Pacifism from 1918 to 1945*. Toronto: University of Toronto Press, 1999.

Brown, Dale W. *Brethren and Pacifism.* Elgin, Ill.: Brethren Press, 1970.

Cadoux, Cecil John. *The Early Church and the World.* Edinburgh: T. & T. Clark, 1925.

Chatfield, Charles. *For Peace and Justice: Pacifism in America, 1914–1941.* Knoxville: University of Tennessee Press, 1971.

Detweiler, Richard C. *Mennonite Statements on Peace, 1915–1966; A Historical and Theological Review of Anabaptist-Mennonite Concepts of Peace Witness and Church-State Relations.* Scottdale, Pa.: Herald, 1968.

Driedger, Leo, and Donald B. Kraybill. *Mennonite Peacemaking: From Quietism to Activism.* Scottdale, Pa.: Herald, 1994.

Driver, John. *How Christians Made Peace with War: Early Christian Understandings of War.* Scottdale, Pa.: Herald, 1988.

Durnbaugh, Donald R., ed. *On Earth Peace: Discussions on War/Peace Issues between Friends, Mennonites, Brethren, and European Churches.* Elgin, Ill.: Brethren Press, 1978.

Dyck, Cornelius J. *An Introduction to Mennonite History: A Popular History of the Anabaptists and the Mennonites.* Scottdale, Pa.: Herald, 1993.

Dyck, Harvey L. *The Pacifist Impulse in Historical Perspective.* Toronto: University of Toronto Press, 1996.

Gingerich, Melvin. *Service for Peace: A History of Mennonite Civilian Public Service.* Akron, Pa.: Mennonite Central Committee, 1949.

Griffin, Keith L. *Revolution and Religion: American Revolutionary War and the Reformed Clergy.* New York: Paragon House, 1994.

Guenter, Lewy. *Peace and Revolution: The Moral Crisis of American Pacifism.* Grand Rapids: Eerdmans, 1988.

Gwyn, Douglas, George Hunsinger, Eugene R. Roop, and John H. Yoder. *A Declaration on Peace: In God s People the World s Renewal Has Begun.* Scottdale, Pa.: Herald, 1991.

Hartill, Percy. *Into the Way of Peace, by Communicants of the English Church.* London: J. Clarke & Company, 1941.

Heering, Gerrit Jan. *The Fall of Christianity: A Study of Christianity, the State, and War.* Translated by J. W. Thompson. London: Allen & Unwin, 1930.

Hiebel, Jean-Luc. *Armed Forces and Churches. Forces armees et eglises.* Strasbourg: Cerdic Publications, 1973.

Hirst, Margaret E. *The Quakers in Peace and War: An Account of Their Peace Principles and Practice.* New York: Garland, 1972.

Homan, Gerlof D. *American Mennonites and the Great War.* Scottdale, Pa.: Herald, 1994.

Hornus, Jean-Michel. *It Is Not Lawful for Me to Fight.* Scottdale, Pa.: Herald, 1980.

Horst, Samuel L. *Mennonites in the Confederacy: A Study in Civil War Pacifism.* Scottdale, Pa.: Herald, 1967.

Jackson, David, and Neta Jackson, eds. *On Fire for Christ: Stories of Anabaptist Martyrs, Retold from Martyrs Mirror.* Scottdale, Pa.: Herald, 1989.

Juhnke, James C. *Vision, Doctrine, War: Mennonite Identity and Organization in America.* Scottdale, Pa.: Herald, 1989.

Juhnke, James C., and Carol M. Hunter. *The Missing Peace: The Search for Nonviolent Alternatives in United States History.* Kitchener, Ont.: Pandora, 2001.

Kauffman, J. Howard, and Leland Harder. *Anabaptists Four Centuries Later.* Scottdale, Pa.: Herald, 1975.

Keim, Albert N. *The CPS Story: An Illustrated History of Civilian Public Service.* Intercourse, Pa.: Good Books, 1990.

———. *The Politics of Conscience: The Historic Peace Churches and America at War, 1917–1955.* Scottdale, Pa.: Herald, 1988.

Lee, Umphrey. *The Historic Church and Modern Pacifism.* New York: Abingdon-Cokesbury, 1943.

Lunger, Harold L., ed. *Facing War/Waging Peace: Findings of the American Church Study Conferences, 1940–1960.* New York: Friendship, 1988.

MacMaster, Richard K. *Christian Obedience in Revolutionary Times: The Peace Churches and the American Revolution.* Akron, Pa.: Mennonite Central Committee, Peace Section, 1976.

———. *Conscience in Crisis: Mennonites and Other Peace Churches in America, 1739–1789: Interpretation and Documents.* Scottdale, Pa.: Herald, 1979.

———. *Land, Piety, Peoplehood: The Establishment of Mennonite Communities in America, 1683–1790.* Scottdale, Pa.: Herald, 1985.

Miller, Richard B. *War in the Twentieth Century: Sources in Theological Ethics.* Louisville: Westminster/John Knox, 1992.

Moomaw, Daniel Crouse. *Christianity versus War: A Presentation of Scriptural and Christian Teaching upon the Subject of Carnal Warfare and the Taking of Human Life, Together with Experiences of Conscientious Objectors in the World War.* Ashland, Ohio: Brethren Publishing Company, 1924.

———. *A Cloud of Witnesses: An Expression of the Deep Conviction of Faithful Men who Are Opposed to War.* Ashland, Ohio: Brethren Publishing Company, 1924.

Nuttall, Geoffrey. *Christian Pacifism in History,* 2nd ed.. Berkeley, Calif.: World Without War Council, 1971.

Schlabach, Theron F. *Peace, Faith, Nation: Mennonites and Amish in Nineteenth-Century America.* Scottdale, Pa.: Herald, 1988.

Schlabach, Theron F., and Richard T. Hughes. *Proclaim Peace: Christian Pacifism from Unexpected Quarters.* Urbana: University of Illinois Press, 1997.

Smock, David. *Religious Perspectives on War: Christian, Muslim, and Jewish Attitudes toward Force after the Gulf War.* Washington, D.C.: United States Institute of Peace, 1992.

Stevenson, William R. *Christian Love and Just War: Moral Paradox and Political Life in St. Augustine and His Modern Interpreters.* Macon, Ga.: Mercer University Press, 1987.

Stone, Ronald H., and Dana W. Wilbanks, eds. *The Peacemaking Struggle: Militarism and Resistance: Essays Prepared for the Advisory Council on Church and Society of the Presbyterian Church (U.S.A.).* Lanham, Md.: University Press of America, 1985.

Swartley, Willard M., and Cornelius J. Dyck. *Annotated Bibliography of Mennonite Writings on War and Peace: 1930–1980.* Scottdale, Pa.: Herald, 1987.

Swartley, Willard M., and Donald B. Kraybill. *Building Communities of Compassion: Mennonite Mutual Aid in Theory and Practice.* Scottdale, Pa.: Herald, 1998.

Weaver, J. Denny. *Becoming Anabaptist.* Scottdale, Pa.: Herald, 1987.

Wengst, Klaus. *Pax Romana and the Peace of Jesus Christ.* Philadelphia: Fortress, 1987.

Theological Studies on Peacemaking

Abrams, Ray H. *Preachers Present Arms.* Scottdale, Pa.: Herald, 1969.

Arnold, Eberhard. *The Peace of God.* Ashton Keynes, Eng.: Plough Publishing House, 1940.

Augsburger, Myron S. *The Peacemaker.* Nashville: Abingdon, 1987.

———. *The Robe of God: Reconciliation, the Believers Church Essential.* Scottdale, Pa.: Herald, 2000.

Bender, Ross, and Alan P. F. Sells, eds. *Baptism, Peace, and the State in the Reformed and Mennonite Traditions.* Waterloo, Ont.: Wilfrid Laurier University Press, 1991.

Boettner, Loraine. *The Christian Attitude toward War.* Phillipsburg, Pa.: Presbyterian and Reformed, 1985.

Bonhoeffer, Dietrich. *The Cost of Discipleship.* New York: Macmillan, 1963.

Branding, Ronice E. *Peacemaking: The Journey from Fear to Love.* St. Louis: CBP Press, 1987.

Brensinger, Terry L., and E. Morris Sider, eds. *Within the Perfection of Christ: Essays on Peace and the Nature of the Church in Honor of Martin H. Schrag.* Nappanee, Ind.: Evangel, 1990.

Brown, Dale W. *Biblical Pacifism: A Peace Church Perspective.* Elgin, Ill.: Brethren Press, 1986.

Brown, Robert M. *Making Peace in the Global Village.* Philadelphia: Westminster, 1981.

———. *Religion and Violence.* Philadelphia: Westminster, 1973.

Brueggemann, Walter. *Living toward a Vision.* Philadelphia: United Church, 1976.

———. *Peace.* St. Louis: Chalice, 2001.

Burkholder, John Richard, and Calvin Redkop, eds. *Kingdom, Cross, and Community.* Scottdale, Pa.: Herald, 1976.

Burkholder, John Richard, and John Bender. *Children of Peace.* Elgin, Ill.: Brethren Press, 1982.

Buttry, Daniel. *Christian Peacemaking: From Heritage to Hope.* Valley Forge, Pa.: Judson, 1994.

Byler, Dennis. *Making War and Making Peace: Why Some Christians Fight Back and Some Don t.* Scottdale, Pa.: Herald, 1989.

Cadoux, Cecil John. *Christian Pacifism Re-Examined.* Oxford: Basil Blackwell, 1940.

Cahill, Lisa Sowle. *Love Your Enemies: Discipleship, Pacifism, and Just War Theory.* Minneapolis: Fortress, 1994.

Clouse, Robert G., ed. *War: Four Christian Views.* Downers Grove, Ill.: InterVarsity, 1991.

Cochrane, Arthur C. *The Mystery of Peace.* Elgin, Ill.: Brethren Press, 1986.

Culliton, Joseph T., ed. *Non-Violence, Central to Christian Spirituality.* New York: E. Mellen, 1982.

Culver, Robert Duncan. *The Peacemongers.* Wheaton, Ill.: Tyndale House, 1985.

Dear, John. *Disarming the Heart: Toward a Vow of Nonviolence.* New York: Paulist, 1987.

Dombrowski, Daniel A. *Christian Pacifism*. Philadelphia: Temple University Press, 1991.

Douglas, James W. *The Non-Violent Cross: A Theology of Revolution and Peace*. New York: Macmillan, 1966.

Drescher, John M. *Why I Am a Conscientious Objector*. Scottdale, Pa.: Herald, 1982.

Dunne, John S. *The Peace of the Present: An Unviolent Way of Life*. Notre Dame, Ind.: University of Notre Dame Press, 1991.

Egan, Eileen. *Peace Be with You: Justified Warfare or the Way of Nonviolence*. Maryknoll, N.Y.: Orbis, 1999.

Eller, Vernard. *The Promise: Ethics in the Kingdom of God*. Garden City, N.Y.: Doubleday, 1990.

Ellul, Jacques. *Violence: Reflections from a Christian Perspective*. Translated by Cecelia G. Kings. New York: Seabury, 1969.

Epp, Frank H. *A Strategy for Peace: Reflections of a Christian Pacifist*. Grand Rapids, Eerdmans, 1973.

Fahey, Joseph, and Richard Armstrong, eds. *A Peace Reader: Essential Readings on War, Justice, Non-violence, and World Order*. New York: Paulist, 1987.

Fast, Henry. *Jesus and Human Conflict*. Scottdale, Pa.: Herald, 1959.

Folk, Jerry L. *Doing Theology, Doing Justice*. Minneapolis: Fortress, 1991.

Hadley, Norval, ed. *New Call to Peacemaking*. Philadelphia: Friends World Committee for Consultation, Section of Americas, 1976.

Hardner, Leland. *Doors to Lock and Doors to Open: The Discerning People of God*. Scottdale, Pa.: Herald, 1993.

Hauerwas, Stanley. *The Peaceable Kingdom: A Primer in Christian Ethics*. Notre Dame, Ind.: University of Notre Dame Press, 1983.

———. *Should War Be Eliminated? Philosophical and Theological Investigations*. Milwaukee: Marquette University Press, 1984.

Hellwig, Monika. *A Case for Peace in Reason and Faith*. Collegeville, Minn.: Liturgical Press, 1992.

Hershberger, Guy F. *War, Peace, and Nonresistance*. Scottdale, Pa.: Herald, 1969.

———. *The Way of the Cross in Human Relations*. Scottdale, Pa.: Herald, 1958.

Hormann, Karl. *Peace and Modern War in the Judgment of the Church*. Westminster, Md.: Newman, 1966.

Hostetler, Paul, ed. *Perfect Love and War: A Dialogue on Christian Holiness and the Issues of War and Peace*. Nappanee, Ind.: Evangel, 1974.

Hoyt, Herman Arthur. *Then Would My Servants Fight*. Winona Lake, Ind.: Brethren Missionary Herald, 1956.

Jungel, Eberhard. *Christ, Justice, and Peace: Toward a Theology of the State in Dialogue with the Barmen Declaration*. Edinburgh: T. & T. Clark, 1992.

Kagawa, Toyohiko. *Love, the Law of Life*. Philadelphia: John C. Winston, 1929.

Keeny, William. *Lordship as Servanthood*. Newton, Kans.: Faith and Life, 1975.

Klaassen, Walter. *Armageddon and the Peaceable Kingdom*. Scottdale, Pa.: Herald, 1999.

Klassen, William. *The Forgiving Community*. Philadelphia: Westminster, 1966.

———. *Love of Enemies: The Way to Peace*. Philadelphia: Fortress, 1984.

———. *The Realism of Peace*. Sackville, N.B.: Mount Allison University Press, 1986.

Kreider, Alan. *Becoming a Peace Church*. London: New Ground/HHSC Christian Press, 2000.

Landrum, Kelly J. *Conscientious Objections: Toward a Reconstruction of the Social and Political Philosophy of Jesus of Nazareth*. Lewiston, N.Y.: E. Mellen, 1994.

Lehman, J. Irving. *God and War*. Scottdale, Pa.: Mennonite Publishing House, 1945.

Lehn, Cornelia. *Peace Be with You*. Newton, Kans.: Faith and Life, 1980.

Lewis, John. *The Case against Pacifism*. New York: Garland, 1973.

Lind, Millard. *Answer to War*. Scottdale, Pa.: Mennonite Publishing House, 1952.

Long, D. Stephen. *Living the Discipline: United Methodist Theological Reflections on War, Civilization, and Holiness*. Grand Rapids: Eerdmans, 1992.

Long, Edward LeRoy. *Peace Thinking in a Warring World*. Philadelphia: Westminster, 1983.

Lutz, Charles P., Jerry L. Folk, et al. *Peaceways*. Minneapolis: Augsburg, 1983.

Macquarrie, John. *The Concept of Peace*. New York: Harper & Row, 1973.

Martin, David. *Does Christianity Cause War?* New York: Oxford University Press, 1997.

Merton, Thomas. *The Nonviolent Alternative*. Edited by Gordon C. Zahn. New York: Farrar, Straus, and Giroux, 1980.

Miller, Melissa, and Phil M. Shenk. *The Path of Most Resistance*. Scottdale, Pa.: Herald, 1982.

Minear, Paul. *I Pledge Allegiance: Patriotism and the Bible*. Philadelphia: Geneva Press, 1975.

Moellering, Ralph Luther. *Modern War and the Christian*. Minneapolis: Augsburg, 1969.

Moulton, Phillips P. *Ammunition for Peacemakers: Answers for Activists*. New York: Pilgrim, 1986.

Mumaw, John R. *Nonresistance and Pacifism*. Scottdale, Pa.: Mennonite Publishing House, 1952.

Myra, Harold. *Should a Christian Go to War?* Wheaton, Ill.: Victor, 1971.

Nerburn, Kent. *Make Me an Instrument of Your Peace: Living in the Spirit of the Prayer of Saint Francis*. San Francisco: HarperSanFrancisco, 1999.

Niebuhr, Reinhold. *Love and Justice: Selections from the Shorter Writings of Reinhold Niebuhr*. Louisville: Westminster/John Knox, 1992.

Nouwen, Henri J. *The Road to Peace: Writings on Peace and Justice*. Edited by John Dear. Maryknoll, N.Y.: Orbis 1998.

Nyce, Dorothy Yoder. *Jesus Clear Call to Justice*. Scottdale, Pa.: Herald, 1990.

Olson, Theodore W., and Lynne Shivers. *Training for Nonviolent Action*. London: Friends Peace and International Relations Committee, War Resisters International, 1970.

Peachey, Paul, ed. *Peace, Politics, and the People of God*. Philadelphia: Fortress, 1986.

Peck, M. Scott. *The Different Drum: Community-Making and Peace*. New York: Simon and Schuster, 1987.

Raven, Charles E. *The Theological Basis of Christian Pacifism.* New York: Fellowship Publications, 1951.

Redekop, Ben and Calvin Redekop. *Power, Authority, and the Anabaptist Tradition.* Baltimore: Johns Hopkins University Press, 2001.

Runyon, Theodore. *Theology, Politics, and Peace.* Maryknoll, N.Y.: Orbis, 1989.

Russel, Elbert W. *Christianity and Militarism.* Oakville, Ont.: Canadian Peace Research Institute, 1971.

Rutenber, Culbert. *The Dagger and the Cross.* Nyack, N.Y.: Fellowship Publications, 1958.

Schaeffer, Francis A., Vladimir Bukovsky, and James Hitchcock. *Who Is for Peace?* Nashville: Thomas Nelson, 1983.

Schipani, Daniel. S. *Freedom and Discipleship: Liberation Theology in an Anabaptist Perspective.* Maryknoll, N.Y.: Orbis, 1989.

Schrag, Martin H., and John K. Stoner. *The Ministry of Reconciliation.* Nappanee, Ind.: Evangel, 1973.

Shannon, Thomas, ed. *War or Peace?: The Search for New Answers.* Maryknoll, N.Y.: Orbis, 1980.

Shelly, Maynard. *New Call for Peacemaking.* Newton, Kans.: Faith and Life, 1979.

Shenk, Calvin E. *When Kingdoms Clash: The Christian and Ideologies.* Scottdale, Pa.: Herald, 1988.

Sider, Ronald J. *Christ and Violence.* Scottdale, Pa.: Herald, 1979.

Sinclair, Karen Kennedy. *The Church Peace Union: Visions of Peace in Troubled Times.* New York: Garland, 1993.

Snow, Michael. *Christian Pacifism: Fruit of the Narrow Way.* Richmond: Friends United, 1981.

Stanton-Rich, Diane. *Becoming Peacemakers: An Introduction.* Elgin, Ill.: Brethren, 1987.

Steiner, Susan Clemmer. *Joining the Army that Sheds No Blood.* Scottdale, Pa.: Herald, 1982.

Stotts, Jack L. *Shalom: The Search for a Peaceable City.* Nashville: Abingdon, 1973.

Stoutzenberger, Joseph. *The Christian Call to Justice and Peace.* Winona, Minn.: St. Mary's Press, 1987.

Stringfellow, William. *An Ethic for Christians and Other Aliens in a Strange Land.* Waco, Tex.: Word, 1973.

Swartley, Willard M. *Essays on Peace Theology and Witness.* Elkhart, Ind.: Institute of Mennonite Studies, 1988.

———, ed. *Essays on War and Peace: Bible and Early Church.* Elkhart, Ind: Institute of Mennonite Studies, 1986.

———, ed. *The Love of Enemy and Non-retaliation in the New Testament.* Louisville: Westminster/John Knox, 1992.

———, ed. *Violence Renounced: Rene Girard, Biblical Studies, and Peacemaking.* Telford, Pa.: Pandora, 2000.

Sweet, Leonard. *The Lion s Pride: America and the Peaceable Community.* Nashville: Abingdon, 1987.

Teichman, Jenny. *Pacifism and the Just War: A Study in Applied Philosophy.* New York: B. Blackwell, 1986.

Thompson, Joseph Milburn. *Justice and Peace: A Christian Primer.* Maryknoll, N.Y.: Orbis, 1997.

Tillich, Paul, *Theology of Peace.* Louisville: Westminster/John Knox, 1990.

Toews, John E., and Gordon Nickel, eds. *The Power of the Lamb*. Hillsboro, Kans.: Kindred, 1986.

Valentine, Foy. *Peace! Peace!* Waco, Tex.: Word, 1967.

Valliere, Paul. *Holy War and Pentecostal Peace*. New York: Seabury, 1983.

Walsh, James P. M. *The Mighty from Their Thrones*. Philadelphia: Fortress, 1987.

Webster, Alexander F. C. *The Pacifist Option: The Moral Argument against War in Eastern Orthodox Moral Theology*. San Francisco: International Scholars, 1998.

———. *The Price of Prophecy: Orthodox Churches on Peace, Freedom, and Security*. Washington, D.C.: Ethics and Public Policy Center; Grand Rapids: Eerdmans, 1995.

Wenger, John C. *The Way of Peace*. Scottdale, Pa.: Herald, 1977.

Will, James E. *A Christology of Peace*. Louisville: Westminster, 1989.

Willard, Dallas. *The Divine Conspiracy*. San Francisco: HarperCollins, 1999.

Wink, Walter, ed. *Peace is the Way: Writings on Nonviolence from the Fellowship of Reconciliation*. Maryknoll, N.Y.: Orbis, 2000.

Winn, Albert Curry. *Ain t Gonna Study War No More: Biblical Ambiguity and the Abolition of War*. Louisville: Westminster/John Knox, 1993.

Yancey, Philip. *The Jesus I Never Knew*. Grand Rapids: Zondervan, 1995.

Yoder, John H. *The Christian Witness to the State*. Newton, Kans.: Faith and Life, 1964.

———. *Nevertheless: The Varieties and Shortcomings of Religious Pacifism*. Scottdale, Pa.: Herald, 1992.

———. *The Original Revolution: Essays on Christian Pacifism*. Scottdale, Pa.: Herald, 1972.

———. *The Priestly Kingdom: Social Ethics as Gospel*. Notre Dame, Ind.: University of Notre Dame Press, 1984.

———. *Reinhold Neibuhr and Pacifism*. Scottdale, Pa.: Herald, 1963.

———. *The Royal Priesthood: Essays Ecclesiological and Ecumenical*. Grand Rapids: Eerdmans, 1994.

———. *What Would You Do? A Serious Answer to a Standard Question*. Scottdale, Pa.: Herald, 1992.

———. *When War Is Unjust: Being Honest in Just-War Thinking*. Minneapolis: Augsburg, 1984.

Zorrilla, Hugo. *The Good News of Justice: Share the Gospel: Live Justly*. Scottdale, Pa.: Herald, 1988.

Applications of Peacemaking

Adeney, Bernard T. *Just War, Political Realism, and Faith*. Philadelphia: American Theological Library Association; Metuchen, N.J.: Scarecrow, 1988.

Arnett, Ronald C. *Dwell in Peace: Applying Nonviolence to Everyday Relationships*. Elgin, Ill.: Brethren Press, 1980.

Augsburger, David W. *Caring Enough to Confront*. Scottdale, Pa.: Herald, 1980.

Augsburger, Myron S., and Dean C. Curry. *Nuclear Arms: Two Views on World Peace*. Waco, Tex.: Word, 1987.

Aukerman, Dale. *Darkening Valley: A Biblical Perspective on Nuclear War*. New York: Seabury, 1981.

———. *Reckoning With Apocalypse: Terminal Politics and Christian Hope.* New York: Crossroad, 1993.

Baers, Arthur Paul. *On Earth as in Heaven: Justice Rooted in Spirituality.* Scottdale, Pa.: Herald, 1991.

Beachey, Duane. *Faith in a Nuclear Age: A Christian Response to War.* Scottdale, Pa.: Herald, 1983.

Beaver, R. Pierce. *Envoys of Peace: The Peace Witness in the Christian World Mission.* Grand Rapids: Eerdmans, 1964.

Bernbaum, John A. *Perspectives on Peacemaking: Biblical Options in the Nuclear Age.* Ventura, Calif.: Regal, 1984.

Brown, Dale W. *The Christian Revolutionary.* Grand Rapids: Eerdmans, 1971.

Buttry, Daniel. *Peace Ministry: A Handbook for Local Churches.* Valley Forge, Pa.: Judson, 1995.

Chapman, G. Clarke. *Facing the Nuclear Heresy: A Call to Reformation.* Elgin, Ill.: Brethren Press, 1986.

Dalton, Harlon L. *Racial Healing: Confronting the Fear between Blacks and Whites.* New York: Doubleday, 1995.

Donaghy, John. *Peacemaking and the Community of Faith: A Handbook for Congregations.* New York: Paulist, 1983.

Duffey, Michael K. *Peacemaking Christians: The Future of Just Wars, Pacifism, and Nonviolent Resistance.* Kansas City, Mo.: Sheed & Ward, 1995.

Durland, William R. *No King but Caesar? A Catholic Lawyer Looks at Christian Violence.* Scottdale, Pa.: Herald, 1975.

Franz, Marian C. *Questions that Refuse to Go Away: Peace and Justice in North America.* Scottdale, Pa.: Herald, 1991.

Friesen, Duane K. *Christian Peacemaking and International Conflict: A Realist Pacifist Perspective.* Scottdale, Pa.: Herald, 1986.

Gandhi, Mahatma. *Non-violent Resistance (Satyagraha).* New York: Schoken, 1961.

Grannis, J. Christopher, Arthur J. Laffin, and Elin Schade. *The Risk of the Cross: Christian Discipleship in the Nuclear Age.* New York: Seabury, 1981.

Graybill, Beth, Marilyn McDonald, and Bill Price. *Building Christian Community: Pursuing Peace with Justice.* Washington, D.C.: World Peacemakers, 1983.

Gros, Jeffrey, and John D. Rempel, eds. *The Fragmentation of the Church and Its Unity in Peacemaking.* Grand Rapids: Eerdmans, 2001.

Haleem, Harfiyah Abdel. *The Crescent and the Cross: Muslim and Christian Approaches to War and Peace.* New York: St. Martin's, 1998.

Hanks, Gardner C. *Against the Death Penalty: Christian and Secular Arguments against Capital Punishment.* Scottdale, Pa.: Herald, 1997.

Heggen, Carolyn Holdenread. *Sexual Abuse in Christian Homes and Churches.* Scottdale, Pa.: Herald, 1993.

Herr, Judy Zimmerman, and Robert Herr, eds. *Transforming Violence: Linking Local and Global Peacemaking.* Scottdale, Pa.: Herald, 1998.

Hollenbach, David. *Nuclear Ethics: A Christian Moral Argument.* New York: Paulist, 1983.

Jackson, David. *Dial 911: Peaceful Christians and Urban Violence.* Scottdale, Pa.: Herald, 1981.

Kaufman, Donald. *The Tax Dilemma: Praying for Peace, Paying for War.* Scottdale, Pa.: Herald, 1978.

———. *What Belongs to Caesar?* Scottdale, Pa.: Herald, 1969.

King, Martin Luther Jr. *Where Do We Go from Here: Chaos or Community?* New York: Harper & Row, 1967.

Kissinger, Warren S. *The Buggies Still Run.* Elgin, Ill.: Brethren Press, 1983.

Kraybill, Donald. *Facing Nuclear War: A Plea for Christian Witness.* Scottdale, Pa.: Herald, 1982.

Kreider, Robert S., and Rachael Waltner. *When Good People Quarrel: Studies of Conflict Resolution.* Scottdale, Pa.: Herald, 1989.

Landis, Susan Mark. *But Why Don t We Go to War? Finding Jesus Path to Peace.* Scottdale, Pa.: Herald, 1993.

McCarthy, Colman. *I d Rather Teach Peace.* Maryknoll, N.Y.: Orbis, 2002.

McGinnis, James B. *Parenting for Peace and Justice.* Maryknoll, N.Y.: Orbis, 1981.

McGinnis, James B., et al. *Educating for Peace and Justice: Global Dimensions.* St. Louis: Institute for Peace and Justice, 1984.

McGinnis, James B., and Thelma Burgonio-Watson, et al. *A Call to Peace: 52 Meditations on the Family Pledge of Non-violence.* Liguori, Mo.: Liguori Publications, 1998.

Merton, Thomas. *Passion for Peace: The Social Essays.* Edited by William H. Shannon. New York: Crossroads, 1996.

Miller, Marlin E., and Barbara Nelson Gingerich. *The Church s Peace Witness.* Grand Rapids: Eerdmans, 1994.

Miller, Melissa A. *Family Violence: The Compassionate Church Responds.* Scottdale, Pa.: Herald, 1994.

Moltmann, Jurgen. *Creating a Just Future: The Politics of Peace and the Ethics of Creation in a Threatened World.* London: SCM Press, 1989.

Mosley, Don and Joyce Hollyday. *With Our Own Eyes.* Scottdale, Pa.: Herald, 1996.

Peachy, Lorne J. *How to Teach Peace to Children.* Scottdale, Pa.: Herald, 1981.

Perkins, John. *With Justice for All.* Ventura, Calif.: Regal, 1980.

Ramseyer, Robert L. *Mission and the Peace Witness: The Gospel and Christian Discipleship.* Scottdale, Pa.: Herald, 1979.

Raymond, Alan, and Susan Raymond. *Children in War.* New York: TV Books, 2000.

Redekop, Calvin W. *Creation and Environment: An Anabaptist Perspective on a Sustainable World.* Baltimore: Johns Hopkins University Press, 2000.

Redekop, John. *Making Political Decisions: A Christian Perspective.* Scottdale, Pa.: Herald, 1972.

Redekop, Vernon W. *A Life for a Life? The Death Penalty on Trial.* Scottdale, Pa.: Herald, 1990.

Rohr, John A. *Prophets without Honor: Public Policy and the Selective Conscientious Objector.* Nashville: Abingdon, 1971.

Ruth-Heffelbower, Duane. *The Anabaptists Are Back! Making Peace in a Dangerous World.* Scottdale, Pa.: Herald, 1991.

———. *The Christian and Jury Duty.* Scottdale, Pa.: Herald, 1991.

Schlabach, Gerald W. *And Who Is My Neighbor? Poverty, Privilege, and the Gos-*

pel of Christ. Scottdale, Pa.: Herald, 1990.

Schrock-Shenk, Carolyn, and Lawrence Ressler. *Making Peace with Conflict: Practical Skills for Conflict Resolution.* Scottdale, Pa.: Herald, 1999.

Shearer, Jody Miller. *Enter the River: Healing Steps from White Privilege toward Racial Reconciliation.* Scottdale, Pa.: Herald, 1994.

Sider, Ronald J. *Completely Pro-Life: Building a Consistant Stance on Abortion, the Family, Nuclear Weapons, the Poor.* Downers Grove, Ill.: InterVarsity, 1987.

———. *Preaching on Peace.* Philadelphia: Fortress, 1982.

———. *Rich Christians in an Age of Hunger*, 3rd ed. Dallas: Word, 1990.

———, and Richard Taylor. *Nuclear Holocaust and Christian Hope: A Book for Christian Peacemakers.* Downers Grove, Ill.: InterVarsity, 1982.

Simon, Arthur R. *Harvesting Peace: The Arms Race and Human Need.* Kansas City, Mo.: Sheed & Ward, 1990.

Spaeth, Robert L. *No Easy Answers: Christians Debate Nuclear Arms.* Minneapolis: Winston, 1983.

Stassen, Glen Harold. *Just Peacemaking: Ten Practices for Abolishing War.* Cleveland, Ohio: Pilgrim, 1998.

———. *Just Peacemaking: Transforming Initiatives for Justice and Peace.* Louisville: Westminster/John Knox, 1992.

Stoner, John K. *Letters to American Christians.* Scottdale, Pa.: Herald, 1989.

Swartley, Willard M. *Slavery, Sabbath, War, and Women: Case Issues in Biblical Interpretation.* Scottdale, Pa.: Herald, 1983.

Tooley, Michelle. *Voices of the Voiceless: Women, Justice, and Human Rights in Guatemala.* Scottdale, Pa.: Herald, 1997.

Vanderhaar, G. A. *Enemies and How to Love Them.* Mystic, Conn.: Twenty-Third, 1985.

Vincent, John J. *Christ in a Nuclear World.* Rochdale, U.K.: Crux, 1962.

Wagner, Donald E. *Anxious for Armageddon: A Call to Partnership for Middle Eastern and Western Christians.* Scottdale, Pa.: Herald, 1995.

Wallis, Jim. *Peacemakers: Christian Voices from the New Abolitionist Movement.* San Francisco: Harper & Row, 1983.

———. *Waging Peace: A Handbook for the Struggle to Abolish Nuclear Weapons.* New York: Harper & Row, 1982.

Weigel, George. *Peace and Freedom: Christian Faith, Democracy, and the Problem of War.* Washington, D.C.: The Institute on Religion and Democracy, 1987.

Wengerd, Al. *Life after Prison.* Scottdale, Pa.: Herald, 1984.

White, C. Dale. *Making a Just Peace: Human Rights and Domination Systems.* Nashville: Abingdon, 1998.

White, Ronald C. Jr., and Eugene J. Fisher, eds. *Partners in Peace and Education: Roman Catholic-Presbyterian/ Reformed Consultation IV: Text and Discussion Guide.* Grand Rapids: Eerdmans, 1988.

Wolterstorff, Nicholas. *Until Justice and Peace Embrace.* Grand Rapids: Eerdmans, 1983.

Wuliger, Joel. *The Biblical Basis for Selective Conscientious Objection; and a Case for Nuclear Pacifism.* M.A. thesis, Ashland Theological Seminary, 1981.

Yantzi, Mark. *Sexual Offending and Restoration.* Scottdale, Pa.: Herald, 1998.

Zehr, Howard. *Changing Lenses: A New Focus for Crime and Justice.* Scottdale, Pa.: Herald, 1990.

Stories of Peacemaking

Bauman, Elizabeth Hershberger. *Coals of Fire.* Scottdale, Pa.: Herald, 1954.

Boulding, Elise. *One Small Plot of Heaven: Reflections on Family Life by a Quaker Sociologist.* Wallingford, Pa.: Pendle Hill, 1989.

Dear, John. *Our God Is Nonviolent: Witnesses in the Struggle for Peace and Justice.* New York: Pilgrim, 1990.

Duffey, Michael K. *Sowing Justice, Reaping Peace: Case Studies of Radical, Religious, and Ethnic Healing Around the World.* Franklin, Wis.: Sheed & Ward, 2001.

Dyck, Peter. *A Leap of Faith: True Stories for Young and Old.* Scottdale, Pa.: Herald, 1990.

Friedman, I. M. *Helping Resolve Conflict: True Experiences of a Christian Anthropologist.* Scottdale, Pa.: Herald, 1990.

Gish, Arthur G. *Hebron Journal: Stories of Nonviolent Peacemaking.* Scottdale, Pa.: Herald, 2001.

Hallock, Daniel. *Hell, Healing, and Resistance: Veterans Speak.* Farmington, Pa.: Plough, 1998.

Heydt, Barbara von der. *Candles Behind the Wall: Heroes of the Peaceful Revolution that Shattered Communism.* Grand Rapids: Eerdmans, 1993.

Hostetler, Marian. *They Loved Their Enemies: True Stories of African Christians.* Scottdale, Pa.: Herald, 1988.

Hunter, Allen A. *Courage in Both Hands.* New York: Ballantine, 1962.

Jones, E. Stanley. *A Song of Ascents: A Spiritual Autobiography.* Nashville: Abingdon, 1968.

Lederach, John Paul. *The Journey toward Reconciliation.* Scottdale, Pa.: Herald, 1999.

Meyer, Mary Clemens. *Walking with Jesus.* Scottdale, Pa.: Herald, 1992.

Miller, Ella May. *The Peacemakers: How to Find Peace and Share It.* Old Tappan, N.J.: Fleming H. Revell, 1977.

Nolan, Liam. *Small Man of Nanataki: The True Story of a Japanese Who Risked His Life to Provide Comfort for his Enemies.* New York: E.P. Dutton, 1966.

Oe, Kenzaburo. *Hiroshima Notes.* Tokyo: YMCA Press, 1981.

Perkins, John. *Let Justice Roll Down.* Glendale, Calif.: Regal, 1976.

Perkins, Spencer, and Chris Rice. *More than Equals: Racial Healing for the Sake of the Gospel,* rev. ed. Downers Grove, Ill.: InterVarsity, 2000.

Sharp, John E., ed. *Gathering at the Hearth: Stories Mennonites Tell.* Scottdale, Pa.: Herald, 2001.

Shearer, Tobin Miller, Regina Shands Stoltzfus, and Iris de Leon-Hartshorn. *Set Free: A Journey toward Solidarity against Racism.* Scottdale, Pa.: Herald, 2001.

Sider, Ronald J. *Non-Violence, the Invincible Weapon?* Dallas: Word, 1989.

Swalm, E.J., ed. *Nonresistance under Test: A Compilation of Experiences of Consci-*

entious Objectors as Encountered in Two World Wars. Nappanee, Ind.: E.V. Publishing House, 1949.

Watson, C. Hoyt. *DeShazer.* Coquitlam, B.C.: Galaxy Communications, 1998.

Wells, Ronald A. *People behind the Peace: Community and Reconciliation in Northern Ireland.* Grand Rapids: Eerdmans, 1999.